The Journey of Advaita

Contemporary Researches in Hindu Philosophy and Religion, no. 19

The Journey of Advaita

From the Ṛgveda to Sri Aurobindo

Priti Sinha

DK PRINTWORLD
Publishers of Indian Traditions

Cataloging in Publication Data — DK
[Courtesy: D.K. Agencies (P) Ltd. <docinfo@dkagencies.com>]
Sinha, Priti, author
The journey of Advaita : from the Ṛgveda to Sri Aurobindo / Priti Sinha.
pages cm (Contemporary researches in Hindu philosophy and religion; no. 19).
Includes bibliographical references and index.

1. Advaita – History. 2. Śaṅkarācārya. 3. Ghose, Aurobindo, 1872-1950. I. Title. II. Series: Contemporary researches in Hindu philosophy and religion; no. 19.

LCC B132.A3S56 2017 | DDC 181.482 23

ISBN: 978-81-246-0934-7
First published in India, 2018

Printed and published by:
D.K. Printworld (P) Ltd.
Regd. Office : *Vedaśrī*, F-395, Sudarshan Park
(Metro Station : ESI Hospital), New Delhi - 110 015
Phones : (011) 2545 3975, 2546 6019
e-mail : indology@dkprintworld.com
Web : www.dkprintworld.com

To my husband

Shri Ashok Kumar Varma

a companion, an anchor, an inspiration

who stood firm with me at trying times,

encouraging me to strive for the best

Preface

The present work, *The Journey of Advaita,* intends to elucidate the profundity of Advaitic philosophy which is but the most exquisite philosophical tradition of India. Vedāntists by their significant contribution have enriched the area of Indian philosophy with their understanding of the mystery of human life, the dimension of human existence and its destiny.

Advaita Vedānta is not a later development of thought as one of the six systems of Indian philosophy. Right from the Vedic period Indian philosophical thought has exhibited its Advaitic strand. The general belief is that there is polytheism and not monism in Veda as Vedic *ṛṣi*s worshipped different gods and goddesses in anticipation to get their prayer rewarded in the form of material benefits, but in the Vedic dictum, *ekam sad viprā bahudhā vadanti,* we can find a spiritual prevision of Advaita philosophy too. There is incessant flow of Advaitic thought right from the dawn of civilization. Yes, sometimes it is in disguised form.

There was echo of unity in some of the hymns of Vedas, Upaniṣads picked up this echo and sought to realize this unity amidst diversity by meditation and spiritual experiences; hence in Upaniṣads there is shifting of this centre from the outer to the inner. Since the world is an emanation and not creation of God there is no duality between the creator and the creation. The identity of *Brahman* with the universe resolves all duality. In Upaniṣads *ātman* too is *Brahman* in the sense of identity and not in the sense of community. In the journey from Vedic philosophy to Upaniṣadic philosophy there is a distinct sign of transformation from God to self, from prayer to philosophy, from polytheism to monotheistic mysticism which worked as foundation of later Advaita. In Upaniṣadic philosophy we find a first sketch of Advaita philosophy, Śaṅkara's Advaita is only a growth of the Advaitic strands found in Upaniṣads in a very logical and systematic way.

Śaṅkara, the most precious gem of Indian philosophical thought, illumined with his logical acumen the firmament of Advaita which lulled the erudite scholars for centuries to come. The galaxy of Advaitic authors like Sureśvarācārya, Vācaspati Miśra and Citsukhācārya contributed immensely to make the roots of Advaita strong but it could not serve as a solace for those who had a tender heart and not a strong rational mind. They looked for emotional appeasement where *bhakti* was more acceptable than *jñāna*. Rāmānuja's Viśiṣṭādvaita, Madhva's Dvaita, Nimbārka's Dvaitādvaita and Śuddhādvaita of Vallabhācārya sought to satisfy the aspirant religious soul which aspires loving communion with God. As a result Bhakti-Vedānta came into existence which served as a transitional link between Kevalādvaita of Śaṅkara and Integral Advaitism of Sri Aurobindo which is said to be "the Vedānta of tomorrow". Bhakti-Vedānta does not cancel the world as *māyā* as it is creation of God. His creatorship is not incompatible with His Absoluteness. Sri Aurobindo goes even further; he presents an integral approach, "a dynamic truth vision". His Integral Advaita reconciles the becoming of the world with the being of God. As the manifestation of *Brahman* the world is divine in nature. Both being and becoming are real. In onward march of evolution, the lower is not to be rejected as Śaṅkara thinks, but to be uplifted. Sri Aurobindo thinks for the salvation of the whole universe and not only of human being. What the ancient seers said in mystic way is being accepted by the modern scientists also. Modern physics has not refuted Advaita philosophy rather it has revitalized it. It is also taking Advaitic stand when it accepts that matter is a kind of non-material energy. "The fact of matter is that it is no longer a fact." Modern science believes that the Universe is a field of energy, any material cannot be the cause of the Universe and "the input of human consciousness cannot any longer be ignored". It is consciousness and not matter which is the building block of the Universe, the ground of all beings. All things – mass and energy – are no longer antithetical. Like Śaṅkara they too accept that the spatio-temporal world can never be final. "There is something ineffable about the real", which is to be explored by intuition and not by reason. Albert Einstein says: "I can never like a work if it cannot be intuitively grasped." There is no ontological absolute reality in quantum particles. The rhythm of the world consists in the unity of unity and diversity. Quantum physics has allowed us to enter into the era where metaphysics and philosophy are no longer antithetical. It can be happily said: "The earliest formula of wisdom promises to be the last."

My book is an effort to elucidate the journey of Advaita philosophy right from the Vedas, Upaniṣads, Bhakti-Vedānta to that of Integral Advaitism of Sri Aurobindo, and that it doesn't end here but its philosophy is being increasingly advocated and explored by modern science too.

This book will be incomplete without recording my gratitude to my mentor late Dr K.N. Mishra who finetuned my understanding of Advaita philosophy. I would also like to extend my gratitude to Dr Vashishtha Narain Tripathi (Former HOD, Kashi Vidyapeeth) for his relentless encouragement and help. My heartfelt appreciation and thanks to Dr Ashish Pandey for his constant support without which this book wouldn't have seen the light of day. In the last to my daughters Shriti, Shriya and Saumya, whose love and support ensured me enough time to indulge in my writing.

With my limited knowledge, this effort of mine is like an oblation in the *jñāna yajña*. I request all the enlightened scholars to overlook the shortcomings if any.

Priti Sinha

Contents

Preface v

Abbreviations x

Introduction **1**

1. Traces of Advaita in Ṛgveda **9**

2. Advaita in Upaniṣads **10**

Advaita Vedānta as Independent School 26

3. Kevalādvaita of Śaṅkara **29**

Meaning of the Word "Brahman" 29

Saguṇa and Nirguṇa Brahman 30

Sat (Existence) 36

Brahman as Consciousness 39

Brahman as Bliss 42

Saguṇa Brahman or Īśvara 46

Proofs for the Existence of God 49

Śaṅkara's Conception of Man and His Bondage 53

Jīva and Ātman 58

Jīva and Sākṣin 59

Īśvara and Jīva 61

Tat Tvam Asi 63

Three States of Jīva 68

The Doctrine of Māyā 70

Māyā and Avidyā 83

Adhyāsa 85

Is Avidyā One or Many? 89

World 89
Triple Reality 91
Śaṅkara's Conception of Liberation 96
The Way to Liberation 99
Karma and Jñāna 103
Bhakti and Jñāna 110
Jīvanmukti and Videhamukti 112

4. Schools of Theistic Vedānta **120**
Viśiṣṭādvaita of Rāmānuja 120
The Nature of Ultimate Reality 121
Para Manifestation 129
Antaryāmī Manifestation 129
Arcā Manifestation 130
The Human Soul and Its Bondage 130
Destiny of Man and the Ways to Attain It 135
Dvaita Vedānta of Madhvācārya 145
Concept of Ultimate Reality 145
Brahman 146
The Concept of Jīva and His Bondage 151
The Reality of World 155
The Concept of Mokṣa 156
Dvaitādvaita Vedānta of Nimbārka 161
The Nature of Reality 161
The Nature of Jīva 166
The Nature of the World 170
The Concept of Salvation and Ways to Attain It 171
Śuddhādvaita of Vallabhācārya 178
The Nature of Soul and Its Bondage 184
The Nature of the World 189
Liberation 192
Divine Grace of Puṣṭi Mārga 196

5. The Integral Advaitism of Sri Aurobindo **201**
Existence (Sat) 202

Conscious-Force 205
Bliss 211
Integral Advaitism 218
The Concept of Supermind 220
The Supermind as Creator 222
Supermind as Truth-Consciousness 224
The Absolute and the Supermind 227
The Triple Status of Supermind 229
Supermind and Overmind 233
Sri Aurobindo's Conception of Man and His Bondage 235
The Concept of the Individual Self 235
The Double Soul 240
Evolution 242
Spiritual Evolution 244
Triple Character of the Process of Evolution 250
The Triple Transformation 254
Psychic Transformation 256
Spiritual Transformation 259
Higher Mind 260
Illumined Mind 261
Supramental Transformation 265
The Destiny of Man 266
Gnostic Being 273
Place of Personality in the Gnostic Being 278
Divine Life 280

6. A Summing Up of the Journey of Advaita from Śaṅkara to Sri Aurobindo 282

7. Advaita and Modern Science 293

Bibliography 299

Index

Abbreviations

Ai.U.	*Aitareyopaniṣad*
Apa.	*Aparokṣānubhūti*
B.G.	*Bhagavadgītā*
B.G.R.B.	*Bhagavadgītā Rāmānuja Bhāṣya*
B.G.Ś.B.	*Bhagavadgītā Śāṅkara-Bhāṣya*
B.S.	*Brahmasūtra*
B.S.M.B.	*Brahmasūtra Madhvācārya-Bhāṣya*
B.S.S.B.	*Brahmasūtra Śāṅkara-Bhāṣya*
Bṛ.U.	*Bṛhadāraṇyakopaniṣad*
Bṛ.U.Ś.B.	*Bṛhadāraṇyakopaniṣad Śāṅkara-Bhāṣya*
C.I.P.	*Contemporary Indian Philosophy*
Chā.U.	*Chāndogya Upaniṣad*
Chā.U.Ś.B.	*Chāndogyopaniṣad Śāṅkara-Bhāṣya*
G.K.	*Gauḍapāda Kārikā*
G.K.Ś.B.	*Gauḍapāda Kārikā Śāṅkara-Bhāṣya*
H.I.P.	*History of Indian Philosophy* by S.N. Dasgupta
Īśa.U.	*Īśopanisad*
K.U.	*Kaṭhopaniṣad*
K.U.Ś.B.	*Kaṭhopaniṣad Śāṅkara-Bhāṣya*
Ke.U.	*Kenopaniṣad*
Ke.U.Ś.B.	*Kenopaniṣad Śāṅkara-Bhāṣya*
M.U.	*Muṇḍakopaniṣad*
M.U.Ś.B.	*Muṇdakopaniṣad Śāṅkara-Bhāṣya*
Māṇḍ.K.	*Māṇḍūkya Kārikā*

Māṇḍ.U.	*Māṇḍūkyopaniṣad*
Naiṣ.	*Naiṣkarmyasiddhiḥ*
P.I.	*The Philosophy of Integralism* by Haridas Chaudhary
P.R.	*Prameya-ratnārṇava*
Pra.U.	*Praśnopaniṣad*
Pra.U.Ś.B.	*Praśnopaniṣad Śāṅkara-Bhāṣya*
S.D.S.	*Sarva-Darśana Saṁgraha* by Mādhavācārya
Śaṁ.Śā.	*Saṁkṣepa Śārīraka*
Sū.Mā.	*Śuddhādvaita-Mārtaṇḍa*
Sve.U.	*Śvetāśvataropaniṣad*
Sve.U.S.B.	*Śvetāśvataropaniṣad Śāṅkara-Bhāṣya*
T.D.N	*Tattvārtha-dīpa-nibandha*
T.U.	*Taittirīyopaniṣad*
T.U.Ś.B.	*Taittirīyopaniṣad Śāṅkara-Bhāṣya*
Up.Sā.	*Upadeśasāhasrī* by Śaṅkara (tr. Swami Jagadananda)
V.C.	*Vivekacūdāmaṇi*
V.E.	*Vedānta Explained* by V.H. Date
V.K.	*Vedānta Kaustubha* by Roma Bose
V.P.	*Vedānta Paribhāṣā* by Dharmaraja Dhvarindra
V.P.S.	*Vedānta Pārijāta Saurabha* by Roma Bose
Viv.	*Vivekacūḍāmaṇi*
Y.A.	*The Yoga of Sri Aurobindo* by Nolini Kanta Gupta

Introduction

ADVAITA is not only a philosophical discourse but a vision: a vision of spiritual experience which takes into its fold philosophical illumination as well as moral exaltation. Reality is not only to be thought of but to be lived, a person has to become one with it. The focus of Advaita is on immanent potency and infinite possibility of human soul. There is no numerological calculation in its domain. The reality is one and only one. It includes both matter and spirit, both being and becoming.

Many persons generally believe that Vedic philosophy is mainly polytheistic in character. They ignore the fact that different gods and goddesses in *Ṛgveda* are worshipped not only in their individual capacity but as manifestations of the ultimate Reality; that behind gods and goddesses there is a pronounced unity. Even monotheism failed to satisfy their inquisitive mind. Their questioning mind started thinking in terms of *kasmai devāya haviṣā vidhema*. And in their search they came to the neutral term which exceeds all monotheism. In Nāsadīya hymns we get the picture of speculative monism of highest order, *tad ekam*. In later period all divinities were conglomerated in one supreme reality. Thus the urge to visualize the Ultimate God is distinctly perceptible in Vedas. It is said that *Ṛgveda* is the "original storehouse of Indian Idealism where there is substantial message of unity in germinal form".

In the journey from Vedic philosophy to Upaniṣadic philosophy, there is a transfer of interest from God to self, from prayer to philosophy. There is continuity of thought running from God to self, from Saṁhitās, Brāhmaṇas and Āraṇyakas to Upaniṣads. The more they walked, the more they realized the unity of self with *Brahman*. Upaniṣadic seers picked up monistic suggestions from Vedic hymns and strengthened them into the philosophy of Advaita. The interest was transformed from the outer to the inner. God is to be realized in the inner recesses of one's heart, one has not to seek God but to see Him. The ultimate question for the Upaniṣadic seers was, what is that by knowing which everything is known, and their search for reality endlessly goes till they come to the ultimate conclusion *tat tvam asi* which assures us that we have the capacity to become Divine. The reality is both the essence of cosmic phenomena as well as psychological self. It is not to be rationally understood but intuitively realized, they realize the truth by direct awareness.

Although all the later systems of philosophy derive their thought also from Upaniṣads, Advaita Vedānta is entirely based on them. The concept of self is the special legacy of Upaniṣad to later systems. *Ekam sad* gets proper explanation in bequeathed Upaniṣadic philosophy. Upaniṣads were never compiled as treaty, they are only records of the inner experience of the seers received by intuition. They are the first recorded experience of the seers at a systematic and rational philosophizing. Bādarāyaṇa, Śaṅkara and later Vedāntists introduced an order by giving them a more systematic shape. Upaniṣads adhered to this continuity but at the same time they gave fillip to new schools of thought. The mystic hedges of Upaniṣads give rise to different suggestions taken by later systems but Vedānta is entirely based on them where unity is more important than duality.

In this way the caravan of Advaita Vedānta went incessantly flowing through different schools of Bhakti-Vedānta setting its full height in Integral Advaitism of Sri Aurobindo.

For Śaṅkara, the real is one and indubitable. By real he means that which is present in all times, *kālatraya-sattāvat*. The empirical world is not *trikāla satya* as its reality will be sublated by the knowledge of unity. As only gold is real and not the ornament, only *Brahman* is real. Moreover, an eternal thing cannot have a beginning.[1] For him granting reality to the world will mean to accept fundamental dualism which is a false metaphysics. He

---

[1] *na hi nityaṁ kenacid ārabhyate loke yad ārabdhaṁ tadnityaṁ iti*। — T.U.Ś.B. 1.1.

sticks to Advaitism and follows it in every sphere.

Ātman is verily *Brahman*. *Brahman* realization means self-realization. Śaṅkara stands pledged to the doctrine of oneness. Liberation is another name of cosmic expansion of self (*sarvātma bhāva*). The identity of self is not only bare identity, it is identical with *Brahman* in all its fullness (*pūrṇatva*) and in all its richness of contents. "It is perception by *ātman*, in *ātman* and of *ātman*, *ātmanā ātmani*, *ātmānam*." Śaṅkara never promises liberation on the other side of the grave. It can be realized here and now, the only need is to see him but not to seek him.

He built Advaita doctrine on the firm foundation of Śrutis. He accepts that *Brahman* can be realized through revelation but intellect is not looked down upon; rather it is kept as an ancillary to revelation on vital metaphysical principle. When he asserts that intellect is insecure it is *kutarka* he is condemning. Reasoning for him was both offence and defence against his opponents and at the same time it was helpful in interpreting the scriptures which was his great passion. He constantly defends Śruti with reason. He provides a rational foundation to the great doctrine of Vedānta. The genius of Śaṅkara gave final shape to Advaita though the background was created long ago. After Śaṅkara, the great theistic Vedāntists, Rāmānuja, Madhva, Nimbārka and Vallabha rose against the concept of *Nirguṇa-Brahman*. Rather they attempt a harmonious synthesis of Absolutism with personal theism as what they want is a personal relation with *Saguṇa Brahman*. Since *bhakti* for them is the chief source of *mukti*, they need personal relationship with God. The world as a creation of God can't be rejected.

In the Viśiṣṭādvaita of Rāmānuja, unity is qualified by diversity. Soul and matter are His attributes, *Cidācidviśiṣṭa Brahman* is the absolute Supreme Reality while the world is His *viśeṣaṇa*. He accepts the world as *anitya* and not false. Dependence does not mean the unreality. *Brahman* manifests himself both in *cit* and *acit*. For Him the world is too great and meaningful to be lightly dismissed as product of *avidyā*. There is inseparable relation (*apr̥thak siddhi*) between *Brahman* and soul. He believes not in self-effacement but in self-surrender to personal god. He has emphasized the religious side but not at the cost of philosophical wisdom.

Madhva, the champion of Dvaita Vedānta, is the "born foe" of Śaṅkara's Absolutism. His conception of God emphasizes two aspects of divinity: the perfection of being (*sarva guṇa pūrṇatva*) and freedom from all defects and limitation (*sarva doṣa gandha vivarjita*). *Nirguṇa* texts cannot nullify the qualities which Śrutis themselves describe: "His activity is the consequence of his overflowing perfection." Madhva identifies God with Viṣṇu. Lakṣmī is His consort as eternal as Lord Himself. She is personification of God's creative energy. Creation is a metaphysical fact. *Nānātva* is real and is dependent on God. He condemns all the three reasons of Śaṅkara to prove the falsity of the world in cognizability (*dṛśyatva*), materiality (*jaḍatva*) and the fact of being a part (*aṁśatva*). God is both inherent (*samavāyī*) and efficient (*nimitta*) cause of the world. His view neither is Vivartavāda nor Pariṇāmavāda, it is *avikṛta* Pariṇāmavāda. The word of Śruti that "by knowing one you know all" does not propound the falsity of the world, rather it advocates the cause–effect relation between God and the world (*nahi satya-jñānena mithyā jñānam sambhavati*). *Tat tvam asi* does not advocate identity. Madhva interprets *sa ātmā tat tvam asi*, as *sa ātmā atat tvam asi* (*na dvaitvam bhrānti-kalpitam*).[2] Creation is a reality though it is dependent on God. The soul is real, *Brahman* is real; the difference between them too is real. In liberation the soul lives in harmony with God but it is not completely merged there.

Nimbārka advocates the doctrine of Bhedābhedavāda (the doctrine of difference and non-difference). God possesses innumerable qualities which can be virtually classified as attributes of majesty and attributes of sweetness. Lord is both transcendental and immanent, all powerful as well as merciful. His might and majesty are as important as his love and sweetness. Some of his qualities are *sauśīlya* (to meet all without considering his status and position) and *vātsalya* (not to pay heed to devotee's mistakes). *Brahman*, world and soul – all the three principles – are

[2] *Sarva-Darśana Saṁgraha*, p. 269.

real; creation is His sport. He creates out of fullness of his nature and abundance of bliss. He asserts the relation of identity and difference between world and *Brahman* and again between soul and *Brahman* (*ubhaya vidhivākyānām tulya balatvāt*). *Brahman*, world and soul are neither absolutely identical nor absolutely distinct. Like Rāmānuja, Nimbārka too emphasizes identity as well as difference, but while Rāmānuja emphasizes identity more than difference, for Nimbārka both are equally important.

Vallabha's Advaita is Śuddhādvaita, pure non-dualism. There is only one *Brahman* who is Kṛṣṇa who is both the inherent (*samavāyī*) and efficient (*nimitta*) causes of the universe. *Māyā* is not a principle of creation but a power of God which is one with Him. He is "warp and woof" of all that exist. Neither is his view Vivartavāda nor Pariṇāmavāda but *avikṛta* Pariṇāmavāda. A desire for self-expression is innate in *Brahman*. The world springs out of God, as spark springs out of fire, lustre from jewels, rays from lamp. As cotton spreads itself as thread, God spreads Himself as the world.

In liberation, soul enjoys affinity with God but it does not lose its identity in Him as Śaṅkara thinks. He gives creative freedom to them to do right or wrong action for his own sport. He is merciful to let his devotee enjoy supreme bliss and to attain affinity with Him. He stresses a life of unqualified love for God. For liberated soul there is no difference among world, soul and God. *Tat tvam asi* is literally true not figuratively. He emphasizes identity and subordinates difference.

The school of Bengal Vaiṣṇavism of Caitanya is known as Acintya-bhedābheda-vāda. Madhva was his spiritual *guru* and Caitanya himself thought that he was preaching Madhva's dualism, but in fact there is his close affinity with Nimbārka as what he practised actually was difference in non-difference. Hari, the personal god of love and grace, is the Ultimate Reality. He reverses Śaṅkara's position. *Brahman* as the creator, the Lord is the complete truth. He is necessarily Saccidānanda. His inner power which forms this essence is manifested as threefold power: as *sandhinī* (which is existence), as *saṁvit* (which is consciousness) and as *āhlādinī* (which is bliss). Through His higher energy, He becomes the efficient cause of the world and through His lower energy, He becomes the material cause of the world. He assumes many forms of which the chief is Lord Kṛṣṇa. Rādhā is the essence of delight-giving power. The souls are infinite and remain distinct even in liberation. They are manifestation of God's energy. If the lots of *jīva*s would have been decided by the work done by them, God would have lost His sovereignty. He gives creative freedom to them to do right or wrong action for his own spirit.

In liberation the soul is not submerged into *Brahman;* only the wrong notion of soul vanishes. World too, like *jīva,* comes out of God through His power of being. They are dependent on God but they are separate and distinct from Him. *Bhakti* is the sole means of liberation which means the eternal enjoyment of this blissful love for Kṛṣṇa in His *nitya vṛndāvana dhāma.*

Theistic Vedānta accepts the reality of experience at all levels. They do not differentiate *Brahman* of logic from the God of religion and reconcile the demand of logic with the needs of religious feelings. Their concept of *bhakti rūpa jñāna* meets both ends, the demand of metaphysics and supreme call of love. Śāṇḍilya thinks that the cause of repeated transmigration of soul is not ignorance but lack of devotion.

Sri Aurobindo

Theistic Vedānta served as the transitionary link between Śaṅkara and Sri Aurobindo. They accept the reality of the world but not of indeterminate Absolute. Sri Aurobindo accepts both. He builds Advaitic edifice in new texture of modern age. He comprehends new values and opens up new vistas of human progress. Śaṅkara denies the multiplicity, Rāmānuja denies unqualified oneness, Madhva fails to recognize unity in multiplicity but Sri Aurobindo says: "Real monism accepts all things as one *Brahman,* it does not bisect it into two incompatible realities as self and not self, as *Brahman* and not *Brahman.*" If it is true that the self alone exists it must also be true that all is self. In spite of major difference with Advaitic Vedānta, it is vivid that Advaitic Vedānta created background for Sri Aurobindo's dynamic philosophy.

Identifying with the divine within is not enough. One has to achieve identity with the divine without. The Divine which manifests in the individual is manifested in the universe also. Not only the individual is to be spiritualized but the whole cosmos. Salvation means perfection of man as well as the whole universe. *Kaṭhopaniṣad* too says: "*Brahman* is attained here in this world (*atra brahma samaśnute*)." The world is not a product of *māyā* to be sublated by real knowledge, it has the potency to be divinized.

In the onward march the lower is not rejected but uplifted. Involution of spirit precedes the evolution. *Ātman* is verily Saccidānanda. Thus Sri Aurobindo envisages the possibility of the salvation of the human race as a whole and not only of the individual. This seems to be a significant contribution of Sri Aurobindo to the ancient and traditional Hindu concept of liberation.

Even today, Advaita philosophy is acceptable equally to science and philosophy both. With dauntless logical acumen and spiritual insight, Śaṅkara propounded the theory of Advaita Vedānta which is fully acceptable to modern scientists also. During the period of classical physics, philosophy and science were two different disciplines. The scientists believed that they cannot incorporate philosophy into their domain which is not subjectively verifiable; but with the appearance of quantum physics their field of research widened. They are no more confined to the formalistic view of reality. The classical physics was deterministic and mechanical. Isaac Newton gave a static model of the world which was deterministic, but by reducing the physical world to a dynamic unitary substratum, modern physics opened an understanding of the mystic view of the world. They started thinking that "we cannot know anything unless we know everything", and that knowledge can be gained through intuition only. This gives the grasp of the world as a whole and not in fragmentation of mind and matter, within and without. Modern physicists are realizing that their knowledge is not "a catalogue of properties of nature" only. Max Planck, the father of quantum physics, felt that science is progressing towards the aim which is to be perceived intuitively and not rationally. They are realizing the basic oneness of the universe. They are getting at the point that consciousness is more fundamental than matter. Erwin Schrödinger's world view has affinity with Vedānta when it says that there is only a single consciousness of which we are only different parts. Like Advaita Vedānta he accepts that we cannot find consciousness in plural. What Vedānta says in mystic way has started drawing attention of the scientific genius of today. Modern science is taking a quantum jump from wisdom to intuition. The scientists are going back to the philosophy of unity. The whole universe is one is not only the belief of Vedānta, it can be scientifically demonstrated now. It is said that in this materialistic world, the scientific workers are only profoundly religious people.

What we need today is a dynamic interplay between mystical intuition, which studies the roots, and scientific attitude, which understands the branches.

1

Traces of Advaita in Ṛgveda

INDIAN philosophy is a "perennial river" flowing incessantly down the ages. Philosophy here is a spiritual way of life; even the universe is also supposed to be spiritual in its intrinsic nature. The Indian tradition draws its inspiration, both spiritual as well as moral, from the very fountain source of all inspirations, i.e. Śruti. The unique character of Indian philosophical systems is that they are not isolated systems claiming their independent origin; instead they are only different stages in the development of thought. The scholars humbly accept that they are only the authorized successive exponents and outstanding spokesmen of their respective systems which have been traditionally handed down to them from time immemorial. They are simply their best codifier. A.E. Gough (1903: 258) comments:

> The philosophy has had its virtual pre-existence in each previous stage. What has been more implicit becomes more explicit, but has been no addition from without, no interpolation from foreign elements.

The spiritual temper that had set in under the unbridled spirit of inquiry in *Ṛgveda* crystallized in different currents of Indian thought. Vedas are the ultimate source of inspiration in all fields of life but this faith is not mere "hypnosis induced by undiluted veneration", not mere blind faith but "a tentative belief terminating in an assured conviction begotten by logical ratiocination".

Usually we conceive polytheism or henotheism, a term coined by Max Müller, to express the manyness of gods and goddesses in *Ṛgveda* but the fact is that like other Indian philosophical schools the keynote of Vedic hymns too is spiritual monism. To perceive different "isms" – anthropomorphism, polytheism, henotheism and monotheism – in the Vedas is like, to borrow a phrase from

Gauḍapāda, "to see the footprint of a bird in the sky" (Sharma 1952: 16). The Vedic seers worshipped naturalistic and anthropomorphic Gods in the hope that they would listen to their prayers, accept the sacrifices and after being appeased, they would bestow their blessings. But soon they realized the inadequacy of their thought. The crowd of gods and goddesses proved weariness for them. They started realizing through the veil of manyness the unity which was underlying it.

> The scattered rays dispersed among the crowd of deities are collected together in the intolerable splendour of the One nameless God who alone could satisfy the restless craving of the human heart and the sceptic mind.
>
> – Radhakrishnan 1966, vol. I: 98

The Ṛgvedic growth of thought, embodied in different concepts of gods, can be tentatively put in the following hierarchical order:

(a) Dyaus, the god of natural worship.

(b) Varuṇa, the moral god.

(c) Indra, the jealous conqueror who wanted to dominate.

(d) Prajāpati, the god of monotheists.

(e) Brahman, the one maximized essence of each of the gods of the preceding stages.

This has not been arranged in the chronological as well as the logical order of gods. In fact when the texts of *Ṛgveda* were written, these stages had already passed away. After exploring all possible metaphysical aspects – materialistic, atheistic, nihilistic, theistic and idealistic – the monistic view was approved. They started believing that polytheistic beliefs are only different expressions of one all-comprehending unitary power. When the idea of creator God appeared, He was recognized as "the One" of speculative monism. In this way from the pluralistic view of the origin of the world, the monistic view arrived. There is only One being, the wise call it by various names: *ekam sad viprā bahudhā vadanti* (ṚV I.164.46). It is again said *ekam vai idaṁ vivabhūvasarvam, santam bahudhā kalpayanti* (ṚV X.114.5).

In the texts of *Ṛgveda* there are innumerable references

dissimilated in hymns, advocating philosophical monism. For example, each of the twenty-two hymns of Sūkta 55 of Maṇḍala 3 says that "the great divinity of the gods is One". The generic feature common to all these texts is "a pronounced unity (*ekatvam*) coupled with Omniformity (*viśvarūpam*), i.e. unity in variety". Vivekananda also feels that *ekaṁ sad viprā bahudhā vadanti* is the ground explanation that is given to all subsequent thoughts of India, the one that will be the theme of the whole world of religions. He further says that here lies the secret not only of Vedic hymns, but of all religious life of Indian thoughts.

The gods were never worshipped in *Ṛgveda* in their individual capacities, but as the divine manifestations of that Ultimate God. "Hence, there is no development from polytheism through monotheism to monism, but only of monism from the first *mantra* portion to the last Upaniṣadic portion" (Sharma 1952: 16). The prayers were not offered separately to different gods, but to all of them. Their address name might have been different like Agni, Varuṇa and Mātariśva, but they are the expressions of the same God. Later on they were comprehended by one name as Viśvadeva which may be said to be an anticipation of later Vedānta. To quote T.M.P. Mahadevan (1957: 173):

> It was rather by way of harmonization, by discovering the underlying unity of the different conception of godhead that the Vedic sect arrived at the idea of one God.

The later religious and philosophical thought developed out of "crude ideology and suggestion of early thinkers". *Brahman* is the sole reality, and yet a place is found for the multitudes of gods as the manifestation of *Brahman*. The gods are praised only as manifestation of the Supreme, and not as individual identities different from the Supreme.

The hymns in *Ṛgveda* are not addressed to these natural forces like sun, moon and sky independently. Kokileshwar Sastri (1931: 200) comments:

> It is remarkably strange to imagine that the intelligent race of people like the Hindus should exhibit such a lamentable lack of even common sense in allowing the hymns and *mantras*

addressed to inert, non-intelligent natural phenomena to form an essential part of their religion.

He further says that if "Ṛgvedic hymns contained nothing but prayers for the fascinating objects of the nature only to inspire awe and admiration, then its value is surely diminished" (ibid.). He is of the firm belief that the importance of *Ṛgveda* lies in the fact that it is "the original storehouse of the Indian idealism which subsequently gave rise to Vedānta". He further feels that like the description of *Brahman* in the Upaniṣads as *prāṇasya prāṇah*, as *manaso manaḥ*, as *sūryyasya sūryyaḥ*, in Vedas too there is an invisible form of gods as personification of the forces of nature. There is at the same time growing a tendency for a monistic interpretation of the universe. From "the babbling of the child-humanity, they pass on to the utterances of the truth of highest order". Monotheism, which was still a matter of faith in many quarters, failed to satisfy the later Vedic seers. Monotheistic belief had to answer to the queries like whether God had created the world on his own, or had applied His creative skills on some pre-existent matter. Undoubtedly the Ṛgvedic thought started with "infinite wonder", but soon ensued the reflective thought which introduced an order in the "lawless mythologizing and God-making", leading to monism. All the crowding of gods and goddesses began to cause weariness to the intellect, so a tendency was soon shown to identify one God with another. We see in the hymns the practice of combining gods possessing similar characteristics such as Indra–Soma, Indra–Vāyu, Indra–Pūṣan and Indra–Viṣnu.

On some occasions, three gods are represented working as one like Aryaman, Mitra and Varuṇa, and Agni, Soma and Gandharva. This shows a clear tendency for the search of a common divine reality which could ascend them from multiplicity to unity. And this unity of godhead was achieved by taking Him to be the Supreme God. Such a deity was called by the name of Viśvakarmā, who was the father, the creator; He was granted the highest position in the later Vedic period. Bṛhaspati (the divine teacher), Prajāpati (the lord of the people) and Hiraṇyagarbha (the golden womb) are also given the status of the Supreme God in some hymns. Though the metaphysical form of thought was not so well developed in *Ṛgveda* as in the Upaniṣads, the *ṛṣis* felt instantly the existence of this unitary principle behind the working of the universe. They went further to find ultimately the infinite power as the cause of the universe *tad ekaṁ* (that one) they displaced the idea of polytheistic anthropomorphism by spiritual monotheism. However, later on, monotheism too failed to satisfy them, thus they finally kept gods and goddesses under one higher being. The Vedic seers tried to explain the mysteries of the world by three different methods: theological, metaphysical, and psychological.

The first is the theological method which they realized through devotion. But their God of devotion is ultimately not less than the transcendental principle which is at the back of the whole universe. The sages contemplated the theistic view of creation in their hymns towards Prajāpati and Viśvakarmā. Metaphysically in their comprehension of the Ultimate Reality they could realize Him as the *Parama Puruṣa* (the Ultimate Being), the whole universe being his body. He had a thousand heads (*sahasraśīrṣā*), innumerable eyes (*sahasrākṣa*) and a thousand legs (*sahasrapāda*). From the concept of God as personal being, the seers finally arrived at the concept of Him as utterly impersonal. God is the ultimate energy in and behind all creation, but is never identical with it. Though the ontological thought is not so well developed during the Vedic period, there is at least enough proof to show that they had in their mind the glimpses of the transcendental reality as the ground of the temporal and the relative. The psychological approach to the problem was more extensively discussed in the Upaniṣadic period, but the roots are found in *Ṛgveda* too. The identity of the individual soul with the Cosmic Soul is clearly mentioned in two dialogues of Ṛṣi Vāmadeva and Ṛṣikā Vāc. Vāmadeva says, "I am the Sun, and I am the intelligence" (ṚV IV.26.1-2). And Vāc says "I am the queen of the whole universe. The omnipotent possessor of all wealth" (ṚV X.125.3). Such supreme psychological realization on the part of a woman at the dawn of human civilization is unparallel in the history of the world.

Nāsadīya Sūkta presents the most advanced theory of creation where the *ṛṣis* conceive the infinite power as the cause of the universe. The Ultimate Reality behind the universe cannot be said to be either existent or non-existent, neither self-conscious, like "I", nor unconscious, like "not-I". It is higher than both, it is the transcending consciousness. It breathed by itself without breath, other than it there was nothing. It is one nameless God beyond time and space, beyond death and immortality. We cannot express "what it is except that it is". Although this hymn baffles exact translation, John Muir has well attempted to translate it in the following words:

> *Then there was neither Aught, nor Naught,*
> *no air no sky beyond*
> *What covered all? Where rested all?*
> *In waterly gulf profound.*
> *Nor death was then nor deathlessness,*
> *nor change of night and day*
> *The one breathed calmly, self-sustained,*
> *naught else beyond it lay …*
> *A self supporting mass beneath, and energy above,*
> *Who knows, who ever told,*
> *from whence this vast creation rose?*
> *No gods had then been born – who can ever the truth disclose?*
> *Whence sprang this world,*
> *and whether framed by hand divine or no*
> *Its lord in heaven alone can tell,*
> *if even he can show.*
>
> – *Ṛgveda* X.121

Nāsadīya hymn resolves the dualistic metaphysics of nature and spirit into higher monism. Saroj Kumar Das (1937: 68) comments:

> The Nāsadīya hymns may therefore be said to stand at the crossway, pointing on the one hand to religion, and on the other to philosophy, making, in effect, the transition from religion to philosophy.

He further says:

> . . . the Nāsadīya hymns may be taken as the very texts of uncompromising monotheism rounding itself off in characteristic speculative monism of the agnostic or mystical type with its inevitable ignorance in the end.

In this *sūkta*, we stand on the threshold of Upaniṣadic monism. Here we have the quintessence of monistic thought.

Puruṣa Sūkta, on the other hand, propounds the pantheistic view of creation making room for metaphysical understanding. In this *sūkta*, the Vedic seers visualize, perhaps for the first time in human history, the organic unity of the whole universe. "In Him all this is, has been, and will be" (ṚV X.121, X.81-82). The *ṛṣis* emphasize the greatness of God by giving Him great dimension. He has sacrificed Himself in creating the universe. Nowhere does this hymn contradict the idea of creation by one Absolute. In this act of creation *Puruṣa* is the victim as He sacrifices himself by creating. The Supreme Spirit becomes the active *Puruṣa*. "*Puruṣa* is thus the begotter as well as the begotten. He is absolute as well as the self-conscious I" (Radhakrishnan 1923, vol. I: 105).

The hymns of *Ṛgveda*, on the other hand, contain the germinal point of the Vedānta, providing at least a foothold for the later Vedānta to trace out its ideologies in this earliest scripture of human hisory. It is said that the main concept of the Vedānta is prefigured in *Ṛgveda*. We have only to discover the idea, and not the words. With the concept of the manyness of gods and goddesses, as personifying the forces of nature, there is a growing aptitude for the acceptance of the one Supreme God. Robert Ernest Hume here rightly remarks "... the scholars should never forget how easy it is to weed a field which has been ploughed and how difficult to plough unbroken soil."[1] The later Vedāntins similarly developed the ideas hidden in the Vedas in the latent form. Thus, in the making of the Vedānta, the importance of *Ṛgveda* lies in providing the ground for it. "The contribution of *Ṛgveda* is what is aspired to be, and not in actuality". It is said that we are all "born Vedāntists". The doctrine of "universal immanence of an intelligent monism" is the most fundamental belief which is implicitly or explicitly acceptable to almost all schools of Indian philosophy. The concept of the ultimate unity of the material and spiritual reality, which was the result of the long circuitous journey of the Indian thoughts, was foreseen long before in *Ṛgveda*. There was a

[1] Hume (tr.), 1921, *The Thirteen Principal Upanishads*, vol. 1, Preface.

scholarly shift from the concepts of personal gods and goddesses to the utterly impersonal reality.

Das (1937) comments that Vedānta, in particular Advaita, is implanted in the Vedas – *vede vedāntaḥ supratiṣṭhitaḥ*. He puts a beautiful simile:

> The laws of development never permit the flower to remain along with the fruit. The decay of the flower is the precondition for the appearance of the fruit. But here, there is no season. All at once it bears its leaves, fruits and blossoms.

In Vedic hymns, from the beginning to the end there is a sustained message of unity of a clear-cut Advaitism.

Naturalism and anthropomorphism seem to be the preliminary stage of Vedic religion. Later on, reason started ascendency over fancy, and as a result they started a search for a permanent reality. The nucleus of the Vedic hymns is spiritual monism, the indestructible Absolute embracing both monism and pluralism within its fold, though this concept blossoms fully in the philosophy of the Upaniṣads and the Vedānta.

There may not be any positive contribution of *R̥gveda* in making Vedānta, but definitely its contribution lies in preparing its background. It is rightly said

> The Veda has always stood as the distant and unchanging background and as the ultimate source of inspiration for all Indian achievements in any field of life.
>
> – Belvalker and Ranade 1933, vol. 2: 1

It is the origin source of later Vedānta though in very germinal form.

2

Advaita in Upaniṣads

THE journey from the Vedic philosophy to Upaniṣadic philosophy is a process of the transfer of interest from God to self, from imagination to reason, from prayer to philosophy, from hymnology to reflection and from henotheistic polytheism to monotheistic mysticism.

The Upaniṣads form the basis of the enlightened faith of India. Upaniṣadic seers work on the concepts that are found in the germinal stages in Saṁhitās, their works are only to refine them and to bring them to a higher plinth. Their aim is not to enjoy the unalloyed bliss of heaven as it is not everlasting, the bliss they want to realize is the Ultimate Bliss based on inner experience and mystic realization, on intuitive cognizance and psychological revelation.

Upaniṣads do not stand for a single doctrine or a set pattern of thought; rather they supply various initiations of thought which are later sprouted into different fully grown-up systems thus they are known as "Berecynthia of all later systems of Indian philosophy". R.D. Ranade (1968: 131) comments:

> Upaniṣads constitute the lofty eminence of philosophy, which from its various sides gives birth to rivulets of thoughts.

These rivulets are only different stages in the evolution of thought and not a revolt against their tenets. Every Indian scholar looks up to Upaniṣads for their support and inspiration.

There is continuity of thought running from Saṁhitās, Brāhmaṇas and Āraṇyakas to the Upaniṣads but the Upaniṣadic philosophy is the first recorded effort of *ṛṣis* at systematic philosophizing where the realization of infinite is its pivotal principle. In Upaniṣadic philosophy we find an advance on "Saṁhitā mythology, Brāhmaṇa hair-splitting and even the Āraṇyaka theology" and still they have their set place in it. Brāhmaṇas, like Upaniṣads, takes the sacred texts and rituals as their starting point for a new interpretation of the spiritual thought but its task is "the conservation of the forms" rather than the revelation of the soul of Vedas like Upaniṣads.

> Brāhmaṇas labour to fix and preserve the minutiae of the Vedic ceremony, the conditions of their material effectuality in symbolic sense . . . – Sri Aurobindo 1998, vol. 15: 14

In Āraṇyaka period again there was a shift from ritualism to philosophical thought which got its full bloom in Upaniṣads.The Upaniṣadic seers sought to recover the lost or waning knowledge by meditation and spiritual experience and they used the texts of the ancient *mantra*s as a prop or an authority for their own intuitions and perceptions, or else the Vedic Word was seed of thought and vision by which they recorded old truths in new forms (ibid.).

In their treatment of the question of the Ultimate Reality, the Upaniṣadic seers replace the objective vision of the Vedic seers by subjective one. Sharma (1952: 15) says:

> The *mantra* portion has been called the religion of the Nature, of the poets; and the Brāhmaṇas ritualism, the religion of law, of the priests; the Upaniṣadic portion the religion of the Spirit, of the philosophers . . . Then gradually polytheism yielded place to monotheism and later to monism.

It is visible at every step the transfer of priority from God to self. Their treatment of the problem is not so much metaphysical as psychological. The circuitous journey to reach the ultimate unity of reality was visualized much earlier by Vedic seers but their dream was fulfilled in Upaniṣads. *Ekaṁ sat* of Veda gets its strength in Upaniṣadic metaphysics only. Undoubtedly the monistic idea was conceived earlier in *Ṛgveda* but Upaniṣads enrich it more logically, more methodically. In Upaniṣads we get more the consistency of intuition than reason; still we find there the first sketch of philosophical system. To quote Radhakrishnan (1966, vol. 1: 144):

> The advance of the Upaniṣads on the Vedas consists in an increased emphasis on the monistic suggestions of the Vedic

> hymns, a shifting of the centre from the outer to the inner world, a protest against the externalism of the Vedic practices and an indifference to the sacredness of the Veda.

The mechanical "give and take" relation of man with God of Vedic age converged into spiritual identity of *Brahman* and *ātman*. Reality is not divine individual which is to be worshipped. The Upaniṣadic philosophy "sought to square a growing idealistic philosophy with the dogmas of a settled theology". The vision of cosmic person of *Ṛgveda* (Viśvadeva) is replaced by the vision of *ātman* in the Upaniṣads as the concept of Viśvadeva could not impress the Upaniṣadic saints for the reason that it could not touch the innermost being which was the matter of great concern for them. Vedic *ṛṣi*s seek God in external forces, Upaniṣadic seers see God in themselves. They believe that "life exhibits the greatest truth in the centre rather than at its surface". They were well aware of the underlying unity of all beings which was accepted by the later thinkers. Upaniṣads lay all stress on identity, identity of self with the Absolute, with the universe. The life is to be realized "in its fullness and glory and not in parts". This is the complete (*pūrṇamidam*), the complete is substracted from the complete, the remainder is again the complete (*pūrṇamevāvaśiṣyate*). The Upaniṣadic couplet expresses "the mystic promise in the most effective way. Life is actively emerging for fullness. The spirit cannot bear division" (Sircar 1934: 47). There are three concepts regarding the relation of God and the universe in the Upaniṣads.

The first concept is that *Brahman* is the soul and the universe in the body and the duality of God and the universe persists, they are not one. To refer *Īśopaniṣad* (verse 1), one spirit is inhabiting and governing the whole universe of movement and the rule of divine life for man is "enjoyment of all by renunciation of all through the exclusion of desire". We have to be the One Being without ceasing to see the many. Becomings for them are existent and are included in *Brahman*'s view of Himself (Aurobindo 1951b). The seers have before their mind that a duality between *Brahman* and the universe persists, only it is to be perceived with knowledge and not with ignorance. *Śvetāśvataropaniṣad* IV.2-4 says:

He is Sun, He is Agni, He is Vāyu, He is real, He is eternal, immortal, He is the one goal to be attained.

To quote *Muṇḍakopaniṣad*:

Brahman is the innermost self of all *sarvabhūtāntarātmā*. – II.1.4

Prāṇa, mana, sense organs, *vāyu, ākāśa*, fire, water and the earth, which bear the whole world, emanate from that *Akṣara Puruṣa*. – II.1.3

The second concept which has apparent support in Upaniṣads is – there is no longer the question of *Brahman* and the universe, there is only *Brahman*. Duality has been resolved into identity. What is without is also within, there is no modification in reality, it is only in word and speech, only the clay is real and not its modification.[1] The reality is eternal, is all-pervading, the whole universe is His manifestation, His production.[2] He is the innermost self of the world. The knower of *Brahman* has not only the joy of light as the result, he has some immense gain also. Duality is resolved into identity (*tad etat satyam*). Upaniṣads is well aware of the underlying unity of all beings which was most accepted truth for the later thinkers. Śaṅkara particularly drew his philosophical concept of advaita from such sources only.

The third concept is – *Brahman* escapes all descriptions, all definitions. There is no affirmation whatsoever regarding *Brahman*. The reality can be reached not by thought but by *turīyāvasthā* of highest immediacy *prajñānam brahma* (Ai.U.III.3). Speech with reason returns by not finding Him.[3] He is not seen by eyes nor heard by ears, rather eyes see, ears hear only with His help. Duality and externality persist at intellectual level only. The reality is beyond the *tripuṭī* of *jñātā, jñeya* and *jñāna*. *Ānanda* is the highest result where all these three become one. The knower of *Brahman* becomes *Brahman* himself.[4]

---

1 (a) . . . *vikāro nāmadheyaṁ mṛttiketyeva satyam* |
(b) *vikāro nāmadheyaṁ lohamityeva satyam* | – Chā.Up. VI.1.4-5

2 *anādimattvaṁ vibhutvena vartase yato jātāni bhuvanāni viśvā* – Śve.U. IV.4

3 *yato vāconivartante aprāpya manasā saḥ* | – T.U. 2.4.1

4 *brahma veda brahmaiva bhavati* – M.U. III.2.9

Brahman is not a Being to be worshipped by us but the Being from which the breath is drawn. *Prāṇa* in Upaniṣads is a "bio-psycho-ontological principle". It is "life from biological point of view, consciousness from psychological point of view and *ātman* from ontological point". The whole universe is the permeation of that *Brahman*. To quote Āruṇi's answer to Śvetaketu – we don't see him as we don't observe salt melted in water but it is there (Bṛ.U. VI.13.1). As the salty water is at the bottom, at the middle and at the top, similarly God is everywhere immanent in the world. Thus all the three views are present in Upaniṣad. The more the Upaniṣadic seers advance towards intense mystic exhilaration the more they realize that *Brahman* escapes all descriptions, all definitions, it is not this, it is not this (*neti, neti*). It is ungraspable, undefinable, all inclusive *Brahman*. To quote Ranade (1968: 160):

> . . . the Upaniṣadic characteristic of the Absolute passes from the negative stage of neither–nor, through the affirmative stage of inclusiveness of the transcendental state of either–or.

The antithesis between matter and mind, between the world and soul vanishes in the realm of *Brahman*. *Brahman* is the unity of both the physical as well as the mental. He is "without earlier, without later". In their comprehension of reality, there is total synthesis of the knowledge of without with the knowledge of within. "Reality in fact does not know the language of inside and outside, it is ever full" (Garg 1978: 35). The ultimate question which the Upaniṣadic seers ask is what is that by knowing which everything is known. Having failed in getting the answer in cosmological domain they turned up to psychological domain. Yājñavalkya asserts forcefully that *ātman* is only the knower, *vijñātāramare ken vijāniyāt* (Bṛ.Up. IV.5.15).

This search for reality tirelessly goes till the Upaniṣadic seers come to the highest conclusion: *tat tvam asi*. *Brahman* is not only the essence of the cosmic phenomena but of the psychological self also. The foam, the bubbles, the ripples, the waves of sea are all but sea itself. *Ātman* is *Brahman* not "in the sense of community but in the sense of identity". Upaniṣadic mystics see the spirit in its essence as well as in expression, in its transcendence as well as in immanence. The many emerges from the One and returns into the One. The same light illumines both the soul of man as well as the cosmos. This consciousness is "the paradise regained, i.e. the recovery of the paradise lost" (Sircar 1934: 105). The absolute is existence with inexhaustible potentiality – and manifests actuality. Reality is not to be realized by reason rather it is intuited by a person to whom it reveals its nature.[5] Upaniṣadic philosophy is not a calculated construction of logic but spontaneous outflow of mystic experience and such mystic experience is not static in nature rather it is a process, an incessant flow of thought. As it is in itself *jñānarūpa*, it does not require any other source of knowledge.[6]

The Upaniṣadic concept that the world is permeation of God never conveys the pantheistic view of Western philosophy where God is all, and all is God. By pantheism they mean necessary and eternal coexistence and coextension of the world and God. Swami Prabhavananda (1963) comments:

> The Hindu sees God as the ultimate energy in and behind all creation, but never either in ancient or in modern time as identical with it.

Permeation here only means that there is nothing independent of him. To say that the universe is in God does not mean that the universe is God. The world is only the expression of God. A.S. Geden describes Indian pantheism as "idealistic pantheism".

The Upaniṣadic[7] seers have never accepted that every object we perceive in this world "in the state of apparent isolation and self-subsistence" is *Brahman*. The whole universe is *Brahman* only. He illumines the whole universe. The irony of Western pantheism is that it believes in eternal coexistence of God and the world. But

---

[5] (a) K.U. I.3.12. (b) *Gītā* VII.25.

[6] *prakāśasya prakāśāntarāpekṣayānasambhavaḥ tadvat* – Ke.U.Ś.B.2

[7] (a) *tasya bhāsā sarvamidaṁ vibhāti* । – M.U. II.2.10

(b) *brahmaivedam .... viśvamidaṁ variṣṭam* – ibid. II.2.11

(c) *ekastathā sarvabhūtāntarātmā rūpaṁ rūpaṁ pratirūpo bahiśca*

– K.U. II.2.10

(d) *eko vaśī sarvabhūtāntarātmā ekaṁ rūpaṁ bahudhā yaḥ karoti*

– Ibid. II.2.12

according to Upaniṣads *Brahman* exists apart from relationship as well as in relationship. It is not only "empty intellectual conception void of spirituality" as Gough has remarked, it is the fullest reality; it is not only a possibility but inevitability. There is no difference between the outer reality and the inner reality, between the physical and the psychological. To quote *Kaṭhopaniṣad*, "death to death goes he who perceives difference". There is no longer the question of *Brahman* in the universe, there is only *Brahman*. What is without is also within. There is no difference between "the Cosmic Being without and the vivifying soul within". He is the One, the innermost self of all. As thousands of scintillation arise from well-lit fire and again get resolved into it, the world comes into existence and again is merged into it.

In Upaniṣads there is nothing like sensible or suprasensible for life is one and integral.

> The charm of the Upaniṣads lies in the transvaluation of the values in the light of the eternal truth and in reading every move of life in this light. The sensible finally resolves into the suprasensible when the mystic sense dawns upon us.
>
> –Sircar 1934: 188

Brahman is *jñānarūpa* thus it is not dependent on anything for its being known.[8] Those who claim that they know *Brahman* in fact do not know Him.[9] There is hardly any suggestion in the Upaniṣads to prove the unreality of the world. As the revelation of God there is rhythm, there is harmony in the world thus they are in no mood to reject the reality of the world as merely a phenomenal appearance. Hiraṇyagarbha of Upaniṣads is suggestive of the idea that there is One Eternal Being in whom we live, move and have our being.

The Vedic concept of Viśvadeva could not appease the soul of Upaniṣadic seer as it cannot touch the inner being. The central theme of Upaniṣads is to see unity in the midst of diversity. *Brahman* is the innermost self of all (*sarvabhūtāntarātmā*). Radhakrishnan (1953, vol. I: 145) comments:

---

[8] *yena sarvavijānoti tekena vijānīyat.*

[9] *avijñātam vijānataṁ vijñātamavijānatām* – Ke.U. 2.3

> . . . the Upaniṣads sought to square a growing idealistic philosophy with the dogmas of a settled theology.

Upaniṣads which are known for their "sublime simplicity and rich suggestiveness" are always aware of the underlying unity of all beings. The doctrine of "the universal immanence of an intelligent monism" is the most fundamental presumption of their speculation and as such they never deny the reality of the world, the world as "the countenance of God" is as necessary for Him as He is for the world. The world process, according to Upaniṣads, is not chaotic as it has its base in the Absolute. The Reality which is itself timeless, manifests itself in and through time. The law and order of the universe guarantees the Absolute behind the whole scene.

Whenever the problem of the relation between the multiplicity and unity is discussed, Upaniṣads put forward different similes and symbols and not a definite answer. The world is an emanation of *Brahman* and not creation. Thus there is no distinction between the creator and the created. The belief that *Brahman* is the sole reality includes that the finite world is *Brahman* and it is relatively real. For the belief in the absolute, the denial of the relative is not necessary. The absolute includes as well as transcends the relative world. There is no question of *Brahman* in the world, there is only Brahmā.[10] What is emphasized in the Upaniṣads is the self-sufficiency of *Brahman* and the mode of Its relation with the world. The Upaniṣads never suggest that the entire universe of change is "a baseless fabric of fancy, a mere phenomenal show or world of shadows rather it is His revelation" (*ānandarūpam amṛtam yad vibhāti*). "The inexplicability of the relation between the two is assumed by the Upaniṣads and the later Vedānta gives to it the name of *māyā*" (Radhakrishnan 1953, vol. I: 186). The contention of Upaniṣads is, the stage of manyness does not constitute the Ultimate Reality thus for the knowledge of the Ultimate Reality the manyness should be reduced into one. On the basis of such contention Śaṅkara grabs the opportunity to declare the manyness as illusive in character. He has never based his thought on any

[10] (A) Bṛ.U. V.14-15. (B) Chā.U. VI.1.5.

particular Upaniṣad rather he has linked the threads of different Upaniṣads and woven them into the contexture of his doctrine of *māyā*. He has to discover the idea and not the word. Scholars comment that in no sense Advaita is a school propounded by Śaṅkara, the credit goes to him only for its successful development in a new garb. In fact, the non-dualistic philosophy existed long before its emergence. Nāgārjuna holds that the world from the ultimate point of view (*pāramārthika dṛṣṭi*) is neither born nor exists nor disappears. Gauḍapāda, who formulated his Vedānta on the basis of the philosophy of *Māṇḍūkya Upaniṣad*, integrates the thought of Nāgārjuna in his philosophy with the difference that while in Buddhist philosophy there is no ontological basis, for Gauḍapāda they are all rooted in Absolute Being. Gauḍapāda, the spiritual ancestor of Śaṅkara, did not take this idea further, this task was accomplished by Śaṅkara himself.

Śaṅkara assumes the existence of *māyā* but never proves it. Nowhere has he committed to how does he come to the doctrine of *māyā*. He loudly proclaims that it is an eternal principle but never has proved it. He argues against the pluralists, the theists, the deists but when he comes to the doctrine of *māyā* he maintains discreet silence. Gauḍapāda did not mind him being called a Buddhist but Śaṅkara has great objection to it. Kokileshwar Sastri (1926: Preface) comments:

> It was in no sense a school founded by Śaṅkara. His credit lies in his successful attempt at systematization, development, elaboration and methodical philosophical treatment under which the doctrine appeared in what may be characterized as an altogether new garb in which he clothed it with a master hand. A large part of its principles existed embedded in the hymns of *Ṛgveda*. . .. It was mainly Śaṅkarācārya who first discovered and then brought it out from its unmerited obscurity into the clear light of the day adding to it the lustre which has gathered around it.

A Western scholar comments that Śaṅkara's philosophy is a philosophy of Upaniṣads "only in sharper outlines and in fresher colours". It is styled as "Aupaniṣadic Mīmāṁsā". Although all the six systems claim to derive their authority from Upaniṣads,

Vedānta is entirely based on them as it lays more emphasis on identity than on contradiction.

The Upaniṣads were not compiled as treatises, they are exposition of the innermost experience of seers over a span of several years. The Upaniṣadic *ṛṣis* get at truth by direct awareness, by intuitive experience, or by spiritual exhilaration thus they lack the systematic presentation of thought.

It is a fact that no metaphysics is valid till it has the support of logic. *Brahmasūtra* endeavoured to take this job. Bādarāyaṇa introduced an order in them and presented them systematically. *Brahmasūtra* intends to present the salient thoughts of Upaniṣads in a lucid and methodical manner. During those days the cryptic way of writing was more in vogue. It was difficult for the commoners to understand the underlying thoughts of the aphorisms without a commentary. Thus the different commentators came forward with their interpretation in the light of their own preconceived notion. The chief commentators were Śaṅkara, Rāmānuja, Madhva, Nimbārka and Vallabha propounding the different schools of Vedānta verily known as Kevalādvaita, Viśiṣṭādvaita, Dvaita, Dvaitādvaita and Śuddhādvaita respectively, after Śaṅkara all the later Advaitists added some prefix to the word Vedānta.

The caravan of Advaita in a way finds its completion in the Pūrṇādvaita of Sri Aurobindo where the matter and spirit, *saṁsāra* and *paramārtha*, both are given their due without denying the importance of one or the other. He presents an integral approach, "a dynamic truth vision". His Advaita presents a happy reconciliation of being and becoming. His ideal is "to divinize the human", "to immortalize the mortal" and "to spiritualize the material".

Advaita Vedānta as Independent School

Though the philosophy of Advaita is present both in Vedas and Upaniṣads, Śaṅkara philosophy presents it with more dazzling glory satisfying both the practical and metaphysical needs of man. As Vivekananda comments, Advaita is the fairest flower of philosophy and religion engulfing the whole range of Upaniṣads.

It is "the most satisfying formation of the distinctive spirit of Hinduism" influencing its historical evolution. It towers like a pyramid over all philosophical schools making them almost insignificant on some of the places.

Advaita is not idealism in the general sense of the term but Brāhmanism. As Max Müller puts it, "it is the native philosophy of India". There is a general misconception that it discards all ceremonies, Vedic or post-Vedic, but the fact is, it implies no rejection but only a reinterpretation of the religion. There is no "professional contempt for the traditional worship". What it wants to emphasize is that the truth is to be felt inwardly as a self-expression. It shifts the point of gravity of Indian philosophy from the outer to the inner, from the external God to the soul of man. Gauḍapāda calls Advaitism an accommodating doctrine (Nirvirodhavāda). It can accommodate all placing each in its proper place in the panorama of world thought leading all to the Ultimate Reality of Oneness.

As a single word Advaita means what is devoid of duality; in Upaniṣad it is *ekamevādvityam* (one without the second) but when combined with the word Vedānta it speaks volume about the nature of non-duality having the whole range of Upaniṣadic philosophy on its side. In fact, the entire edifice of Vedānta was built upon the Upaniṣadic philosophy. It is said that the final and the fairest texture of Upaniṣad is "the golden web of Vedānta". To quote Satkari Mukherjee (1975: 298):

> Śaṅkara derived his monistic inspiration direct from the Upaniṣad and only worked out the negative logic in order to vindicate his position.

The philosophy of Advaita generalizes the whole universe into one. This oneness is the rationale of all ethos and all spirituality. ". . . nothing gives such strength as the idea of monism. Nothing makes us so moral as this idea of monism" (Bhattacharya 1986). In fact, the infinite oneness of soul is "the eternal sanction of all morality".

There is general tendency to reject it as an abstract concept denying the reality of the phenomenal world, but the fact is that

Advaita does not accept the complete unreality of difference but only its Ultimate Reality. Apparent unreality lies in its relativity; it is relatively real. For the belief in the Absolute the denial of the relativity is not necessary. Being and becoming "that which is and that which is to be are identical". "*Brahman* is in the world and yet not the world". *Gītā* IX.19 too says: "I am two in one by nature *sat* and *asat*." In fact, the main interest of Advaitism is in establishing the undivided *ātman* and not in explaining away the facts of the empirical world. Non-dualism does not allow the entry of number in its domain. *Vyāvahārika* is only *pāramārthika* in waiting. Indian philosophy realizes universally the necessity of Śaṅkara's Advaita for the correct understanding of the Absolute being and for the evolution and perfection of man who has not only to end as man but as a divine spirit. This philosophy discovers the immanent potency and possibility of human soul. "Advaita is non-different from *vijñāna*, eternal and self-luminous; that is the ever-present knowledge of *Brahman*. It is the highest truth and it never really arises" (Murty 1947). *Śrutirevādvaitapramāṇaṁ*, an Advaitic vision, according to Śrī Harṣa, has immediate and undoubted result.

Some scholars are of the opinion that philosophy of Advaita is not the original contribution of Śaṅkara, it is securely lodged in Veda like oil in the sesame seeds. It is said that Vedānta is directly based on the speculative aspect of Vedas, Śaṅkara has only put it in a new garb. Kokileshwar Sastri (1931: 216) accepts that *Ṛgveda* "is not a book of hymns composed of primitive Indian tillers of soil, but it is a storehouse of Māyāvāda too from which Śaṅkara borrowed the main idea of his philosophy".

Indian philosophers lived their philosophy and later handed down to the successive generation for further development and understanding. Padmapāda, Sureśvara, Vācaspati Miśra and others gave further development to Advaita philosophy.

3

Kevalādvaita of Śaṅkara

VEDĀNTA is a science of reality. The ontological notion of reality is different from the ordinary view of reality. For a common man there is nothing more real than the phenomenal world. As C.E.M. Joad (1924: 6) says:

> The attitude of the ordinary man in the street to the universe is that of an uncompromising Realist.

He finds no reason to doubt the reality of the world. A.E. Taylor (1961: 4) says:

> Metaphysics sets itself more systematically than any other science to ask what after all is meant by being real.

Śaṅkara gives a metaphysical view of reality. According to him, real is "that about which our understanding does not vary".[1] Again he says, real is "that the ascertained nature of which does not undergo any change".[2] At another place he says that "that object which necessarily remains what it is, is truly real".[3] And that Ultimate Reality in Śaṅkara's Advaita is styled as *Brahman*. Thus, Śaṅkara's conception of *Brahman* is logically reducible at once from his conception of real as immutable, self-existent and self-identical being.

Meaning of the Word "Brahman"

The word *brahman* is derived from the root *bṛh* which means "to grow or let grow or to be great, to increase, to expand well", "that which has reached its ultimate evolution, development, expansion

---

[1] *yadviṣayā buddhirna vyabhicarati tatsat* – B.G.Ś.B. II.16

[2] *yadrūpeṇa yanniścitaṁ tadrūpaṁ na vyabhicarati tat satyam* – T.U.Ś.B. II.1

[3] *eka-rūpeṇa hyavastho 'thaḥ sa paramārthaḥ* – B.S.Ś.B. II.I.11

or growth". Thus according to Śaṅkara if we follow the derivative meaning of the term, to be great, etc. "its connotation consisting of eternal purity, etc. gets at once conveyed to us" (Naulakha 1964: 67). Because of its greatness, the Absolute is called *Brahman*.[4] It is known as *Brahman* as it is "fully accomplished and the greatest of all".[5] Again it is known as *Brahman* as "it is (fully) grown and makes other things grow".[6] "By him who analyses the meaning of the word *brahman*, there are cognized meanings eternal, pure, etc. because of confromity with the sense of the root *bṛh*."[7]

There is difference of opinion among writers like Paul Deussen, Rudolph von Roth, Hermann Oldenberg, Alfred Hillebrandt and S. Radhakrishnan about the etymological and chronological meaning of the word *brahman* but that does not count much. Call it by whatever name one likes "absolute", "the great", "world producing energy", etc. the word *brahman* is finally taken in the sense of Ultimate Reality to which phenomenal reality and its evolution is due. "Any way, so far as Śaṅkara is concerned we can definitely say that to him *Brahman* is "the great", "the absolute", "the self-existent", and the one ground and support of all that grows or is of the nature of becoming" (ibid.: 68).

Saguṇa and Nirguṇa-Brahman

Brahman is described in the Advaita Vedānta in two ways: (i) *svarūpa lakṣaṇa* (essential nature), i.e. by definition with reference to the essence;[8] and (ii) by *taṭastha lakṣaṇa* (accidental nature), i.e. by definition with reference to accidents. Normally a definition of a thing marks its difference from others by pointing to its differentia. But in *svarūpa lakṣaṇa* the essence of *Brahman* and not its attribute is chosen as the content of definition. Creatorship, etc.

---

4 *bṛhattvād brahmeti* – Ke.U.Ś.B. I.4

5 *bṛhattamatvādbrahma* – T.U.Ś.B. II.1

6 *bṛṁhati bṛṁhayati tasmāducyate paraṁ brahmeti* – Śve.U.Ś.B. I.1

7 *brahma-śabdasya hi vyutpādyamānasya nitya-śuddhatvādayo 'rthāḥ* | *pratīyante bṛhaterdhātorarthānugamāt* | *sarvasyātmatvācca bṛahmāstitvaprasiddhiḥ* | – B.S.Ś.B. I.1.1

8 *svarūpameva lakṣaṇaṁ svarūpa-lakṣaṇam, yathā satyādikaṁ brahma-svarūpa-lakṣaṇam* – V.P., p. 156

are *taṭastha lakṣaṇa* of *Brahman*, whereas *satyaṁ, jñānam, anantam* are its *svarūpa lakṣaṇa*.[9]

Śaṅkara distinguishes *viśeṣaṇa* from *lakṣaṇa*, i.e. adjective from indicative mark "by maintaining that while the former distinguishes a thing which it qualifies from other things belonging to the same class or falling under the same genus, the latter distinguishes the thing it characterizes from all other things".[10] An adjective has meaning only when there are many things belonging to different groups and possessing many a quality. Thus only *lakṣaṇa* indicates primary significance or the very core of it, not the *viśeṣaṇa*.

There are few minor differences regarding the exact nature of the *svarūpa lakṣaṇa* whether *satyam, jñānam* and *anantam* are to be taken together or each of these should be taken as separate definition.

In the opinion of Brahmānanda Sarasvatī, the author of *Ratnāvalī*, an authoritative gloss on *Siddhāntabindu*, taking them separately will mean three independent realities, thus they constitute the *svarūpa lakṣaṇa* when taken together. *Vedānta Paribhāṣā* maintains that these three may be taken as three independent definitions of the one and the same *Brahman* as there is absolutely no possibility of plurality in *Brahman*. In the case of *Brahman*, truth or existence, knowledge or consciousness are but one and the same thing.

Some thinkers are of opinion that the assertion about *Brahman* as the cause of origin, etc. of the world gives *svarūpa lakṣaṇa* of *Brahman* as Bādarāyaṇa has stated it in the second *sūtra* of *Brahmasūtra*[11] immediately after his assertion in the first *sūtra*[12] there of that *Brahman* "should be the highest object of our inquiry". But it is not so. It may be well explained by pointing out

---

9 *satyaṁ jñānamanantaṁ bṛhmeti brahmaṇo lakṣaṇārthaṁ vākyam* ।
– T.U.Ś.B. II.1

10 *samānajātīyebhya eva nivartakāni viśeṣaṇāni viśeṣyasya* । *lakṣaṇaṁ tu sarvata eva yathāvakāśapradātrākāśamiti* । – Ibid. II.1

11 *janmādyasya yatah* – B.S. I.1.2

12 *athāto brahmajijñāsā* – B.S. I.1.1

the appropriateness of such step. At the primary stage the aspirant should be told such things about unqualified, indeterminate *brahman* to make some image of it in his mind to start with. And this purpose can be served by giving a *taṭastha lakṣaṇa* of it. Śaṅkara says in his commentary on *Taittirīya Upaṇisad,* that the words *sat,* etc. are not related to each other for they are meant for other. These adjectives qualify the subject, *Brahman*. They do not depend on each other rather they are related directly to *Brahman: satyaṁ brahma, anantaṁ brahma, jñānaṁ brahmeti.*[13]

Eliot Deutsch (1968: 10) says:

> *Sat, cit, ānanda* – these terms are really being used properly not so much in a logical as in a phenomenological manner, for the problem is not so much one of defining *Brahman* as it is one of describing the fundamental features of man's experience of oneness.

Svarūpa lakṣaṇa and *taṭastha lakṣaṇa* are of almost universal application and probably all things can be defined in both the ways.

Advaitic *Brahman* signifies the spirit which is the ultimate ground of everything. Following the spirit of Upaniṣads, Śaṅkara makes distinction between *Brahman* as it is in itself and *Brahman* as is conceived by us in relation to the world. The former is called *Para-Brahman,* the latter *Apara-Brahman*. The former is called *Nirguṇa-Brahman,* the latter is called *Saguṇa-Brahman*. It will be a gross error to suppose here that *Nirguṇa-Brahman* is a mere negation. It is not void or mere blank.

Radhakrishnan (1966, vol. II: 536) says:

> When the Absolute is said to be *nirguṇa,* this only means that it is trans-empirical, since *guṇa*s are products of *prakṛti* and the Absolute is superior to it. The *guṇa*s qualify the objective as such and God is not an object.

Kokileshwar Sastri (1926) says:

> The word *nirguṇa* is a technical term. The term *guṇa* is employed to denote what is phenomenal and hence *nirguṇa* means that

---

[13] T.U.Ś.B. II.1.

anything phenomenal does not constitutively belong to *Brahman*.

According to Śaṅkara, *Nirguṇa-Brahman* is also called *paramārtha-tattva* (the highest entity),[14] *sat*,[15] without attributes,[16] *bhūmā* (unexcelled),[17] self-identical, unifrom in nature, real and yet devoid of the nature of the world, without part, *vibhu*,[18] pure and perfectly stainless,[19] though beyond time and space everything is permeated by it. It is devoid of name and from. It is strictly one. It is devoid of self-expression (*āvirbhāva*) and self-concealment (*tirobhāva*), devoid of non-apprehension and misapprehension. It is eternal light of consciousness (*cinmātra-jyotiḥ*). It is inner self of all creatures. It is that by knowing which nothing else remains to be known[20] It is immediate and direct,[21] the innermost self.[22] It is of the nature of eternal knowledge, without interior or exterior, consisting only of the knowledge, all-pervading like the ether and of infinite power, the self of all. It is the unseen seer, the unheard listener, the unthought thinker, the unknown knower.[23]

All these negative epithets do not suggest that *Brahman* is mere blank, an abyss which swallows up all the finites but rather it is fullness of being. To quote Hiriyanna (1955: 163):

> What is meant by speaking of *Brahman* as featureless is that it transcends the distinction between substance and attributes. So the Upaniṣad says, *nirguṇo guṇi*.

A definition must be "per genus et differentia". But *Brahman* neither has genus nor differentia. Śaṅkara admits that even the definition of *Brahman* as *saccidānanda* is imperfect though it

---

[14] *paramārtha-tattvaṁ brahman* – B.G.Ś.B. II.59

[15] *sadākhyaṁ brahman* – ibid. II.17

[16] *nirguṇaṁ satvarajastamāṁsi guṇāh taiḥ varjitam* – ibid. XIII.14

[17] *bhūmā mahān niratiśayam* – ChāU.Ś.B. VII.23.1

[18] *Vividhaṁ brahmādi-sthāvarānta-prāṇibhedair bhavatīt vibhum* – M.U.Ś.B. I.1.6

[19] *Vividhaṁ brahmādi-sthāvarānta-prāṇibhedair bhavatīt vibhum* – M.U.Ś.B. I.1.6

[20] *nirañjanaṁ nirlepam* – Śev.U.Ś.B. VI.1 9

[21] *yatsākṣādaparokṣādbrahma* – Bṛ.U. III.4.1

[22] *ya ātmā sarvāntaraḥ* – ibid.

[23] Bṛ.U. III.7.23.

expresses the reality in the best way possible. Only *brahmānubhāva* gives the insight into *Brahman* and the best way to express oneself is to keep silence.

Śaṅkara reports in his commentary on *Brahmasūtra* (III.2.17) that Bādhva, when asked by Bāṣkali for a definition of *Brahman*, expounded it in the language of silence. When repeatedly pressed for a definition he cried out, "We are telling you, only you do not understand, this *ātman* is silence".[24] Bergson too says: "No amount of concepts can exhaust the nature of finite individual even what to tell of the Absolute."[25]

The natural effect of the negative account of *Brahman* is to give rise to a suspicion that *Brahman* is pure abstraction, "an uncomfortable night of nothingness", "an indeterminate blank". But the truth is not this. Śaṅkara conceives it as the highest reality. Nalini Mohan Mukherji–Sastri(1942: 113) says:

> It is a demand for logical consistency that makes such a negative description inevitable. It is a limitation of the intellect. This is all the more reason why we should guard against committing the error of imagining *Brahman* as almost nothing.

"The logical thought has always a negative moment." Negation is affirmation's correlate. Radhakrishnan (1966, vol. II: 536) says, "It does not follow that it is pure nothing since the negative has its meaning only in relation to the positive." An assumption that nothing is intelligible unless qualified by a quality will land us in infinite regress as that quality will need further quality to qualify it.

Brahman, according to Śaṅkara, beggars all descriptions. Although *Brahman* is immanent in all that is experienced yet nothing which is an object of experience can be predicated of it. Radhakrishnan says: "A demand for theoretical consistency requires us to describe the Absolute by a set of negation, neither personal, nor moral, nor beautiful, nor true as F.H. Bradley does." It can be described, according to Śaṅkara, neither as this nor as that (*neti, neti*). P.M. Modi (1985: 92) in his translation of *Daśaślokī* says:

---

[24] B.S.Ś.B. III.2.17.

[25] Quoted from *Review of Philosophy and Religion*,1934, 5: 59.

> *Brahman* neither is white, nor black, nor red, nor yellow, nor thick, nor short, nor long.

Whatever is experienced in any way is limited, impure, non-intelligent, by the knowledge of these cannot be defined the nature of *Brahman*.[26]

According to Alfred Hillebrandt *na* is not the negative but an affirmative particle signifying "in truth", "it is", or as M. Eckhart expresses it, "The formula can be rendered as *na iti na, iti, Brahman* 'is not not', is the negation of negation, is 'a denial of a denial' " (Deussen 1966: 149). Śaṅkara's explanation, according to Deussen, is already offered in *Bṛhadāraṇyaka Upaniṣad*. Eliot Deutsch (1968) says:

> The via negativa of Advaita Vedānta also safeguards the unqualified oneness of that state of being called *Brahman* and silence all arguments that would seek either to demonstrate or to refute it. Human language has its source in phenomenal experience, hence, it is limited in its application to the state of being that is beyond that experience.

Some supporters of *Nirguṇa-Brahman* have tried to show that the conception of *Saguṇa-Brahman* will land us in "flagrant inconsistency" because if we state *Brahman* has qualities, we have to clarify whether these qualities are different or not from it. In case the qualities are different from *Brahman*, *Brahman* in itself will have to be admitted as something devoid of them, i.e. as *nirguṇa*. And in the case where the qualities are not different from *Brahman*, they will be identical with it. There it would be wrong to say that *Brahman* has them or is qualified by them, since on being so conceived the qualities would go to constitute its very being and consequently would not be its qualities. Thus there is nothing wrong in presumption that *Brahman* is *nirguṇa* "because the assertion that *Brahman* has qualities is either found to be a wrong assertion or to be one which is tantamount to saying that *Brahman* is not, strictly speaking, possessed of qualities (Naulakha 1964: 71). *Nirguṇa-Brahman* is, in Deussen's words, "the last

---

[26] *na tenopalabdhena tadviruddhasya nitya-śuddha-budha-svabhāvasya brahmaṇaḥ svarūpaṁ śakyaṁ lakṣayitum*. – *Bhāmatī*, on B.S.Ś.B. I.1.2, p. 84

unknowable origin of the existent." Negation of quality "does not mean negation of existence of *Brahman*". *Brahman* is *kūṭastha nitya* as against *pariṇāmī nitya*. *Amarakoṣa* defines *kūṭastha nitya* as "one who remains uniform in all times".[27]

Brahman, according to Śaṅkara, is free from all kinds of distinctions *sajātīya–vijātīya* and *svagata bheda*. Rāmānuja admits only *svagata bheda* in *Brahman*. It is both the material and the efficient cause of the world but for Śaṅkara there is no distinction in *Brahman* either homogeneous, heterogeneous or internal.

Sat (Existence)

Though the definition of *Brahman* as existence, consciousness and bliss is imperfect, it expresses the reality in best possible way. What is *sat*? That which abides in all times. *Sat kim? kālatraye 'pi tiṣṭhati iti sat* (that which exists in all the three periods). *Cit kim? jñāna-svarūpam* (it is of the nature of consciousness). *Ānandaḥ kaḥ? sukha-svarūpaḥ* (it is of the nature of bliss).[28]

In Advaita, *sat* is the same as reality and reality is identical with Truth. The term real is often used in Western philosophy in a very wide sense. "All thinkables such as universals, relations and propositions are said to be real." But in Advaita Vedānta reality is not used in ordinary sense. It is *trikāla-satya, trikālābādhita* (not sublated in any period). There is nothing real which is not existent. *Brahman* is the essence of existence, *satyasya satyam* (Bṛ.U. II.3.6).

Vedānta regards existence neither as the appearance of reality nor as a species of the real but as the characteristic nature of the Absolute (Mahadevan 1957: 114). Existence is not an attribute, it is rather the very nature of the being. Existence is *Brahman*.

For Hegel being is the emptiest notion of reason it is the least adequate interpretation of reality and thus there is demand to develop it to make it adequate to most authentic reality. But for Advaita Vedānta being is to be understood not as a notion of

---

[27] *eka-rūpatayā tu yaḥ kālavyāpi sā kūṭasthaḥ* | – *Amarakoṣa*, v. 1118

[28] Quoted by V.J. Kirtikar in *Studies in Vedānta* from Śaṅkara's *Tattvabodha*, p. 53.

reason, but as reality itself.

> Being is the only thing that is real and non-ideal. It is the thing-in-itself. It is not an exaggeration to say that all things are made out of being, live in being and go back to being. Being is their very stuff and substance. It is the only ultimate reality there.
>
> – Malkani 1916: 40

> Advaita Vedānta thus reverses the whole Hegelian position. What was for Hegel the emptiest of ideas is for Advaita Vedānta the most real reality. – ibid.: 41

The concept of empty being is reached through abstraction from the concrete manifold world but Advaita Being, which is *Brahman*, is the ultimate source of this manifold world, by knowing Him everything is known.

Further light on *Brahman* as *satya* may be gathered from Śaṅkara's commentary on the text of *Chāndogya Upaniṣad* VI.2.1.[29] Śaṅkara says that not only before world manifestation but even now *sat* alone is real.

It may be borne in mind that according to Upaniṣads as well as Śaṅkara both, *Brahman* neither is being nor non-being in the ordinary sense of the term with which we are acquainted in the phenomenal world. *Brahman* and *sat* are the two ways of speaking about one thing.

> The word *Brahman* directs us to the ground of the world and something that is great and infinite while the word "being" or *sat* directs our attention to what is eternally real and can never be cancelled in any subsequent knowledge like all things illusory.
>
> – Malkani 1916: 42

Like T.H. Green (1906: 29) who said that "whatever anything is really, it is unalternably", Śaṅkara defines reality as that about which our intellect does not vary.[30] There is difference of meaning in these two terms but there is coincidence in significance.

Plurality of reality is a myth. What is real can never be many; in that case real will be limited and a limited real cannot be

---

[29] *sadeva somyedamagra āsīdekāmevādvitīyam* | – Chā.U. VI. 2.1

[30] *yadviṣayā buddhirna vyabhicarati tatsat* – B.G.Ś.B. II.16

sat (existence) (Mahadevan 1957: 118). Being (*sat*) points to the "ontological principle of unity to the oneness not constituted of parts, to the existential substratum of all subjects and objects".

There is nothing different from *sat*. What is not *sat* must be *asat* but

> the *asat* cannot be the counter correlate of the *sat*, since it is non-existent and unreal. Hence there can be no entity different from and opposed to the *sat*. Real existence is one without a second. It has no genus, it possesses no properties, and it is unrelated to anything else. – ibid.

Negative meaning of being can be more easily understood in different context of experience:

(i) The concept of hare's horn is completely imaginary;

(ii) the concept of son of a barren woman is self-contradictory; and

(iii) there are entities which appear to be real but later on cancelled by real knowledge, i.e. illusory.

The illusory has a "borrowed kind of being", not being in real sense. Only being (*sat*) is real for all times. It is *trikāla-satya,* not to be contradicted by or replaced by experience whatsoever. Real is one.[31] Deutsch (1968) says:

> *Brahman* is experienced as pure unqualified being. In fact, it alone truly exists – which is to say that its manner of being is not comparable to the supposed existence of anything else.

Nihilists conclude everything to be void. They set the example of *Chāndogya Upaniṣad* IV.2.1: "Non-existence alone was in the beginning" and of *Taittirīya Upaniṣad*, "this was *asat* in the beginning, *sat* came out of it",[32] but they are sadly mistaken. What *Chāndogya Upaniṣad* means is, the phenomenal world was non-existent, i.e. undifferentiated before creation and not that, non-existent is the "parent of the world". The words *sat* and *śūnya* are diametrically opposed to each other.

---

[31] *ekameva hi paramārtha-satyaṁ brahma* – T.U.Ś.B. II.6

[32] *asadvā idamagra āsit* | *tato vai sadajāyata* – T.U. II.7

Brahman as Consciousness

The whole edifice of Advaita is built on one of the fundamental tenets that reality is intelligence. *Brahman* is pure existence (*sat*). But this existence must be of the nature of Pure Consciousness too as any kind of real being must have inwardness and depth. And "there can be nothing deeper and more inward in being than intelligence". *Brahman* as *sat* is nothing different from *Brahman* as *cit*.

Śaṅkara says that in scriptures for many times intelligence is ascribed to the principle of world creation. "He designed (*aikṣata*) I will become many, I will procreate."[33] "He designed: I will create the world."[34] We may easily deduce from these that *Brahman* is Pure Intelligence, is pure spirituality.

What type of intelligence is this? In human being, intelligence is known through its functions of feeling, volition, thought, desire, etc. These are *vṛti*s of mind. They have borrowed intelligence only. But when one says *Brahman* is intelligent, it is intelligence in-itself. It is pure intelligence, intelligence as such and not a borrowed one. "By whom can the knower be known."[35]

Brahman without intelligence will be inert. *Brahman* is not an agent of knowing, it is not merely accessory to the act of knowing. Had it been an agent of knowing it could not be *satya* (immutable) and *ananta* (infinite). Ordinarily an act of knowing is inconceivable without an object to be known (*jñeya*). In the case of *Brahman*, it will jeopardize its infinitude. Everything is permeated by *Brahman*. There is nothing beyond *Brahman* to serve as an object of *Brahman*'s knowledge. Reality is free from the three factors (*tripuṭī*) of the knower, the known and the knowledge. It is eternal, indeterminate, infinite consciousness.[36] *Brahman* may not be supposed to know itself for activity in regard to one's own

---

33 *tadaikṣata bahu syāṁ prajāyeyeti* – Chā.U. VI.2.3

34 *sa īkṣata lokānnu sṛjā iti* – Ai.U. I.1.1

35 *vijñātāramare kena vijānīyāt?* – Bṛ.U. IV.5.15

36 *jñātṛ-jñeya-jñāna-śūnyam anantaṁ nirvikalpakam* |
kevalākhaṇḍacinmātraṁ paraṁ tattvaṁ vidurbudhāḥ || – *Vivekacūḍāmaṇi* 239

self is self-contradictory – *nātmani kriyāstitvam*. The hypothesis of Bhāṭṭa Mīmāṁsā that the self is partly sentient and partly inert is, of course, "inadmissible, for *Brahman* is a partless integral whole of intelligence". It is *prajñānaghana* (Bṛ.U. IV.5.13).

In his commentary on *Kena Upaniṣad* Śaṅkara says that *Brahman* is the essence of knowledge (*saṁvedana-svarūpam*). There is neither knowing by itself nor by another (neither *svasaṁvedyāt* nor *para-saṁvedyāt*). In *Brahmasūtra-Bhāṣya*, he says: "It is of the nature of constant consciousness."

Deussen refers Sāṅkhya's objection and Śaṅkara's reply to it that an eternal cognition in *Brahman* would take away the freedom of *Brahman* with reference to the action of cognition. To this Śaṅkara replies that it is only an eternal, actual and not a potential cognition (such as Sāṅkhyas ascribe to the *sattva guṇa* of their primordial matter). A cognition of this kind does not take away the freedom of *Brahman* for in the case of sun we see, it continuously gives us light,"it shines", "it warms" still it does this on its own accord.

The second objection is: Cognition is possible only when there is also an object of perception which was not the case before the creation. The answer is: As the sun shines even when there is nothing to shine upon, so *Brahman* might know without an object of cognition.

The third objection is: cognition cannot proceed without organs of perception, body, senses, etc. The answer is: Reality is consciousness as such; consciousness as it is in itself. Cognition is its very essence. It requires no organ for this effect. Self-revelation is not an act which would require an agent and an object but a fact.

Brahman is light, *svayaṁ-jyotiḥ*, thus naturally it can be deduced from it that *Brahman* is of the nature of consciousness (*caitanya-svabhāvam*). Just as "existence runs like an infinite thread through all particulars of experience",[37] intelligence also remains one and the same despite the plurality of its objects in the states of waking

---

[37] *yeṣu vyāvartamāneṣu yadanuvartate tat tebhyo bhinnaṁ yathā kusumebhyaḥ sūtram* | – *Bhāmatī* on *Adhyāsabhāṣya*

and dream.[38]

Intelligence itself is styled as *saṁvit* in *Pañcadaśī*; it remains homogeneous and integral.[39] Through many months, years, ages . . . consciousness is the same, it is self-revealing.[40] Consciousness is to *Brahman* as illumination is to the sun.[41]

Consciousness and existence are always experienced together. Consciousness is permeated by existence and vice versa. The denial of one leads to the denial of the other. They are one and the same.

Śaṅkara agrees with the Sāṁkhya thinkers when they say that there is one ultimate cause of the world but he does not agree with their assertion that this cause is unintelligent. According to him, non-intelligent *prakṛti* cannot be the cause of this nicely planned universe. A non-intelligent cause cannot produce anything without being guided by intelligent being. How can this world be created by a non-intelligent principle[42] when planning of this world far excels even the intelligence of a skilled architect? For the production of a jar not only clay is required; the potter is not less important. Further, on the basis of cause and effect relation we cannot draw the conclusion that all effects have a non-intelligent principle for their antecedent as we see the relation exists in the case of coaches and chairs also, intelligent principles preside over them (B.S.Ś.B. II.2.1).

The non-intelligent chariots, clay, etc. cater into activities only when they are acted upon by intelligent cause such as the horses and potter. Thus the activity, which is the cause of the world, would be impossible without an intelligent cause. Śaṅkara does not assert that the activity does not belong to non-intelligent thing, he only asserts that it is caused by intelligent agency. "Motion can

---

38 *śabdasparśādayo vedyā vaicitryājjāgare pṛthak* ǀ
tato vibhaktā tatsaṁvidaikarūpyānna bhidyate ǀǀ – *Pañcadaśī*, I.3

38 *tatobhedo 'tastayoḥ saṁvidekarūpa na bhidyate* ǀ – Ibid. I.4

40 *māsābdayugakalpeṣu . . . ekāsaṁvideṣā svayaṁ-prabhā* ǀ – Ibid. I.7

41 *brahmaṇovijñānaṁ tat savitṛ-prakāsávadagnyuṣṇavacca brahma-svarūpāyatiriktaṁ svarūpameva tat* ǀ – T.U.Ś.B. II.1

42 *ato racanānupapatteśca hetornācetanaṁ jagatkāraṇ am anmātavyaṁ bhavati* ǀ
– B.S.Ś.B. II.2.1

be reconciled with the doctrine of an all-knowing first cause; but not with the doctrine of a non-intelligent first cause."[43]

The flow of milk and water cannot support Śaṅkara's viewpoint as water flows because of declivity of soil and cow makes her milk flow because of motherly love for the calf (B.S.Ś.B. II.2.3). A non-intelligent cause cannot explain "the original impetus, the first push, the elan". The simile of blind and lame also does not help them as both are intelligent and active beings, but *prakṛti* is unconscious and *puruṣa* conscious, there cannot be any contact among them. The simile of grass turning into milk also does not explain their position as only when grass is eaten by female mammal animal it is turned into milk and not when eaten by a bull. On these reasons the spontaneous modification of the *pradhāna* cannot be proved.[44] Even if we admit the spontaneous activity of *pradhāna*, the purpose of creation will remain unexplained. If release is the purpose of *pradhāna*, its activity is useless as the soul is in the state of release already. The objects themselves do not possess pleasure, pain and infatuation which can plea for *triguṇātmikā prakṛti* as the ultimate cause. These objects impart such feelings only on account of desire and mental disposition of man. Thus Śaṅkara concludes that unless an ultimate intelligent principle is presupposed, the process of creation cannot be explained. On the basis of scriptures and on the basis of reasoning in accordance with the scriptures, only conscious *Brahman* can be the material and the efficient cause of the world.[45]

Brahman as Bliss

This consciousness, which is our self, is of the nature of Supreme bliss. *Brahman* is unexcellable bliss. *Ānanda* is not that what *Brahman* has but what *Brahman* is.

There are many passages in Upaniṣads which attribute bliss

---

[43] *tasmātsambhavati pravṛttiḥ saravajñakāraṇatvena tvacetana kāraṇatve* |
– B.S.Ś.B. II.2.2

[44] *tasmānna tṛṇādivatsvābhāvikaḥ pradhānasya pariṇāmaḥ* | – B.S.Ś.B. II.2.5

[45] *ata āgamavaśenāgamānusāri-tarkavaśena ca cetanaṁ brahma jagataḥ kāraṇaṁ prakṛtiśceti sthitam* || – B.S.Ś.B. II.1.11

as the characteristic of *Brahman*. "That which is infinite is bliss, there is no bliss in the finite."[46] "All infinite is full of nature of bliss, because it is free from all desires that lead to suffering." Śaṅkara could not help but believe that *ānanda* is essential to *Brahman*.

> By the characterization of *Brahman* as *ānandamaya*, it is not, however, to be construed that *Brahman* becomes transformed into bliss as suggested by the use of the suffix *mayaṭ*, but is the infinite source of bliss. – Mukherji 1942: 118

In his *Bhāṣya* on *Brahmasūtra* (I.1.12) Śaṅkara, in a series of arguments, examines the opponent's possible objection on the basis of *Taittirīya Upaniṣad* that the self which is characterized by *ānandamaya* is not the Supreme Self (T.U.Ś.B. II.5). The opponents say that it is only *jīvātman* and not *Brahman* because in the first place the *ānandamaya* comes last in the series of lower *ātman* such as those made of food, mind and intelligence. Second, it has joy, etc. as its limb, e.g. "joy is its head". Third, unlike *Brahman*, it has body, viz. the preceding *ātman* is made up of intelligence.

In reply to this Śaṅkara says *ānandamaya* means the highest *ātman* (B.S.Ś.B. I.1.12). "After introducing the topic of *ānandamaya* as an embodied one, it is further said to constitute the essence of flavour, *rasa*. It is after getting this *rasa* that one finds the bliss."[47] *Brahman* is figuratively depicted as a being whose head is joy. *Taittirīya Upaniṣad* itself refers: "He reaches the self, consisting of bliss."[48] "He who knows the Bliss of *Brahman* fears nothing."[49] "He understands that Bliss of *Brahman*." In *Bṛhadāraṇyaka Upaniṣad* too, it is mentioned that knowledge and bliss are *Brahman*. Śaṅkara says as a man, when he has to point out the star Arundhati, points it in the last after showing other stars which are not Arundhati, similarly self consisting of bliss is the real self, it is pointed at last on account of its being the innermost. Thus *ānandamaya ātman* is

[46] (a) *yo vai bhūmā tatsukhaṁ, nāpe sukhaṁ asti* | – Chā.U. VII.23.1

(b) *raso vai saḥ* – T.U. II.7

(c) *ānando brahmeti vyajānat* | – T.U. III.6.1

[47] Date 1954: p. 44.

[48] *etam ānandamayam ātmānam upasaṅkrāmati* – T.U. II.8.5

[49] *vijñānam ānandaṁ brahma* – Bṛ.U. III.9.28

the highest *Brahman*.[50]

Commenting on *Brahmasūtra*,[51] he meets the objection that component *maya* of the compound *ānandamaya*, i.e. of the nature of bliss means *vikāra* (modification), just as *annamaya* and similar words do and *Brahman*, according to Śaṅkara, cannot undergo any sort of modification. He says *maya* may be used also in the sense of abundance[52] and *Brahman* is called *ānandamaya* since it is full of Bliss, abounding in Bliss. *Taittirīya Upaniṣad* (II.8) refers that bliss of *Brahman* knows no measure. Thus *maya* here denotes only abundance.[53]

He strengthens his contention in his commentary on *Brahmasūtra* I.1.14. The suffix *maya* of *ānandamaya* means only abundance and the compound itself is attributed to *Brahman*. He quotes *Taittirīya Upaniṣad* in his support "He, who bestows Bliss himself, abounds in Bliss".[54]

Brahmasūtra (I.1.15) gives Śaṅkara another opportunity to reiterate his contention that *Brahman* is of the nature of Bliss. He refers to the theory of gradual understanding of self which he names as *koṣa*. There is always a self inner and higher than the previous one. There is nothing inner and higher than the self which is bliss. It is self (*paramātman*) which is *ānandamaya* who has created the world.

In his commentary on *Brahmasūtra* I.1.17, Śaṅkara concludes that the self consisting of bliss cannot be identical with the transmigratory soul for the reason that "it (self-consisting of bliss) is a flavour; for only after perceiving a flavour can this (soul) perceive bliss". (Thibaut 1957: 69). This *ānandamaya Brahman* is the cause of the world and not the inert *prakṛti* of Sāṁkhya (B.S.Ś.B. I.1.18).

In *sūtra* I.1.19, Śaṅkara has just reversed the conclusion drawn in the previous *sūtras*. After explaining the *sūtras* from I.1.12 to

---

[50] *eṣa eva param ānandaḥ* – Ibid. IV.3.33

[51] *vikāraśabdānneti cenna pracuryāt* – B.S. I.1.13

[52] *Pāṇini Sūtra* V.4.21.

[53] *prācūryārthe mayat* – B.S.Ś.B. I.1.13

[54] *eṣa hyevānandayāti* – T.U. II.7

I.1.18 in the sense of *Brahman* as blissful, Śaṅkara critically reviews the entire question again. Why should the suffix *maya* be used in the sense of transformation (*vikāra*) in the case of *annamaya*, *prāṇamaya*, etc. and in the sense of abundance in the case of *ānandamaya*. Referring to *Taittirīya Upaniṣad* II.5, where it is said with reference to *ānandamaya* that joy is its head, satisfaction is its right wing, delight is its left wing, *ānanda* (bliss) is its soul and *Brahman* is its tail and support, Śaṅkara just reverses his previous assertion (*tasmādānandamaya para evātmā*) and says that the self-consisting of Bliss is not the Ultimate *Brahman*, it is rather an effect of *Brahman* which is also the cause of the entire aggregate of effects. Thibaut says that this is an exceedingly forced interpretation that *ānandamaya* is not *Brahman*. Deussen says that the second part of the *sūtra* I.1.19, where the interpretation is put forth to the effect that *ānandamaya* is not *Brahman*, is interpolation. Radhakrishnan too says that here Śaṅkara offers a strained interpretation and that the *sūtrakāra* evidently means that *Brahman* is full of Bliss. According to A.G. Warrier, the whole trouble centres round the problem whether "*Brahman* has bliss or is Bliss" and Śaṅkara's objection aims at the expression of *ānandamaya* and not at *ānanda*.

Any way I have not to indulge here in an inquiry or to make a textual evaluation. What is important is, Śaṅkara conceives *Brahman* as Bliss. He has himself asserted against this conclusion in his commentary on *sūtras* III.3.11, 12 and 13. So unshakable is the intuition of *Brahman* as Bliss that they cannot deprive *Brahman* of Bliss for a moment. He observes: "The empirical or the finite bliss is also a part of the Bliss of *Brahman*."[55] All the beings of the universe are dependent on the Bliss of *Brahman* for their existence (Bṛ.U.Ś.B. IV.3.32). Who indeed would breathe, who will live, if this Bliss were not the ether? (T.U. II.7).

Deussen calculates in *Philosophy of Upanishad* that a human bliss is just a hundred billionth part of the Bliss of *Brahman*. This assertion shows that Bliss of *Brahman* surpasses all our worldly conceptions and enjoyment of bliss.

Thus Śaṅkara has conceived Pure Existence, Pure Consciousness

---

[55] *laukiko 'pyānando brahmānandasyaiva mātrā* – T.U.Ś.B. II.8

and Pure Bliss as constituting the very essence of *Brahman*. The very fact that every conscious being desires to be and never not to be indicates that existence and consciousness are inseparably one with happiness or bliss.

Saguṇa Brahman or Īśvara

Brahman associated with *māyā* is represented as the cause of the world.

> If now we choose to look upon them as together constituting the source of the world, their blend or combination becomes what is known as the qualified (*Saguṇa*) *Brahman*, comprehending all the diversity of experience including the experiencing selves.
>
> – Hiriyanna 1955: 163

Īśvara is the determinate (*Saguṇa*) *Brahman*. He is the Supreme Personality. *Saguṇa-Brahman* is not other than *Nirguṇa-Brahman* conceived with the adjunct of *māyā*. The moment we try to think of *Brahman* in terms of intellectual categories, the moment we try to make this ultimate subject an object of our thought, it is converted into determinate God. *Īśvara* is the "personal aspect of the impersonal *Brahman*". "After showing the nature of *Brahman* unconditioned by an adjunct, Śaṅkara describes the attributes of *Brahman* as omniscience and omnipotence due to the adjunct of *avidyā*."[56]

Brahman is indeterminate Pure Being, Pure Consciousness (*caitanyamātrasattākam* – Ke.U.Ś.B. I.5), *Īśvara* as such is being-in-becoming. While *Brahman* is inactive, *Īśvara* is active. God to an Advaitist is the personal aspect of the Absolute and the Absolute the impersonal aspect of God (Ranade 1968: 159). He is the Lord of *māyā*. *Īśvara* is known as *Apara-Brahman*, *Brahman* is known as *Para-Brahman*. In *Nirguṇa-Brahman* "all distinctions are obliterated and are overcome, in *Saguṇa-Brahman* they are integrated, a duality in unity is present here".

Śaṅkara reconciles lower and higher "in his own masterly way by a subtle process of logical reasoning which is at once beautiful

---

[56] *Bhāmatī* 1.11.

and convincing" (Mukherji 1942: 109)

Nirguṇa-Brahman is a state of "spiritual enlightenment" (*jñāna*), *Saguṇa-Brahman* is a state of "vital loving awareness (*bhakti*)". While God necessarily requires world and individual soul to be ruled by Him, *Brahman* is beyond all these. "*Saguṇa Brahman* is the content of loving experience of unity, *Nirguṇa-Brahman* is the content of intuitive experience of identity" (Deutsch 1968).

God, according to Śaṅkara, is endowed with all auspicious qualities. He is omnipotent, omniscient, the cause of the origin, sustenance and dissolution of the entire world. He is the object of worship. He sees without eyes, listens without ear.[57] As luminosity is the nature of sun, His nature is of eternal knowledge. He is the cause of all effects. He is *satya-saṅkalpa, sarvajña, sarvaśakti-śamanvita*, the Supreme Spirit. He is above all evil (B.S.Ś.B. I.2.18). He is *antaryāmī*, pervading the subjective and objective worlds. All the perfections – metaphysical and moral – are ascribed to him. He is the crown of moral perfection.

Radhakrishnan (1966, vol. II: 545) says:

> The reality of Īśvara, in Śaṅkara's philosophy, is not a self-evident axiom, is not a logical truth, but an empirical postulate which is practically useful.

With the imagination of phenomenal God, Śaṅkara could reconcile the conception of *Nirguṇa-Brahman* with a creator *Brahman*. *Īśvara* is both the material and the efficient causes of the world, is both suggested and directly expressed in different Upaniṣads. As spider prepares its cobweb out of its own saliva – it is both the efficient and the material causes of it – *Īśvara* is the cause of the world (M.U.Ś.B. I.1.7). He is the first cause since he has no origin (B.S. II.3.9). God of Nyāya is only the efficient cause of the world. Śaṅkara criticizes their concept of God in his *Brahmasūtra-Bhāṣya* II.2.37-41.

> The conception of *Īśvara* is not an irrelevant intruism, tertium quid, an unnecessary intervening between the highest Reality and *jīva*. On the other hand, the conception serves many practical purposes. – Iyer 1964: 82

---

[57] *paśyatyacakṣuḥ sa sṛṇotyakaraṇaḥ* – *Śvetāśvataropaniṣad* 3: 19.

It is the connecting link, the immediate step in the realization of the Pure Spirit. The diversity of the world must be dissolved into identity before it finally submerges into Pure Unity, i.e. *Brahman*. Though *Saguṇa-Brahman* is not the highest possible experience, it is an extremely valuable experience. Worship of *Īśvara* makes our road to *Brahman* clear and swift. At an early stage mind refuses to grasp the notion of immutable, indescribable absolute. At this stage the idea of merging their personal identity and losing their individuality is unpalatable to them. The worship of God prepares our mind to feel this unity, to realize the identity, to visualize it is all *Brahman*.[58] "The affirmation of *Saguṇa-Brahman*, however, is not merely an acknowledgement of human limitations, it is also the name for that spiritual experience that harmonizes rather than obliterates distinctions."[59]

God is both the immanent and the transcendent causes. *Bhagavadgītā* narrates:

> He is without and within all being. He is free from the dispositions of nature and yet He enjoys them.

A.N. Whitehead (1925) too speaks of God both as immanent and transcendent:

> . . . something which is a remote possibility and yet the greatest of present facts, something that gives meaning to all that passes and yet eludes apprehension, something whose possession is the final goal and yet is beyond all reach.

This something is Vedāntic *Īśvara* only; it is not "beyond all reach".

Śaṅkara presupposes that prior to its creation the phenomenal world existed in the mind of *Īśvara* as its object. Śaṅkara says, "the work of creation becomes the subject matter of the knowledge of *Īśvara* before creation" (B.S.Ś.B. I.1.5). God is not impelled by any special motive but for *līlā*. He comes out spontaneously from the nature of God (ibid. II.1.33). He is always conscious of underlying unity though He manifests diversity through His accessory *māyā*.

It is not that Śaṅkara points *Brahman* first, *māyā* next, then

---

[58] *sarvaṁ khalvidaṁ brahma* – Cha.U. III.14.1

[59] *Brahmasūtra*, p. 14.

conjoins the two into *Saguṇa-Brahman* and lastly derives the world of being and things from it. He simply analyses the given and comes to his concept of *Brahman* and *māyā* (Ray Chaudhuri 1950).

Śaṅkara accepts two forms of *Brahman* – *Para-Brahman* and *Apara-Brahman*. He unhesitatingly makes this distinction in his commentary on *Brahmasūtra* I.1.19-20; 1.2.2; I.2.14; I.2.21; etc. in his *Bhāṣya* on *Bṛhadāraṇyaka* II.3.1 and *Praśna Upaniṣad*[60] but that does not mean he believed in two different forms of *Brahman*. It is one and the same viewed from two different points, one phenomenal, the other noumenal, the one being true for devotion and the other for knowledge. Max Müller (1967: 82) truly says:

> The exoteric *Brahman* was substantially the same as the esoteric, that there was in reality and that there could be one *Brahman* only, not two.

Saguṇa Īśvara is being-in-becoming, identity-in-difference so He cannot be called truly real; but it is as much a logical necessity as the conception of *Brahman*. Malkani (1916: 190) says:

> The Advaitic God or *Īśvara* is not to be understood in an external way as a real God, existing prior to this creation. He is a functional God. If creation, then God, what exists prior to creation is the unqualified *Brahman*.

Such a God is necessary for religion not for philosophy. According to R. Otto (1932), Śaṅkara's Advaitic philosophy represents theism of high type, it is not simply the theism of old monastic Upaniṣad. Thus *Īśvara* in Advaita is "a spiritually significant principle from which derive all life and its value" (Warrier 1961: 258.5). *Īśvara* is *Brahman* himself deprived of qualities.

Proofs for the Existence of God

The proofs advanced by Śaṅkara in respect of God's existence, according to Deussen, may be classified under four heads – (i) cosmological, (ii) physico-theological, (iii) psychological, and (iv) ontological (Kirtikar 1924: 123). According to J.N. Sinha (1952: 512),

---

[60] *oṁkārasya paraṁ cāparaṁ ca brahmetyabhedaśruteḥ* | – Pra.U.Ś.B. V.3

> Śaṅkara gives the cosmological, ideological and moral arguments for the existence of God.

According to cosmological proof, the world is an effect, we presume a cause of it and the cause is none but God. He Himself is the uncaused cause of the world.[61] The other name of physico-theological proof is the argument from design. There must be some teleology behind the planned creation. Moral proof presumes that God is the Lord of the law of *karma*. He produces the fruit of action. Mīmāṁsā's theory of *apūrva* is not acceptable to Śaṅkara as it is a non-intelligent principle; God is the source of scriptural injunctions and prohibitions. Vedas are His breath. This is a moral proof for the existence of God.

S.N. Dasgupta (1922, vol. I: 438) says: "The reasons that Śaṅkara adduces for the existence of *Brahman* may be considered to be threefold." (1) *Brahman* is the cause from which the "world has sprung into being". But it cannot be thought that *Brahman* itself has originated from something else – that will lead us to the theory of infinite regress (*anavasthā doṣa*). (2) A non-intelligent source cannot be the cause of law and order of the universe – and that intelligent source is none but *Brahman*. (3) *Brahman* is the consciousness which shines as self through the objects of the world. It is our essence. To deny *Brahman* is to deny ourselves.

In fact, Śaṅkara believes that God cannot be proved by reason. His approach to the Ultimate Reality is not rationalistic. He showed the futility of proofs for the existence of God as Immanuel Kant did much later. Kant says all proofs lead to *antinomies*. Śaṅkara believes that if we say that *Brahman* is the cause of the world it is on the authority of the Upaniṣads and not on the basis of reasoning. Even if we admit the universality of causal relation, the category of causality cannot be applied to supra-rational reality. Cosmological argument can promise only a "finite creator of this finite creation". If *Īśvara* is the cause, he must fall within space and time, he will no more be infinite or omnipotent. The teleological proof can only point out the fact that a conscious principle is working at the root of creation. The ontological proof can give an idea of God and

---

[61] Śve.U. VI.9; Cha.U. VI.22.

not God as a real object. Deussen, too, does not think high of this argument. He remarks:

> Indians are never ensnared into an ontological proof. On the other hand, we find a new proof in which the concept of God blends with the concept of the soul. – Kirtikar 1924: 123

But Radhakrishnan (1966, vol. II: 534) does not agree with him and he remarks, "So far as any logical proof of *Brahman* is available in Śaṅkara's writings, it is undoubtedly the ontological proof". To him the idea of perfection leads to Reality that is *Brahman*. *Mokṣa* is only the other name for it.

However, for the existence of God "as Kant falls back on faith, Śaṅkara falls back on Śruti" (Sharma 1960: 396). He says that *Brahman* is proved on the basis of testimony of scriptures. Perception is not an adequate means for knowing *Brahman* as *Brahman* cannot be an object of experience,[62] nor can it be known by *anumāna* (T.U.Ś.B. II.1.1). Reasoning too has no solid foundation as it depends upon human mind.[63] Reason is insecure.[64] The question of *upamāna* does not arise as its field is very limited. In fact, the *pramāṇas* hold good only in the phenomenal world of *avidyā*.[65] They rest in *jīva*. How can these *pramāṇas* produce the sense and knowledge of reality in us. In reply, Śaṅkara points out that

> the *pramāṇas* do succeed in producing right knowledge, even as lines straight and crooked and letters such as *a*, *i*, become instrumental in the production of the cognition of real sound for letters.[66]

Thus reason, according to Śaṅkara, is only "ancillary to revelation". Only Śruti can provide proofs for the existence of God.[67] He

---

62 (a) *na pratyakṣam atīndriyatvāt* I – S.D.S., p. 789

(b) *nāyamarthaḥ pratyakṣa-gocaraḥ . . . nānumānādīnām* I – B.S.Ś.B. II.1.11

63 *na pratiṣṭhitatvaṁ tarkāṇāṁ śakyamāśrayituṁ puruṣamativairūpyāt* I – B.S.Ś.B. II.1.11

64 *tarkastvanavasthito bhrānto 'pi bhavati* I – K.U.Ś.B. I.3

65 *avidyāvadviṣayāṇi . . . pratyakṣādi pramāṇāni* I – B.S.Ś.B. I.1.1

66 Devaraja and Hirematha, 1971, *A Source Book of Śaṅkara.*

67 *tad brahma vedānta-śastrādevāvagamyate . . . tasmātsiddhaṁ* I – *brahmaṇāḥ*

puts *śruti* on the highest dias because it is a record of realized experience which "can fetch for us goal earlier than by logical understanding". At best, arguments can point out the possibility of God and at worst, they make atheism plausible, but they cannot help us in realizing the vision of God. But setting aside proofs for the existence of God does not mean denial of God altogether. Radhakrishnan (1966, vol. 2: 544-45) says:

> Śaṅkara's point is that no purely rational argument for the existence of God as a personal supreme being is finally acceptable. At best the "proofs" only tell us that God is a possibility. The reality of God transcends our rational power of conceiving as well as comprehending, only if we resort to the spiritual insight of seers as recorded in the scriptures can we be certain of God.

The doctrine of *Īśvara* has been a hard nut to crack for the followers of Śaṅkara. According to Pratibimbavāda "*Īśvara* is the reflection of *Brahman* in *māyā*, while *jīva* is the reflection of *Brahman* in *avidyā*". According to Avacchedavāda, *Brahman* conditioned by *māyā* is *Īśvara* while *Brahman* limited by *avidyā* is *jīva*. Some other followers regard *jīva* as the reflection of *Īśvara*. Again Ābhāsavāda regards *Īśvara* and *jīva* as inexplicable appearances of *Brahman*. Sharma (1960: 397) says: "The post-Śaṅkarites have indulged in needless hair-splitting. The problem was not at all taxing to Śaṅkara." He uses different similes as the reflection of sun or moon in waves, the reflection of space in jars, of red flower in the crystal, only "as a metaphor for their suggestive value". Śaṅkara seems to advocate Abhāsavāda theory as *Īśvara* and *jīva* are only appearances (*vivarta*) of *Brahman*. *Brahman* is God to those who are still under the spell of *avidyā*.

Not understanding properly the concept of *Brahman*, some Western philosophers have indulged in uncharitable criticism of Śaṅkara's conception of *Brahman*. Hegel described Indian *Brahman* as "a characterless nothingness", "an empty abstraction", "a purposeless empty power without wisdom and without activity". Another critic describes *Brahman* as "an abyss of

---

śāstrapramāṇakatvam | – B.S.Ś.B. I.1.4

negative infinitude", still another "an abyss which swallows all finite being", "a cave of lion in which all loot-steps lead but none lead out again", "practically useless in the development of man and society". It is nothing but "picturesque recklessness" to hurl such criticisms against Śaṅkara. In the language of Max Müller (1893: 534), "they have made an abyss between the human and the divine and they dare not cross it". Kirtikar says that they belong to a different plane of thought.

Śaṅkara's *Nirguṇa-Brahman* is not like Baruch Spinoza's substance, because the latter possesses attributes. It is not like J.H. Fichte's Absolute Ego, for in Fichte the anstoss or the principle of self-limitation of the Absolute Ego is real. Evidently it has no similarity with Hegel's Absolute. It is not like Kant's *Ding an sich*. For Kant does not posit its objective existence. The concept of noumenon is merely the correlative of phenomenon and limits the sphere of sensibility . . . the best analogue of *Nirguṇa-Brahman* in European philosophy is the Eleatic Being.[68]

According to Kirtikar (1924: 30), the Vedāntic *Brahman* is in the Hegelian mode of expression,

> an absolute self-conscious, self-determining spirit of thought which reveals itself in the unified difference of the finite world . . . a Being which has in it the impulse (*sphūrti*) to realize itself in all the manifold.

The old gods (Viśvakarmā, Prajāpati and Varuṇa) were abandoned not because "the ancient Āryan believed or desired less but because Śaṅkara believed and desired more". To quote Max Müller "It is not so much atheism as adevism". *Brahman* is the positive ground, it is the "fullest reality", the "completest consciousness".

Śaṅkara's Conception of Man and His Bondage

The cornerstone of Vedāntic philosophy is the "primal, eternal, immutable facthood of the *ātman* (the self) or *Brahman*". The moment *Brahman* is associated with *māyā*, *jivātman* and God are simultaneously posited. According to Śaṅkara, the pure subjective

[68] Shastri 1911: 115.

is the pure objective. Śaṅkara adheres to the concept of unity without any difference and follows it logically in every sphere. He has not only established the concept of soul of Upaniṣad, he has also attached much more importance to it.

> It is not a microcosm to him in a macrocosm, it is the macrocosm itself. It is not merely a true index to the reality proper according to him, but it is reality itself – Mukherji 1942: 156. He thus identifies the soul per se with the *Brahman* itself.
>
> – Mukherji 1942: 156

It is eternal, indivisible, immutable, self-luminous, "undifferentiated being–consciousness–bliss", inactive, partless and one.[69]

Ātman is the universal self. Its existence cannot be denied. One who denies it is none but *ātman*. It is there even in the act of denial of its existence. It is not a matter of inference or it is not to be deduced from empirical knowledge or a postulate demanded by experience, it is verity of direct experience. It is self-manifested, self-revealed. The *ātman* is self-luminous by its own power.[70]

It is not proved by *pramāṇa*s rather it is the presupposition of all *pramāṇa*s. To quote *Naiṣkarmyasiddhiḥ*: "How can that by which all the *pramāṇa*s are established, be itself established by the *pramāṇa*s."[71] "*Ātman* being itself of the nature of knowledge does not depend on any knowledge."[72] It is established earlier than the operation of *pramāṇa*s. "Consciousness, according to the Advaita thinkers, being the ultimate principle of revelation cannot stand in need of a mere ulterior principle of its own revelation. That which is the prime of the knowable objects cannot itself be conceived as an object among other objects much as the light which reveals everything does not require a second light for its own manifestation."[73] The same truth is expressed by Descartes in his famous dictum *cogito ergo sum* (I think therefore I am), but

---

[69] *ekastathā sarvabhūtāntarātmā rūpaṁ rūpaṁ pratirūpo bahiśca* |

– K.U. II.2.10

[70] *atrāyaṁ puruṣaḥ svayaṁ jyotiḥ* – Bṛ.U. IV.3.9

[71] *yato rāddhiḥ pramāṇānaṁ sa kathaṁ taiḥ prasidhyati* | – Naiṣ. 11.37

[72] See B.S.Ś.B. II.3.7; also K.U.Ś.B. II.2.4.

[73] Mukerji 1943: 129.

> Śaṅkara starts with the existence of the *Ātman*, the universal self, which is the ontological reality of the individual self whereas Descartes starts with the existence of the individual self.
>
> – Sinha 1952: 486

It is not transcendental in its negative significance of non-empirical rather the whole universe is permeated by consciousness. It is of the nature of undifferenced consciousness (*nirviśeṣa caitanya*). It is trans-empirical (*niṣprapañca*). It is of the essence of consciousness and bliss (*caitanyānandaghana*). It is devoid of enjoyment (*bhoktṛtva*) and activity (*kartṛtva*).

By what means can the knower be known?[74] The question of knowability of the self was first put up by the Sage Yājñavalkya in the history of world philosophy. May *ātman* ever be an object of knowledge? Śaṅkara raises this question while discussing the possibility of *adhyāsa*. K.C. Bhattacharyya (1909: 30) says: "The Vedāntic self is incapable of being caught in any determinate mode of knowledge."

In its essential nature *Ātman* is eternal,[75] homogeneous consciousness, witness of all cognition and their knower. It cannot be the effect of anything because it is self-proved (B.S.Ś.B. II.3.7).

Being, Consciousness and Bliss constitute the very essence of the self, they are not adjectival to the self. Being means that which cannot be negated. It is *sat*, *sat* for all the times. The self is consciousness as such whose light never ceases or wanes. It is not an adventitious quality, rather the very being of the self (B.S.Ś.B. II.3.29). It never rises or sinks. *Cit* (consciousness) has no English equivalent. It is not mind, not sentiency. It may be called consciousness, says Woodroffe, if by consciousness we mean "atomic or physical consciousness, comatose or trance like consciousness of plant life, animal consciousness and man's complete self-consciousness". It can neither be the substrate nor the object of consciousness. And if consciousness be self-luminous, the soul which is not different from it, is also self-revealing. *Ātman* is homogeneous consciousness, *nityabodha-svarūpa*.

---

[74] *vijñātāram are kena vijānīyāi?* – Br.U. IV.5.15

[75] M.U. I.1.6; Bṛ.U. IV.4.25, etc.

The self is bliss as such. Pleasure and pain are the properties of mind but bliss is of self. In dream stage and waking stage, we do not realize the blissful nature of self. In dreamless stage self shines with its inherent glory because it is here, it is totally detached from non-sentient objects.

Self-love is palpable. Man loves everything not for their sake but for his own sake (Bṛ.U. II.4.5). They are "ancillary accessories which serve the purpose of self-pleasure". Ācārya Śaṅkara says:

> I am not an individual life-monad (*jivo nāham*), I am the Blissful one (*śivo-'ham*), I am Śiva (the peaceful one) whose form is spirituality and bliss. – Zimmer (1953: 462)

Being, Consciousness and Bliss are not the determinations of the self. The self cannot be conceived as a substance possessed of attributes, since the substance–attributes notion signifies a relation and a relation implies distinction between the relata. Distinction is a category which is a product of *māyā* – the self is beyond the tentacles of *māyā* (Ray Chaudhuri 1955: 100-01). In *Upadeśasāhasrī*, Śaṅkara says that like ornament all these qualifications of self are superimposed through ignorance, when self is known, they prove to be unreal (VI.3). He again says that all the qualities are similar to the arms cut off and thrown away as they are all non-self. So the self is free from all qualifications (VI.2).

The self is all-pervading. It is one, not many, it is ubiquitous. Self is the knower not by dint of any activity in it but by its mere existence. Devaraja (1972: 189) says:

> The self is merely the principle of revelation in experience, and there can be no experience without revelation or illumination. Just as there is no meaning in speaking of vision without light, similarly it is meaningless to speak of experience without consciousness.

The self which is the nature of consciousness is ever present in experience. Its absence is unthinkable, since in its absence there will never be any experience. *Jñeya* is different from *jñāna*, thus the absence of *jñeya* never proves the absence of *jñāna* (Pra.U.Ś.B. VI.2). The *ātman* is known as the presupposition of all knowledge

(Ke.U.Ś.B. II.4). Sureśvarācārya in *Naiṣkarmyasiddiḥ* II.64 compares "the self with gem which shines in the presence of other objects as well as in their absence without undergoing any change". This self illumines all acts of the mind but remains itself unaffected by the change of mental states.

It is neither an active agent nor an object of activity. It is by nature inactive as activity is of the nature of pain and an active *ātman* cannot be liberated, pleasure and pain belong to empirical self. It is beyond space and time causality.

S.N.L. Srivastava says:

> What is taken as the first and foundational principle in Vedāntism is not a problematic something, an inaccessible noumenon, but the deepest and most undeniable verity of our experience. At the very start Vedāntism steers clear of all kinds of acosmism and transcendentalism.[76]

It is a remarkable fact that even scientists of today are well aware of the fact that consciousness is the most certain fact in experience. "Mind", says Arthur Stanley Eddington, "is the first and most direct thing in our experience, all else is remote inference". Vedānta gives the challenging truth that the consciousness which illumines all and which being everything is in our very self, the inmost core of our being.[77]

To Kant, self is a "necessary logical postulate of our experience", "an object of moral faith and not a determinate fact". He speaks of the noumenal self but it is unknown and unknowable, thus later philosophers cancelled this view. It is not like the Vedāntic self which cannot be known but then there is no demand to know it as an object. It is to be known intuitively not logically. It is not known as an object, but this never means the self is unknown and unknowable. A.C. Mukerji (1943: 310) says:

> Deussen's interpretation of Śaṅkara's theory of self on the agnostic lines seems to be due to the fact that he construes such phrases as "not knowable as an object" and "unknown as an

---

[76] "What Vedantism Is?", *Prabuddha Bharata*, 1937, vol. XLII, p. 532.

[77] Ibid.

object" as equivalent of entirely inconceivable and unknowable.

Self is knowable par excellence. Thus there should not be any confusion with agnostic position.

Jīva and Ātman

The difference between *jīva* and *ātman* is not transcendental but phenomenal due to "limiting adjunct" *avidyā* (B.S.Ś.B. I.2.20). *Jīva* is the Absolute in association with *upādhi* or psychological complexes. It is not ontologically real but only "imaginary construction of the adjunct of *buddhi*". It is the systematic unity of the conscious experiences of a particular individual centre, which is itself defined or determined at the outset by the bodily organism and other conditions (Radhakrishnan 1966, vol. II: 603). It is the embodied self. It has *sthūla śarīra* (a gross body), a *liṅga śarīra* (subtle body) and *kāraṇa śarīra* (a causal body).

Deutsch (1969: 51) says:

> The *Jīva* is a combination of reality and appearance. It is reality so far as *ātman* is its ground and appearance so far as it is identified as finite, conditioned.

While *jīva* is the object of self-consciousness (*ahaṁ-pratyaya-viṣaya*), the *ātman* reveals self-consciousness. The *ātman* is the witness which reveals the *jīva*. It is self-luminous, it is pure self to be known only by supra-intellectual intuition. Though *ātman* and *jīva* are ontologically one, the difference is created due to adjuncts. How does the real become the phenomenal is an oft-repeated question. *Ātman*, due to its association with body, mind, senses and sense objects, accounts for the phenomenal self. But the relationship between *ātman* and *jīva* is inexplicable, mysterious. How can an eternally free, ever conscious *ātman*, which is purely inactive and desireless, be the source of *jīva*? To this Śaṅkara says as magnet, devoid of motion, moves iron. *Jīva* is a composite of self and not self. It is the limited form (*upahitarūpa*) of *ātman*. It is *ātman* itself, but we do not realize its real nature since it is covered by *upādhi* (M.U.Ś.B. II.2.1). *Ātman* is the Universal Self, *jīva* is the empirical self.

Though the relation between *ātman* and *jīva* is indescribable, it admits no logical articulation, still Śaṅkara has suggested some analogies which later on developed into independent theories. The simile of cosmic space and space occupied by jar well establishes the relationship between the individual self and the Cosmic Self. When the limitation caused by jar, etc. is removed, the limited space is submerged into the Absolute Space, so is the *jīva*. Different names are given to space occupied by different adjuncts – in fact there is only one *ātman*. Space is neither produced with jar nor does it affect the Universal Space. Similarly *jīva* does not affect *ātman*.

The crystal seems to be red in its relation with the real flower lying besides it (B.S.Ś.B. III.2.15). The empirical self is an object of "I" cognition while *ātman* is the witness which reveals the empirical self (Sinha 1963: 375).

Ātman is all-pervading, subtle, partless like *ākāśa*. The same *ātman* is *jīva* like *ghaṭākāśa*. There is no fundamental difference between them.

Jīva and Sākṣin

According to Pāṇini,[78] the word *sākṣin* means direct percipient, spectator.[79] "It witnesses all objects and experiences, but is itself witnessed by none. It is the unobjectifiable permanent subject of all knowledge and shines forth by its own light (Naulakha 1964: 139).

Vedānta Paribhāṣa distinguishes *jīva* and *sākṣin* by the following lines. The *jīva* is Pure Consciousness qualified by *antaḥkaraṇa* (internal organ) while *sākṣin* is consciousness qualified by *antaḥkaraṇa* as an adjunct of *upādhi* only.

The term *sākṣin* appears very late in Upaniṣadic philosophy but the idea is found in early Upaniṣads also. In his commentary on *Bṛhadāraṇyaka Upaniṣad* III.4.2, Śaṅkara points out two kinds of *dṛṣṭis*, *laukika* and *pāramārthika*. *Laukika vṛtti* is "modification of internal organ when it operates". "It is transitory as it is produced by contact with sense organ and object, but as fire never loses heat and light, the native sight of *ātman* or *jīva* is immutable

[78] *sākṣād draṣṭari saṁjñāyāṁ* – *Paṇini Sūtra* V.2.91

[79] *sarveṣām bhūtanāṁ sākṣī sarvadraṣṭa* – Śve.U.Ś.B. VI.11

being its very nature." Thus according to Śaṅkara, apart from *antaḥkaraṇa vṛtti* which is responsible for cognitive, emotive and conative experiences, there is a *sākṣin*, the witness consciousness. It is the eternal consciousness. It is presuppossed by objective consciousness. Mukerji (1943: 120) says: "*Sākṣin* is the witness of all objects and all changes in the objects, it is *sarvapratyayadarśī* and *citśaktisvarūpamātra*."

Hiriyanna compares *sākṣin* with *puruṣa* in Saṁkhya-Yoga (1955: 165):

> It is the *Jīva* viewed in its true character – not as one with or even as related to any of its adjuncts, but as aloof from all of them. It is transcendental ego as distinct from empirical ego.

Śaṅkara refers to three states of *jīva*: waking state, dream state and deep-sleep state. These states are of *jīva* and not of the *sākṣin* which is their illuminator.

> *Sākṣin* is not an objective cognition (*vṛtti jñāna*), which is a modification of the internal organ, but is the very form of consciousness (*svarūpa-jñāna*). – Radhakrishnan 1957, vol. I: 28

It is a spectator not an actor. It neither acts nor enjoys. It is ever liberated pure self whereas *jīva* is empirical self which is doer and enjoyer (*kartā* and *bhoktā*) (Pra.U. IV.9). We should not bear in mind that *sākṣin* and *jīva* are two distinct facts. Both are distinct from empirical point of view; in *Brahman*, the Ultimate Reality, all are one. The fact of self-consciousness is well experienced and it is easily understood by supposing distinction between *sākṣin* and *jīva*. In self-consciousness the same self is both the subject and the object of the act of knowing. It seems paradoxical at first sight,

> but on viewing the empirical self or *jīva*s as a sort of synthesis of the *sākṣin*, the subject or witness of all knowledge and the internal organ, which is an objective element, the difficulty in the explanation of the self-consciousness is considerably removed. For on this view one and the same self contains a subjective as well as an objective element in it. – Naulakha 1964: 140

It is *ātman* that is witness of self-consciousness, self-consciousness cannot reveal *ātman*. J.N. Sinha (1952: 493) says:

> In fact, Śaṅkara does not make any distinction between *ātman* and *sākṣin*. He regards the *ātman*, the eternal universal self in the *jīva*, as the witness (*sākṣin*) of all cognitions (*sarvapratyaya sākṣin*) or mental modes (*buddhipratyaya sākṣin*).

Vācaspati too regards the *ātman* conditioned by the mind–body aggregate as the *jīva* and the pure *ātman* as its witness. Thus, this transcendental *ātman* is the witness self, which is the ontological reality in the empirical. Therefore, there is practically no difference between *ātman* and *sākṣin*. The difference was created by later Vedāntins.

Vidyāraṇya defines the *sākṣin* as immutable consciousness which is the substratum of gross and subtle bodies. It controls both the bodies without being affected by them. Vidyāraṇya is clear that witness self is not to be identified with *jīva* which participates in life affairs. He compares it with lamp on the stage which equally illumines all, the stage manager, the actor, the audience and shines in their absence too.[80] Thus witness self, according to Vidyāraṇya, illumines the empirical self. *Siddhāntaleśasaṁgraha* too differentiates *sākṣin* from *jīva*.

The author of *Tattvapradīpikā* defines "the witness self as the pure, unqualified *Brahman*, which is the substratum of all *jīva*s and which wrongly identifies with all *jīva*s".

Madhusūdana Sarasvatī defines "*sākṣin* as consciousness reflected either in *avidyā* or its product".

Īśvara and Jīva

Though both *Īśvara* and *jīva* are products of *Brahman*, ontologically of the same nature, phenomenally there is difference between them due to limiting adjunct (B.S.Ś.B. I.2.20). According to Śaṅkara, soul in its essential nature is identical with *Brahman*, so is *Īśvara*. But their transcendental unity cannot overlook the phenomenal unbridgeable gulf between *jīva* and *Īśvara*. While *jīva* is an agent, an enjoyer, feels pleasure and pain, accumulates pleasure and pain, *Īśvara* is indifferent to all these. God is God only to the *jīva* who is still under the spell of *avidyā*. He Himself never feels to

[80] *Pañcadaśī* V.10.11.

be God as distinct from *Brahman*. God is the Lord of *māyā*, *jīva* is troubled by *ātman*. God enjoys bliss of *Brahman*, *jīva* suffers pain and is vexed by *avidyā*. *Muṇḍaka Upaniṣad* III.1.1 declares: "One bird (*jīva*) eats the sweet fruit while the other (*Īśvara*) merely looks on." *Īśvara* is the ruler, *jīva*s are ruled, *Īśvara* is limited by the *upādhi* of pure *sattva* of *māyā*, *jīva* by impure *upādhi* of *avidyā*. They are master and servant. *Jīva* enjoys (*pibati*) while *Īśvara* makes him enjoy (*pāyayati*). The difference between *jīva* and *Īśvara* is like the difference of reflection of sun in pond and in *śarāva*.[81] That very consciousness overpowered by *bimbatva dharma* is *Īśvara* and overpowered by *pratibimbatva dharma* is *Jīva*.[82] God is *upakāraka*, *jīva* is *upakārya* (B.S.Ś.B. I.2.4). The limiting adjunct of *jīva* is *avidyā*, of *Īśvara* is *māyā*. Both are extraneous if *jīva* and *Īśvara* are rid of them, there will be nothing to distinguish *jīva* from *Īśvara* and both from *Brahman*. Their difference is only in respect of their adjunct (*upādhi*) as the difference between king and servant on stage is only of dress.[83] *Jīva* and *Īśvara* finally lose their individuality and merge in Pure Spirit. God is omniscient, omnipotent, there is no limit to his divine excellence. He is an object to be attained while *jīva* is the obtainer (B.S.Ś.B. I.2.4). The one is thinker and the other an object of its thought (B.S.Ś.B. I.2.12). The one is knower, the other is the object of its knowledge (B.S.Ś.B. I.3.5). While the limiting adjuncts of *Īśvara* are eternal and unexcelled knowledge and power, the limiting adjuncts of *jīva*s are ignorance (*avidyā*), desire (*kāma*) and psycho-physical organism qualified by actions.[84] Vidyāraṇya says that limiting adjunct of *Īśvara* is *māyā* characterized by its pure *sattva guṇa*, of *jīva* is *avidyā*.[85]

According to *Prakaṭārtha-Vivaraṇa*, *Īśvara* is the reflection of *Brahman* in *māyā* and *jīva* is the reflection in *avidyā*, which is a part of *māyā*. For the author of *Tattva-viveka* the reflection of the *Brahman* in the *sattva* aspect of *mūla-prakṛti* is *Īśvara* and in other aspect is

---

81 V.P., p. 379.

82 Ibid.

83 *Collected Works of Śaṅkara*, vol. XIV, st. 246.

84 Bṛ.U.Ś.B. II.8.12; B.S.Ś.B. I.3.14, 3.18

85 *Pañcadaśī* I.16-17.

jīva (Radhakrishnan 1957: 295). The author of *Saṅkṣepaśārīraka* holds that "there is no feeling of egoity in *Brahman* and *jīva* cannot think of being omniscient, *Īśvara* is without egoity, *jīva* is with egoity.[86] He does not distinguish between *māyā* and *avidyā*, and thinks that "when the *cit* is reflected in *avidyā* in its total aspect as cause, we get *Īśvara* and when reflected in *antaḥkaraṇa* – a product of *avidyā* – we have *jīva* (individual self)".[87]

Tat Tvam Asi

Śaṅkara, following the tradition of Upaniṣad (Chā.U. VI.8.7), speaks of realization of *Brahman* in and through the relation of one's own self. *Tat tvam asi,* the ultimate identity of an individual self with *Brahman* is "as much a presupposition of the subjective approach to the Reality as it is the culminating point of this approach to it" (Naulakha 1964: 96). Duality is always painful. There is only one reality underlying and he identifies that reality with soul in unequivocal terms: *brahmaivāham, ayamātmāhibrahmaiva, svātmā brahma, idaṁsarvaṁ yadayamātma,*[88] etc. are the leading slogans used by Śaṅkara very frequently to advocate Advaita. Soul merges in the absolute like water in water, fire in fire.

Max Müller (1964a: 122) says:

> The *tat* is what we saw shadowed forth in the Upaniṣads as the *Brahman*, as the cause of the world, the *tvam* is the *ātman*, the self in its various meanings from the ordinary "I" to the divine soul or self, recognized in man and it is the highest aim of Vedānta to show that these two are in reality one. This fearless synthesis, embodied in the simple words *tat tvam asi* seems to me the boldest and truest synthesis in the whole history of philosophy.

It is most fundamental idea of Śaṅkara's philosophy and its realization is the *summum bonum* of human being. *Pañcadaśī* says that *Brahman* is referred as "that", when the supreme *Brahman* superimposes on itself *avidyā*, that is *sattva* mixed with *rajas* and *tamas*, creating desire and activities in it, then it is referred as

---

[86] *Saṅkṣepaśārīraka* 178 and 185.

[87] H.I.P. vol. 1, p. 476.

[88] *Pañcadaśī* I.45.

"thou" (Bṛ.U. II.4.6).

But "thou art that" never assures an unqualified identity of man and God. There is no identity between "thou" and "that" if the word "thou" is taken in the sense of the empirical individual limited by body and "that" is taken in the sense of reality beyond the world. "Thou" here means Pure Consciousness underlying man. There is potential identity between "thou" and "that" and not actual identity. "Thou art that" is not mere tautology.

> They are the concrete representation of a movement of thought from one ontological level (of particularity) through another (of universality) to get another (of unity) wherein the attainment of the latter negates the distinction between the former. One begins with individual consciousness (*tvam*), passes on to universal consciousness (*tat*) and arrives at the pure consciousness that overcomes the separative reality of both the individual and the universal and that constitutes their ground. *Tat tvam asi* means the affirmation of a common ground, viz. consciousness to the individual and *Brahman*. – Deutsch 1969: 49

Man, according to Śaṅkara, is not merely a conditioned being with his emotions, desires, mental activities, etc. He is spirit, he is consciousness, he is free and timeless being.

Tat tvam asi is a significant proposition only when we grasp their basic underlying identity and deny their reality as such. *Saṅkṣepaśārīraka* 305 says *tat* means *pratyaktva*, both are interdependent.

Radhakrishnan (1960: 147) says:

> The text "that thou art" means that the Divine is all that we are capable of becoming and we must strive on and on till our life becomes an expression of the Divine.

Devadatta of today is the same Devadatta of yesterday or of a day before yesterday, though the conditions of Devadatta of yesterday cannot be exactly the same as the conditions of Devadatta of today. Man, viewed apart from different conditions, is none but *Brahman*.

What is illusorily taken as different is really one. It is the real identity which appears only as different. The identity of *ātman* and

Brahman is an "eternally accomplished identity". Difference is not a problem for us, problem is unity. And this knowledge of unity is what is rewarding. There is one real substance which appears before us as two: *jīva* and *Brahman*.

> Only we must reject those characters of each which are incompatible with the essential reality of other. *Brahman* must lose its outsideness and distantness, and *jīva* must lose its embodied character and the finitude that comes from it.
>
> – Malkani 1916: 74

The empirical self is neither a part of *Brahman* since *Brahman* is partless, nor a modification of *Brahman*, since *Brahman* is unchangeable, it is the substratum of the empirical self and the entire universe which cannot exist apart from *Brahman*. Their non-difference is primary while their difference is merely secondary. Thus the final import of this *mahāvākya* is when *avidya* falls away what remains is pure spirit. The import is brought out by the process of clarification of the concepts "that" and "thou". The clarification takes place in three stages. These two terms denote different objects "*Īśvara*" and "*jīva*" "but since they are in grammatical apposition we conclude that in some manner the two terms must denote the same thing". This is the first stage of interpretation called "knowledge of apposition between the terms (*samānādhikaraṇya jñāna*), the second stage is called (*viśeṣanaviśeṣya-bhāva*) – the relation of substance and attributes". In "that thou art" the relation of substance and attributes is between spirit characterized by mediacy and spirit characterized by immediacy. But there is a difficulty involved here. If we take the literal meaning of the two terms, they cannot be related as substance and attributes for "That" stands for spirit characterized by mediacy and "thou" stands for spirit characterized by immediacy. "That" (*Īśvara*) is omniscient and "thou" (*jīva*) has very limited knowledge. We have therefore to abandon the primary meaning and go in for the secondary meaning. We have not, however, to abandon the primary meaning completely. We retain a part of it and for the other part go in for the secondary meaning. This principle of interpretation is called "*bhāga-tyāga-lakṣaṇā* (partial implication)" (Iyer 1964: 125-26). We abandon mediacy and immediacy and go beyond them to the spirit underlying. This stage of interpretation is called *lakṣya–lakṣaṇa-bhāva* (the relation of the implied and the implying). Thus the final import of "thou art that" is non-duality which discards all qualifications.

Tat means Universal Consciousness and *tvam* means particular consciousness. The difference between *tat* and *tvam* is due to limiting adjuncts which are not real.[89] When this limiting adjunct is discarded properly no difference is left. Śaṅkara sets an example: state is adjunct of a king and armour is of a soldier and when they are deprived of their conditions there is none like king or soldier.[90]

This realization of identity cannot "be objected to on the ground either of uselessness or of erroneousness because first it is seen to have for its result the cessation of ignorance, and because, second, there is no other kind of knowledge by which it could be sublated".[91]

It is objected that there is essential difference between the two, how can there be identity? The greatest obstacle in way to this identification is apparent individualization of the soul. How can the soul working under such limitations be identified with the one indivisible Absolute? This difficulty is solved by Śaṅkara himself, individuality is attributed to the working of *māyā*. It has no intrinsic basis, it is only an appearance (B.S.Ś.B. II.3.17). He suggests further that this identity of which the scriptures speak should be taken in the same sense in which Viṣṇu, etc. are taken to be identical with their idols (B.S.Ś.B. IV.1.3). The difference between *vijñānātmā* and *paramātmā* is conditioned by *avidyā*, the distinction is phenomenal and not the ultimate point (ibid. I.4.22). I am always the Supreme *Brahman*, as if free from bondage, unborn and devoid of duality.[92] I am the lord always the soul in all beings.[93] Soul per se is essentially consciousness (ibid. II.3.18). As space does not admit any real chasm or division, consciousness does not admit any division or difference.

---

[89] Viv. (*Vivekacūḍāmaṇi*) 245.

[90] Ibid., 246.

[91] Deussen 1906: 1.

[92] Up.Śa. VIII.2.

[93] Ibid.

This identification caused much misunderstanding and objections were raised against it. Kirtikar has mentioned principal objections raised by European thinkers:

i. That it is revolting to common sense and blasphemous for humanity to claim complete identity and equal rank with the Eternal Absolute.

ii. That the said conception presupposes the fictitious character of the individual soul or the annihilation of that individual soul.

iii. That it involves the destruction of Nature and is thus one-sided.

iv. That this conception is inconceivable and absurd.

v. That it means pantheism, with a decidedly antitheistic and immoral tendency.

vi. That it does violence to the Christian ethical ideal which is acceptable to all mankind.

vii. That it is mystic in its character and can furnish no guide either to philosophy or theology for general acceptance.

viii. That as leading to a life of quietism it is practically useless in the development of man or in the progress of society.

But does Vedānta mean every man we meet in street is God? It will be the height of arrogance to identify man with all his finitude with God. Vedānta does not promise that soul, in its "apparent isolation and self-subsistence is *Brahman*". The identity only promise there is a germ in man which will lead to affinity with God if he enkindles in himself the fire of knowledge. He must be God-like to become God. They are perhaps forgetting the biblical phrase, "lose life so that you might gain it". Does Meister Eckhart not very frequently describe the mystical union with God as an absorption of the soul in God. Kirtikar (1924: 76) says:

> Hegelianism admits the potential identity of man with God in the single element of knowledge. Is there no blasphemy in that conception?

Western philosophers try to understand Śaṅkara from their own plane of thought. Max Müller (1893: 534) rightly remarks that they have created an abyss between the human and the divine and they dare not cross it. The often-repeated sentence *tat tvam asi* means, says Max Müller (1967: 92), "not that the soul is a part of *Brahman* but that the whole of *Brahman* is the soul".

After perfection "Man will be a pillar in the temple of God shall go out no more".[94] He will be a God in Platonic sense. This is precisely the view presented by Herbert Spencer as the "consummation of human evolution when absolute power and supreme knowledge result". J.R. Ballantyne says, it will be "mischievous cruelty to hurl such criticism against Vedānta". To consider Vedānta as spokesman of pantheism on this line would mean to condemn St. Paul.

How is it the annihilation of soul if the soul is gaining his real nature and returning to its natural abode? E. Caird has distinctively admitted that there is no extinction of the self in this conception. Another objection against *tat tvam asi* is of Acosmism. But Advaita Vedānta is most scientific in its approach. James Fitzgerald says, "It is impossible to resist to the conclusion that all Nature is living thought". Gottfrid Wilhelm Leibnitz too agrees with it. "It is only a cerebral phenomenon" according to Arthur Schopenhauer. Śaṅkara denies the reality of the world from the ultimate point of view, but at the same time he makes it permeated by spirit – whole world is *Brahman* because that which is imposed is not something different from its substratum.[95] Thus there is no conflict between the famous *mahāvākya* and the ethical ideas.

Three States of Jīva

In the empirical condition of *jīva*, three stages are distinguished – *viśva* (i.e. *jāgrata* or awakened stage), *taijasa* (i.e. dream stage) and *prājña* (i.e. deep sleep stage or *suṣuptāvasthā*). In the first stage the soul is well aware of the external objects and enjoys worldly things and objects. He thinks himself identified with the gross body, as well as external and internal organs. In the second stage the senses are at rest but *manas* is active. In the third stage both mind and senses are at rest. The *jīva* does not have any idea of the

---

[94] Revelation 3: 12.

[95] Viv. 233; Up.Sā. XI. 7.

object, thus he ceases to be knower as well. The polarity of subject and object, between knower and known vanishes altogether. Yet consciousness does not cease altogether otherwise how could he remember at all on awaking from sleep that he had such a peaceful sleep having no dream. *Māṇḍūkya Upaniṣad* mentions four stages. The fourth stage is *turīyāvasthā*. The individual soul becomes one with the Universal Soul. These three vestures are spoken of as the gross (*sthūla*), subtle (*sūkṣma*) and causal (*kāraṇa*) bodies of *jīva*. Self is not exhausted by these three stages. The fourth is *turīya* which includes and transcends them.

Jīva is covered by different layers of the not-self. In order to know the true nature of the self one must look through the coverings which are called *koṣa*s and discard them. These are *annamaya, prāṇamaya, manomaya, vijñānamaya* and *ānandamaya*. *Annamaya* is identified with the sheath of food, *prāṇamaya* with the sheath of vital air, *manomaya* with the sheath of mind, *vijñānamaya* with the sheath of self-consciousness and *ānandamaya* with bliss. *Annamaya* survives by food and in its absence it cannot survive. The *prāṇamaya,* endowed with five organs of action, is called the sheath of vital air.[96] All animal beings breath and live through this second sheath. Its cosmic counterpart is Hiraṇyagarbha. In third stage, man's real self is identified with *manas* (mind) by a process of superimposition, as before it was with the gross body and the vital breath. Its cosmic counterpart is *sūtrātmā*. *Jñānendriya*s and *manas* are responsible for the concepts like myself, mine, etc.[97] All the dualities are carried on by *manas* which is enkindled by desires and emotions.[98] In the state of *suṣupti* at the dissolution of *manas*, nothing is left.[99] *Vijñānamaya* is the cause of man's transmigration.[100] *Ānandamaya* is the Supreme Bliss.

A similar scheme is worked out in the case of *Īśvara* also. M.K. Venkataraman shows it (Table 3.1). The psychological analysis

---

[96] Viv. 167.

[97] Ibid. 169; T.U. III.4.

[98] Viv. 170.

[99] Ibid. 173.

[100] Ibid. 186.

of the sheath will show that they are one inside the other. When these *koṣa*s are pierced, the soul reveals itself as foundational consciousness (*prājña Brahman*). *Ātman* cannot be identified with any of these sheaths since it is beyond all adjuncts (*upādhi-rahita*).

Some followers of Śaṅkara believe in Ekajīvavāda (e.g. Prakāśānanda), some in Anekajīvavāda (e.g. Vidyāraṇya), but Śaṅkara definitely supports Anekajīvavāda. He never says that *jīva* limited by *ajñāna* is one, for in that case on liberation of one *jīva*, all would have been liberated and mundane existence would have come to end. *Brahman* limited by different psychological organisms like body, sense organ, mind, *antaḥkaraṇa*, born of *avidyā*, become divided into many individual souls. The theory of one soul will make it impossible to distinguish between the soul aspiring *mokṣa* and soul incurring bondage. No doubt, from the ontological point of view plurality is not the real existence of *jīva*. *Jīva* is an empirical fact, a mundane existence so is the existence of many *jīvas*. Plurality of *jīva* is a stern fact from the point of view of the worldly existence. His view is of Ekātmavāda, and not Ekajīvavāda. *Vedānta Paribhāṣā* quotes that according to Ekajīvavāda the reflection in *avidyā* and according to Anekajīvavāda the reflection in *antaḥkaraṇa* is called *jīva*.[101] Thus, *jīva*s according to Śaṅkara are many, each inhabiting a body of its own. They are as many as *antaḥkaraṇa*s. These *upādhi*s constitute the difference of the soul. The Upaniṣadic passages too say that the particular individual attains freedom.

The Doctrine of Māyā

The doctrine of *māyā* is the very pivot over which the whole philosophy of Advaita Vedānta rotates. It is based on the facts of experience and is not a "mere hypothesis or gratuitous assumption". That the reality of things is different from their outward appearance is almost a trite saying. A straight stick appears bent in water. Plants from a running train seem to be moving, but in fact it is not so.

The Upaniṣadic conception of *Brahman* as *nirguṇa* will be inconceivable if the conception of creatorship is real. Again, if the world of multiplicity is real, how can it be proved as false at

---

101 V.P., p. 385.

Table 3.1: Three States of Īśvara

Waking State	*Physical Body*	*Sheath of Food*
Dream State	Subtle body	Sheath of vital air, the mind and self-consciousness
State of deep sleep	Causal body	The sheath of bliss

the dawn of consciousness? The knowledge of reality can never be sublated by any knowledge whatsoever. The postulation of the doctrine of *māyā* saves Śaṅkara from all these difficulties. *Brahman* being associated with *māyā* creates the world. Again, if we suppose the world to be an illusion, a *māyā*, its validity, till we are in ignorance and its falsity when we are awake, will be easily made clear to us. Thus *māyā* is the coping stone of Advaitic edifice. Viewing *Brahman* from the worldly point of view brings in "simultaneous positing of the doctrine of *māyā*".

The word *māyā* is nothing new in Śaṅkara's Advaita. It is to be found even in *R̥gveda*, though the meaning is somehow different. To take most common and popular example of its occurrence in *R̥gveda*, we may refer to the hymn (VI.47.18) which means "Indra assumes many forms through mysterious power". There are other hymns too referring to *māyā*, "Through *māyā*, Mitra and Varuṇa send rain and guard their law" (V.63.3.7), "Sun and moon succeed each other in virtue of *māyā*" (X.85.8). Sometimes it is used to denote the power of demons too. "By overcoming the *māyā* of the demons, Indra won the Soma."[102] *Atharvaveda* too refers to the word *mayā*. "Sun and moon follow one another by *māyā*."[103] Thus in *R̥gveda* the word *māyā* is used generally to indicate the supernatural power attributed to gods, especially to Varuṇa, Mitra and Indra.

S.N. Dasgupta (1922, vol. I: 469) says:

> The word *māyā* was used in the *R̥gveda* in the sense of supernatural power and wonderful skill and the idea of an inherent mystery underlying it was gradually emphasized in the *Atharvaveda* and it began to be used in the sense of magic or illusion.

---

[102] Quoted from *Encyclopedia of Religion and Ethics*, p. 503.

[103] Ibid.

Sāyaṇa notes that its most common meanings in *Ṛgveda* are *prajñā* and *kapaṭa* (deceit).[102] In *Ṛgveda* X.52.2 the concept of *māyā* has close resemblance to Advaitic conception. "O, Indra, then all thy battles of which men tell were but a product, a creation of *māyā* (ṚV X.52.2)."

There are definite traces of this doctrine in Upaniṣadic philosophy. *Bṛhadāraṇyaka Upaniṣad* quotes the famous *mantra* of *Ṛgveda*.[103] There apparently the word *māyā* meant power instead of illusion, a sense in which it was later used by Śvetāśvatara Upaniṣad when it describes its God as a "*Māyin*, a magician, a powerful Being who creates this world by His power while the other, namely the individual soul is bound down again by *māyā*".[104] Again in *Śvetāśvatara Upaniṣad* it is said: "*Māyā* is the *prakṛti* and Maheśvara is the wielder of *māyā*."[105] *Śvetāśvatara Upaniṣad* further says "only by meditation upon God, by union with him and by entering into his being at the end there is cessation of *māyā*" (Śve.U. I.10). In *Praśnopaniṣad*, it is said only those persons can attain *Brahman* in whom there is no deceit, falsehood and *māyā* (Pra.U. I.16).

Some scholars are of the opinion that the word *māyā* is older than the idea of *māyā* but P.D. Sastri says that they are sadly mistaken. The idea of *māyā* is very old – certainly older than the word *māyā*.[106] Ranade (1968: 162-63) opines:

> He (Śaṅkara) may definitely be said to have gone back to the Upaniṣads to find his inspiration there. Śaṅkarācārya only elaborated the idea that he found in the Upaniṣads and wove them into the contexture of his Advaitic-philosophy.

Date says: "Śaṅkara only fixes the place and function of it in his system." Thibaut (1957: cxxv) says:

---

[102] Sāyaṇa on *Ṛgveda* III.27.7.

[103] *indro māyābhiḥ pururūpa īyate* – Bṛ.U. II.5.19

[104] *asmānmāyī sṛjate viśvametat tasmiṁścānyo māyayā sanniruddhaḥ* – Śve.U. IV.9

[105] *māyāṁ tu prakṛtiṁ vidyān māyinaṁ taṁ maheśvaram* – Śve.U. IV.10

[106] Shastri 1911.

> The later growth of *māyā* doctrine on the basis of the Upaniṣads is therefore quite intelligible and I fully agree with Mr. Gough when he says regarding it that there has been no addition to the system from without but only a development from within, no graft but only growth.

We may more fairly trace the idea of *māyā* in different Upaniṣads rather than the word. *Īśopaniṣad* tells that truth is veiled in this universe by a vessel of gold and the grace of God is evoked to lift up the golden vessel and allow the truth to be seen (Īśa.U. 15). In *Kaṭhopaniṣad* we have description of people living in ignorance, but thinking themselves to be wise move wondering like blind men following the blind, in search of reality which is to be seen easily if they would have lodged themselves in knowledge instead of ignorance (K.U. I.2.4-5). *Chāndogya Upaniṣad* shows how knowledge is power and ignorance impotence. In *Bṛhadāraṇyaka Upaniṣad* there is famous prayer where the devotee is praying to lead him to the path of *sat*, from *asat*.[107] Then again in the famous conversation of *Chāndogya Upaniṣad* (IV. 4) between Śvetaketu and Āruṇi, it is told that besides *ātman* everything is merely a mode, a word and a name.

On the basis of examination of various passages in the Upaniṣadic philosophy we may conclude with Ranade that

> even though the word *māyā* may not have been used for many times in the Upaniṣads, still the conception that underlies *māyā* is already present there even though we do not find there the full-fledged doctrine of illusion in its philosophical aspects as in Gauḍapāda and later writers, still we do find in Upaniṣads all the material that may have easily led Śaṅkara to elaborate a theory of *māyā* out of it. – Ranade 1968: 165

In post-Upaniṣadic period we do not find the doctrine expressed in the terms in which Gauḍapāda and Śaṅkara state it. In the great epic *Mahābhārata* the following references are found (i) *purāvikurute*[108] *māyām*, (ii) *māyāṁ mohinīṁ samupāśritaḥ*, and (iii) *apsarā devakanyā vā māyā*. In *Gītā* (XVIII.61), *māyā* is used in the

[107] *asato mā sadgamaya, tamso mā jyotirgamaya, mṛtyormā-mṛtaṁ gamaya* ।

[108] Quoted from Shastri 1911.

sense of magical power, God the great magician. He revolves all *jīvas* by the power of his divine magic. Kṛṣṇa says in *Gītā* (IV.6) that "though He is unborn, He comes into being through His power (*māyā*)". Again He says "the divine *māyā* is hard to overcome but those who take refuge in Him cross beyond it" (VII.14). In *śloka* VII.15, He refers to the persons whose minds are carried away by illusion.[109] Veiled by this creative power (*yogamāyā*), He is not revealed to all (VII.25). The word *māyā* has been used in three senses in *Gītā*, viz.

(a) the mysterious power of the Supreme Lord,

(b) the worldly effects of this power, and

(c) the ignorance of the individual soul.

Ranade (1968: 165-66) says that in *Gītā* "nor does the theistic – mystic trend of the argument leave much room for a philosophical development of the conception of *māyā*".

In fact, Gauḍapāda's use of the term *māyā*, crystallized its meaning as "illusive power in reality, does not exist". He treats the world not only as appearance but he goes further and says the world was never created (the theory of non-origination, Ajātivāda). No *jīva* is born, there is no cause for it, this is the supreme truth, nothing whatever is born (G.K. III.48).

He further says "duality is only *māyā*, non-duality is the only reality" (G.K. I.17). Gauḍapāda employs several expressions to indicate the illusory nature of the world and its things – *māyā*, *vitatha*, *mithyā*, *kalpita*, *ābhāsa*, *viparyaya* and *saṁvṛtti*, etc. (Mahadevan 1954: 154). In Alātaśānti Prakaraṇa, Gauḍapāda says:

> Creation has been recommended by the sages for the benefit of those who cannot but find the world to be real (*upalambhāt*), and who must need be led on the path of good conduct (*samācārāt*).

Ranade (1968: 166) says:

> This shows however Gauḍapāda has to take some cognizance at least of the world as real, though it may be for the perfection of mystical endeavour or ethical conduct even though,

---

109 *māyayāpahṛtajñānā*.

philosophically, he may regard it as not having been created at all.

Paul David Devanandan (1950: 87) says:

> Gauḍapāda uses the word with freedom and latitude of meaning. . . . He seems to be more concerned in proving the unreality the world. To him, therefore, the term *māyā* helps to establish the illusory multiplicity of life rather than the sole reality of the ultimate. It is the negative aspect of formula of *māyā* that fascinates the mind of Gauḍapāda.

Śaṅkara is profited by all these conceptions and "weaves his full-fledged doctrine out of the stands left at his disposal by the Upaniṣads and Gauḍapāda" (Ranade 1968: 167). It is certainly a growth and not a "graft", "a development from within".

Prabhu Dutt Shastri (1911) gives many derivative meanings of the term "*māyā*". The word *māyā* is derived from *mā*, to measure *mīyate anayā iti*, i.e. by which it is measured, meaning thereby as tradition has it, that illusive projection of the world by which the immeasurable *Brahman* appears as if measured. The same root gives further the sense of "to build" leading to the idea of "appearance" or "illusion". Shastri mentions Sāyaṇa's explanation of *R̥gveda* II.27.7. He derives it from *mā* to know or to measure and adds *mimīte jānīte, karma mīyate anayeti vā māyā, karmaviṣayābhijñānam*. That is √*ma*, means to know, by which ritual, etc. are known. Again *mā* means to measure, by which the ritual, etc. are measured. Another fanciful derivation he gives – *mā yā* that which is not but appears to be.

Another way to derive it would be *māti* (*svātmānam*) *darśayati iti māyā*, i.e. that which shows itself – that which appears to our view (without having any real existence). Here √*ma* is to show.

Hence the conception of *māyā* as the causal willpower (*īkṣā śakti* or *prajñāna*) may be derived from √*ma*, i.e. to know and as the effectual state of the world as illusion from *ma*, i.e. to measure, to build.

In the whole of the Advaita literature *māyā* is indicated as *avidyā*, *adhyāsa*, *adhyāropa*, *anirvacanīya*, *vivarta*, *nāma-rūpa*, *avyakta*, *ajñāna*, *bhrama*, *bhrānti*, *bījaśakti*, *mūla-prakr̥ti*, etc. used more or less equivalents; of these *māyā*, *avidyā*, *adhyāsa* and *vivarta* are used mostly as interchangeable words.

Māyā is the seed of the world of difference and multiplicity. This *avyakta* state of the world is called *māyā* by Śaṅkara who defines it as

> This undeveloped prior state of the world which is inexplicable because it is the same and also not the same, is called *māyā* and it is dependent on God (*Īśvara*). – B.S.Ś.B. I.43

In fact, *māyā* is not different from *Brahman* for it is *Brahman* as *satkāryābhimukha*,[110] as *sargonamukha*,[111] that is to say it is *Brahman* about to manifest itself. It is *Brahman* in *vyācikīrṣitāvasthā*,[112] i.e. as desiring to differentiate itself. It is *Brahman* as *jāyamānaprakṛtitvena nirdiśya*[113] as *prakṛtisvarūpamātmānam*, i.e. it is *Brahman* only looked upon as the material cause of the world.

> *Māyā* is *Brahman* itself in a particular state. . . . Because a slight distinction arose, a separate name *māyā* was given.
>
> – Sastri 1931: 36

When *Brahman* distinguishes itself as its objects from itself as subjects, the object is known by the name *māyā* in Advaita Vedānta.

Māyā is described in *Vedāntasāra* as neither *sat* nor *asat*, i.e. it is indescribable. It is *triguṇātmikā*, contrary to knowledge and positive.[114] *Māyā* is not real as real things cannot be sublated. By real Śaṅkara means *trikāla-satya*. It transcends all empirical existence. It is free from all differences of space and time It is not real because it has no existence apart from *Brahman*. Giving an independent place to *māyā* will mean accepting fundamental dualism between *Brahman* and *māyā*. Nor is it unreal for it projects the world of appearance, it is true at least till it lasts. "It is not real to constitute a limit to *Brahman* and yet it is real enough to give rise to the world of appearance" (Sharma 1960: 387). It is *sadasadanirvacanīya*. It

---

110 Chā.U.Ś.B. III. 19.1.

111 *Ratnaprabhā* I.1.5.

112 M.U.Ś.B. I.1.8.

113 B.S.Ś.B. I.2.21.

114 *Vedāntasāra*, p. 18.

is indescribable.[115] *Māyā* is category which baffles the ordinary logical division of existence and non-existence and the principle of excluded middle (Dasgupta 1922: 442). The word *anivacanīya* has a positive significance in Advaita Vedānta. Devaraja (1972: 162-63) says:

> According to Vedānta, the presentation of the false is a fact of experience, a fact which is *sui generis*, and the word *anirvacanīya* simply embodies that fact in language. Far from being a negation of definition the term *anirvacanīya* is itself a definition. Paradoxical as it may appear, the application of the epithet *anirvacanīya* to the phenomenal object is an attempt at its *nirvacana*, even as the ring-finger is sought to be named by the designation *anāmikā* or nameless.

Māyā has two aspects. In its negative aspect it conceals the reality and in its positive aspect it projects (*vikṣepa*) the world of multiplicity on *Brahman*. While *āvaraṇa* is mere negation of knowledge, the second is positive generation of error. We not only do not perceive the absolute but we perceive in its place something else. *Jagat* is the totality of names and forms which *māyā* assumes. It is not merely absence of apprehension but misapprehension as well. As a small piece of cloud seems to cover the sun which is million times bigger in size, *ajñāna* covers the soul.[116] Robert Browning is expressing Śaṅkara's view when he says:

> *Some think creation's meant to show him forth*
> *I say it's meant to hide him all it can.*
>
> – Browning 185

It is *triguṇātmaka*[117] because the *guṇa*s or their effects (pleasure, pain and indifference) are found in the evolutes of *ajñāna*. It does not have the three *guṇa*s, but it is itself the three *guṇa*s. *Śvetāśvatara Upaniṣad* refers to *ajāmekāṁ lohita-śukla kṛṣṇām*. Lohita denotes *rajas*, *śukla*, *sattva*, *kṛṣṇa* and *tamas*.[118]

The attribute *triguṇātmaka* implies that in spite of its

[115] B.S.Ś.B. II.1.14, 27

[116] *Vedāntasāra*, p. 30.

[117] *Vivekacūḍāmaṇi*, *śloka* 110.

[118] Śve.U. IV.5

> *anirvacanīyatva, ajñāna* is not an absolutely unintelligible concept. *Sattva, rajas* and *tamas* may also be conceived as attributes inhering in *ajñāna*. This suggests that *ajñāna* is different from false knowledge.
> – Malkani 1933: 86-87

The power of projection is caused by *rajoguṇa*,[119] but *āvaraṇa śakti* is caused by *tamoguṇa*.[120]

Māyā is *jñāna-virodhinī*. It is cancelled after knowledge of its substratum. Both *jñāna* and *ajñāna* are opposed to each other when they have the same object and the same locus. Thus it is not opposed to pure *cit*, but *cit* as reflected in *vṛtti*. It disappears at the dawn of knowledge as the true knowledge of rope removes the illusion of snake.[121]

Ajñāna is *bhāvarūpa* (a positive entity). For Nyāya-Vaiśeṣika and others *ajñāna* is a negative entity being just the absence of *jñāna*. But for Śaṅkara it is positive. It is not negation of all knowledge, for a negation requires previous knowledge of what is negated and the locus of the negation. Had it been pure nullity, it could not have been experienced at all. Śruti declares that "*jñāna* or *māyā* is the matrix of the manifold".

Warrier (1961: 312) says:

> In fact, the philosophical signifiance of describig *avidyā*, as a positive entity, seems to be that, thereby, a degree of reality is lent to the objective world of which *avidyā* is the material cause.

Vidyāraṇya says that *māyā* may be envisaged from three different standpoints:

1. from the standpoint of revealed experience (*śrauta*) it is negligible,
2. from the standpoint of reasoning (*yauktika*) it is indefinable, and
3. from the standpoint of ordinary man (*laukika*) it is real.

For the first standpoint it is *tuccha*, for the second, it is

---

119 *Vivekacūḍāmaṇi, śloka* 113.

120 Ibid., *śloka* 115.

121 Ibid., *śloka* 112.

anirvacanīya and for the third it has all importance.[122]

Ajñāna, according to Śaṅkara, is beginningless (*anādi*). It may be argued that it is not beginningless for it is "a mere illusory imagination of the moment caused by some imperfection (*doṣa*)". But this is not true about the primordial *ajñāna*. If it is taken as a temporary imperfection, then some other imperfection must be assumed to explain it and then a third one till ad infinitum. In order to avoid this infinite regress, *ajñāna* must be regarded as existing from eternity. Moreover, being the material cause it cannot be said to have beginning in time. "If primeval source also has an origin, it cannot be extended in its effects. An effect is not seen to abide in other effects." R. Das says:

> My ignorance of things which I never know and do not know is beginningless as the non-existence of object before it is created (*prāgbhāva*). Moreover, ignorance is beginningless in the sense that there is nothing objective prior to ignorance. All things including time among them, being product of ignorance.[123]

Ajñāna again is not partless. As partless thing can never be a source of anything and as we know, *jñāna* is the material cause of the world. Nor can it be said that it has parts for then it will become a produced thing (*sādi*) and *brahma-caitanya* reflected in it will not be infinite. Obviously *ajñāna* is neither. Once again we can take the liberty to say, it is *anirvacanīya*.

It is the inherent power or potency (*śakti*) of *Brahman*. Just as pure water appears as dirty foam – *Brahman* appears as manifold through its agency of *avidyā*. It has a phenomenal and relative character (*vyāvahārika sattā*). It is appearance only (*vivarta*).

Śaṅkara says that to ask What is *avidyā*? Whose is *avidyā*? Where does it appear, etc. are meaningless questions (B.G.Ś.B. XIII.2). For if *avidyā* is not known, these questions cannot be solved, and if the true nature of *avidyā* is realized, its locus and object are realized (ibid.). It is not a hypothesis but a statement of fact.

---

122 *tucchā 'nirvacnīyā ca vāstavī cetyasau tridhā* |
jñeyā māyā tribhirbodhaiḥ śrautayanktikalaukikaiḥ ||
– *Pañcadaśī*, Citradīpa, 130

123 Malkaniet al., 1933, *Ajñāna*, p. 87.

The term *avidyā* has two different uses in Śaṅkara's philosophy, individual *avidyā* and cosmic *avidyā*. Due to individual *avidyā* we superimpose the world of *nāma–rūpa* on *Brahman;* but cosmic *avidyā* is *māyā* or *prakṛti*. The former may be destroyed but not the latter (B.S.Ś.B. III.2.21).

Śaṅkara argues, the locus and the object of *avidyā* are none but *Brahman*, yet *Brahman* is not affected by them like a magician who is unaffected by his magic or as colourless *ākāśa* which is untouched by the dark colour attributed to it, but scholars differ at this point.

For Vācaspati, *jīva* is the locus of *ajñāna* while the absolute is its object. Some Śruti says that *Brahman* is pure, its purity will be affected if it is said to be the locus of *ajñāna*. But this conception is untenable as we already know that *jīva* itself is due to *ajñāna*. This assertion will involve the fallacy of *petitio principii* meaning thereby that a thing depends upon itself.

Now the question is: are they mutually dependent? Madhusūdana Sarasvatī comes out with a definite no as reciprocal dependence in respect of the existence of things may occur in two ways: (i) when two things are interdependent on each other, and (ii) when the existence of one is inconceivable in the absence of the other. Both these types are absent here.

Vivaraṇa school says *cit* is the locus of *ajñāna*. Sarvajñātmamuni, Prakāśānanda, Iṣṭasiddhikāra and others also hold that pure *cit*, devoid of the distinction between *jīva* and *Īśvara*, is the locus of *ajñāna* (Hastings 1910, vol. II: 86). Sarvajñātmamuni says that the illusory distinction between *jīva* and *Saguṇa-Brahman* is due to *ajñāna*, hence the possibility of *ajñāna* is to be admitted.[124]

Still others hold that *Saguṇa-Brahman* is the locus of *ajñāna*. The assertion that *Brahman* is omniscient will not be possible if *Brahman* is regarded as the locus of *ajñāna*.

Some again distinguish *māyā* from *avidyā* and say *māyā* is the adjunct of *Īśvara*, *avidyā* is of *jīva*. *Māyā* can only project but *avidyā* can both project and obscure. Thus the locus of *māyā* is *Īśvara*, of *avidyā* is *jīva*.

---

[124] *Śaṅkṣepaśārīraka*, chap. I, *śloka* 319.

But, as I have stated, Śaṅkara admits *Brahman* to be the locus of *ajñāna*. So far as the question of object of *ajñāna* is concerned, all thinkers are of opinion that *Brahman* is the object. "*Māyā* accounts for everything other than *Brahman*." It accounts for the world in space and time, manyness of individuals, everything subjective and objective.

Māyā is twofold. In its undivided state (*avibhaktāvasthā*), it is real, indistinguishable from *Brahman*. It is not separate (*anya*) from *Brahman*. This is its universal aspect (*sāmānyāvasthā*). But differentiated in the form of its effects or *vikāra*, it is *asat*. Here it is separate from *Brahman*. It is its *sāmānyāvasthā* (particular aspect). In its *sāmānyāvasthā*, it is nothing different from *Brahman*, in its *viśeṣāvasthā* it is designated as multiple world of name and form, something separate[125] from underlying reality and supposed to be self-sufficient.[126] It is the universal (*sāmānyāvasthā*) which assumes the particular (*viśeṣa*) form, the former is the cause, and the latter is the effect.

Māyā is used in the sense of illusion both as a principle of creation, as *śakti* or accessory cause, and the phenomenal creation itself, as the illusion of world-appearance. In the Hegelian mode of expression *māyā* may be said as the "Non-Being of the Absolute Being, the negative aspect explaining the Becoming".

Māyā is the "principle of unifying contradiction" – the contradiction between the self and the non-self, the subject and the object, the cause and the effect, *Brahman* and the world, ego and non-ego. But no explanation is possible unless contradiction is somehow or other reconciled. *Māyā* is the principle which mysteriously or inexplicably reconciles the contradictions, and makes experience possible. V.S. Ghate describes it as "the principle of illusion served like a two-edged sword to cut asunder all kinds of opposition" Nalini Mohan Mukherji–Sastri (1942: 138) says:

> *Māyā* is a link between *Brahman* per se and the manifold world, reconciles the two diametrically opposed perception of *Brahman* by explaining how this is caused.

---

125 B.S.Ś.B. II.1.19.

126 Ibid. I3.41.

The essential nature of *māyā* is to hide the real (*āvaraṇātmakatvād avidyā*). There are three ways of its operation:

(a) as positive wrong knowledge (*viparītagrāhika*),

(b) as doubt (*saṁśyopasthāpikā*), and

(c) as absence of knowledge (*agrahaṇātmikā*).[127]

Māyā does no harm to reality as mirage water does not make the sandy water muddy.[128] The Absolute is not touched by *māyā* at all.[129] As when the illusory knowledge of snake is dispelled, only rope is left, when *māyā* leaves, *Brahman* alone is left.

To express how *māyā* neither is *tat* nor *atat*, Kokileshwar Sastri refers the lines of Māgha's *Śiśupālavadha* for a nice illustration to this effect. "He is the same man, yet he is not the same." Śiśupāla is the same Rāvaṇa but he seems not to be the same man as he has now concealed himself in the name of Śiśupāla.

Radhakrishnan (1952, vol. I: 279) points out six different meanings of the word *māyā*, used in Śaṅkara's systems.

1. That the world is not self-explanatory shows its phenomenal character, what is signified by the word *māyā*.
2. The relation between *Brahman* and world is a problem. We intuit *Brahman* to be unitive principle and demand its relation with the world on logical grounds. The riddle is solved by the term *māyā*.
3. *Brahman* is the cause of the world only in the sense that it rests on *Brahman* without affecting it in any way and the world which rests on *Brahman* is called *māyā*.
4. The principle assumed to account for the appearance of *Brahman* in the world is also called *māyā*.
5. If we confine our attention to the empirical world and employ the dialectic of logic, we get the conception of a perfect personality (*Īśvara*) who has the power of self-expression. This power or energy is called *māyā*.

---

127 B.G.Ś.B. XIII.2.

128 Ibid.

129 B.S.Ś.B. II.1.9.

6. The energy of *Īśvara* which is the material cause of the universe is called *māyā*.

Māyā and Avidyā

The conception of *māyā* is a "great stumbling block" in the proper understanding of the Advaita system. It baffles all attempts to make clear understanding about its true nature. It is "the metric of undeveloped seed of name and form". Londhe (1930: 8) says: "*Māyā* remains *māyā*, a veritable mystery in spite of all philosophical scrutiny." The word *māyā* originally meant power and the idea of mystery has always been associated with it. And *avidyā* literally means absence of knowledge. It cannot be denied that the world has also sometimes been spoken of by Śaṅkara as being *avidyātmaka* (consisting of *avidyā*), *avidyā-kalpita* (imagined by *avidyā*), *avidyā-pratyupasthāpita* (presented by *avidyā*), *avidyākṛta*, *avidyāropita*, *avidyā-nimitta* and so on in his *Bhāṣya*. Now naturally the question creeps in whether *māyā* and *avidyā* are identical or different. There is difference of opinion. According to Thibaut (1957: xxv), these two terms in Śaṅkara's Vedānta are interchangeable:

> *Brahman* . . . is associated with a certain power called *māyā* or *avidyā* to which the appearance of this entire world is due.

But Jacob is quite emphatic on the fact that *māyā* is not synonymous to *avidyā*. He says:

> I think, therefore, that it is clear from the *Bhāṣya* itself that *māyā* is not used there as a synonym of *avidyā* but is regarded as an illusion produced by it. – Jacob 1934: Preface

D.G. Londhe (1930: 42) asserts:

> *Māyā* is not at all a synonym for *avidyā* according to Śaṅkara and the passages lose all their point and force if the word *avidyā* is substituted for the word *māyā*.

Malkani (1916: 157) says that, *ajñāna* and *māyā* are not two different things:

> The explanation of illusory world is supposed to stop with the conception of ignorance (*ajñāna*) or the conception of *māyā* (power of illusion making), each must be understood to be a

sufficient and final explanation of the appearance of an illusory world. The two powers are intimately connected.

The followers of other schools, who treat *māyā* and *avidyā* as different, put in their favour the following points:

i. *Māyā* is positive in character. It is the inseparable power of *Brahman* to which the phenomenal creation of the world is due. But *avidyā* is negative in character, being the absence of reality.

ii. *Māyā* conditions *Īśvara* who is unaffected by *avidyā*, but *avidyā*, the individual ignorance, conditions *jīva*. *Brahman* reflected in *māyā* is *Īśvara* and *Brahman* reflected in *avidyā* is *jīva*.[130] Individual *avidyā* is dispelled by knowledge but *māyā* being the inherent nature of *Brahman* cannot be disposed of.

iii. They say that the predominating *guṇa* in *māyā* is *sattva*; in *avidyā* are all the three *guṇas* – *sattva*, *rajas* and *tamas*. Sarvajñātmamuni, Prakāśānanda (in *Siddhāntamuktāvalī*) and Vidyāraṇya (in *Vivaraṇaprameyasaṁgraha*) see no difference between *māyā* and *avidyā* or *ajñāna* but in *Pañcadaśī* and *Prakaṭārtha-Vivaraṇa*, distinction is made between *avidyā* and *māyā*. In *Pañcadaśī*, *māyā* is held to be the adjunct of *Īśvara* and *avidyā* of individual soul only.[131]

C.D. Sharma (1960: 385) says:

> The general trend of the Advaitins including Śaṅkara himself has been to treat these two terms as synonymous . . .

Radhakrishnan (1966, vol. II: 587) too says that as *Ātman* and *Brahman* are one so are *māyā* and *avidyā* one: "When we look at the problem from the objective side we speak of *māyā*, and when from the subjective side we speak of *avidyā*." He again says:

> It is called *avidyā* since it is dissolvable by knowledge, but the objective series is called *māyā*, since it is co-eternal with the supreme personality. . . . *Īśvara*, the omniscient, who controls his *māyā* has no *avidyā*, and if Śaṅkara here and there lends countenance to a different theory, it is in the figurative sense

130 *kāryopādhirayaṁ jīvaḥ kāraṇopādhir īśvaraḥ* ।

131 *Pañcadaśī* I.16.

> that *Īśvara* has the power which leads to *avidyā* in the individual.
> – Ibid.: 588-89

Mukherji–Sastri says:

> Looked at from the subjective point of view this *māyā* is again *avidyā*. It is false perception that creates the appearance of plurality. Looked as the objective world of experience, it is *māyā*, but looked at as a mental factor that causes this distorted perception of reality, it is *avidyā*. In this sense *māyā* is the objective result of the finitizing process of *avidyā*. The latter is the cause and the former is the effect. These are therefore practically the same thing viewed differently. For a better appreciation of the close relation of the two we might even identify them and say that they are identical. The tendency of our mind to see reality, which is one, as many, is *avidyā*, and the appearance of the one as *māyā*. What is *māyā*, from the objective side is *avidyā* from the subjective side.[132]

Deussen holds that to Śaṅkara, *avidyā* is the causal principle of the world of appearance, while *māyā* is the effect of appearance itself. It is true that later Vedāntin distinguishes them but for Śaṅkara *māyā* is both the principle of creation and creation itself. Kokileshwar Sastri (1926), too gives similar view in his Advaita philosophy.

The distinction between *avidyā* and *māyā* is only a popular concept. *Ajñāna* endowed with projecting capacity which is under the wishes of *Īśvara* is *māyā*, which covers the element of *jñāna* is *avidyā*.[133]

Adhyāsa

Adhyāsa is defined as "the appearance of a thing where it is not". To attribute to the real what is different from it, is what Śaṅkara calls, *adhyāsa*. What is called *adhyāsa* is the cognition as something of what is not that.[134] When the rope appears as snake we have *adhyāsa*. In all illusions there is some sort of projection, there is projection of snake in the rope, of the world in *Brahman*.

---

[132] Mukherji–Sastri, 1942, *A Study of Śaṅkara*, pp. 141-42.

[133] S.D.S., p. 855.

[134] B.S.Ś.B., *Adhyāsa-bhāṣya*.

In modern psychological terminology, a process of this kind is called projection. In all illusions there is always such projection (*adhyāsa*), the serpent is projected by imagination on the rope and the world on *Brahman*.

> The principle *adhyāsa* therefore is such as has no reason to exist and yet is most indispensable for all human affairs. It is the law that regulates all our actions and all our movements, nay it is the law that makes the world what it is. Although it is indefinable yet it is not abstraction and has a most concrete existence so far as the phenomenal world is concerned.
>
> – Bhattacharyya 1937, vol. III: 241

Adhyāsa according to Mādhavācārya is of two kinds: *arthādhyāsojñānadhyāsaśceti.*[135] *Arthādhyāsa* means superimposition of one object on another. *Jñānādhyāsa* means superimposition of false knowledge (*mithyā jñāna*) on *ātman*. Again *adhyāsa* may be characterized into two: *nirupādhika*[136] and *sopādhika.*[137] *Adhyāsa* also may be *saṁsargādhyāsa* (superimposition of an attribute of one thing on another) and *tādātmyādhyāsa* (identification of one thing with another).

The different schools of Indian philosophy have tried to define *adhyāsa* in their own characteristic ways. For example, Nyāya-Vaiśeṣika school has defined it as the superimposition of the attributes of something on something else. According to Mīmāṁsakas, it is that error which results from the non-recognition of the difference between what is superimposed and what it is superimposed on. In the opinion of Mādhyamika Buddhism, it consists in "the fictitious assumption of attributes contrary to the nature of that thing on which something else is superimposed". On taking a comprehensive view, one may sum like this "superimposition essentially consists in an apparent presentation of the attributes of something in something else". Śaṅkara has defined it as the apparent presentation, in the form of rememberance, to consciousness as something previously observed

135 S.D.S., p. 801.

136 Ibid.

137 Ibid.

in some other thing.[138] Frankly speaking the real characteristic of *adhyāsa* has been rightly pointed out by Govindānanda as *paratarāvabhāsa ityeva lakṣaṇam*.[139] In the illusion of rope and snake, snake is not actually present but it was previously observed. It only exists in our mind as an impression.

Ajñāna lies at the root of the *adhyāsa* which is the basis of life and experience. *Ajñāna* has *bheda* (difference) as its characteristic and is the source of all misery and pain. Vācaspati Miśra says that there can be no superimposition both when there is complete apprehension and when there is total non-apprehension.[140] When there is superimposition of one on another, it is a "delusion conditioned by non-apprehension of their distinctness".

The dualistic metaphysics does not properly explain the relation between mind and body, soul and matter. Śaṅkara gives the solution of this problem by supposing that one is superimposed upon the other, the body is superimposed on soul, matter on spirit, world on *Brahman*. Since the body is superimposed on soul, this can be easily sublated in the stage of *mokṣa*.

The doctrine of superimposition helps us in understanding the causal relation in a new light. Words like *vivarta* and Vivartavāda are hardly used by Śaṅkara. He applies the theory of *adhyāsa* as much to explain the production of the jar from clay as that of the world from *Brahman*. Modification is not real according to Śaṅkara. The effect is false. It has no real existence apart from the cause. The whole modification is real so far it partakes the nature of *sat*, but it has no independent reality. The newness of effect is nothing but "metaphysically considered, a fictitious superimposition upon the cause". "The world with all its multiplicity is inherent in *Brahman* as jar is inherent in clay. The principle of Advaita is undoubtedly present in the Upaniṣads but the theory of *adhyāsa* is "strange to the Upaniṣadic thinker".

Sāṁkhya philosophy takes shelter under as if when they are to

---

138 *smṛtirūpaḥ paratra pūrvadṛṣṭāvabhāsāḥ* । – B.S.Ś.B., *Adhyāsa-bhāṣya*

139 *Ratnaprabhā* 1.1.1.

140 *tasmādatyantograhe 'tyantāgrahe ca nādhyāsa iti siddham* ।
– *Adhyāsa-bhāṣya Bhāmatī*, p. 37

explain how does insensible body appear to be as conscious, how does the indifferent *puruṣa* appear to be the agent. Śaṅkara found the explanation quite easy by installing *adhyāsa* as the explanatory principle. The co-mingling of the subject and the object, this mixing up of truth and errors, this coupling of the real and the unreal is called *adhyāsa*. *Adhyāsa* is the root of the world process. It is begnningless (*anādi*) and unending (*ananta*). Superimposition is one stern fact and not an object of mere hypothesis.

Mahadevan (1957: 226) points out five factors working in *adhyāsa*:

> In order that superimposition may be possible, there must be (1) the residual impression brought about by the cognition of a real object; (2) defect in the object of knowledge; (3) defect in cognizer; (4) defect in the instrument of valid knowledge; and (5) a knowledge of the general nature alone of the substrate without a knowledge of its particularities.

Objection is raised, how can objects and their attributes be imposed on the *ātman* which is non-objective in its character, which is of the nature of existence, consciousness and bliss. In general illusion one object is confused with another whereas here the self is confused with the object. The answer to this objection is, it is not a universal rule that an object may not be superimposed on self. Colour is superimposed on imperceptible *ākāśa*. The superimposed quality does not affect in the least the substratum. Superimposition of the blue colour on *ākāśa* does not affect the imperceptible sky. Similarly, in spite of the universal illusion of self on not-self, the self shines in its glory and is unaffected by any objective limitation.

Karmakāṇḍa has its basis in *avidyā*, unless the distinction of caste, *āśrama*, etc. is not superimposed upon the *ātman*, there will be no possibility of the performance of sacrifice. But *jñāna* is beyond all these. Soul is supposed to be *kartā*, *bhoktā*, etc. due to this superimposition. Thus in order to remove *adhyāsa*, a study of Vedānta is essential so that we may understand the real nature of things. We cannot trace the origin of illusion which is not artificially induced and we cannot also visualize its end.

Is Avidyā One or Many?

Some people are of opinion that there are many *ajñāna*s as there are many *jīva*s. They argue that in case there is one *ajñāna*, if one person is liberated, all are liberated but this is not the case. T.R.V. Murti says that the determination of the oneness or otherwise of *ajñāna* depends on the nature of its locus (*āśraya*), the person deluded and the object (*viṣaya*).

Ajñāna in *jīva*s is ultimately one. In Śruti the word *māyā* is used in singular number as well as in plural number. The singular number is in the following Śrutis: *ajāmekāṁ lohitaśuklakṛṣṇāṁ, māyāṁ tu prakṛtiṁ vidyāt, taratyavidyāṁ vitatām*, etc. Again we find '*indro māyābhiḥ pururūpa īyate*', here the plural number is used.

The author of *Vedānta Paribhāṣā* says that *māyā* or *jñāna* is one. The use of plural number in Śruti shows *vicitra śakti* of *māyā* or reference to the three *guṇa*s of *māyā* – *sattva, rajas* and *tamas.*[141] According to *Tattva-Viveka, māyā* and *avidyā* are two forms of *mūla prakṛti* (original matter), which has three *guṇa*s (attributes) – *sattva, rajas* and *tamas. Mūla prakṛti* with *sattva* predominating is *māyā*, but with *sattva* overpowered by *rajas* or *tamas* is *avidyā* (see Radhakrishnan 1952, vol. I: 294).

Again the author of *Vedānta Paribhāṣā* says: "If we take *māyā* as one then there will be simplicity of thought (*kalpanā-lāghava*)." According to *Vedāntasāra, jñāna* may be viewed in both ways. It is one and also many. It is one with reference to the aggregate (*samaṣṭi*). From the aspect of *sāmānya*, it is one, from the aspect of *viśeṣa*, it is many. According to Vācaspati, *jīva*s are the locus of *avidyā* while Absolute is its object.

All agree unanimously that the object of ignorance is *Brahman*. *Brahman*-knowledge alone cancels the world-illusion. *Ajñāna* is not cancelled but merely put off (*nivṛttimātra*).

World

The time-honoured examples for showing the world to be unreal are the simile of rope–snake, *śukti-rajata*, the dirty surface of the

---

141 V.P., p. 102.

sky, the city of the mythological *gandharvas* (*gandharvanagara*), the dream (*svapna*), the bubble of the water, the foam of the water, the fire circle created due to the fast rotation of the fire, the magical elephant, the illusion of double man created when the eyeball is pressed, the pure magic (*indra-jāla*). By real, Śaṅkara means something eternal, *trikāla-satya*, real for all times. It is freedom from all considerations (*bādhārahita*) and by unreal he means absolutely unreal like barren woman's son, hare's horn. Following his criteria of reality, *Brahman* alone is real. But when he says *brahma satyaṁ jaganmithyā*, he does not deny total reality to the world. When he says that world is *mithyā* he means it is not real in the sense of *trikāla-satya*. *Mithyā* connotes in Advaita Vedānta a special meaning. It is a technical term of Vedānta philosophy. It is wrong to translate it as illusory or illusion. The *mithyā* has a mermaid sort of reality, it is really false and falsely real. In other words, it exists because it appears but it is not real because it later disappears. Unreality (*asattvam*) here means non-eternity (*trikālabādhitvam*), not real for all the times, past, present and future. Therefore by falsity of the world is meant that it has not eternal existence incapable of sublation while at the same time, it does appear in its locus, i.e. *Brahman*. *Advaitasiddhi* says, *asattva* means unfitness to appear as existent in any locus. It is real till we are in bondage, when knowledge dawns upon us we realize it is nothing but unreal. Das et al. (1933: 86) says: "In fact, Advaitism is so realistic that it grants some reality even to illusory objects." It builds its "philosophical edifice on the firm rock of realism".

Śaṅkara did never separate the world from *Brahman* both after and before its manifestation, he never separated many from the unity. Śaṅkara has said that nothing is *asat* anywhere, since "*sat* alone is wrongly taken to be differentiated into plurality".[142] He further says that he never thinks of anything different from *sat*.[143] All the names and forms are nothing but, *sat*.[144] All the things of

---

[142] *sata eva dvaitabhedenānyathāgṛhyamāṇatvānnāsattvaṁ kasyacitkvaciditi brūmaḥ* । – Chā.U.Ś.B. VI.2.3

[143] Ibid.

[144] Ibid.

the world before production are nothing but *sat*.[145] This, the world of duality is *māyā*, reality is Advaita.[146] After creating the world He entered into it.[147] *Vivekacūḍāmaṇi* (*śl.* 233) says that this world is an expression of *Brahman;* it is *Brahman* because the existence of superimposed is not different from its substratum. Mukherji-Sastri says:

> Looked at from the perpetual stage of subject–object relation, the world of sense perception is in the truest sense an objective reality. Looked at from the higher plane of vision which cares only for logical consistency and thorough unity, this universe is resolved to an abstract unity which is indivisibly one. It is really a question of rising to a different plane of vision. Looked at from the point of view of absolute unity, the dualism of the subject–object relation appears to be a distortion. It is the one appearing by some mysterious agency as the manifold of sense perception which is *māyā*. Looked at from the empirical standpoint of practical life this *māyā* or finitizing agency is no more an illusion but an objective truth testified to by the senses.[148]

The world has pragmatic value. It is the "scene of retribution". *Māyā* implies a "philosophy of relative reality". The facts of experience should be evaluated from the point of view of that abiding reality called *Brahman*. The creation of the unreal thing is never to be seen like hare's horn.

Triple Reality

In order to understand clearly the real nature of this world, it is necessary here to mention Śaṅkara's conception of *sattā* (existence). According to Śaṅkara there are three types of *sattās* – *prātibhāsika sattā*, *vyāvahārikā sattā* and *pāramārthika sattā*, i.e. the illusive reality, the empirical reality and the metaphysical reality, respectively.

Prātibhāsika sattā means merely apparent existence. It is sublated by right knowledge, e.g. the perception of snake in

---

[145] G.K.Ś.B. 1.6

[146] G.K. 1.17.

[147] T.U.Ś.B. II.6.

[148] Mukherji–Sastri 1942, p. 151.

rope or silver in conch shell. This rope–snake knowledge is not baseless like sky-flower or son of a barren woman. We impose the knowledge of snake on rope which is to be sublated later on by the knowledge of rope as rope itself. *Prātibhāsika sattā* is not absolutely non-existent. Absolute non-existence has neither its cause nor any being underlying them. They are selfless (*nirātmaka*) and have no ground to sustain them (*nirāspada*) and nothing that is of this type is fit to serve any practical purpose.[149] *Prātibhāsika sattā* has always a ground. No one has perceived it without ground. It is not really there but appears to be there. Its apparent reality is some how contradicted. They are not real but at least "they serve to point to some reality underlying them". The knowledge of snake is sublated but not the consciousness one has of snake is sublated.

By empirical reality (*vyāvahārika sattā*) Śaṅkara means the reality which is seen in day-to-day life. According to *Dṛgdṛśyaviveka*, things possess five qualities: (i) *asti*, (ii) *bhāti*, (iii) *priya*, (iv) *rūpa*, and (v) *nāma*. The former three are but the characteristics of *Brahman*, the last two characteristics are of the empirical world.[150] The objects of dream are our private experiences and exist in our mind but objects of the empirical world are facts of common experience. *Prātibhāsika sattā* serves no practical purpose of ours, mirage water cannot quench our thirst. But *vyāvahārika sattā* has practical importance. A common man never doubts the objects of his experience. Only at the dawn of reality he thinks this world to be false.

According to Śaṅkara, *pāramārthika sattā* is the sole reality. It is *trikāla-satya*. It is none but *Brahman* who is the only reality, the really real.[151] Mādhavācārya says that *Brahman* is the metaphysical reality, *ākāśa*, etc. empirical, *śukti-rajata*, etc. *prātibhāsika*.[152] That which is to be sublated by *laukika pramāṇa* (*pratyakṣa*, *anumāna*, etc.) is *prātibhāsika sattā*. The *jñātā* remains even after the knowledge of *prātibhāsika* is sublated. That which is to be sublated by Vedic *pramāṇa* is *vyāvahārika sattā*. Here *jñātā* too is sublated when this

[149] See, B.G.Ś.B. IX.4.

[150] *āsti bhāti priyaṁ rūpaṁ nāma cetyaṁśapañcakam । ādyatrayaṁ brahmarūpam jagadrūpaṁ tato dvaym ॥* – *Dṛgdṛśyaviveka* 20

[151] B.S.Ś.B. II.1.14.

[152] S.D.S., p. 851.

sattā is sublated.[153]

Devaraja (1962: 205) says:

> His doctrine of the phenomenality of the world is primarily an attempt to rationalize, first, the scriptural declaration that reality is one-without-a-second and second, the faith that ultimate release can be brought about by right knowledge.

Some of Śaṅkara's arguments for the unreality of the world are as follows:

1. The real is that which maintains a uniform nature. To Śaṅkara as to Plato "true knowledge should be related to an object which has a constant nature or an immutable essence". The world is ever changing, it is sublated by knowledge of reality. Thus it is unreal. It is real only from the empirical point of view. It holds good for all practical purposes. Transcendentally it is unreal.
2. Objects of the world are unreal since they do not exist in the beginning and in the end like illusory object.[154] Plato too says that the real is eternal. Worldly things appear to be real but are unreal in fact.
3. The real is always present. *Brahman* is never absent this is not the case with the world.
4. *Brahman* is not limited in space, time and causality. They are empirical categories. They are not metaphysically real. Thus world is unreal expressing itself in space, time and causality. It is relative, *sāpekṣatvāt mithyā*.
5. The perishable world is the object of knowledge. Objectivity is then the other reason for the illusive character of the world, *viṣayatvāt mithyā*.
6. All objects of perception are known and what is known (*dṛśya*) is unreal, *dṛśyatvāt mithyā*.[155]

---

153 S.D.S., p. 852.

154 *Aparokṣānubhūti* 56.

155 *jāgraddṛśyānāṁ bhāvānāṁ vaitathyamiti dṛśyatvāditi hetuḥ* ।

– G.K.Ś.B. II.4

7. The most important consideration in favour of unreality of the world is "unless this hypothesis is accepted, release would be impossible".
8. The world is an effect, and an effect is always unreal. All effects of clay are mere names originating from speech only.[156] The effect does not exist apart from the cause.
9. It is non-intelligent, therefore illusory, *jaḍatvāt mithyā*.

Nāgārjuna too has attempted a similar classification of existence. For *prātibhāsika sattā* of Śaṅkara he uses the world *alokasaṁvṛti* and for empirical reality (*vyāvahārika sattā*) and Ultimate Reality (*pāramārthika sattā*) he uses the words *lokasṁvṛti* and *pāramārthika satya* respectively.

If *Brahman* is absolutely separated from the world and if He is not accepted as the ground (*adhiṣṭhāna*) of the world, this world will be but utterly unreal. Śaṅkara says that the world of *nāma–rūpa* is to be looked upon in connection with *Brahman*, and not cut off from him. K. Sastri (1931: 22-23) says:

> We find from all these discussions that Śaṅkara's idea was that there are indeed statements in the Śruti about the creation no doubt, but its object is not to describe creation or deduction of the world from unity so much as to show that *Brahman* is present (*anugata*) in the world which is its revelation, and to show its unity with *Brahman* and its non-separability from *Brahman*.

Śaṅkara everywhere advocates the fact that the world of *nāma–rūpa* is to be taken as the revelation of *Brahman* because:

a. If *Brahman* is entirely separate from the world, he will not be the material cause as Śruti asserts. He is not an external cause. Śruti says: "Previously it was *Ātman* only."[157]
b. How can the world be separated from *Brahman?* As in that case the knowledge of the world will fall beyond

---

[156] *vācārambhaṇāṁ vikāro nāmadheyaṁ mṛttiketyeva satyam* ।
– Chā.U. VI.1.4

[157] *ātmaivedamagra āsīt* । – Bṛ.U. I.4.1
brahmaivedamamṛtaṁ purastād brahma paścad । – M.U. II.2.11

the knowledge of the *Brahman*, and world will not be an expression of *Brahman*, but Śaṅkara everywhere asserts along with Śruti that the world is a revelation of *Brahman*, *ātmabhūte iva nāmarūpe*.

c. *Brahman* is called in Vedānta as *sattāprada*. If the world is supposed to be *sattā*, it will be independent of *Brahman*.

d. The object of his will is not outside Himself and He is not limited by anything outside Himself.

In its continuous transformation the world remains as it is, for its content is always the same, for this reason it is *pariṇāmī nitya*. But as there is transcendental element behind it, also other than what it is and this transcendental element is none but *kūṭastha nitya*.

Sastri (1931: 50) says that we can never understand the world "as becoming merely, but as being that is becoming. *Vikāra*s are not mere changes but movements to a definite end or goal, a progress."

Śaṅkara never separates the effect from the cause. Cause is also superior to the effect.[158] There is no world separate from *Brahman*, its independent existence is illusory like snake in the rope. How can there be reality in imposed object. The locus itself is giving an impression.[159] Radhakrishnan (1966: 583) says:

> The world is not so much negated as reinterpreted. The conception of *jīvanmukti*, the idea of *kramamukti*, the distinction of values, of truth and error, of virtue and vice, the possibility of attaining *mokṣa* through the world of experience, imply that there is Reality in appearances; *Brahman* is in the world, though not as the world.

Thus we see the world in Vedānta is not totally unreal as critics misunderstand it. R. Das (1935) has very clearly pointed out this fact:

> When Vedānta says that the things of the world are real, merely denies of the things the sort of reality that belongs to the Absolute. And when common sense says the sort of reality that

---

[158] Chā.U.Ś.B. VII.12.1.

[159] *Vivekacūḍāmaṇi*, *śloka* 237.

> can be given in sense experience and is needed for the practical purpose of life.

He further says:

> Thus it is clear that a judgement about reality by common sense is a judgement of fact but the Vedāntic judgement about the unreality of empirical object is a judgement of value, that a judgement of fact does not contradict and is not contradicted by a judgement of value, because their significance is different.

Vedānta is not "a science of positive fact" but "a science of spiritual ideal". It enunciates a spiritual ideal and leaves it to us to realize it in ourselves. There is no reason to call the world unreal before the knowledge of oneness of *ātman* is attained.[160] The world is unreal because it is logically unsatisfactory or indefinable.

Śaṅkara's view of the *mokṣa* is supported by his view of the world. The state of release consists not in the persistence or annihilation of plurality, but in the incapability of the pluralistic universe to mislead us. After release the world is not destroyed, only the vision of the world is destroyed or changed. Whenever Śaṅkara denies the reality of the phenomenal world, he uses words like "different from *Brahman*" or "different from the cause". It is not illusion in ordinary sense. The factor that is responsible for this distorted view is not a mere subjective factor. It is psychological constituent of every perceiving mind, it is a defect in constitution of our intellectual faculties.

Śaṅkara's Conception of Liberation

"The Advaita Vedānta is primarily a science of freedom"(Das et al. 1933: 83) Max Müller's remark on Indian philosophy that "it looks upon metaphysics as the natural outcome of religion" most faithfully describes the Vedāntic position. According to Śaṅkara, the greatest good of man lies in the realization of *Brahman* in man. The aim of Śaṅkara's Advaita is "the psychological identity of self is to be lost or immersed in the metaphysical reality or transcendence".[161]

---

160 *Naiṣkarmyasiddhi* II.66.

161 *brahmāvagatirhi puruṣārthaḥ* । – B.S.Ś.B. I.1.1

Brahman, according to Śaṅkara, is not only perfect being but also perfect bliss. There is no gain greater than that of *Brahman*, no bliss or knowledge better than the bliss or knowledge of it.[162] The knowledge of it is the *summum bonum, parama puruṣārtha* of life. When the idea of cosmic expansion of self (*sarvātmabhāvaḥ*), which is another name of Vedāntic liberation, bestows upon the philosophical pilgrim, he is filled in with new outlook. Otto's (1932) remark that the Vedānta is not metaphysics but a doctrine of salvation is hardly an exaggeration. He aptly remarks about Śaṅkara and Meister Eckhart that none of them is concerned with knowledge "out of curiosity to explain the world, but each one is impelled by a longing for salvation".

Mukti is derived from the root *muc* meaning "to let go", "to discharge", "release"; it signifies in the first instance deliverance and release from pain and penalities of any kind.

> It was not an actual addition to the sum of human possession and enjoyment, a new fact breaking forth, where nothing has been before, but the removal of a barrier and the entering into the secure realization of a permanent inalienable truth.
>
> – Hastings 1910

Vedānta Paribhāṣā defines it as "the realization of *ānandasvarūpa Brahman* and absolute cessation of agony of life is called *mokṣa*".[163]

The concept of *mukti* has two sides: (i) a negative side, viz. having got lose from or rid of (*apāpa, niṣkāma, vi-jara, agarīra, vi-duṣkṛta*), and (ii) a positive side, general sense of expanded outlook (Rhys Davids 1967), realization of God in man. *Mokṣa* is a positive state of being and not merely a negative condition of absence of miseries. It is nothing external to us. It is realization of our own nature and not the acquisition of anything that we do not possess already. It is not a matter of new attainment but gain of that which is already with us (*prāptasya prāptiḥ*). It is like the search of the

[162] *yallābhānna paro lābho yatsukhānna paraṁ sukham* ।
yajjñānanna paraṁ jñānam tadbrahmaivāvadhārayet ॥
– *Ātmabodha* 54

[163] *ānandātmakabrahmāvāptiśca mokṣaḥ śokanivṛtiśca* । – V.P., chap. VIII

necklace which is lying in neck but is searched for everywhere[164] (*aprāptamiva prāpnoti*).[165] To know the real self is the greatest attainment according to the scriptures and reasoning.[166] It is the greatest value of human life. It is the highest ideal of human being. The worth of all our actions is to be judged by this standard only.

Heaven is not the ultimate goal according to Śaṅkara. Heaven is all the time here. The only thing important is to caste off the veil of ignorance. Radhakrishnan (1966, vol. II: 636) says:

> The enfranchisement of man from all his self-wrought bondage, the glory which is utterly beyond all grasp of thought, the peace that is the very purpose of all our striving, lies nearer to us than our nearest consciousness.

Nirvāṇa of the Buddha, *apavarga* of Nyāya, *niḥśreyasa* of Vaiśeṣika, *kaivalya* of Yogin, *mukti* of Sāṁkhya all the schools differ so far as the positive side of *mokṣa* is concerned, as to its negative conclusion they all accept that the state of release implies a complete freedom from the shackle of empirical existence. *Śāstradīpikā* says:

> The spirit, the body which is the centre of enjoyment, the senses which are the instruments of enjoyment, and the objects of enjoyment such as sound, and the rest, complete dissolution of this threefold bond is release.[167]

Release is the supreme state of beatitude or blessedness – a supra moral state of fulfilment. It neither has beginning nor end. If it would have beginning, there would be an end, and it would be a misnomer to call it release. Again if it is predicated to be accompanied by an act, in that case its relation to body, senses, etc. would have to be predicated and it would be capable of increase and decrease, and that which is subject to increase and decrease is not imperishable.

On the point of *mokṣa*, Śaṅkara differs from other Vedāntists

---

[164] *ātmā tu satataṁ prāpto 'pyaprāptavadavidyayā* ।
tannāśe prāptavadbhāti svakaṇṭhābharaṇaṁ yathā ॥ – *Ātmabodha*, p. 44

[165] T.U. I.2 and B.S.Ś.B. I.1.4.

[166] *ātmalābhaḥ paro lābha iti śāstropapattayaḥ* । – *Upadeśasāhsrī* XVI.44

[167] *Śāstradīpikā*, p. 125.

at least in one important aspect. According to Śaṅkara, it is *sādhya* in common sense of the term.

> It is not brought into being anew like *dharma* nor does it involve a modification in the character of the individual self or any readjustment of its relation to the highest principle in the universe, as other Vedāntists think. It is *siddha* or self-existent according to him. – Hiriyanna 1952: 89

If *Nirguṇa-Brahman* is the highest value, may it not be asked that *mokṣa* practically means repudiation of all the values of life. The answer is negative; ultimate self is not only *sat* and *cit* but also *ānanda*. *Mokṣa* transcends different orders of life. Transcendence is not negative. It does not negate the values of life:

> The entire Advaita system is permeated with value question and in such a way that an independent separate treatment of them is unnecessary. Value questions do enter, however implicitly into every ontological and epistemological analysis.
>
> – Deutsch 1968: 99

Identification of self with body (*dehātma-buddhi*) is the root cause of all miseries. In *mokṣa*, man transcends this sense. It is a positive state of bliss and not merely the negative condition of the absence of misery. It is not external, it is realization of our own nature and not the acquisition of anything new that is not possessed already. Radhakrishnan (1966, vol. I: 209) says: "The Vedāntic God in man is a task as well as a fact is as much a problem as a possession." *Brahman* within and *Brahman* outside is one and the same. Date (1954: 454-55) says:

> The glory, as described by Śaṅkara, is that the meeting point of these two is in man and the ultimate value of the one transcendental, real object of inquiry and realization is to be found in the innermost recess of the heart by restoring to moral purity, devotion and spiritual contemplation. . . . Man becomes *Brahman*.

The Way to Liberation

The antecedent conditions, necessary for undertaking the study of Vedānta, are said to be four in number (*sādhana-catuṣṭaya*):

(i) The discrimination between what is abiding and what is not abiding, *nityānitya-vastu-viveka*.

(ii) Non-attachment to mundane and extra-mundane objects of pleasure and pain, *virāga*.

(iii) Possession of tranquillity, restraint and other virtues, *śama-damādi-sādhanasaṁpat*.

(iv) Desire for final liberation, *mumukṣutva*.[168]

The first condition amounts to a general sense of discrimination between things that are permanent and thing that are impermanent. It consists in acquiring the knowledge that I am true, eternal (*nityamātmasvarūpam*) but the objects of my knowledge are of opposite nature.[169] Such determination as *Brahman* is truth and the world is false, is called *nityānitva-vastu-viveka*.[170]

Virāga means absence of desire for seen and unseen enjoyable objects, which arises by scrutinizing these objects from ultimate standpoint.[171] *Virāga* also means renunciation of desire to enjoy the fruits of one's own action. It develops an attitude of aversion for all-worldly objects and "requires to feel as little interested in the highest of them, such as the status of Brahmā, as in the lowest, such as the excrement of a crow".[172] Naciketā, moved by the same spirit of divine discontentment, says, "not with wealth is a man to be satisfied" (K.U. I.1.27). Maitreyī too asks Yājñavalkya whether the whole wealth of the world, if it is owned by her, will provide immortality to her. Yājñavalkya gives in answer a definite no. Thus mind can concentrate on the reality only if it is detached from worldly enjoyment and prosperity (Bṛ.U. II.4.2).

The third prerequisite condition for an Advaita *sādhaka* consists in cultivation of six virtues, viz. *śama*, *dama*, *uparati*, *titikṣā*, *samādhi*

---

168 *nityānityavastuvivekaḥ ihāmutrātha bhogavirāgah, śamadamādi- sādhanasaṁpat, mumukṣutvam ca* । – B.S.Ś.B. I.1.1

169 *nityamātmasvarūpaṁ hi, dṛśyam tadviparītagam* ।
evaṁ yo niścayaḥ samyag viveko vastunaḥ sa vai ॥ – Apa. 5

170 *Vivekacūḍāmaṇi*, *śloka* 20.

171 B.G.Ś.B. VI.35.

172 Apa. 4; also *Vivekacūḍāmaṇi*, *śloka* 21.

(or *samādhāna*) and *śraddhā*.

Śama means "restraint of the inner sense organ".[173] It connotes a constant attempt to give up one's craving for object.[174] The reality cannot be grasped in true sense so long as the inner sense organ is restless.[175] Govindānanda defines it as *laukika-vyāparat manasaḥ uparatiḥ*.[176]

Dama means restraining of the external sense organs.[177] A seeker of true knowledge must draw away his sense from worldly objects as the tortoise draws in its limbs.[178] Kṛṣṇa says in *Gītā*:

> Even though a man may ever strive (for perfection) and be ever so discerning, O son of Kuntī (Arjuna) his impetuous sense will carry off his mind by force.[179]

Govindānanda defines it as "restraining outgoing activities of the senses".

The withdrawal of the senses from their objects when affected is called *uparati*.[180] A person is *uparata* when he is free from all desires for worldly objects.[181] According to Govindānanda "to emancipate the mind from an inflexible routine of ritual duties which have not for their end the supreme goal of life – the realization of the highest truth is *uparati*".[182] Not taking shelter in

---

173 *antarindriya-nigrahaḥ śamaḥ* । – S.D.S., p. 435

174 *sadaiva vāsonā-tyāgaḥ śamo 'yamitiśabditaḥ* । – *Aparokṣānubhūti* 6

175 B.G.Ś.B. II.66.

176 Quoted from S.N.L. Srivastava's article "What Vedāntism Is", *Prabuddha Bharata*, vol. XLII: 532, 1937

177 (a) *damo bāhyendriyopaśamaḥ* । – B.G.Ś.B. X.4

(b) *nigraho bāhyavṛtīnāṁ dama ityobhidhīyate* । – *Aparokṣānubhūti* 6

(c) *bahirindriya-nigraho damaḥ* । – S.D.S., p. 435

178 B.G.Ś.B. II.58.

179 Radhakrishanan's translation of *Gītā* II.60.

180 (a) *viṣayebhyaḥ parāvṛttiḥ paramopanavṛhi sā* । – *Aparokṣānubhūti* 17

(b) *vikṣepābhāva uparatiḥ* । – Sadanand 1967: 11

181 Bṛ.U.Ś.B. IV.4.23.

182 Quoted from S.N.L. Srivastava's article.

the objective world is called *uparati*.[183]

Titikṣā[184] is "stoic endurance of dualities like pleasure and pain, heat and cold". The stoic forbearance of the trouble, without being moved by worries and sorrow, is *titikṣā*.

Samādhi or *samādhāna* is the concentration of one's own mind on *sat*.[185] And *śraddhā* is feeling of respect for Śāstras and teacher.[186] Some of the Western thinkers do not advocate the import of *śraddhā* in the field of philosophy. Descartes starts his philosophy with doubt thus faith has no place in it but in Indian philosophy it plays an important role. Deussen says that a philosophical genius must be excited then only he can create genius in the field of philosophy but Advaitic *sādhaka* is advised to cultivate the spirit of "stern detachment" (*virāga*) which is rather unfit for a philosopher. "*Śraddhā* seems to Deussen to be an unphilosophical trait of the mind" (Warrier 1961: 421). But Jean James has himself maintained that "imitation and invention are the two legs on which human race have historically walked."[187] The following lines of Max Müller (1967: 36) may give an apt reply to Deussen "that the sea must no longer be swept by storms if it is to reflect the right of the sun in all its divine calmness and purity". Thus Advaitins as well as Kant believe that there are many things which are not to be grasped by human understanding and there we seek guidance from faith.

Mumukṣutva is strong desire for one's own liberation. We must have the earnest desire to cast off the veil of ignorance. *Mumukṣutva* "is deep seated and unshaky active attitude of mind which is inquisitive about the means of one's liberation from one's bondage

---

183 *bāhyānalambanaṁ vṛttereṣoparatirūttamā* । – *Vivekacūḍāmaṇi*, *śloka* 24

184 See Bṛ.U.Ś.B. IV.4.23; Apa. 7 and *Vivekacūḍāmaṇi*, *śloka* 25.

185 (a) *sarvadā sthāpanaṁ buddheḥ śuddhe brahmaṇi sarvathā. tatsāmādhānamityuktam* – *Vivekacūḍāmaṇi*, *śloka* 27

(b) *cittaikāgrayaṁ sāmādhānam* – Sadanand 1967: 11

186 *śāstrasya guruvākyasya satya-buddhyāvadhāraṇam* । *sā śraddhā kathitā* . . .
– *Vivekacūḍāmaṇi*, *śloka* 25

guruvedānta-vāke viśvāsaḥ śraddhā । – Sadanand 1967: 12

nigamācārya-vākyeṣu bhaktiḥ środdheti ***viśruta*** ।

187 Quoted in "Śaṅkara's Brahmavāda".

in the world".[188] It is not an easy task to feel earnest desire for realizing one's own self. According to *Vivekacūḍāmaṇi* (verse 3), it is difficult to get a *mumukṣu puruṣa*. But desire is not enough. With such background for the intellect, emotion and will, one may start the study of Vedānta from a teacher who has realized *Brahman*. This study is a threefold process. *Śravaṇa* (listening to the teacher's preachings), *manana* (understanding those preachings through reason till all doubts are resolved) and *nididhyāsana* (repeated meditation of the truth thus accepted). The deep-rooted ignorance cannot be easily uprooted. Only repeated meditation can purify our mind and set us free from the clutches of ignorance. The teacher preaches the secrets of the Advaita doctrine *tat tvam asi* to his *mumukṣu* disciple. Since then he meditates on this truth and his repeated thinking makes him realize the truth.

Karma and Jñāna

The word *karma* is derived from the root *kṛ* which means to do or perform an action. Thus the etymological meaning of the word is "what is done" or "an action". Apart from this dictionary meaning, it connotes sepecial significance in the field of religion and philosophy. In broad sense of the term *karma* includes both the physical and mental activities indiscriminately. During Vedic period, *karma* mainly denoted performance of Vedic sacrifice. S.N. Dasgupta says:

> The law of *karma* is universally regarded as an ethical law by which each person was bound to reap the good and bad effects of his deeds.[189]

It is a relative idea. In a nutshell, we may say, *karma* means: we reap as we sow.[190]

According to Śaṅkara the realization of true self is the highest goal of our life. Realization of *Brahman* is the sheet anchor of Advaitism. Śaṅkara says, *brahmāvagatirhi puruṣārthaḥ* (B.S.Ś.B. I.1.1).

---

[188] See Apa. 9 and *Vivekacūḍāmaṇi*, *śloka* 27.

[189] Dasgupta, 1933, *Indian Idealism*, p. 3.

[190] *avaśyameva bhoktavyaṁ kṛtaṁ karma śubhāśubham* ।
nābhuktaṁ kṣīyate karma kalpa-koṭisatairapi ॥

Liberation is the same as being of *Brahman*: *brahmabhāvaśca mokṣaḥ*. To realize *Brahman* as the true essence of all is the *summum bonum* of life and it is of the nature of eternal knowledge. The worth of all actions is to be judged by this standard. Realization of *Brahman* will not only set ourselves free from the "evils and afflictions" it will provide us the highest beatitude, the highest bliss too. But it never means the denial of other values. Of course, they are only secondary means, inferior to self-realization. Śaṅkara has used the word *abhyudaya* for all these values. It literally means rise or upliftment – not only moral upliftment – as it leads towards the realization of one's highest end. Śaṅkara speaks of *bhoga* and *abhyudaya* as being a *puruṣārtha* along with that of *mokṣa* called *apavarga* or *niḥśreyasa*.[191] *Abhyudaya* cannot be the ultimate end of life. It is unenduring. Even enjoyment in heaven soon comes to an end, then what to tell of earthly pleasure. Value of the world, in the words of Naciketā, lasts till tomorrow only (*śvobhāvaḥ*). Destruction is the inevitable end of every finite thing.

Sureśvarācārya says in *Naiṣkarmyasiddhiḥ* (I.24) that act is performed in ignorance and so action, having its scope only within ignorance, cannot itself destroy ignorance. World passion is not to be quenched. Pouring of butter into fire will not satisfy its hunger for more and more of it.[192]

Thus the highest goal of human life, according to Śaṅkara, is the infinite bliss, the infinite existence and the infinite knowledge, and the sole sufficing means for obtaining the end of all persuits is the true knowledge of the self. Knowledge of *Brahman* is the only means of attaining immortality.

Karma is the name for all activities which will lead to existence hereafter. *Mokṣa* cannot be brought by means of action. *Karma* is always based on egoism, *karmahetuḥ kāmaḥ syāt*.[193] Saroj Kumar Das (1937) says: "Injunctions are but frail resources like insecure rafts in the matter of crossing the bar of mundane existence into

[191] T.U.Ś.B. II.1 and B.G.Ś.B. X.18.

[192] B.G. III.39.

[193] T.U.Ś.B., Introduction.

the land of the life everlasting." Action is thus indirectly useful in removing ignorance. But it cannot directly remove ignorance like knowledge because there is an opposition between action and ignorance. Thus *karma* is the subsidiary means for *mokṣa*. It prepares the ground by purifying our mind (*sattvaśuddhi*), it calms down our mind, cultures our emotion. Its effect always seems to be either as the creation or modification or change or obtainment of something.[194] *Mokṣa* or *Brahman* is none of these. Thus it is to be known only by *jñāna*.

Not only this, Śaṅkarācārya has denied Jñāna-karma-samuccaya-vāda too, according to which "*karma* and *jñāna* are equally contributory to, i.e. coordinate causes of *mokṣa*". This theory is supported by Nyāya, Vaiśeṣika, Rāmānuja, etc. but for Śaṅkara, *jñāna* needs no auxiliary as to support it. The *samuccaya* (coordination) of *jñāna* and *karma* is not possible according to Śaṅkara, because in the first phase there is opposition between them with regards to their cause, nature and effect (*svarūpa-phala-virodhāt*) and second, because like the knowledge and ignorance of a rope, their coexistence is not possible (*saha-saṁbhavānupapatteḥ*). The cause of *karma* is attachment while that of *jñāna* is non-attachment. *Karma* is but nature *jaḍa* (bereft of consciousness) but *jñāna* is self-shining like light. The fruit or effect of *karma* is *svarga*. Knowledge does not require *karma* or anything to supplement it[195] because its result is definite and certain as darkness cannot help light in doing its work. Śaṅkara says, "actions which arise from *avidyā* cannot coexist with a true knowledge of spirit".[196]

The antagonism between *karma* and *jñāna* is evident from the fact that while the former necessarily involves the feeling of egoity on the part of the doer, the latter is accompanied by the absence

---

194 *utpādyam āpyaṁ saṁskāryaṁ vikāryaṁ ca kriyāphalam* ।
naivaṁ muktiryataḥ tasmāt karma tasyāḥ na kāraṇam ॥
– *Naiṣkarmyasiddhi* 1.53

195 *naṇu dhruva-phalā vidyā nānyat kiñcidapekṣate* ।

196 T.U.Ś.B., Introduction.

of that feeling. *Karma* which is *ajñānamaya avidyā*, is *jñānamaya*.[197] Moreover an action (*karma*) is dependent upon its doer, it may be performed or not performed or performed otherwise. Knowledge, on the other hand, is dependent upon the objects known.[198] All the works are rooted in desire and ignorance. The subject of *jñāna* is *karma*, but the subject of *jñāna* is *jñānaniṣṭhā*.[199] The difference between *jñāna* and *karma* is as unshakable as a mountain. Thus there cannot be any coordination between *jñāna* and *karma*. Prosperity is the fruit of knowledge of religious duty and it depends on observance, *niḥśreyasa* is the result of *brahma-jñāna*, and it does not depend upon observance.

Sureśvarācārya (1970: 13) says:

> If knowledge and action are to constitute the whole cause (knowledge being subordinate) both of them must be available at the same time. But we find action and knowledge cannot be found at the same time, because knowledge being an effect of action can come into being only when action is over. —1.54

Again he says:

> Knowledge cannot be joined with action even as an equally important fact (in the complete cause) because knowledge and action being incompatible with each other cannot be had in one place. – 1.55
>
> Knowledge is incompatible with action, it is clear from the fact that action is a product of ignorance and ignorance cannot stand before knowledge. There can be no combination of light and darkness. – 1.56

They are contradictory (*viparīte*) and are poles apart (*duramete*). Śaṅkara in his *Bhāṣya* on *Bṛhadāraṇyaka Upaniṣad* says "*jīva*s incur bondage by *karma* and liberation by *jñāna*"; in this way contradiction is known between *karma* and *jñāna*. *Brahmavidyā* is not associated

---

197 *karmaivadayāsvarūpayor vidyāvidyātmakayoḥ prutikūlavartanaṁ virodhaḥ* ।
– Bṛ.U.Ś.B. II.4.1

198 *vastvadhīnā bhavedvidyā kartradhīno bhavedvidhiḥ* ।

199 *avidyākamabījanaṁ hi sarvam ecva karma . . . avidvādviṣayaṁ karma vidvādiṣayā ca sarvakarmasaṁnyāsapūrvikā jñānaniṣṭhā* ।
– B.G.Ś.B. XVIII.66

with any other means for *puruṣārtha*. It is contradictory to all other means, it is the sole means for *puruṣārtha*.[200]

Maṇḍana Miśra, the author of *Brahmasiddhi*, does not see any contradiction in *jñāna-karmasamuccaya*. The text in *Īśopaniṣad*, *vidyāṁ cāvidyāṁ ca yas tadvedobhayaṁ saha* is interpreted by Maṇḍana Miśra as meaning that "*karma* is the means (*upāya*) and *jñāna* is the end (*upeya*). The two should go hand in hand. *Karma* is helpful in leading to the attainment of *jñāna* quickly". Maṇḍana Miśra does not see any opposition between *jñāna* and *karma*. For Śaṅkara, the two are opposed to each other like darkness and light. But it should be clearly thought that this opposition is from the point of view of unitive consciousness and not at early stage. At early stage *karma* purifies our mind and prepares way for *jñāna*. Śaṅkara knew that cognition, conation and affection cannot be kept in watertight compartments.

It never means that he discredits *karma* altogether. *Karma* has its own contribution and value. Śaṅkara has definitely recognized the value of those actions which are called technically *sādhāraṇa* and *varṇāśrama-dharma*. *Sādhāraṇa* and *varṇāśrama dharmas* are the common duties of man irrespective of his caste, creed and social status, e.g. *satya, asteya, akrodha, kṣamā, dhairya, śauca* and *ahiṁsā*. *Varṇāśrama-dharma* or *Viśeṣa-dharma*, are the duties which are related to one's station and status in society. These duties are hiding on all persons alike. The performance of these duties is a necessity of good human life itself.[201] Śaṅkara endorses the idea of *Kaṭhopaniṣad* that "one who has not perfectly ceased to do or rather to think of doing, whose mind is not perfectly pure and at peace, cannot obtain his true self through knowledge". *Cittaśuddhi* is an essential condition for knowledge and this *cittaśuddhi* can be affected only through the performance of one's duties for their own sake or for the sake of God. Thus disinterested performance of these duties has been regarded as mediate or remote condition of self-realization. Śaṅkara advocates *Gītā*'s view that a deed

200 *tasmānna sādhanāntarasahitā brahmavidyā puruṣārtha-sādhanam, sarvavirodhāt, sādhana-niropekṣaiva puruṣārtha-sādhanamiti* ।
– Bṛ.U.Ś.B. I.4.1

201 Bṛ.U.Ś.B. IV.4.22.

performed by a person never fails to bear its fruits.[202] Action, good or bad, results in the transmigration of soul. Śaṅkara says that one must follow *karma-yoga* before one gets *ātmajñāna*.[203] *Yogī* performs action for the purification of inner self (*antaḥkaraṇa*).[204]

Varṇāśrama-dharma is duly recognized by Śaṅkara but the knowledge of *Brahman* is not restricted to any particular caste. "A temple of truth is open to all." Muirhead (1892: 45) said once, "an artisan or artist or a writer who does not do his best is not only an inferior workman but a bad man". The concept of *Varṇāśrama-dharma* lies in Thomas Carlyle's saying, "Do the duty that lies nearest thee".

> There is activity prior to knowledge when we are adjusting the instruments of knowledge, there is activity after knowledge, when we are trying to put our knowledge to use. There is no activity within knowledge as such, which is a revealing of reality whole and entire.
> – Malkani 1916: 274

All these activities end in knowledge.[205] When sin is ripe by performing good action (*satkarma*), *jñāna* originates.[206] Kṛṣṇa says in *Gītā* that the fire of knowledge destroys all sorts of *karma*.[207] Action merely prepares ground for knowledge and gives necessary qualification for it.

All systems of Indian philosophy, except Cārvāka, believe that *mokṣa* is possible though knowledge. But Śaṅkara goes further and says, "Saving knowledge is essentially the knowledge of reality". *Jñāna* is used in broader sense than its English equivalent or its dictionary meaning. According to Śaṅkara *mokṣa* is attained through "the mental spiritual discipline of *jñāna-yoga*". *Jñāna*

---

202 *avasyam hi kṛtam karma phalamarabhate eva* । – B.G.Ś.B., Introduction

203 B.G.Ś.B. III.16.

204 (a) *sattva śuddhaye karma kurvanti* । – B.G.Ś.B. II.10

(b) *karmaṇām viśuddhihetutvāt* । – Bṛ.U.Ś.B. IV.4.22

(c) *yajño dānaṁ tapaścaiva pāvanāni manīṣiṇām* । – B.G. XVIII.5

205 V.P., p. 423.

206 Ibid.

207 *jñānāgniḥ sarvakarmāṇi bhasmasāt kurute* । – B.G. IV.37

is here not an intellectual pathway to perfection but spiritual wisdom. It is knowledge of unitive consciousness.[208] Man knows only the surface of his being. There is much behind the surface reality which is to be visualized by knowledge. According to Śaṅkara, there is no other resource than *jñāna* for the realization of *Brahman*.[209]

Karma which is a product of ignorance cannot destroy its parent (Mahadevan 1957: 257). Ignorance and delusion can be removed by knowledge only.[210] The action may be done, misdone or left undone.[211] Rituals, injunctions and prohibitions depend on our thinking only but knowledge leaves no option to us. It is not in our hand, rather it is dependent on *Brahman*. Knowledge, according to Śaṅkara, is "*vastutantra* and not *puruṣatantra*".[212] The knowledge of *Brahman*, like the perceptual knowledge of past, is dependent mainly on the self-revealing character of the object itself and not so much on the attitudes and interests and effects of man. The question may be raised here whether knowledge can be said to be purely objective in character, or it has some subjective element too? Every knowledge has subjective element in it. What Śaṅkara means by *vastutantra* is that *brahma-jñāna* is a category in itself. It transcends the empirical categories of knowledge, knower and known. As sun shines even when there is nothing to shine upon, the *vastu* (*ātman* or *Brahman*) would be self valid by its own criteria of self-conscious activity. It is a "homogeneous experience". Śaṅkara never puts the questions "knowledge for whom? and knowledge for what?". It is the knowledge for itself and the knowledge by itself.[213] *Brahman* is not a percipient being thus *brahmānubhāva* is never knowledge of an object. *Brahman* is *vastu* independent of all empirical categories of the judgement and value.

---

208 *tadātmānamevāvedahaṃ brahmāsmi* । – Bṛ.U. I.4.10

209 See Śve.U. III.8; T.U. II.1.1; *Ātmabodha* 2, etc.

210 *vidyaivājñānahanaya na karma 'pratikūlataḥ* । – Upa.Sā. I.6

211 B.S.Ś.B. I.1.2.

212 Ibid.

213 Date 1954, vol. II: 452.

Hiriyanna (1955: 165) says:

> In common with other systems the discipline here also consists of two parts – the first meant for cultivating detachment (*vairāgya*) and the second, for acquiring knowledge (*jñāna*) of the ultimate reality and transforming that knowledge into direct experience.

Knowledge has no other result than casting off ignorance. This *ātmajñāna* is not to be acquired by any other means except by knowledge.[214]

Upadeśasāhasrī describes:

> The cause is ignorance, knowledge brings it to an end, when ignorance, the cause will be removed, you will be liberated from transitory existence.

Knowledge is not to be acquired for its own sake and not for regulating and guiding religious conduct. It is itself sufficient to fetch *mukti* for us.

K.C. Bhattacharyya (1937: 250) says:

> It prescribes knowledge as its distinctive *sādhana* and regards it as self-sufficing and requiring no supplemention (*samuccaya*).

Jñāna does not depend on anything else for giving its effects. It wishes only its origination and nothing else.[215] Knowledge of *Brahman* culminates in fact.[216] The knowledge of *Brahman* depends on *Brahman* itself. True knowledge cannot be produced by hundreds of injunctions and prohibitions. It is not a mental activity, because it depends on the existent being and not on mind.[217] It is the highest means according to Śaṅkara.

Bhakti and Jñāna

Bhakti carries us a long way towards *mokṣa* and its relative value is not denied by Śaṅkara. Bratindra Kumar Sengupta (1953-54:

---

[214] Sam.Śā. IV.4.

[215] Ibid. IV.26.

[216] B.S.Ś.B. I.1.2.

[217] Ibid. III.2.21.

377) says:

> The attitude of devotion is not incompatible even in Advaita Vedānta if we acquiesce to recognize stages or strata of self-realization.

Śaṅkara says:

> Chief among the causes of freedom is devotion, the intentness of the soul on its own nature or devotion may be called intentness on the reality of the self.[218]

In his commentary on *Śvetāśvatara Upaniṣad,* Śaṅkara interprets "the luminous principles of Savitā and Agni in clear exposition of self-surrender to them and their condescence to get that homage".[219] In his commentary on the same Upaniṣad he prays God "to have vision of qualified *Brahman*",[220] and "to look upon him that is to take him to the path of righteousess (*śreyas*)".[221]

Śaṅkara emphasizes in the introduction to his *Bhāṣya* on *Gītā* that only *jñāna* can vouchsafe to us the ultimate goal. But while interpreting the devotional *śloka*s, Śaṅkara has not the least hesitation in accepting that complete self-surrender in and through all our actions can carry us a long way towards the ultimate goal that is self-realization. *Brahman* himself in space and time is made the object of worship and none else. Thus the object of worship does not conflict with the highest principle.

In his commentary on *Brahmasūtra* Śaṅkara recognizes the value of devotion in three ways:

1. It engenders some superhuman and supraphysical power like complete freedom in one's own earthly life (*abhyudayārthāni*).
2. It serves as a stepping stone towards gradual self-realization (*karmamuktyarthāni*).
3. It helps to make our action better and nobler

[218] *mokṣa-kāraṇasāmagrayāṁ bhaktireva garīyasī.*

[219] Śve.U.Ś.B. II.1.

[220] *sākāraṁ brahma pradarsayet* । – Ibid. III.5

[221] Ibid. III.5.

(*karmasamṛddhyarthāni*).[222]

Śaṅkara never denies the relative importance of devotion. He himself, in a high moment of devotion, has composed so many verses in praise of Goddess Durgā, Viṣṇu, Śiva, etc. These *stotras* speak of his devotional attitude par excellence. V.J. Kirtikar (1924: 112) says:

> The keynote of the practical Ethics of Vedānta is *abheda* as the keynote of its philosophy and theology is Advaita. Advaita means oneness without a second, so *abheda* means oneness without destruction of "I" and "thou", "mine" and "thine". The world *abheda* when correctly understood means love in its purity and fullness.

Jīvanmukti and Videhamukti

Enlightenment may come at any time and when it comes a man is called *jīvanmukta*. *Jīvanmukta* is liberated while yet in flesh, in embodied condition. *Videhamukti* is the final release which is obtained after death. Radhakrishnan (1960: 215) says, "*Jīvanmukta* is not close proximity to final release but it is final release". We need not doubt whether such a consummation is possible or not while surviving in flesh and blood. It has full support of Śruti.[223] A man has to wait for final release till the fall of the body.[224] Just as a potter's wheel goes on revolving for some time even after the push is withdrawn, similarly the body may continue to exist even after knowledge has dawned though all attachment with the body is cut off.[225] Like an arrow shot from the bow, the body continues to reap the fruit until it expires but no new actions are accumulated.[226] There is one passage in the Upaniṣad which speaks of three kinds of *karmas* but asserts that when the highest is realized all the *karmas* come to end, thus there is no such thing as *jīvanmukti* in this Upaniṣad. They view that release is consequent only on

---

[222] Quoted from B.K. Sengupta, 1953-54, "Devotionalism in Adavaita Vedanta" in *Vedanta Kesari*, vol. XL.

[223] Bṛ.U. IV.4.6; K.U. VI.14.

[224] Chā.U. VI.14.2.

[225] B.S.Ś.B. IV.1.15.

[226] Cha.U.Ś.B. VI.14.2.

bodily death is sought to be found in *Śvetāśvatara Upaniṣad*[227] and in *Kaṭhopaniṣad.*

But this difficulty is more apparent than real. *Prārabdha karma* does not literally come to an end only *sañcita* and *āgāmī karma*s are nullified and not *prārabdha*. *Prārabdha karma* is exhausted only by its *bhoga*.[228] *Prārabdha karma* is the life-force which is bound to work itself and is exhausted only after it has discharged its effect even on living realizer. Self-realization can destroy *sañcita karma* but *prārabdha karma* which has already borne effects cannot be eliminated. The *jñānin* is free from any possibility of incurring new circle of *karma* but he is living on fructifying *karma*. Śaṅkara like the Buddha, Jaina, Sāṁkhya and other Indian thinkers believes that perfection can be reached here and now, it is not an extra-mundane prospect to be attained hereafter. Rāmānuja, Vallabha and Nimbārka do not believe in *jīvanmukti*. They believe in *sālokya*, *sāmīpya*, *sārūpya*, *sāyujya*, etc. types of *mukti*. But Śaṅkara says that a *mumukṣu puruṣa* first gets *jīvanmukti*, then *videhamukti*.[229] He further says that the person, who realizes by virture of blessing of his teacher that he is *Brahman*, is *jīvanmukta*.[230] A *jīvanmukta*, till his *prārabdha* is over, lives in the world peacefully. Since egoism is over he is beyond duality, *nitya-śuddha*, *nityatṛpta*.[231] A *jīvanmukta* understands that he neither is body nor organ, he neither is *manas* nor *buddhi*, nor *prāṇa* as all these are material, and how can a conscious *ātman* become material. He realizes that he is conscious, *sākṣī*, Śiva and the substrate of the whole universe.[232] Sadānanda describes *jīvanmukta*'s *lakṣaṇa* as

After acquiring knowledge of *brahma-jñāna* by *śravaṇa*, *śruti*,

---

227 Śve.U.Ś.B. I.10.

228 *prārabdhaṁ balavattaraṅ khalu vidāṁ bhogena tasya kṣayaḥ* ।
samayagjñānahutāsanera vilyaḥ prāksañcitāgamnām ।
– *Vivekacūḍāmaṇi*, *śloka* 454

229 *jīvanamuktirmumukṣoḥ prathamamatha tato muktirātyantikī ca* ।
– *Śataślokī*, v. 42.

230 Ibid. v. 91.

231 Ibid. v. 96.

232 Ibid. v. 92.

> etc. after getting rid of all (*ajñāna*) in connection with Brahman, bondage is shattered and that man becomes *jīvanmukta*.[233]

A *jīvanmukta* will be a law unto himself. The code of ordinary morality, nay even Veda will cease to bind him. He will rise above both *dharma* and *adharma* alike because both lead to bondage and transmigration. He will not be affected by praise and blame.[234] Morality is the very condition of his existence as he is beyond sin. There will be ever a smile on his lips to show his inward enjoyment of the bliss of *Brahman*. He enjoys constantly *ātmānanda*.[235] He resolves the multiplicity of the world into unity, reduces the duality of soul and non-soul, mind and matter, etc. into pure and simple essence.

"He, whose cares about the phenomenal state have been appeased, who though possessed of a body consisting of parts is yet devoid of parts, whose mind is free from anxiety", is a *jīvanmukta*. His worldly desires are pacified. He ever feels blissfulness of *ātman* and his intellect (*prajñā*) is always fixed.[236]

Looking everywhere with an eye of equality in this world[237] owing to his mind being engrossed in tasting the bliss of *Brahman*,[238] complete absence of ideas, interior and exterior, living unconcerned with the ideas of "I" and "thine",[239] freedom from bondage of transmigration,[240] are the characteristics of a *jīvanmukta*. There are some common factors in both *suṣupti* and *jīvanmukta* but the major difference between them is while a *suṣupta puruṣa* again regains his previous consciousness and finds himself in worldly troubles, a *jīvanmukta* never returns to worldly allurement as his *saṁskāras* are destroyed. In *jīvanmukta* the body and the world are indispensable factors. A *jīvanmukta* never aspires for

[233] *Vedāntasāra*, p. 111.

[234] B.G. XIV.24-25; *Vivekacūḍāmaṇi, śloka* 441.

[235] *Vivekacūḍāmaṇi, śloka* 429.

[236] Ibid.

[237] Ibid., *śloka* 435.

[238] Ibid., *śloka* 436.

[239] Ibid., *śloka* 437.

[240] Ibid., *śloka* 438.

breathing. The entire psycho-physical organism continues as usual but the actuating force or the energizing principle, i.e. *avidyā*, disintegrating influences and their evil consequences, is not there.

M.K. Iyer (1964) says that the practical advantages of the conception of *jīvanmukta* are mainly two:

(i) The conception of *mukti* attainable in this life is positive and real whereas posthumous *mukti* is hypothetical. *Mukti* here and in this life will serve as a more powerful incentive for moral and spiritual effort.

(ii) *Jīvanmukta* will furnish a living example in selfless activity. He will set an ideal before others.

The ideal of *niṣkāma karma* will be in his flesh and blood, it will no more be a mere idea on paper.

Vidyāraṇya defines *jīvanmukta* as one's awareness of the absence of all *adhyāsa* though the psychophysical organism continues to exist as long as the *prārabdha karma* lasts.[241]

Nayanaprasādinī, a commentary on the *Citsukhī* remarks that if the state of *jīvanmukta* is not accepted, *mukti* cannot stand. A question naturally creeps in, what is the use of such persons in the society? They set burning examples before others and show the path to others. Kṛṣṇa too says in *Gītā*, there is no work for him in "the three worlds which has not been obtained" yet he is engaged in work.[242] Both the ordinary soul and *jīvanmukta* work but while the fromer works for worldly prosperity and gain, the latter works disinterestedly relinquishing the desire of fruits of action. He has to transcend even the consciousness that he has realized *Brahman*. The Buddha compares the activity of *jīvanmukta* with fried seeds which do not bear fruit. *Pañcadaśī* (13) narrates: "As water does not stick to the leaves of lotus, after realization, actions do not incur bondage."

Jīvanmukta acts with liberating knowledge that he is only an

---

241 Com. on *Jīvanmuktiviveka*, pp. 103-04.

242 (a) *na me pārthāsti kartavyaṁ triṣu lokeṣu kiñcana* ।
nānavāptamavāptavyaṁ varta eva ca karmaṇi ॥ – B.G. III.22

(b) *lokasaṁgrahamevāpi sampaśyankartumarhasi* । – Ibid. III.20

instrument of the Lord. He realizes "I do nothing".[243] He does work in perfect manner. He is the perfect channel for the flow of Divine energy. He never loses equanimity, his *titikṣā* never leaves him. He works as a master and not as a slave. *Chāndogya Upaniṣad* says, "He delays only so long as he is not free (from the body) then he attains (oneness)". Thus *jīvanmukta* is a transitory stage in Vedānta. Sarvajñātmamuni advocates *sadyo-mukti*. For him the idea of *jīvanmukti* only encourages the *sādhaka*. He criticizes Śaṅkara for *jīvanmukti*. Sureśvara too says that *jīvanmukta* is only the so-called *mukti*. Real *mukti* is *videhamukti*, which is "concommitting with total annihilation of the world". Veermani Prasad Upadhyaya (1959) says that "strictly speaking the attainment of *mokṣa* in a particular period of time whether on death or in life has no meaning for a released soul; it is purely a creation of those who are still crawling in *avidyā*". For the person who is liberated, time factor has no value. He is one with *Brahman* who is beyond time, not because "time committed suicide in time", but because for him the appearance of time was not, is not, and will not be.

Suryanarayan Sastri (1961: 251) holds that the distinction is useless:

> A proper presentation may rid Advaita, at least, of the duality of *muktis*, there is only one since there is nothing else to contrast it with and dissolution of the body is neither inevitable precondition nor integral feature of mukti.

Jīvanmukti is the only a legitimate concept for those who believe in release through the dawn of wisdom.

A *jīvanmukta* embodies "an exalted ideal of superman". But he is not a superman in the sense in which it was used by Nietzsche. There is a wide difference between ruthlessness of Nietzsche's superman and *sarvātma bhāva* of *mukta*. The liberated soul "shares life in the spirit of divine *līlā*, like a god, while Nietzsche's superman, like the *asura* or Titan, struggles violently to overthrow and crush all oppositions".[244]

---

243 *naiva kiñcitkaromīti* – Ibid., V.8

244 Warrier 1961: 502.

A class of writers has, however, held that morality has no place whatsoever in the Vedāntic scheme of liberation. J.N. Farquhar (1920: 230) says: "Emancipation is not conceived as being dependent on morality in any way. It arises altogether from knowledge." He further tells us that in Vedānta:

> *Brahman* is declared to be reality, consciousness, bliss but he is never said to be righteousness or as being the source or centre of the moral order (1920: 229).

Deussen (1912: 403-04) too says:

> Christianity sees the essence of man in will, Brāhmanism in knowledge, therefore for the former, salvation consist in a Transformation of will . . . for the latter in a Transformation of knowledge, in the dawning of consciousness that one is not an individual but *Brahman*, the totality of all Being. . . .

Both Farquhar and Deussen are sadly mistaken. An answer to the question, what is knowledge according to Vedānta and how is it obtained will set aside all misunderstandings. By knowledge Vedānta means "spiritual insight", "an awakening of the individual soul or consciousness to the fundamental unity of all existence". And such a deep sense of unity cannot be acquired except though self-discipline, self-control and purity of heart. Only a pure in heart, a moral person can deserve such morality. Morality is a stepping stone and not a stopping place. Morality is a boat which is to be used indispensably but to be left ultimately when one has crossed the stream. Moral discipline, though is not sufficient to get *mokṣa*, is at least a necessary aid to it. To try to realize liberation without moral perfection is, to use the words of Ranade (1968: 559), to enact the drama of *Hamlet* without the prince of Denmark.

Thus nothing will be more preposterous than the assumption that in Vedāntic scheme of liberation there is nothing like morality. *Muṇḍaka Upaniṣad* says that only pure in heart can see *Brahman*. In Vedānta we find, according to Max Müller (1967: 170), "Ethics in the beginning, ethics in the middle, and ethics in the end". A complete and everlasting transformation of the will and moral rebirth is possible through true knowledge, or spiritual awakening, through a living sense of unity with humanity. Thus in Vedāntic emancipation true knowledge and morality are interwoven, they go hand in hand. Malkani (1916: 286) says:

> Morality in Advaita Vedānta prepares the ground of knowledge and gives the necessary qualification for it. There its function is over.

Fantasy has evidently been allowed to run riot, when Farquhar and other philosophers of West tell us that in Vedānta, *Brahman* is declared to be reality, consciousness and bliss, but he is never said to be "righteousness" as being source or centre of the moral order. There are hundreds of places where Śaṅkara used such expressions as "pure", "without blemish", "spotless", "stainless", etc. Only a man pure in heart can secure liberation. Moral laws are not rendered nugatory. He obeys them when he is a seeker of knowledge and when he has acquired it.

> He is moral throughout his life. He is moral as an aspirant, he is moral as an adept. Morality, in fact, is the very soul of Brahmavāda. – Naulakha 1964: 265

Max Müller says: "Though knowledge alone can in the end lead to *mokṣa*, virtue is certainly presupposed."[245] Another objection against Vedānta is that the metaphysical identity of an individual and the Absolute leaves no scope for ethics. But they do not know perhaps that Śaṅkara did never say that everyman we meet in the street is God. Identity only means we have potentiality to equate ourselves with *Brahman*. There is constant struggle on the part of man to cast off the veil of finitude in which infinite has dressed ourselves. We struggle with imperfection and behave well to reach our native country. Max Müller (1967: 163) says:

> Vedāntic philosophy, so far from merely supplying a metaphysical explanation of the world, aims at establishing its ethics on the most solid philosophical and religious foundation.

In *Brahman* morality is not negated but transcended as all duality is transcended. Moral life belongs to the realm of duality.

It is supposed that there is no encouragement to social life and

[245] Quoted in Hiriyanna 1955.

civic duty in Śaṅkara's world-negating philosophy. If the world is mere illusion, a dream, what is the necessity to take interest in it. "There is no incentive to improve the existing social institutions." The critics here are sadly mistaken. We can easily run away from the world but it is not easy to run away from one's own self.

> His attitude will be not world-seeking or world-saving. The perfect man lives and dies not for him but for mankind.
>
> – Radhakrishnan 1953: 633

Śaṅkara advises us to be in the world but not to be of it like a lotus leaf. What is essential is the transvaluation of the empirical world and not the transformation of it. C.E.M. Joad's (1984: 145) assertion that "For a condition in which I shall cease to exist to feel as an individual or indeed to be an individual is a condition in which I shall cease to be at all. Why should I hope to realize such a condition unless my individual personality is of no account", is a typical representation of the Western view about Vedāntic liberation. They do not realize that to lose individuality in *Brahman* is not a loss but a gain. "The *jīva* returns to its native land." *Mokṣa* is not a fruit to be achieved after a long travelling. It comes as a sudden enlightenment.

4

Schools of Theistic Vedānta

Viśiṣṭādvaita of Rāmānuja

No doubt, "the paragon of all monistic systems is the Vedānta philosophy of Hindostan" but such philosophy does not justify the fundamental religious instinct of man. Philosophy is rooted in man's practical need. The dauntless logic of Śaṅkara leaves no room for loving communion with God. There is no warmth of compassion that can cheer up the devotee in despair. It may be a speculative diversion but not a solace for spirit in distress. The immutable all-pervading unexcelled *Brahman* of Śaṅkara disappoints the devotees who expect a helping hand of grace. The Absolute is unaware of love and total surrender of devotees as the historical monuments are unaware of admiration. Radhakrishnan (1953, vol. II: 659) remarks:

> For all those who regard the goal of religion as the goal of philosophy – to know God is to know the real – Śaṅkara's view seems to be a finished example of learned error.

Śaṅkara's relentless logic, his astounding dialectic acumen kept the intellectuals under its spell for centuries to come and consequently they took Advaita as the last word in philosophical analysis. The galaxy of post-Śaṅkarite authors like Sureśvara, Vācaspati Miśra, Sarvajñātmamuni and Citsukhācārya contributed immensely towards Advaita. Yet its inherent weakness exposed itself to many who had a soft heart but not a strong mind. To those who have a theistic bent of mind, it appeared to be a dark night which belittles all differentiations and distinctions. Reduction of God to phenomenal entity, of *jīva* to an appearance of the truly Real, of world to illusion, converted ethics and religion to useful fictions. The theistic attitude of mind abhors the identity philosophy of

Śaṅkara where individual is not left apart to enjoy the loving awareness of his Lord. The Absolute of Śaṅkara turns out to be a closed system. The supremacy of *Brahman* cannot be defended with human experience. Philosophy revolts against slavish allegiance to dogmatic theology but religious faith is infallible on account of spiritual authority. Śaṅkara's relentless logic and dialectical acumen subordinate personal value to impersonal ones. Pure identity is as deceptive as pure difference. Truth, beauty and goodness are not reality in abstraction. An abstract, indeterminate and indifferentiated *Brahman* cannot do justice with religious mind. God is not only the highest reality but He is the Supreme value too. *Satyam*, *Śivam* and *Sundaram* are attributes of *Brahman* and that a substance possessing an attribute cannot but be qualified. The Supreme Real is not only Absolute of metaphysics but also God of religion. He is not only to satisfy a dauntless logician but also an aspirant religious soul. Man is a unity of conation, cognition and volition. Logic satisfies his rational need whereas emotion kindles in him an intense yearning for the Supreme Value and he has at the same time to discipline his will too into a benevolent character, into constant contemplation of the infinite glory of God.

The theistic religion of the Vaiṣṇava developed as a protest against ritualism of Mīmāṁsakas and intellectualism of Śaṅkara. Though Śaṅkara did never mean to support a barren and theoretical learning, his disciples made religion "an affair of the head than of the heart or will". Hence a need of the theistic Vedānta was the cry of the day. The four schools of theistic Vedānta, i.e. Viśiṣṭādvaita of Rāmānuja, Dvaita Vedānta of Madhva, Śuddhādvaita of Vallabha and Dvaitādvaita of Nimbārka, sought to cater to demands that were extra philosophical and won the day. In spite of their doctrinal disparity, they agree on some of the facts: (a) *Brahman* is qualified God; (b) soul is atomic in size, it is identical with *Brahman* not in entity but in nature; (c) *mukti* means loving communion with God, and (d) devotion is the only means, etc.

THE NATURE OF ULTIMATE REALITY

Reality, according to Rāmānuja, is a determinate whole. He elaborates the conception of quantitative *Brahman* until it is identified with unqualified *Brahman*. From his epistemology, it follows that the real cannot be a bare identity. It is a determinate whole which maintains its identity in and through difference. The Absolute contains many. It is not bereft of many. The spirit of synthesis is the hallmark of Rāmānuja's philosophy. The Supreme Reality is the loving God of religion and not the metaphysical Absolute. It expresses its fullness through the richness of experience. Reality is one Advaita, but it is not indeterminate or *nirviśeṣa* but qualified (*viśiṣṭa*) – qualified by the conscious soul and non-intelligent matter. God exists in threefold forms as *cit*, *acit* and *antaryāmī*. *Cit* and *acit* form His body. He is their ground controller and principal (*śeṣin*). He is the inner self of unconscious matter and conscious souls, a self of all. He is static in its essential nature but dynamic in its attributive aspects. All such modifications take place in *acit* aspect of His body. He is "untarnished by the incessant moral upheavals of the phenomenal world". Rāmānuja has the support of scriptures on his part. The doctrine of *antaryāmī* God of *Bṛhadāraṇyaka Upaniṣad* gives a classical exposition of this view.

Taittirīya Upaniṣad also supports the view of Rāmānuja when it describes how God, the one, transforms Himself in the manifold world. "Having created the world He entered into it and both became the defined and the undefined, the reality and unreality. . . ." Rāmānuja does not state one for many or many for one but believes one to be impregnated with the many. His Absolute is not bare abstraction. We cannot help believing in one all inclusive unity but at the same time we cannot deny the existence of this manifold diversity. Reality is too rich and complex to be confiscated within the narrow limits of identity. Rāmānuja unites personal theism with the philosophy of Absolute. He is a monist not of second grade in comparison to Śaṅkara. There is nothing other than *Brahman* but by other he does not mean *svagata bheda* but only *sajātīya bheda* and *vijātīya bheda*. The Absolute of Rāmānuja is the whole which does not deny its parts, a substance which does not deny its attributes, a ground which does not deny consequent. Unity and diversity, substance and attributes, whole and parts are integrated in it. Determinations and limitations are in it but not of it. They are coeval and coeternal with the unity.

Finite is a moment of its own existence. He is an organic whole. "He is above all, in all, and through all. All are in Him out of Him and unto Him." The Absolute is not exhausted by many. It is not being completely identified with them but "reserves an exhaustive amount of reality – whereby it transcends them".

Rāmānuja shows unparallel philosophical maturity and religious sincerity in the interpretation of Upaniṣadic text on the matter of God. *Nirguṇa-Brahman* in Upaniṣads does not mean a barren abstraction, a ground with no content. *Nirguṇa* Śrutis deny the inauspicious qualities as *Brahman* while *saguṇa* texts describe *Brahman* as exhaustive home of all perfection. Rāmānuja attaches equal importance and value to both *saguṇa* and *nirguṇa* Śrutis. *Saguṇa* texts ascribe the positive attributes to Him, the *nirguṇa* texts seem to negate the physical qualities of *Brahman*, and there is no contradiction in these two sets of passages.

Brahman is the highest person, a treasury of an infinite number of excellent qualities. He is the supreme glory, the supreme spirit and the host of lovely qualities like *mādhurya*, brilliance, compassion and beauty. On the authority of *Viṣṇu Purāṇa* he mentions six other attributes of *Brahman*, viz. *jñāna*, *bala*, *aiśvarya*, *virya*, *śakti* and *tejas*. *Saulabhya* (easy accessibility) and *sauśīlya* (graciousness) are two more attributes of *Brahman* which exhilarate Rāmānuja. All the attributes are coordinative and not contradictory. God's auspicious qualities are eternal. They are coeval with and inherent in His being (*svarūpa*) which is eternal. These qualities are boundless. To quote Bhatt (1975: 37), according to Rāmānuja:

> *Brahman* is metaphysically the ground of all existence, religiously their final refuge, morally their inner controller and aesthetically the beauty and bliss inhering in them. He is the whole of metaphysics, the "Holy" of religion and the Abode of all ethical and aesthetic values.

The Advaitin draws distinction between *Para-* and *Apara-Brahman*, the transcendental esoteric *Brahman* and empirical exoteric God, the one being true for knowledge, the other for devotion. *Nirguṇa-Brahman* is a state of spiritual enlightenment which far excels *Saguṇa-Brahman* who is determinate. But Rāmānuja does not admit any distinction between the higher *Brahman* and the lower *Brahman*. Supreme Reality is simultaneously *nirguṇa* and *saguṇa*, *nirguṇa* in the sense that *sattva*, *rajas* and *tamas* do not exist in His essence (*svarūpa*) and *saguṇa* in the sense that all auspicious qualities such as compassion, beauty, omniscience, affection, generosity (*audārya*) belong to Him. According to Rāmānuja, the oft-quoted assertion of monists that there is no diversity, only means to imply the unification of the attributes and denial of any source other than *Brahman*. Without intellectual contradiction he successfully identifies *Brahman* with Viṣṇu. He is the religious counterpart of the only tenable philosophical position. There cannot be incurable contradiction between higher religion and higher philosophy. The Absolute of philosophy and God of religion cannot be different. There is no justification in the claim that identity text is superior to the one which speaks of manifold. Rāmānuja's identification gave stability and dignity to the faith of Vaiṣṇavism. God is the object of our worship and the end of all our religious aspirations. Rāmānuja tries to justify Pāñcarātra theism by means of Upaniṣadic Absolutism. Rāmānuja's Absolute is Śaṅkara's *Brahman* bound to this world.

Reality is not homogeneity of consciousness exclusive of all divisions and determinations. Rāmānuja proves this, on the following grounds.

1. *No Proof in Experience*: Undifferentiated and indeterminate substance. Whenever we will try to verify it, we will differentiate it. The Advaitins themselves believe that different attributes belong to consciousness.
2. *Nor in Śabda*: Speech is operated with words. A sentence always expresses some meaning. It never denotes undifferentiated reality.
3. *Nor in Perception*: In all apprehensions some specific characters are discerned. Even the first apprehension is not devoid of difference.
4. *Nor in Inference:* Inference is based on perception and since perception reveals difference as real, inference cannot come to contrary results.

5. *Nor in the Nature of Knowledge*: Thought apprehends reality and not identity devoid of difference. The very nature of thought as a synthetic activity propounds at once its relational character.
6. *Nor in Śrutis, Smṛtis and Purāṇas*: Scriptures never propound *Brahman* devoid of all differentiations. Rāmānuja's contention is that *nirguṇa* texts deny only undesirable predicates to *Brahman*. *Brahman* is unapprehended means. *Brahman* eludes the human grasp. The text which denies plurality means the denial of separate and independent existence of things. The supreme spirit is the soul of all (*sarvasyātmatayā*). All things are *svarūpa* (essence) and *vibhūti* (manifestation) of *Brahman*. All terms are thus connotations of Him by the rule of *samānādhikaraṇya* or the rule which expresses the inseparable relation existing between substance and attributes, or the invariable co-existence of subject and predicates.[1] This principle of *samānādhikaraṇya* neither endangers the reality of the world nor of *Brahman*. He is Absolute in the sense that nothing else can be supposed to exist than He. He is Absolute as He is the ground of all (*ādhārādheya bhāva*). Bradley confesses the inability of human thought in explaining how one contains many. But with Rāmānuja there is no problem because of his installation of *samānādhikarṇya* doctrine which holds that unity and diversity can coexist and be in intimate relation. God is Absolute as he is untarnished by imperfection. He is Absolute in the sense that all else are real only when referred to him. God is Absolute also in the sense that "He eternally possesses fullest realization of all spiritual values manifested in man's cognitive, aesthetic moral acts" (Vidyarthi 1978b: 78).

God is the sole sufficient cause of the world. God of Nyāya-Vaiśeṣika and Yoga is only the efficient cause of the world. But for Rāmānuja, God is material, efficient and assisting cause of the world.

---

1 B.G.R.B. VII.7.

> Thus substance that undergoes change of states in the form of effect is called *upādāna*, that which causes the *upādāna* to undergo changes is the efficient cause and that which acts as the assisting factor is called *sahakārī-kāraṇa*. – Sengupta 1967: 158

God is *upādāna-kāraṇa* in association with *cit* and *acit*, is *nimitta-kāraṇa* as He resolves that "I shall be many". And with His quality of power and knowledge, He is the *sahakārī-kāraṇa* of the world. There is modification in adjective part (*viśeṣaṇāṁśā*) of *Brahman* and not in noun part (*viśeṣyāṁśa*). By modification only *acit* aspect of *Brahman* is affected and by moral imperfections only *cit* aspect is influenced but *Brahman* remains unaffected and immutable under all modifications.

Brahman for Rāmānuja is not only principle but a person too. He is perfect personality as He is independent and contains all experiences within Himself. The Supreme Reality is also the Supreme God. Only a god with personality can satisfy a monotheistic mind. The philosophy of Rāmānuja will be a contradiction in terms if we maintain the notion of personality and Absolute as propounded by F.H. Bradley, John M.E. McTaggart and Bernard Bosanquet. According to Bradley, to use personality in infinite sense is misnomer. To him infinity and personality are mutually exclusive. Freedom from relation is the sign of perfection. But Hermann Lotze thinks that personality can properly be attributed to God only. Of course, the personality will not mar the impersonal aspect of *Brahman*. Scriptures deny only *aprākṛta* attributes and forms. The Divine attributes and the Divine form are essentially inseparable. Rāmānuja has the support of scriptures. Some devotional scriptures had nicely delineated the beauty and elegance of Deity. *Chāndogya Upaniṣad* has compared the Deity's eyes with lotus (*puṇḍarīkākṣa*). *Viṣṇu Purāṇa* has compared the colour of the Deity with blue lotus. *Mahābhārata* tells us that His colour is like the flower of *atasī*. The passage of *Ṛgveda* depicts deity as young despite His being the most ancient in age. All these support deity with form and personality. William Temple says: "The heart of religion is not an opinion about God, such as philosophy might reach as its conclusion of its argument, it is a personal relationship with God." Religion without belief in personality either in man or in God is inconceivable. Rāmānuja gives sympathetic treatment to this religious consciousness of commoner by giving them a personal God whom they can adore and worship and in lieu of that He will be kind and benevolent to them. God of Viśiṣṭādvaita is a self-conscious principle. In his anxiety to exalt *Brahman* as the only reality, Śaṅkara relegates even personal God to *avidyā*. But in Rāmānuja's philosophy, theism runs parallel to the monistic tendency: *Brahman* is the Supreme Reality as well as an object of religious consciousness. The more perfect the entity is, the more relations it has. Like the Infinite to Hegel, the personality of God is all inclusive. Many has its station in the scheme of Absolute. "Rāmānuja's philosophy is not the philosophy of either–or, but of both–and" (Vidyarthi 1978a: 182). Both one and many are equally real. Many is not declension from the One. He makes the claims of both philosophy and religions coincide. His approach is synthetic and not analytic. Sri Aurobindo (1970, vol. I: 352-53) too says:

> Existence, itself has no meaning without an Existent, consciousness has no standing place if there is none who is conscious, delight is useless and invalid without any enjoyer, love can have no foundation or fulfilment if there is no lover.

The abstract reality is barren in its content. Thus the Absolute of Rāmānuja is not non-relativistic, devoid of all relations. Unity is not subversive of multiplicity. His three cardinal principles of co-ordination – *samānādhikaraṇya*, *apr̥thak siddhi* and *śarīra-śarīrī bhāva* – speak high of Rāmānuja's justification both with philosophical genius and religious aspiration. The principle of *apr̥thak siddhi* renders God to be a person in the fullest and the truest sense of the term and synthesis is its distinct feature. *Śarīra-śarīrī bhāva* makes God a Supreme Ethical will. He is both immanent and transcendent.

The concept of *avatāra* (incarnation) plays an important role in Vaiṣṇavism. It has been derived from Sanskrit word *avataraṇam* meaning descent. God is not looking down at us sitting high up in the heaven but descends on this earth to participate in the morale upliftment of the world, and to share our feelings. According to Auguste Barth:

> An *avatāra* in the highest, the fullest sense of the word, is not a transitory manifestation of the deity, still less the procreation by the connection of a God with a mortal, of a being in some sense intermediate. It is the presence, at once mystic and real of the supreme being in a human individual who is both truly God and truly man.

The Upaniṣadic conception, that the Supreme Being manifests himself in various forms and that these various gods are one, led to the concept of *avatāra*. *Avatāra* is a mere identification of two gods as He acts as a human being or even as a brute, still He possesses miraculous power of God. He is God grace, God of favour, God who interferes in the worldly affairs not directly but through His incarnation. According to Rāmānuja there are twofold objects of *avatāra*:

(a) To establish righteousness, *dharma*.[2]

(b) To be accessible to His devotees.

He sometimes incarnates Himself in order to honour particular *vaṁśa* like Yaduvaṁśa or Raghuvaṁśa. He is above all kārmic influences. He incarnates on his own accord.[3] Reality is as such beyond all human grasp, only through the incarnation it becomes accessible to man who wants loving communion. It serves the purpose of "intellectual illumination, moral elevation and emotional exaltation". *Avatāra* is the periodic invasion of *kṛpā* into all species. Reality is bearer of values and if values are objectively real then some sort of anthropomorphism too is inevitable. Destitute of human elements, God becomes a mere name. P.B. Vidyarthi, says:

> Not to conceive of God in terms of the best that man knows is to bring him down to a level lower than that of man and to insinuate that He is less than what man is. – 1978b: 86

Anthropomorphism too does not lead to religious fanaticism or bigotry as it is generally supposed by Absolutists.

---

[2] *Gītā* IV.7-8.

[3] *tadā ahameva svasaṅkalpena uktaprakāreṇa ātmānaṁ sṛjāmi* |
– B.G.R.B. IV.7

On the authority of *Viṣṇu Purāṇa*, Rāmānuja believes that Lakṣmī too incarnates along with Viṣṇu. They are ontologically one and only one reality. Their duality is an appearance. She is the creative energy of God, the Divine Mother of the universe. She has two forms of *kriyā* and *bhūti*, i.e. the principle of regulation and the principle of becoming.

Pāñcarātra philosophy draws a sharp distinction between an *avatāra* or *vibhava* and a *vyūha*. While the former is concerned with the individual soul, the latter is concerned with the cosmos. The forms assumed for creation, sustenance and destruction of the cosmos are called *vyūha*s (manifestations). God as creator is Pradyumna, as preserver is Aniruddha and as destroyer, He is Saṅkarṣaṇa. In Vāsudeva, all the six qualities are present but in *vyūha*, only two qualities are manifested. In Saṅkarṣaṇa *jñāna* and *bala* alone get manifested. He exposes the scriptural knowledge to human being by his power *jñāna* and destroys the world by his *bala*.

He propagates righteousness through prowess and creates the world through supremacy. From Pradyumna emanates Aniruddha in whom energy and splendour (*śakti* and *tejas)* predominate. He propagates self-knowledge by the virtue of his splendour and supports the world through His energy.

Besides these two, the Supreme Being manifests itself in three more forms – *para*, *antaryāmī* and *arcā*.

Para Manifestation

This is the very first form of God, the Highest Glory. This is named as Vāsudeva. In *Tattvatrayabhāṣya*, it is called *sāḍguṇyavigraha* – it is the repository of six qualities that are knowledge, power, prowess, supremacy, energy and splendour. To these six qualities Rāmānuja adds two more – *niṣpāpa* and *satya śaṅkalpa*. *Para* is the transcendental aspect. He has His own divine life. He is really not exhausted in the creation.

Antaryāmī Manifestation

In this form only God enters into the human heart as well as in the world. He is the Lord of *karma* who determines the future on the basis of *karma* performed. He is not a manifestation of the Supreme Being but only of Aniruddha. He is the indwelling principle of the world.

Arcā Manifestation

The image of Viṣṇu acquires miraculous *śakti* after it is duly consecrated. The image is the object of our worship. *Bhakti* (religion) believes in duality of *bhakta* and *bhagavān*. A devotee feels the immediate presence of God in it. And for all practical purposes, it is treated as God Himself who is easily accessible to men. The *arcā* manifestation may lack the marvellous subtlety, austere intelligence and remorseless logical justification of Advaitins, but it satisfies the emotional need of a devotee. He is not Absolute looking at devotees with frozen eyes rather He is partaking in their feeling, receiving their obeisance and warmly reciprocating them.

THE HUMAN SOUL AND ITS BONDAGE

Viśiṣṭādvaita advocates identity in and through difference and because of difference, identity and difference (*bhedābheda*). From the ontological position of God as unity inclusive of determinations and differentiations, the reality of *cit* and *acit* is immediately posited. They are modes of God and as such they derive their substantiality and reality from God. Vedāntic psychology is not based on perceptual or conceptual understanding of the self, it is a metaphysical analysis based on the intuitive experience. One of the fundamental tenets of religion is belief in self as a spiritual entity, as a transcendental character. The self is not only a fortuitous concourse of atoms, it is essentially a cognitive agent. It pervades the world with knowledge as the light of the lamp. It is of the nature of infinite bliss. It is the spiritual principle that logically implies that it is self-conscious. Rāmānuja's conception of participation of soul in God may be compared with the model dependence of soul on God in Spinoza and monadic individuality in Leibnitz. As it is Viśiṣṭādvaita, neither its individuality is lost in Absolute nor is it being provided independent status. They are real entities as they are differentiations of God. But to realize this is a veritable Herculean task. *Gītā* (II.29) too speaks of "the rarity of the man who knows the self".

The common characteristics between God and *jīva* are:

(a) *Pratyaktva* (inwardliness) – both soul and God dwell in *acit*.

(b) *Cetanatva* (consciousness) – consciousness is the essence of soul also.

(c) *Ātmatva* (spirituality).

(d) *Kartṛtva* (agency).

Both have the capacity to act; though to act or not to act is dependent on their sweet discretion. The uncommon characteristics are *aṇutva* (atomic), *śeṣatva* (as accessory), *ādheyatva* (supportedness), *vidheyatva* (dependence), *parādhīnakartṛtva*, *paratantratva*.[4]

Self-consciousness is an essential prerogative of spiritual being. The relation of consciousness to *jīva* is like that of a gem which illumines itself as well as other objects. It is not Pure Consciousness of the Advaitins. Soul is essentially a knower, a subject, a conscious principle. Religion is communion between man and Divine – both are persons, and personality inherently implies self-consciousness. Vidyarthi (1978a: 139) says:

> Rāmānuja is of the view that the self is a substance having consciousness both for its essence, *svarūpa* and attributes, *guṇa*, from which follows the distinction between substantive consciousness and attributive consciousness.

It knows itself while it knows things and knows at the same time its distinction from them. It is consciousness and at the same time that which has consciousness.[5] Both *cit*, the subject, and *acit*, the object, have their subsistence and being in the whole scheme of reality.

Rāmānuja regards *ātman* as *aṇu*,[6] otherwise *utkramaṇa* (movement from one place to another) would have been impossible. The word *aṇu* is generally translated as "atomic" but Schraeder (1916: 40) says that it should be translated as "small".

---

[4] *Vedārtha-saṅgrahaḥ*.

[5] *evamātmā cidrūpa eva hi caitenyaguṇakaḥ* I – *Śrībhāṣya*, p. 163

[6] *ato 'ṇurevāyamātmā* I – *Śrībhāṣya* II.3.23

It is small in comparison to the greatness of Supreme Self, "The imperfection of the finite self confirms its atomicity". Scriptures speak of soul as passing out and coming into the body which will be impossible in the case of omnipresent reality. Rāmānuja cites the authorities of *Śvetāśvatara* (V.8-9) and *Muṇḍaka* (III.1.7) *Upaniṣads* in support of his view. He again advocates his case on the fact that since simultaneous perception and non-perception do not take place, the self is atomic. The soul feels the happening in any part of the body because of its attributive knowledge (*dharma-bhūta-jñāna*). *Ātman* and *jñāna* may be logically distinguishable but not physically separable. The *ātman* is blind. Rāmānuja is eager to prove the atomic character of individual self just to avoid Śaṅkara's theory of all-pervasiveness which denies individuality.

The soul has been described as *śeṣa* (accessory) of God, meaning "that which exists for another" (*śeṣaḥ parārthatvāt*). Sudarsana Suri in his work *Śrutaprakāśikā* describes "he is *śeṣa* whose purpose is included in the purpose of another; the other is *śeṣin*". God is *śeṣin* both for *cit* and *acit*, but *cit*, as *śeṣa,* has the privilege of serving his Lord. Soul is fully controlled, supported and protected by God. There is *śeṣa–śeṣī-bhāva* in *jīva* and *Īśvara*. This protects the dignity of individual as well as nobility of God. Soul is *niyamya* (controlled), God is *niyāmaka* (controller). God is the soul of *jīva*. Control of God is not detrimental to the freedom of individual souls. Man is both the master and the slave; he is the master of *kriyamāṇa karmas*, but slave of *prārabdha karma*. *Prārabdha karma* bears fruit according to the direction of God. S.N. Dasgupta opines that here there is some sort of occasionalism as it holds that every action of man is dependent of God's will.

The relationship between God and individual self is one of *prakāra–prakārin*. Souls are *prakāras* (modes) of God. God is "the life of its life". He transmits its perfection to *jīva*. The individual is not an offspring of an error but one whom God Himself prizes as His possession and in the transfiguration of whose soiled career is He deeply interested. The ethical relationship between them is expressed by the term *īśa īśitavya bhāva*.

Ādhāra-ādheya is another expression to indicate intimate

relationship between *jīva* and *Brahman*. *Brahman* is the pulse of every individual. Individuals have their subsistence till the pulse of divine beats in them. Soul hankers after God because God contains it.

The soul is intrinsically blissful, pure and perfect. The apparent limitation is caused by its own *karma*. In the state of *suṣupti* we realize this inherent nature of soul. Only *karma* spoils its inherent glory. It is not ignorance but corrupting nature of egoism which robs its nature.

The individual soul, Rāmānuja maintains, is eternal and immutable. It is real. Birth and death mean its association with and dissociation from physical embodiment. Its essence is unaware of its diminution or addition. It is unity by itself. According to Rāmānuja, the eternity of soul is an essential condition for morality which is a constant need of religion.

Every finite individual has some unsharable experiences – a memory of one person cannot be transferred to other – these are the facts of life. On the basis of such experiences, Rāmānuja proves the existence of many souls. Again this plurality of individual makes room for the realzation of social values too. Human personality is unique in its own way. It is the spiritual centre of divinity and morality. It is "a monad as well as a mode". Vidyarthi remarks:

> If morality is more than a mere exalted conception of God, then both religion and morality involve intimate relations of man to man and man to God and imply in consequence the reality and independence of man against the dead unity of the Absolute.

To make religion significant, the difference of soul is inevitable. It is the core of religious life. *Brahman* comprises within itself the distinct elements of plurality which have claim in the whole scheme of reality. Metaphysical jugglery of words cannot deny their difference.

Rāmānuja believes in triune reality: God, man and nature. In Hegelian mode of expression we may say, "man is transcending nature and both man and nature finding their ultimate reconciliation in God – a unity-in-variety". Even *mahāvākyas* like *tat tvam asi* and *so 'ham asmi* do not bridge the difference between ubiquitous God and finite soul. Rāmānuja interprets the Upaniṣadic assertion with philosophical maturity and religious sincerity. To him, Upaniṣadic assertions only mean similarity between the nature of *Brahman* and *jīva,* and not identity. Bare identity is tautologous. Every judgement presents a synthesis of distinction. In the judgement "*S* is *P*", *S* is neither identical with *P*, in that case, it will be a tautology, nor different from *P* as then the statement "*S* is *P*" will be impossible. Thus it is neither a pure identity nor a pure difference. It is identity of the qualified.[7] "Thou" of "thou art that" stands for God existing in the form of man and "that" for God Himself. It is "identity of the same but differently qualified entity" (*viśiṣṭasya aikyam*), "an identity of two forms of God".

Self, according to Rāmānuja, can never be *Brahman* as a part can never become whole, an attribute can never become substance. The whole does not precede parts, nor do parts succeed the whole. God is the inner substance. It is identity of the one substance existing in two real forms: *ekam eva vastu dvirūpaṁ pratīyate*.[8] The relation between self and God is that of inseparability (*apṛthak sthiti*). "That" is the causal God, "thou" is God as the inner self of *jīva* and both are same but not in the sense of bare identity. In the judgement "This is that Devadatta", this Devadatta and that Devadatta refer to same Devadatta, still there is difference in them regarding time. "This Devadatta" refers the person seen at present and 'that Devadatta' refers the person seen in past though both are one and the same. As modes, *jīvas* are different from God, whereas in essence, they are one with God.

Before the manifestation of the world, in the state of perfect homogeneity, soul exists in a very subtle form as the eternal part of *Brahman*, but in this state also there is no total suppression of its essential nature, it is not a state of coalescence. In its released

[7] *Prakārdvaya-viśiṣṭaika-vastu-pratipādanena sāmānādhikaraṇyaṁ ca siddham* | – *Śrībhāṣya* I.1.1

[8] *Śrībhāṣya* I.1.1.

state also it differs from *Brahman* on two major issues: first, they are atomic hence finite, and second, they cannot participate in creation and cannot rule over the world like God. The difference remains there too. Liberation does not mean identity (*tādātmya*) but equality (*sādharmya*), *nirañjanaḥ paramaṁ sāmyamupaiti*. Individual self finds its meaning within the context of the Absolute, but this does not mean obliteration of its individuality. After liberation it becomes a member of divine society, a spiritual community of God.

According to Rāmānuja, there are three classes of *jīva*, *baddha* (bound), *mukta* (freed) and *nitya* (eternal). *Baddha jīva*s wander in *saṁsāra* because of their selfishness and equity. *Mukta jīva*s are liberated from the clutches of ignorance by dint of their devotion and wisdom. *Nitya jīva*s reside in Vaikuṇṭha and enjoy holy communion with God. They are ever free from the transmigration of soul. They are called *parikara* of Lord. They enjoy bliss.

DESTINY OF MAN AND THE WAYS TO ATTAINT IT

The pivotal issue in all religions is the destiny of man. And the worth of all religious sanction is to be judged from this point of view. Materialistic achievement is not the be all and end all of human endeavour. Every individual has a destiny to achieve, a purpose to accomplish. And this destiny or purpose is to be realized through constant *sādhanā* and rigorous discipline. According to Rāmānuja, expansiveness of the dynamic consciousness with unceasing delight is the destiny of every individual. It is the state of supreme fulfilment. The finite individuals have their source and sustenance in *Brahman* but they forget their divinity and wander in the whirlpool of the world like the prince, who forgetting his rich heritage, lives as a hunter but at last restores his kingdom. Forgetting its divine origin, the individual self also moves round the cycle of birth and death under the great spell of beginningless *avidyā*. Only *tattva-jñāna* (the knowledge of truth) and *tattvābhyāsa* (practice of truth) will help *jīva* in regaining its lost glory.

Rāmānuja differs from other systems so far as the nature of destiny is concerned. Vedic rituals cannot liberate a *jīva* from the fetters of *karma*. The emancipation is not final. When the effect will be exhausted one will have to come back to this world again to suffer the sobs and throbs of life.

Rāmānuja differs fundamentally from Śaṅkara also on ethical points. For him *mokṣa* is not only a negative removal of false knowledge, rather it is a positive attainment. Rāmānuja presents dynamic concepts of reality which retain difference which is not detrimental to integrity. The individuality is not fused in *Brahman* in the state of *mukti*, it is retained there to enjoy that loving communion with God. According to Sāṁkhya and Advaita Vedānta, *kartr̥tva* (agency) and *bhoktr̥tva* (power of enjoyment) do not belong to the real nature of self. They are fictitiously superimposed on soul due to *avidyā*, hence knowledge and action are opposed to each other. But *mokṣa*, according to Rāmānuja, "is the experience of *Brahman* which involves the appropriation and aesthetic enjoyment of His ravishing beauty embodied in His attributes" (Vidyarthi 1978b: 210). He disagrees with the view that *mokṣa* necessarily means isolation from *prakr̥ti*. It is a matter of "aesthetic enjoyment" of divine communion where individuality is not denied. Identity consciousness will mean *satyātmanasa*. God is the highest from the point of view of reality as well as value, thus service to God is the highest destiny of *jīva*. And this servitude is possible only with individuality. In *mokṣa* what is lost is not individuality but egoity. Service to God who is the source and centre of the bliss of others is the most dignified achievement of *jīva*. Vaiṣṇavas especially Rāmānuja deem this devotion and service to God as well as to the world as the most important feature of man's life. In Rāmānuja's philosophy, it is said that "after hundreds of years of the pessimistic influence on Indian life and thought, real interest in the affairs of the world and in the values of personal life was resurrected and revived". Personal value is not submerged and lost into *Brahman* rather it gets a new dimension, opens a new vista and gains a new meaning. Soul experiences the inseparability from God and not identity. It is integration. This state of love is not "ontologically dualistic but experientially unitive". The individual self is elevated, transfigured and not eliminated. To be similar to God does not mean to be identical. Self-luminosity, consciousness, agency and selfhood are common factors of *jīva* and *Brahman* both, still it is different from *Brahman* as here there is distinction between a qualified thing and a qualifying attribute, between a part and the whole, and between an attribute and a substance. Soul and *Brahman* have identity of the ground (*samānādhikaraṇya*) but they are not one and the same. The exalted idea of *mokṣa* of Advaita does not satisfy the religious urge of Rāmānuja, who has all sympathy for mundane existence. "Rāmānuja cannot tolerate the castigation and vilifications of the facts of normal religious life by means of standards of judgement that are abnormal"(Vidyarthi 1978b: 225). Repudiation of world values will lead to "inexcusable monstrosities". This will deprive men from listening to the divine music everywhere in the world. Perfection does not mean annihilation but integration and sublimation. Dependence on God is not contradictory to his inherent freedom and dignity. It is soul's essence. Dependence on any other thing or person may be painful but dependence on God is itself a matter of supreme delight. The liberated soul enjoys all the perfections of Vaikuṇṭha like *sālokya* (identity of abode), *sāmīpya* (remaining near the Deity), *sārūpya* (having a form similar to that of the Deity), *sārṣṭi* (possession of lordship equal to that of the Deity) and *sāyujya* (intimate union). *Sālokya* is the lowest type of spiritual consciousness. The aspirant aspires more and more nearness to deity, i.e. *sārūpya*. *Sārūpya* is still the higher stage when the aspirant realizes similarity with Deity. The highest ideal is *sāyujya* when there is perfect communion between the liberated man and *Brahman*. We may say that *sāyujya* includes all the lower stages as Divine communion is not possible without being in the locality of God and without being in close proximity with God. And since in the state of *sāyujya*, the soul possesses the same contour as Deity, the *sārūpya* state is there. Salvation, according to Rāmānuja, means this eternal fellowship with God. Śaṅkara too used this world "*sāyujya*" but he imparts a different meaning to it. *Sāyujya*, to him, means "numerical identity", fusion of man in God. The liberated man acquires many attributes of *Brahman* but not all. He is atomic in size, he cannot be the creator of the world. Rāmānuja does not interpret the text *brahmavid brahmaiva bhāvati* on the lines of Śaṅkara. He understands it in the sense *brahmavid āpnoti param* (the knower of the *Brahman* attains the Supreme). *Śrī Bhāṣya* (p. 69) quotes:

> One who is released from *avidyā* cannot be essentially identical with God because that which is capable of being the seat of *avidyā* cannot be that for whom it is never possible to be the seat of *avidyā*.

The self maintains its own centrality, its own individuality as well as similarity. Similarity of God does not mean becoming God. God is God, the self is self, the two shall never meet.

As Rāmānuja presents the values of life from a different platform, a divergence in the discipline of *mokṣa* is inevitable. According to Rāmānuja, cancellation of *avidyā* is not the only means to get liberation. In his scheme of reality, nothing is cancelled or denied. It is not only knowledge which leads to *mukti*. Devotion of heart purity of conduct and finally the grace of God are essential prerequisites for liberation. In his scheme of religious discipline there is harmonious blending of all the elements of religious consciousness – conation, cognition and volition. The three paths to liberation *karma*, *jñāna* and *bhakti* are the three successive stages in the final release. *Bhakti* is the final means but *karma* and *jñāna* are preliminaries to *bhakti*. These paths constitute an integral discipline.

According to Śaṅkara, *karma* and *bhakti* are antithetical to each other. He does not even accept *jñāna-karma-samuccaya*. According to him, *mokṣa* can be attained only by knowledge"(B.G.Ś.B. I.1.1). But in Rāmānuja's philosophy ethical discipline is more important than anything else. *Karma* is an integral part of *jñāna* and both *karma* and *jñāna* are contributory to *bhakti* which is the chief source of emancipation. Work is ancillary to knowledge. *Karma-yoga* is the first step towards *mokṣa*. His emphasis on *karma-yoga* is entirely based on the Upaniṣads and *Gītā*. *Kaṭhopaniṣad* declares that "not he who has not ceased from bad conduct can obtain Him by intelligence" (K.U. I.2.24). *Śvetāśvatara Upaniṣad* also emphasizes the yogic practices for the purification of soul. In *Gītā*, *niṣkāma karma* may lead to emancipation.[9] One must perform

[9] *asakto hyācaran karma param āpnoti pūruṣaḥ* | – B.G. III.19

duty for duty's sake only. The Lord himself sets an example of *niṣkāma karma*.[10] The aspirant of *mokṣa* should fulfil some practical requirements. Actions performed with the sole end of worshipping God destroy the sinful acts.

Desireless actions are purifying in effect. It gives rise to purified mind, it cultivates the fervour of divine love which leads to *mukti*. A purely contemplative life is vicious for religious discipline. Religious life is not a barren contemplation. Hedonistic attitude of *karma* is not latent in Rāmānuja's contention. For the knowledge of self, the discipline of *karma-yoga* is a necessity. Not only this, he has to maintain the discipline of *karma-yoga* even after perfection. According to Rāmānuja, the discipline of action is more helpful in knowing the self than *jñāna*.[11]

Action and knowledge are, "the convex and concave of the same circle". Performance of duties disinterestedly is possible only when one knows one's essential nature. *Karma* and *jñāna* interpenetrate each other. *Karma* is preparatory discipline for *jñāna* and *jñāna* embraces *karma*. Spiritual maturity does not decry the importance of *karma*. *Niṣkāma karma* purifies the mind and prepares the atmosphere for the advent of *jñāna*. His concept of *jñāna* is distinctively different from that of Śaṅkara as his *jñāna* shares both the moments of feeling and action whose source is God himself. It is *bhaktirūpāpanna jñāna* (*jñāna* turned *bhakti*). *Jñāna* and *karma* have relative values.

Karma-yoga which means disinterested fulfilment of religious duties and *jñāna* which means knowledge of essential unity with *Brahman* are not sufficient means for liberation. Rāmānuja is against both the "cold intellectualism" of the monists and "blind voluntarism" of Mīmāṁsakas. *Bhakti* is of paramount importance for liberation.[12] It is knowledge of God as well as obedience to His will.[13] It is the organic whole in which *jñāna* and *karma* are inherent.

---

[10] *nānavāptamavāptavyaṁ varta eva ca karmaṇi* || – Ibid. III.22

[11] *karmayogasya ātmaprāptisādhanatve jñānaniṣṭhāyāḥ śaighryam* | – "Introduction", *Śrībhāṣya*, p. 3

[12] *trisatyasya bhaktireva garīyasī* | — *Nārada Bhaktisūtra*

[13] *jñāna karmānugṛhītaṁ bhakti-yogam* | — Rāmānuja, *Gītā Bhāṣya*, p. 4

The knowledge of God is not a barren intellectual achievement. He is not only *cit*, He is ultimate in value. He is *ānanda* par excellence too. To know God means to adore Him, to love Him, to long for His grace. *Bhakti* means loving meditation, it is "meditation on God accompanied by love". Real knowledge is not only verbal knowledge. It is constant remembrance of God (*dhruvā smṛti*). This is differently described as *dhyāna* (meditation), *upāsanā* (prayer) and *bhakti* (devotion). This constant meditation should be there in performance of *karma* as well as *jñāna*.

Bhakti is intensity of love for God, it is constant longing for him. A devotee becomes God-intoxicated. *Bhakti* is religion par excellence. No one can deny the call of emotion in religion but "it is not an intellectual exuberance of feeling, or a fervent glow of emotion or an unrestrained exhibition of erotic element, but it is thoroughly meditative and contemplative". The real knowledge is indentified with highest *bhakti* in Rāmānuja's philosophy. It is "man's reaching out towards a fuller knowledge of God". *Bhakti* and salvation are so related that at every stage of *bhakti* we are perfecting ourselves. It is "salvation in becoming". Since it is its own reward (*phalarūpatvāt*) it is superior to *jñāna* and *karma*. The whole life is transfigured in *bhakti*. Every thought of our mind, each drop of our blood and every inch of our body are surrendered to God. It is love of God with all our mind and with all our heart. God is beyond the ken of logic, beyond the reach of sense, it is to be attained only with wholehearted devotion. It is profound admiration for Divine majesty coupled with deep attachment.[14] Nārada defines it as deep love of God.[15] He lives and has his being in divine love. It is constant longing for the Lord.

It is a permanent disposition towards the Deity. In Upaniṣads *Brahman* is very often mentioned to be bliss. In this case knowledge of *Brahman* cannot be anything except the knowledge of God by love and devotion.[16] Knowledge by love is most complete and sure.

Bhakti according to Rāmānuja is not merely unreasoned

---

14 *sā parānuraktirīśvare – Śāṇḍilya-Sūtram.*

15 *sā tvasmin parama-premarūpā – Nārada-bhakti-sūtram* 2.

16 *Śrī Bhāṣya*, vol. I, p. 194.

ecstasy, it is not a sway of passion, it is not merely outer form of worship, it is rather an inner spiritual attitude cultivated by fulfilment of certain conditions. As an iron piece, covered with dust, needs a good cleaning before it is magnetized, the finite soul needs purification before it becomes God-conscious. Rāmānuja insists on an elaborate preparation for *bhakti* which include:

1. *Viveka* (discrimination) of good, purity of mind and body are effected by food. The criterion for the purity of food is threefold – (a) it should not be *tāmasika* in nature, (b) it should not be served by sinful persons, and (c) it should not be polluted accidentally by any other means like eaten by dog, etc. *Chāndogya Upaniṣad* and *Gītā* claim that the character of man is built in accordance with the food he eats.
2. *Vimoka* (freedom) from slavery to one's passions – infatuation, vanity, jealousy are contrary to spiritual advancement.
3. *Abhyāsa* (continuous thinking) of God – all mental activities should be directed to God only.
4. *Kriyā* (performance) of five great sacrifices. By the performance of these sacrifices, the body is rendered fit for the apprehension of the Lord.
5. *Kalyāṇa* (auspicious deeds) consists in the cultivation of virtues like compassion, straightforwardness, equanimity, purity, fortitude, forgiveness, liberality and mercy.
6. *Anavasāda* (non-dejection) – spiritual man should develop equanimity. He should not lose heart in adverse situations. He must be undisturbed by sobs and throbs of life. Depression is injurious to integration of personality.
7. And the last is *aṇuddharṣa* (absence of elation) – there should be total absence of excitement at the moment of pleasure and depression, at the moment of pain.

In the place of these seven spiritual preparations Radhakrishanan mentions eleven requisite preparations for *bhakti*: *viveka, vimoka, abhyāsa, kriyā, kalyāṇa, satyam, ārjavam, dayā, ahiṁsā, dāna* and *anavasāda*.

All these *sādhanas* aim at physical, mental and moral

development of man and are integral aids of *bhakti*. They lead to *anubhava* which is just prior to *mukti*. When *bhakti* deepens, the soul-hunger for God is not so intense as God-hunger for the soul. This is the state of *parama bhakti*.

Bhakti, according to Rāmānuja, is the result of this *sādhana-saptaka*. It has three stages – *dhruvānusmṛtiḥ* (firm mediation), *asakṛdāvṛttiḥ* (frequent repetition) and *darśana-samānākāratā*.

Rāmānuja has also made reference to the following nine phases:

1. *Stuti* (recital of hymns),
2. *smṛti*,
3. *vacana* (discourse on God),
4. *vandanā* (salutation to God),
5. *smaraṇa* (remembrance of God),
6. *arcanā* (worship of God),
7. *śravaṇa* (listening to Divine attributes),
8. *yātanā* (mortification), and
9. *dhyāna* (meditation).

While *bhakti* is a long and laborious process, it needs elaborate preparation. *Prapatti* is the simplest. It does not need the arduous discipline. It is complete self-surrender to God, it is flinging oneself on the mercy of God totally. It is open to all. It is an essential ingredient of *bhakti* as well as it is an independent discipline. According to southern school (Tengaḷais), *prapatti* is the only way to salvation. No effort is required on the part of the devotee. God takes care of those who have totally surrendered themselves in his hands. It is like kitten's love. The northern school (Vaḍagaḷais) holds that *prapatti* is not the only way. Human effort too is needed. First of all individual has to qualify himself then only God will bestow his grace. Liberation cannot be attained without *prapatti*, whether it is an independent discipline or is an essential part of *bhakti*.

The philosophical doctrine of the self being the servant *śeṣa* of

> the Lord has its ethical and religious fulfilment in the doctrine of *prapatti* where the soul has nothing to worry considering that it is God Himself who is his supreme purpose for whose pleasure he exists.
> – Vidyarthi 1978b: 261

Prapatti is the very spirit of *bhakti*.

Prapatti needs all the three types of surrender: (a) *svarūpa samarpaṇa* or *ātma-samarpaṇa*, (b) *phala samarpaṇa*, and (c) *bhāra samarpaṇa*. *Svarūpa samarpaṇa* means that the individual should surrender himself to God. *Phala samarpaṇa* means the dedication of fruits of action to God and *bhāra samarpana* means the responsibility of protecting the devotee is of God. Divine is the source of perfection. Rāmānuja is emphatic on the point that God can help only those who are morally, ethically and intellectually prepared for receiving the *prasāda*. God does not bestow grace arbitrarily, he acts according to the law of *karma*.[17] A man bereft of these qualities cannot claim God's grace. In *Gītā-bhāṣya* also, Rāmānuja claims that in the operation of divine grace, efforts on the part of both devotee and Lord are required. It is not a one-way traffic. *Prapatti* is only preliminary to *bhakti*.

Six conditions are enumerated as accessories of *prapatti*.

1. *Ānukūlyasya saṅkalpaḥ* – determination to think, will and act in confromity with God's wishes.
2. *Prātikūlyasya varjanam* – not to transgress the Divine command.
3. *Rakṣiṣyatiti viśvasaḥ* – firm faith that God will help. He is the supreme saviour.
4. *Goptṛtva-varaṇam* – the supplication for one's protection. *Mokṣa* is not to be claimed by high ethical aptitude only, it is to be asked for.
5. *Ātmanikṣepa* – absolute self-surrender to God.
6. *Kārpaṇya* – absolute dependence on God. The devotee feels every possession of his, including his self, is dependent on God, and he is nothing before Him. This attitude enables him to act according to the Divine Will. It eliminates all senses

---

[17] *Śrī Bhāṣya* II.3.41.

of difference.

According to Rāmānuja:

> *Prapatti* is actually the final culmination of the method of *bhakti-yoga* and *bhakti-yoga* will not be complete unless it results in pious resignation. – Sengupta 1967: 151

Parama bhakti and *prapatti* both develop an attitude of absolute surrender in the name of God. *Prapatti* opens the gate of liberation even for hard criminals if they surrender themselves wholeheartedly. Moreover since it does not require any elaborate or philosophical knowledge to flourish, persons from every walk of life are welcome. What is needed most is "faith and selfless love accompanied by an attitude of self-surrender and resignation". It democratizes the Hindu religion by making entry into the gate of liberation free for all castes and creeds provided he is a man of faith and devotion.

Bhakti can be classified into *upāya-bhakti* or *sādhana-bhakti* (devotion as means) and *parama bhakti*. *Sādhana-bhakti* is more of the nature of knowledge than of devotion. Still it is not called *jñāna-mārga* because union with God here is not a means of self-realizatian. Here devotee is absorbed in incessant meditation on deity. He is impatient to attain intimacy with Him. He does not want to be lost in Him. But in the stage of *parama bhakti*, the devotee is fully dedicated to God. This *bhakti* is the finest flower of devotion. *Bhagavad-rāga* becomes the tune of his life and he closely enjoys the bliss of God.

Mukti according to Rāmānuja is always *videhamukti*. As there cannot be the feeling of bodilessness while we are in flesh and blood, there cannot be *jīvanmukti*. So long we are alive, the relationship between soul and body cannot be annulled. A living person, according to Rāmānuja, cannot be totally free from the feeling of difference. *Vākyārtha jñāna* cannot make us aware of the blissful communion with God. It only arouses a living faith. Liberation means total destruction of all worldly experiences. *Sāyujya* is the real form of *mokṣa* which is to be attained only when devotee enters into the kingdom of God. He can taste the flashening of immortality at the time of worship but that is not all. The utmost he can attain in this life is the status of *sthita-prajñatā* (stability in mind). Realization of proximity to God is, for Rāmānuja, the matter of highest virtue. In philosophico-religious thought of Viśiṣṭādvaita, knowledge and *bhakti* are blended together.

Dvaita Vedānta of Madhvācārya

Madhva is a rank dualist. The uncompromising realism (Tattvavāda) and perfect dualism of Madhva show the trenchant opposition to Śaṅkara's unflinching idealism. He condemns Śaṅkara for teaching "the false doctrine of Śūnyavāda Buddhism under the cloak of Vedānta". Advaitins for him are "deceitful demons". He is realistic in approach, but dualist in nature. To admit the divine being endowed with all auspicious qualities as a product of *māyā* would be to decry all religious convictions and faith. Our belief in a saviour God will be uprooted which is so dear to religious instinct and ethical practices. The deification of the Buddha in Mahāyāna Buddhism, the personal devotion to *tīrthaṁkaras* in Jainism, the failure of Godless ritualism of Pūrva-Mīmāṁsā – all these speak volume about the necessity of theism for the survival of religion. God is a personal and determinate God in Madhva's philosophy which defends the difference between him and the individual souls. If *bhakti* is the means of liberation, if God is the Supreme Personal Being, then uncompromising pluralism is a logical consequence of Madhva's philosophy.

CONCEPT OF ULTIMATE REALITY

Madhva defines reality as that "which is an object of knowledge (*pramitiviṣaya*)" or "that which is unsuperimposed (*anāropitam*)". Whatever is an object of valid experience has a claim of reality. Apprehension is the immediate evidence of the thing that is apprehended. Madhva is not a "sentimental idealist" who denies existence of everything except mind, he is not an "uncritical realist" who grants reality to everything, rather he is a "rational idealist" who accepts the reality on the evidence of *pramāṇa*s. And this concept sanctions reality not only to soul and God but to insentient objects of the world also. The objects and their difference too are real. Repudiation of difference is not a necessary criterion for maintaining the reality of the One. *Brahman* is one without a second, "not in a dry numerical sense, but in a richer and deeper sense of being the active source of the rich multiplicity of finite reality and the sustaining principle behind it (*sarvasattāpratīti-pravṛtti-nimittam*)". His criterion of reality reduces the universe to the plurality of reals. The difference in the nature of reality does not justify the degree of reality. The reality of all objects is always absolute and the same. Difference is neither a separate quality nor category, it is the very nature or essence of object.[18] If *A* is different from *B*, the difference between them is the essential nature of both *A* and *B*. Difference is the edifice over which Madhva's philosophy depends. He advocates five types of ultimately real and eternal differences: between God and soul, between soul and matter, between matter and matter, between matter and God and between soul and soul. It is not identity through difference (*bhedābheda*) on which Madhva believes. Difference is the very being (*svarūpa*) of the substrate. The difference is identical with its *dharmin*. Madhva accepts a relation of "colourful identity (*saviśeṣābheda*) in respect of coessential attributes and difference-cum-identity (*bhedābheda*) in the case of transient attributes". Reality is what comes directly under human experience.

BRAHMAN

There are two ontological concepts in Madhva's philosophy: *svatantra* (independent) and dependent (*paratantra*). God is the only independent reality while soul and matters are dependent realities, dependent on God for their subsistence. Independences are the most vital point in *Brahman* because it gives *Brahman* the highest ontological status. *Brahman* is Infinite (*pūrṇa*), the Real of all reals (*satyasya satyam*), the Eternal of the eternals (*nityo nityānām*), and the Sentient of all sentients (*cetanaścetanānām*), the source and inspiration of all being. Soul and matter are dependent on God for existence, knowledge and activity. All the things of the world are dependent on one another and ultimately on God.

---

[18] *satyaṁ bhedastu vastūnāṁ svarūpaṁ nātra saṁśayaḥ* | – *Nyāyāmṛtam*

God, according to Madhva, is full of infinite attributes. An unqualified *Brahman* cannot satisfy the ethico-religious needs of man. The term *nirguṇa* does not deny totally the qualities of *Brahman*. Denial or attributes means denial of the three *guṇa*s of *prakṛti*, denial of impure qualities. The attributes are not to be apprehended by moral eyes. There cannot be anything which is utterly attributeless.[19] The very proposition, *Brahman* is without characteristics, would be inconsistent.[20] *Nyāya-vivaraṇa* quotes: "The independent Being must necessarily be infinite in its attributes".[21] Any inquiry about the true nature of *Brahman* can lead to the conclusion that it is absolutely uncharacterizable. Even, *neti* is a characterization. According to Madhva, to think God as *saviśeṣa* should be the necessary precondition of all philosophical inquiry. There is no mutual difference among the qualities of God. The co-inherence of qualities in Him proves their identity with Him. A transcendent *Brahman* of logic will never become an object of thought, it will always be a "wild goose chase". The conception of unity is a pseudo concept, instead, the truth of diversity is amenable to reason and empirically verifiable. Vyāsatīrtha in his *Nyāyāmṛta* wants to know what exactly leads Advaitin to the denial of all attributes in *Brahman*. Is it for want of some reason to justify His qualities or is it proved on some definite grounds? He disagrees with both the possibilities. Scriptures prove the qualified *Brahman*. At the same time there is ample justification for God being determinate. According to Madhva, "the *saguṇa* text is logically self-contradictory". *Saguṇa* text is *upajīvya* (sustainer) of the *nirguṇa* text. The sustainer is naturally more powerful than the sustained. The attributes of *Brahman* are absolute in their character, thus they do not limit them.

According to Madhva, *Brahman* is necessarily *saguṇa* as He is the creator and creatorship presupposes full knowledge of the nature, accessories and result of the effect. Thus the creator must be omniscient, omnipotent and "capable of accomplishing whatever

---

19 *na ca nirviṣayā kācitsaṁvidasti* – *Śribhāṣya* 1.1.1.

20 *niviśeṣ atvoklereva vyāhatatvāt* | – *Nyāyāmṛtam*

21 *svatantrasya pūrṇaguṇatvaniyamāt* | – *Nyāyā-vivaraṇa*, p. 4

He wills". Anywhere in the world we do not find independent potency. Only *Īśvara* guides the soul and matter. He controls their "presence, cognizability and functioning". He is not only passively present in them rather His entry into matter renders its modification possible as matter itself is dull and inert. His presence may be felt everywhere and in everything. This is how the Supreme chooses to reveal his *pūrṇatva*. By this *puruṣa* all this is filled (*tenedam pūrṇam puruṣeṇa sarvaṁ*), *sarvaguṇapūrṇatvam* (perfection of being) and *sarvadoṣa-gandha vidhuratvam* (freedom from all limitations) are the important aspects of God. These two aspects cover all that is great and good in the idea of God.

He is the Supreme Person (*puruṣottama*), the goal of all attainment. He is indescribable because He cannot be completely comprehended. *Muṇḍakopaniṣad* too says:

> He is great and divine and as such a form that is incomprehensible (*acintya-rūpam*). The two important aspects of God in relation to the world, viz. transcendence and immanence, are given equal emphasis in Dvaita Vedānta of Madhva.

Advaita Vedānta denies the knowability of *Brahman* as He is unaccessible to knowledge. But according to Madhvācārya, He is knowable through scriptures. His transcendence does not banish Him to the region of the unknown. *Brahman* is always knowable and obtainable. Knowability is one of His infinite qualities. Of course, we do not know Him in His fullest extent, in all completeness, we can know and realize Him according to our own limits. Though He is not known in His full glory, it does not mean that He is not known at all. Partial knowability establishes at least partial characterizability. An absolutely characterless entity is a chimera. God is the highest form of perfection conceivable by human intelligence.

God, according to Madhva, is only the instrumental cause of the world. *Prakṛti* (primordial matter) alone is the material cause of the world order and not *Brahman*. As the father's desire is the cause of procreation, the desire of *Brahman* is the efficient cause of the world. The desire of *Brahman* creates a stir in the equipoise of *prakṛti* thus the creation sets in. This *prakṛti* forms the body of

God. *Brahman* cannot be the material cause of the world as the attributes of the cause necessarily enter into the effect but the world is non-conscious in its nature. The material cause suffers transformation but the instrumental cause never undergoes any change or transformation. The texts *sa idaṁ sarvaṁ asṛjata* or *yato vā imāni bhūtāni jāyante* imply the force on God. This universe is pulsating in the pores of the Supreme Being.[22] God is the controller of the world order.

Madhva justifies the existence of God on the lines of cosmological proof of the West. He is the first cause of the world. In the absence of His Being the world order cannot be explained. God is the instrumental cause of the creation, sustenance and destruction of the world order. He is the cause of moral order also. He is the cause of man's bondage, at the same time it is through His benediction alone that the soul can enjoy liberation. K. Narain (1962: 123) says:

> The argument from the existence of the moral law to the law-giver, i.e. God is to what Madhva would happily subscribe almost in the same strain as done by Kant in his critiques.

He believes that the world is being controlled by a morally perfect being that has adequate capacity to lead it to the supreme end. And this perfect being is none but God. This may be named as moral proof for the existence of God.

But Madhva does not ensnare teleological proof for the existence of God. He has shown its futility earlier than any Western philosopher. Undoubtedly it points to an "architect" of this stupendous world design but that architect may not necessarily be a creator *Brahman* who is unsurpassed in excellence.

Supreme *Brahman* in Madhva's philosophy is a person as he has his own character. Personality here does not mean psycho-physical organism with its own limitations as it is used in common parlance. Personality does not here mean self-consciousness too. God is person that means the entire universe is to be thought of as an experience of God. B.N.K. Sharma (1962) says:

---

[22] *romakupeṣvanantāni brahmāṇḍani bhavantite* ।

> The Divine personality constitutes such a centrality of reference, endowed with the faculties of cognition, conation and activity, as part of its being.

It is not an indeterminate mass, "it is both knowledge and knower, bliss and the blissful". It is its own goodness. There is no distinction between His essence and His existence. He is a person, means He has "His own instrument of knowledge and activity". There are two aspects in Divine Will, *śakti* and *vyakti*. He perceives things in their own realities. His knowledge is all-embracing. Empirical similes do not describe Him exhaustively. They intend only to draw some picture in our mind. The transcendental cannot be fully represented by the empirical categories and epithets.

Viṣṇu is being identified by Madhva as the Supreme Being and His cosmic powers are eight in number – creation, preservation, dissolution, control, enlightenment, obscuration, bondage and release. Madhva successfully reconciles polytheism with monotheism. The same Supreme Being, who remains with His glory in the state of equipoise, assumes multifarious forms at the time of creation. The first stage of divine manifestation is *caturvyūha* – Vāsudeva, Pradyumna, Aniruddha and Saṅkarṣaṇa – endowed with the activity of redemption, creation, sustenance and destruction. Then the Supreme manifests Himself periodically in different *avatāras*. Madhva's major difference with Rāmānuja on this issue is he keeps all manifestations at par with one another. He does not accept the different degrees of fullness among these manifestations. The same Infinite expresses Itself in all ranks. All *avatāras* are eternal[23] as against Rāmānuja who regards *avatāra* as non-eternal.

Lakṣmī is the consort of God. She is the personification of God's creative energy. She can assume many forms without material body and witness the glory of God through eternity. She is dependent only on God, otherwise She is independent of everything. God creates, sustains and destroys the world through Her. Lakṣmī, in Madhva's philosophy, is "more a theological character than philosophical". She is intelligent *prakṛti*. She is

---

[23] *sarve nityāḥ śāśvatāśca dehāstasya.*

second only to God in "subtlety and the extent of quality".

According to Madhva, pantheism makes God imperfect, monism is obnoxious, and the doctrine of identity in and through difference is illogical. He is a monotheist giving Viṣṇu the status of Supreme Being.

THE CONCEPT OF JĪVA AND HIS BONDAGE

Soul, in Madhva's philosophy, is "the finite centre of conscious experience, each with a unique essence of its own". Consciousness is the very essence of soul. Since we generally believe that nature of a thing is different from its qualities, consciousness as the essence of soul may look inconsistent with his doctrine that knowledge is the quality of *Ātman*. But for Mādhva there is no inconsistency.

Madhva's "die-hard realism" makes him an uncompromising pluralist. He advocates the doctrine of *pañcabheda* (five differences). Difference constitutes the integral part of things (*dharmisvarūpa*)[24] and not only attributes of things (*dharmabhedavāda*). The soul is different not only from matter but from God too. Not only that, the non-transferable immediacy of experience proves the difference among souls also. In spite of so many similarities, one soul is distinct from the other. The Advaitic cancellation of difference as merely a fiction of thought, a product of *avidyā* is not acceptable to Madhva. Difference lies latent in the bosom of everything real. Difference remains among the released souls also.

Soul is not only the form of knowledge (*jñāna-svarūpa*) but is a knower (*jñātṛ*) too. It is self-luminous (*svaprakāśa*). Self-luminosity in Advaita Vedānta refers to a state of pure consciousness where all differences are swallowed. But this theory is not acceptable to Madhva for whom *ātman* is both a knowing subject as well as the object of his own knowledge. Madhva is able to divide consciousness from itself through *viśeṣa*. Soul as conscious personality is the same as God except for the fact that self-luminosity of *jīva* is dependent on the Supreme.[25]

---

[24] *satyaṁ bhedastu vastūnāṁ svarūpaṁ nātra saṁśayaḥ* | – *Nyāyāmṛtādvaita Siddhiḥ*, part 2, p. 1039.

[25] *jivānāṁ svaprakāśatvaṁ tatprasādāt svavedanam.*

In Madhva philosophy "the universe is a vast expansion of animated nature with every atom of space filled up with *jīvas*" (Radhakrishnan 1953, vol. II: 743). He who suffers and enjoys, he who is eligible for bondage and release is *jīva*.

Though the soul at its best is of the nature of consciousness and bliss, they are unmanifested because of *avidyā*. This inherent nature is revealed to *jīva* only through God's grace. The bliss and consciousness of God are different from *jīva*. *Jīva* is dependent on God both in bondage and liberation. Only the released soul feels his metaphysical dependence on God. God is without an equal or superior. Soul is controlled by God. It is not an absolute agent. The deity and devotee are different from each other. Both God and soul are real as well as their difference too is real.

Madhva insists not only on difference among souls but also on their intrinsic gradation based on knowledge, power and bliss. This is called *svarūpatādātmya* which comes more clearly in the released state of the soul. The triple classification is a unique theory of Madhva – (i) *nitya* (eternally free) like Lakṣmī, (ii) *mukta* (those who have freed themselves from the clutches of *saṁsāra*), and (iii) *baddha* (bound). The third category includes both *mukti-yogya*, those who are eligible for *mukti* and those who are fit for it. The latter is again classified under two heads – (i) *tamoyogya* (damnable), and (ii) *nitya-saṁsārī* (ever transmigrating). Some of the *jīva*s are destined for salvation, the others are destined for hell; the third category of *jīva*s keep ever evolving in *saṁsāra*. The triple classification is based on the three *guṇa*s – *sattva*, *rajas* and *tamas*. *Sāttvika jīva* goes to heaven, *tāmasika* goes to hell, whereas *rājasika* revolves in the world. Each has its own status and distinction. God impels them to act according to their *adṛṣṭa*. Even liberated *jīva*s are not exactly alike.

Like other Indian philosophical systems who solve the riddle of universe through moral and religious standard, Madhva too believes in the eternity of *jīva*s. To justify the doctrine of *karma* or the transmigration of soul is a necessary requisite. Soul has a form and body also. Without acknowledging the form of *jīva*, the formal appearance of living being would be inexplicable.

Madhvites call this philosophy Dehātmavāda, which asserts the real and essential identity of the soul and its body. But this identification is not like Cārvāka philosophy which is satisfied only with the physical character of the body. Madhva asserts that the body of *jīvātmā* is not physical rather it is constituted of consciousness and bliss.

Madhva apparently believes that *jīva* in its nature and existence is different from God. God is the cause of *jīva* only in the sense of father as the cause of his son. He is not identical with *Brahman* as Śaṅkara thinks. There is some intrinsic superiority of God over soul. It will be height of blasphemy to think that *jīva*s who realize their potential relation by the grace of God "manage somehow to shoot up to a position of absolute equality with the universal king, overnight". God and soul are never equal in their basic nature and power or in the innate tendencies for good or bad. The doctrine of intrinsic gradation is a legitimate hypothesis suggested by the moral law and supported by reason, revelation and experience.

Madhva accepts quantitative as well qualitative pluralism of souls. The difference in psychophysical, mental and spiritual lives of beings cannot be explained unless we go back upon intrinsic and fundamental difference in the essence of being. The law of *karma* is not a sufficient proof for cosmic differences. If plurality is to be ultimate, it must be grounded on something more than prakṛtic vestures and influences, including *karma*. Madhva explains this on the basis of *svarūpa-viśeṣa*s. Difference is caused by fundamental peculiarity.

Jīva, according to Madhva, is essentially ignorant. It is doer (*kartā*) as well as enjoyer (*bhoktā*). Madhva's contention is that since *jīva* is the subject of knowledge (*jñāna*), it should also be the abode of *jñāna*. Activity, according to Madhva, is to be carried by *jīva*, it is not only superimposition on *jīva*. Sāstras prescribe ethical norms for release. Unless the aspirant practises that injection he would not be liberated. *Kartṛtva* is real. He is independent to choose his line of action (*yathecchasi tathā kuru*). He is enjoyer of the fruit of his action. Like all other Vaiṣṇavites Madhva too believes that the soul is atomic in size. If the transmigration of soul is an acceptable theory, if Upaniṣadic assertion that soul goes upward to the celestial regions through smoky path is acceptable, soul must be atomic in size. As a lamp placed in the corner of the hall illumines the hall, as sandalwood mark on the forehead keeps the whole body fragrant, similarly the soul, though atomic in size is well aware of the condition of the whole body. As the fragrance of the flower is felt even where there is no flower, consciousness is felt all over the body.

Madhva's contention is that the scriptures speak of identity of *jīva* and *Brahman* figuratively owing to *sthānaikya* (their occupying the same place), *mataikya* (identity of their interest) and *sādṛśya* (resemblance is some figurative statements). The statement that *jīva* is God himself means the presence of God in *jīva*. Even passages like *tat tvam asi*, etc. are being interpreted by Madhva in yield to dualism. The perfect God and the imperfect soul cannot merge together. *Tat tvam asi* simply means that "the soul has for its qualities similar to those of God". He reads the passage differently. The passage *sa ātma tat tvam asi* is read as *sa ātmā atat tvam asi*. This reverses the entire significance of the text. The text *ayam ātmā brahma* is simply an eulogy of the *jīvātmā* or it is a subject of meditation.

Madhva presents a beautiful simile of rainbow to explain *jīva* as the *nirupādhi pratibimba* of *paramātman*. Rainbow is caused by the falling of sunlight on the drops of rain water. Similarly, *jīva*s like raindrops are the vehicle for the manifestation of the Divine. B.N.K. Sharma (1962: 224) says:

> The figure of *bimba–pratibimba-bhāva* thus gives meaning, expresses a great philosophical truth and value and establishes an intimacy of relation between man and God, which is the noblest truth of philosophy and religion.

As soon as *bhakti* grows into maturity, *jīva* realizes its metaphysical dependence on God along with the difference. *Jīva* is different from, dependent on and similar to *Brahman*. *Jīva* can realize its true nature only by God's grace. *Jīva* resembles God in small measure. To quote Sharma (ibid.: 227) again:

> Madhva rejects the relation of *bhedābheda* between *jīva* and

> *Brahman*, accepts fundamental difference and substitutes *aṁśatva* for identity. . . . The difference is not of kind but of both degree and order.

Aṁśa symbolically expresses difference and dependence. No merging is possible, nor are they absolutely exclusive. Their difference is eternal but not absolute. Identity text means only transcendental oneness of *Brahman*. The nature (*svarūpa*) of *jīva* has the potency which is actualized by Divine grace. Devotees are the godly men. They may be compared with the raindrops which reveal the concealed majesty of the rays of sun, i.e. God. Soul is atomic in size but at the same time it has the potency to manifest the Divine. The relation with Divine is possible only by virtue of its being conscious and blissful. The *mukta* soul has nature akin to God that is why there is perfect harmony between them in the state of release. Since God is *antaryāmī*, he can never be excluded from *jīva*. The difference between them is eternal not absolute.[26] Vāyu (Madhva) mediates between God and the soul. He helps *jīva* in acquiring saving knowledge which leads to emancipation.

THE REALITY OF WORLD

Reality of the world is one of the fundamental tenets of theistic Vedānta and Madhva is not an exception to it. Creation is not only phenomenally real, it is also a metaphysical fact with *prakṛti* as its material cause and God as the instrumental cause. God creates the world for the sake of promoting the good of *jīva*s. He does not have his own axe to grind. God's will is the main reason for creation. He creates in a very sportive mood.

Madhva proves the reality of the world on perceptual, rational and spiritual grounds. Perception is an infallible organ of knowledge. It cannot be deprived of its validity. It is self-valid. To rob the reality of world will mean unimportance of ethical principles. Our worldly experiences, according to Madhva, have practical utility. *Sākṣīpratyakṣa* is the ground of Madhva's dualistic philosophy. The verdict of *sākṣī* carries with itself the

---

[26] *jīvātmanaḥ paramātmanā ātyāntikabhedaḥ samarthyate parantu na jīvo brahmaṇo ghaṭa iva paṭād atyantabhinnaḥ.*

logical certainty of the world. To doubt this will mean collapse of all philosophical findings and believes. According to him the scriptures support "the reality of creation and of a real world, real souls and real God". Creation is "an actualization of what is in the womb of matter and souls by the action of *Brahman*".

Madhva does not deem the creation of the world at a specific time. Creation is a reality but it is not performed at a particular time. It is continuous creation and depends on God. It has neither beginning nor end.

Madhva believes in the evolution of *prakṛti* from subtle to gross form. He neither accepts Brahma-Pariṇāmavāda nor Vivartavāda. Sharma (1962: 166) says:

> A strict adherence of the logic of facts and the spirit of the Śrutis compels Madhva to reject the profanity of Brahma-Pariṇāmavāda.

Material causality of *Brahman* is never acceptable to Madhva – *Brahman* is partless and indivisible. To accept Pariṇāmavāda will mean the complete loss of the nature of *Brahman*, Vivartavāda is also no theory of causation. It is logically unsustainable and philosophically unacceptable. To prove the "One" it rejects the many.

THE CONCEPT OF MOKṢA

Mokṣa, according to Madhva, is a complete unfolding of self in its full potency. It is the state of unalloyed bliss. B.N.K. Sharma (1962: 336) remarks:

> His is a distinctive view of *mokṣa*, rich in its detail, uncompromising in principle, trenchant in its logic and full of mystic inwardness, in some respects.

In India, philosophy, religion and morality have always been interwoven. The conception of individual souls and their relation with *Brahman* determines the nature of *mokṣa*. Madhva is not an exception to this. His doctrine of inherent difference between the world, soul and God condemns identity philosophy. For him, "*mokṣa* would not be worth-aspiring if the *ātman* does not survive as a self-luminous entity therein". In this state, the soul enjoys the fulfilment of all his desires in the company of the Lord and he is well aware of this enjoyment. Self is *saviśeṣa-svarūpa* even, in the state of *mokṣa*. It is there "in all its richness and entirety of aspects". Only the false sense of independence and separateness is not there. He looks at things through the eyes of God.[27] He finds release from *saṁsāra*.

Indian philosophy unanimously believes that *mokṣa* means cessation of pain. But for Madhva, it is not only cessation of pain, it is at the same time acquisition of positive blessedness, when *avidyā*, the cause of bondage, is destroyed, soul overbrims with unalloyed bliss. This bliss at the most is similar to the bliss of Viṣṇu but never identical as supposed by Advaita Vedāntists. Bliss of *jīva* differs from the bliss of God not only in quality but also in degree. Madhva's contention is that if *mokṣa* would have been devoid of bliss, there would have been no reason for seeking it with so much trouble.

Bliss is not a matter of external possession it is the essential characteristic of soul. Madhva gets support from *Bṛhadāraṇyaka Upaniṣad* which declares *avināśī vā ayamātmā aṇucchittidharmā* when he advocates persistence of individuality in the state of emancipation. It is not bare survival of *ātman*, it survives with its attributes of consciousness and bliss. It is well aware of its deliverance from misery. It realizes its limitations and dependence on God. It is not only God realization, it is at the same time self-realization also.

Bhakti, according to Madhva, is the final means of reaching to God, though knowledge of God is an essential prerequisite for *bhakti*. *Jñāna* is not the sole means of liberation but it is accessory to spiritual realization. *Bhakti* engenders the relation of *jīva* with *Brahman*. This true relation presupposes right knowledge of His Majesty, the Lord. *Bhakti* in Madhva's philosophy is not a wave of foolish sentimentality. It is the fruit of deep reflection and patient study. First of all we have to enlarge "the horizon of the knowledge of God" by *śravaṇa*. *Bhakti* without knowledge is an impossibility.[28]

---

[27] *sa brahmaṇā paśyati, brahmaṇā śṛṇoti brahmaṇaivedaṁ sarvam aṇubhavati* I
– B.S.M.B. IV.45

[28] (a) Rāmānuja too says, *vinā jñānaṁ kuto bhaktir kuto bhaktiṁ vinā ca tat*.

Unless one knows that God is the inherent controller of the whole universe, he can't get liberation. Correct knowledge leads to *jñāna* which finally culminates in love of God.

Another preliminary need for *bhakti* is the virtuous life. Calmness of mind, control of passion and love of God are essential preconditions for *bhakti*. Madhva does not belittle the contribution of *karma*. It is a path of enlightened activity. The light of knowledge cannot be seen unless we lead a virtuous life. A virtuous man performs the duty leaving all interest in its fruits, *niṣkāmaṁ jñāna pūrvaṁ karma*. Enlightened activity is never binding. *Nivṛtti mārga* does not mean to relinquish all duties but "its active performance in a spirit of devotion and dispassion".[29] Śaṅkara does not believe in *karma-jñāna-samuccaya* even because for him there is opposition between them with regards to their cause, nature and effect (*svarūpa-phala-virodhāt*). But Madhva deems virtuous life as a necessary prerequisite for *jñāna* which culminates finally in *bhakti*. He never takes *karma* in its narrow hedonistic or ritualistic sense. Performance of *niṣkāma karma* with devotion to God keeps the door wide open for the rise of *jñāna* and *bhkati* (*karma tu tatsādhanam eva*). It develops insight into truth. According to Jayatīrtha, the knowledge of the greatness of Lord and *virāga* from worldly pleasure produce in us a feeling of love for God. Devotion without virtuous life will be a travesty.

Bhakti, according to Madhva, is the chief source of *mokṣa*. It is intense devotion proceeding from the knowledge of sovereign God. It is profound admiration for Divine Majesty coupled with spontaneous love for the Lord.[30] It is not merely an emotional excitement or eroticism. *Bhakti*, according to Madhva, blends virtuous life and knowledge with intense love. In Jayatīrtha's definition of *bhakti*, all the three aspects – religious, philosophical and emotional – are happily blended. Sharma (1962: 289) translates the classical definition as:

(b) *jñānadhārānugṛhītam* |

29 *niṣkāmaṁ jñānapūrvaṁ tu nivṛttamiha cocyate* | – *Vyāsa-smṛtiḥ*

30 Śāṇḍilya says: *sā parānuraktīrīśvare* – *Śāṇḍilīya Bhaktisūtra, Prathmādhyāya, śloka* II.

> *Bhakti* is, thus, the steady and continuous flow of deep attachment of God, impregnable by any amount of impediments and transcending the love of our own selves, our kith and kin, cherished belongings, etc. and fortified by a firm conviction of the transcendent majesty and greatness of God as the abode of all perfections and free from all blemish and by an unshakable conviction of the complete metaphysical dependence of everything else upon Him.

Madhva's conception of *bhakti* remains at "its exalted intellectual and spiritual level of firm philosophical devotion to the Supreme Lord".

Bhakti helps in realizing the intrinsic nature of soul and its inherent relationship with God (*pratibimbatva*). The devotee loses all charm for the worldly prosperity as he cannot serve two masters, the pleasure of the world and God, at a time.

Madhva believes in gradation in *mukti*. Since *bhakti* and knowledge are different in different *sādhaka*s, the concept of gradation of *mukti* follows consequently. *Gītā* also teaches *adhikārī-bheda*. All persons are not alike in their mental aptitude. There is intrinsic gradation of fitness in the *jīva*, leading to that there is intrinsic gradation in *mokṣa* also. As vessels are filled with water according to their respective size and shape, *sādhaka*s attain fullness of bliss in accordance with their respective intrinsic capacity. This gradation (*tāratamya*) does not lead to any jealous feeling as the *mukta jīva*s are in the state of heavenly blessedness. They are satisfied with their share of bliss in accordance with their capacity.

As Madhva has staunch belief in difference, it is incumbent on him to defend difference even in the stage of *mukti*.

This doctrine of gradation well explains the four types of *mukti*: *sārūpya*, *sālokya*, *sāmīpya* and *sāyujya*. *Sāyujya* is the highest *mukti* where the devotee enjoys ineffable bliss and similarity with the Lord. The other three are lower and not perfect. In *sāyujya mukti* all the binding *karma*s are destroyed and the *jīva*s remain in Vaikuṇṭha. There is no return from there. In *sālokya mukti* the *jīva* enters into Vaikuṇṭha, in *sāmīpya mukti* he obtains proximity with the Lord and in *sārūpya* his enjoyment is similar to God. The highest and the supreme state is *sāyujya*. He is similar to

God and not identical.

Devotion is utmost warmth of love between devotee and deity and can be established in a threefold way, through body, through speech and through mind. Alms-giving, giving shelter to the destitute, helping persons in distress, etc. are bodily activities. Reciting the sacred texts, speaking the truth, speaking the good, etc. constitute devotion through speech. Kindness, faith and desire for service to the Lord are the constituents of devotion through mind.

Madhva speaks of three types of devotee – *uttama bhakta*, *madhyama bhakta*, and *adhama bhakta* – in accordance with the nature and intensity of devotion. In *uttama bhakti* there is ineffable blending of love with knowledge. It is the apprehension of Reality as "the pivot of one's own reality". Devotion is loving attachment born of knowledge.[31]

Mokṣa has two aspects: negative and positive. Negative aspect consists in getting rid of the fetters of *karma*, extinction of all suffering, etc. It is *ātyantika-duḥkha-nivr̥tti*. Positive aspect is the enjoyment of intrinsic bliss, *paramānandāvāpti*. In his *Bhāṣya* on *Brahmasūtra*, Madhva says, "Release consists in shaking of all extraneous associations and regaining one's own selfhood".[32] Sublime *bhakti*, according to Madhva, is not a means but an end in itself for in the state of release also there is loving communion with God. "The intrinsic spiritual relation between the human spirit and God is dynamic in its magnetism that the attraction of the latter becomes more fully manifested in release than in *saṁsāra*" (Sharma 1962: 297).

According to Madhva, effort on the part of *jīva* is not the only decisive factor in *mokṣa*. Divine grace plays the vital role in the final deliverance of *jīva*. Through devotion the devotee invokes Divine benediction. In Advaita Vedānta's scheme of reality there is no scope for Divine intervention. But for Madhva, sheer knowledge or devotion cannot save man from the worldly agony. This alone is not potent enough to lift the veil of ignorance. Only Divine

---

[31] *jñānapūrvaparasneho nityo bhaktiritiryate* – *Mahābhārata Tātparya nirṇayaḥ* 1.107

[32] *muktir hitvā 'nyathā-rūpaṁ svarūpeṇa vyavasthitiḥ* | – B.S.M.B. I.1.7

grace (*Īśvara-prasāda*) can finally reveal to *jīva* "restoration to pure spiritual existence" (*svarūpeṇa vyavasthitiḥ*). God is not forced by any human merit. He simply selects some for redemption. By His *prasāda* only a man can realize his inherent potency and similarity with God. As Hindu tradition does not allow Madhva to hold the view of God's arbitrary selection, he accepts that the grace is bestowed in proportion to the intensity of devotion. In Madhva's philosophy the utility of *bhakti* lies in pleasing God so that he may bestow His knowledge and devotion on his devotee. "Vivid perception of the Supreme Reality as the pivot of one's own reality" is possible only through His grace.

Aparokṣa jñāna is the ultimate fulfilment of all *sādhanā*s, it is the state of final release. It is the culminating state of arduous process of *śravaṇa, manana* and *nididhyāsana*. It casts off the unessential forms (*anyathārūpam*) of *jīva*. In *aparokṣa jñāna* the state of mind is different from the state of *upāsanā* or *dhyāna*. In *dhyāna* only the reflection of Supreme *Brahman* in *citta* is seen. *Aparokṣa jñāna* defies all explicit expositions of *Brahman* in words. It is a "flash like revelation", it is the direct vision of the Lord. "It is the dawn of *mukti*, with it the *sādhaka* realizes the ineffable bliss of self as well as God realization. It is the state of *ātyantika-duḥkha-nivṛtti* and *paramānandāvāpti*."

Aparokṣa jñānī corresponds to *jīvanmukti* of other schools. But the analogy should not be carried too far. *Mukti* still in flesh and blood is not acceptable to any follower of theistic school along with Madhva. *Nyāyāmṛta* puts that a *sādhaka*, though he has visions of truth, remains in flesh till the grace of God is not bestowed upon him. In this state *avidyā* is not destroyed, the effect of *prārabdha karma* is not annulled. *Aparokṣa jñānī* is not merely waiting for the end of body to get final release as it is in the case of *jīvanmukta*. To *aparokṣa jñānī* the prospect of *mokṣa* is not assured. He may have to live some more "lives" if he is not supposed to be fit for *prasāda*. Moreover, "the *mokṣa* would not be worth having if *ātman* would not be a luminous entity therein".

Dvaitādvaita Vedānta of Nimbārka

THE NATURE OF REALITY

Nimbārka presents the doctrine of Dvaitādvaitavāda or Bhedābhedavāda literally meaning the doctrine of difference and non-difference. He is eager to avoid the extremes and wants to work out a happy synthesis. It is not identity in and through difference like Rāmānuja, because for Rāmānuja difference cannot exist independent of "identity which it qualifies and to which it belongs". For Nimbārka *bheda* and *abheda* both are equally real. The noteworthy feature of his philosophy is the spirit of compromise. Like Rāmānuja he also accepts three realities – God, soul and matter. God is independent reality whereas soul and matter are dependent realities, dependent on God. Soul and matter are not different from God, as they are absolutely dependent on Him; they are different as well because their nature and attributes are different from God. Thus Nimbārka's philosophy is not the philosophy of identity of Advaita Vedānta, nor of difference of Dvaita Vedānta, nor of identity-in-and through difference of Viśiṣṭādvaita, it is the philosophy of identity as well as difference. The difference is as natural as identity. The cause is different from the effect as it is not fully exhausted in the effect. The clay is not only jar but so many other things, but the effect is not different from the cause as it is after all clay itself. According to Nimbārka, *bheda* means "difference in attributes of activities from the standpoint of the effect and transcendence over the effect from the standpoint of the cause". *Abheda* means "no-difference of essence from the standpoint of the effect and immanence in the effect from the standpoint of the cause".

This doctrine does not contradict Śrutis, which deny plurality. There is no plurality in the cause of the world, *Brahman*, but the difference between God, soul and the world is incontrovertible.

The highest *Brahman* is identified with Kṛṣṇa, who is the abode of all auspicious qualities, who is free from all five miseries (those are nescience, egoism, attachment, hatred and fear of death), who manifests Himself in many forms, who is beyond the influence of three *guṇa*s and who is unaffected by *karma*. He gives final liberation by getting *jīva*s rid of their sin.[33]

Brahman is indescribable by words. Scriptures alone are the means of knowing or communicating the knowledge of *Brahman*.[34] Scripture apparently seems to depict so many things but "really it depicts only one thing, viz. *Brahman*, for him alone all the diverse scriptural passages find their complete reconciliation".[35]

He possesses six qualities which help Him in creation:

(i) *Jñāna* (knowledge) which makes him *trikāladarśī* (one who perceives everything of all the tree times).

(ii) *Bala* (strength) which helps Him in supporting the world.

(iii) Power (*śakti*) which makes nothing impossible for Him.

(iv) Prosperity (*aiśvarya*) which helps Him in controlling everything.

(v) *Tejas* (energy) which gives Him tremendous energy to work. He is a tireless worker.

(vi) *Vīrya* (prowess) through which He overpowers everything, but is never overpowered.

He possesses some more auspicious qualities, which can be classified under two heads – qualities of majesty such as omniscience, omnipotence, omnipresence, etc. and qualities of sweetness such as beauty, bliss, *vātsalya* (never thinks of the faults of the devotees), *mārdava* (non-endurance of His devotee's pain and suffering), *sauhārda* (will to protect at one's cost), *dayā* (kindness) and *mādhurya* (appealing beauty). He dwells in the inner heart of everyone.[36] He is the supporter of all the *loka*s. He is the object of all our adoration.

Brahman is the creator of the whole universe.[37] He is both the unmanifest and the manifest, both the efficient cause and the material cause of the world because creation means manifestation

---

33 V.P.S. I.1.3.

34 Ibid., I.1.4.

35 V. P. S. and V. K. Expounded by R.B., p. 25.

36 *anena parabrahmanaḥ sarvagatatvaṁ dṛḍhīkṛtam* | – V. P. S. III.2.37

37 *brahmaiva jagatkāraṇaṁ yuktam* | – V. P. S. I.1.3

of his *śakti*. Radhakrishnan (1953, vol. II: 754) says: "What Rāmānuja calls the body of *Brahman* is the *śakti* of Nimbārka." By His will only He is able to create the world. He does not need material (*upādāna*) for creating the world. His subtle potencies are manifested in grosser form. He is the efficient cause of the universe, because He is the Lord of the law of *karma*. He is the inner controller of the souls. Nimbārka disagrees with Rāmānuja when he asserts that "conscious and the unconscious worlds form, together with *Brahman*, a composite personality, which is the material cause of the world". He creates the world with His *śakti*. Modification and changes in the world do not touch His integrity. He is one with the world as the cause but different from the world in nature and attribute. Hegel too says: "There is no God without the world, there is no world without God." It may be urged that the material cause and its effect are of the same nature. How can *Brahman* be the cause of the world as the world is not sentient. But Nimbārka says that there is no such rule that the cause and the effect must always be similar and the world being different in nature from God may not be created by God. *Brahman* is immanent in the world, so by no means the world is different from God.

He is *nityatṛpta*, *nityamukta* and *nityabuddha*. Then a natural curiosity creeps in, why at all God has created the world. It is not some purpose or some inefficiency that motivates God to create. He creates for *līlā*. He creates out of "fullness of his nature, abundance of His bliss". He is an "indivisable mass of bliss". He is the cause of the bliss of soul thus he is called blissful. Scriptures describe the world as originating from bliss, sustained in bliss and dissolved in bliss. He is all bliss and the source of all bliss.[38] He desires to be many to grow forth. When the universe returns to *Brahman*, it ceases to be imperfect; it inheres in Him as His *śakti* (power).

Brahman is Kṛṣṇa. He is the form of all (*svarūpa*). He brings forth and maintains the Universe through bliss. He is the cause of all causes.[39] He is unlimited. We can well imagine the unlimited

38 (a) *ānandamayaḥ paramātmā eva na tu jīvaḥ* | – V.P.S. I.1.13

(b) *jīvanananda-hetutvādapi paramātmaivānandamayaḥ* | – Ibid. I.1.15

39 V.K. III.2.3.

on account of limited as we can perceive the sunlight through the window or through a hole.[40]

He is all-pervading; but is not affected by the merits or demerits of anything as the fetter of *karma* is not binding upon Him. He is like sun being unaffected by the increase and decrease of water in which it is being reflected.[41]

He is neither atomic nor gross. There is nothing which is not in Him. He has a physical body too, otherwise there would have been nothing for the devotees to meditate upon. There would have been no *upāsanā* for which presence of form is a necessity. Nimbārka deems that if God does not have form, the assertion that "God is seen", will be meaningless. He is Kṛṣṇa, Gopāla. Rukmiṇī, Satyabhāmā and other ladies remain in His company. A devotee meditates upon the Lord in this form. He is putting on *kirīṭa* (crown), *vaijayantī* (necklace), *keyūra* (a bracelet) and yellow silken garment. He is having *śaṅkha*, *cakra* and *gadā*. Other gods and goddesses enjoy their sovereignty granted by Him. He is "the ocean of determination or qualities", God is God, Pure and Perfect, in spite of all impurities and imperfection and not excluding them. He pervades and contains everything, yet transcends everything.[42]

He gives award according to the merits and demerits of the *jīvas*. *Karmaphala-dātṛtva* is one of the important qualities of the Lord. He bestows the final emancipation on deserving *jīvas*.

He is identified with the *suṣupti sthāna* where everything is in the state of peace and bliss. He is one in many, many in one. He is the substratum of the world which is His content. Nimbārka does not accept matter and souls as the attributes of God because the attributes either distinguish one thing from the other or make the thing better know. *Acit* and *cit* as the attributes of God do not serve any purpose. God cannot be distinguished from all else as He is all-pervading. Nor be known by these attributes as they do not constitute His essence. Again, *cit* and *acit* cannot form His body

---

40 V.P.S. III.2.34.

41 Ibid., III.2.20.

42 V.P.S. and V.K. expounded by Roma Bose, 1943, p. 23.

too as in that case God will be subjected to all imperfections of the world. Half of God can be reserved for modification and other half for eternity and perfection. Thus *cit* and *acit* are powers of God. The world is an enfoldment of His power. He is independently all-illuminative. He is by nature the knower. He is *bhūmā* (universal) since *bhūmā* is the ultimate object of inquiry. He is one as well as many because of his inconceivable sovereignty.

He manifests himself in infinite forms; some of these are denoted as *vyūha*s while others as *avatāra*s. He manifests himself in *vyūha*s for the purpose of creating the world and for making Himself easily available for His devotees. There are four forms of *vyūha*s: Vāsudeva, Saṅkarṣaṇa, Pradyumna and Aniruddha. Vāsudeva is the *nirguṇa* aspect of *Brahman*. He is also called *kṣetrajña*. He dwells in us as *antaryāmī* in the form of Saṅkarṣaṇa. Pradyumna is the *manas* of all the beings. He is unchangeable and He manifests Aniruddha, who is the cause of the world.

He incarnates Himself in different forms in order to protect the virtuous and to punish the vicious. His potency is not fully manifested during *avatāra*, still He is in His "full *svarūpa*". Sometimes He incarnates Himself fully (*pūrṇāvatāra*), sometimes He manifests Himself partially (*aṁśāvatāra*). *Guṇāvatāra*, *puruṣāvatāra* and *līlāvatāra* are the three types of *avatāra* accepted by Nimbārka.

Thus the Lord is never an immutable, qualityless *Brahman*. He is the abode of innumerable auspicious qualities. God, in His transcendental aspect, is a unity of existence, consciousness and bliss. In His nature as God "He realizes His own infinite joy through the infinite souls which are but constituent parts of Him." He is all powerful on the one hand, on the other He is "all-merciful". He is transcendental as well as immanent. He is all-pervading yet remains in the heart of man, He is a helper as well as a ruler. He has supreme might as well as boundless love. The philosophy of Nimbārka is philosophico-theological. It seeks to give philosophical explanation of the ultimate categories; at the same time, it does not neglect the call of human heart.

THE NATURE OF JĪVA

Jīva is essentially of the nature of knowledge (*jñānas-varūpa*) at the same time it is also the substratum of knowledge (*jñānāśraya*). He is the abode of both substantive and attributive knowledge. There is *dharma–dharmī bhāva*[43] (the relation between qualified and qualification) like sun which is of the nature of light as well as the substratum of light. *Jīva* is not dependent upon anything except upon the Lord for its nature, existence and activities. The liberated *jīvas* are of the nature of light (*svayaṁ jyoti*). It is dependent on God, is supported by God, pervaded by God and controlled from within by God.

The individual souls are atomic in size,[44] therefore infinite in number and partless in nature. Because of its all-pervading knowledge it can feel the various sensations in different parts of the body like a drop of the sandalwood paste.[45]

The existence and activity of human experience are contained and controlled by Him. Transmigration of soul is possible only when *jīva* is atomic. The illumination in body is caused by soul as the illumination in the room is caused by the lamp. Knowledge is a quality which is spread all over like the fragrance of the flower. Knowledgehood is not an independent entity, it is a quality, a *dharma* of *jīva*. This quality cannot be sublated from *jīvātman*. It is its very essence. Thus it is immutable. *Jīva* is a part and parcel of *paramātman* in one sense and different from Him in another sense. There is *bhedābheda* relationship among them. Bhāskara emphasizes unity more than difference and this difference is caused by *upādhi* (conditions) but for Nimbārka unity is as important as difference. Each soul is a "ray of *Brahman* individualized". Against Śaṅkara's doctrine of the unity and universality of the soul, Nimbārka propounds the theory of atomicity and plurality. They do not have independent existence (*svatantra sattābhāva*) so they are not different from God. They have dependent existence (*paratantra sattābhāva*),

---

43 V.P.S. II.3.27.

44 Ibid. II.3.22.

45 *dehaikadeśastho 'pi kṛtsnaṁ dehaṁ candanabinduryathā 'hlādati tathā jivo 'pi prakāśayati* I – Ibid. II.3.23

thus they are different from God. The infinite numbers of souls are not identical with each other like the monads of Leibnitz nor are they identical with *Brahman*. They have their own individuality and separateness which are maintained even in liberated state. They are sustained by the supreme spirit. *Mukti* does not mean annihilation of individuality rather it means fulfilment of its real nature and attributes. Here he is similar in nature and attribute to God, not identical.

In the state of *pralaya, cit* and *acit*, matter and soul dwell in Him in a subtle form. When the world is produced by the *śakti* (energy) of God, each separate soul is embodied according to its *karmaphala* (effects of its deeds).

Jīva is called *aja* (unborn). It is "the Lord's *niyāmya*" (that which is controlled). God is the controller, *jīva* in all its states is of the nature of being controlled (*niyāmya*). *Niyantṛtva* (to govern) is the eternal nature of God. When *jīva* turns away its face from the Lord, it wanders from one birth to another. It incurs bondage due to its association with *avidyā* and *karma*.

Jīva is *aṁśa* of God, but *aṁśa* here does not mean "part" or "reflection" of *Brahman*, it is rather potency of *Brahman*. *Jīva* can never be equated with God in power. It has less power and it is dependent. It is *aṁśa*; the Lord is *aṁśī*.[46] All *jīva*s are His *pāda*, that is *aṁśa*.[47] God is never affected by pleasure and pain of *jīva* like Sun, which is unaffected by impurities in its rays. The Lord is eternal and qualityless. He is as indifferent to the fetters of *karma* as the leaf of Lotus is indifferent to water.[48] Due to the influence of *māyā*, the knowledge of *jīva* is limited in the state of bondage.

There are four stages of *jīva* – (a) waking stage, (b) dreaming stage, (c) the stage of sound sleep, and (d) going out. And *jīva* under the influence of *karma* can be classified under two heads – (a) *baddha* (bound), and (b) *mukta* (free). *Baddha jīva* is in the clutches of the various modifications of *prakṛti* and is devoid of the

---

46 *aṁśāṁśibhāvājjvaparamātmanorbhedaṁ darśayati* | – V.P.S. II.3.42

47 *pādo 'sya viśvābhūtāni* | – Ibid. II.3.43

48 *tatra yaḥ paramātmā 'sau sa nityo nirguṇaḥ smṛtaḥ | na lipyate phalaiścāpi padma-patramivāṁbhasā* | – Ibid. II.3.46

Supreme Bliss. *Baddha* can again be classified under two heads – (a) *mumukṣu* (who is desirous for freedom from cosmic existence), and (b) *bubhukṣu* (who wants to enjoy worldly prosperity). Among *mumukṣus*, there are some, who want to know the true nature of the Lord (*bhagavad-bhāvapatti*), while others want to realize their own nature (*nijasvarūpāpatti*). Again some *bubhukṣus* have got blissful (*bhāviśreyaska*) and others are ever attached to the worldly life (*nitya-saṁsārī*).

Mukta jīvas are those who have realized their true nature by the grace of God and are free from the fetters of *karma*. Among them some are eternally liberated (*nityamukta*). They are again either those who are directly connected with Lord as His flute, His bracelet or His crest or those who are His attendants like Garuḍa.

Jīva, according to Nimbārka, is *kartā* and *bhoktā*. According to Sāṁkhya philosophy, *jīva* is only conscious entity, it is never an active agent but for Nimbārka, *jīva* by its very nature is the doer.[49] He claims the support from the Śrutis: "One should live for hundred years while engaged in doing action."[50] Desirous of salvation, one should submit oneself to the Lord. His doership is present even in the act of breathing. *Taittirīya Upaniṣad* also says: "*Vijñāna* performs sacrifice and other deeds." By *vijñāna* they mean *jīva* only. Nimbārka opines that if *jīva* would not have been doer, he would have merged himself into *Brahman* and taken *samādhi*. He believes that whomsoever He wants to take to the higher *loka*, He persuades him to do good deeds.

Nimbārka does not advocate the indentity philosophy of *jīva* and *Brahman*. He believes in Bhedābhedavāda. The relation is both of identity and difference. Identity is as important as difference. He interprets the text *tat tvam asi* in this light. *Tat* signifies the eternal omnipresent *Brahman*, *tvam* the individual soul who is dependent on God and *asi* points out the relation of both difference and non-difference. The simile of sun and its rays, fire and its sparks may well explain their relation. The soul and matter are one with the Lord at the same time different from Him like water and its wave,

---

49 V.P.S. II.3.32.

50 *Īśopaniṣad*.

like coil of a rope and the rope. What is different is also identical. The individual soul is different from God for it being a dependent entity. It is non-different as it is of the nature of *Brahman*; it cannot exist apart from Him. Whatever is pervaded by an entity is of the nature of that entity. There is non-difference (*abheda*) in them.

Jīva is the doer of the past deeds; he suffers three kinds of pains: *ādhyātmika*, *ādhibhautika* and *ādhidaivika*. If it were identical with *paramātman*, He too would have to suffer these pains. *Sarvaṁ khalvidaṁ brahma* (all this is indeed *Brahman*) simply means that the whole non-conscious reality comes out of Him. The precious stones like emerald, adamantine are the modifications of earth, thus they are rightly called earthy, yet they are quite distinct from earth.[51] Like that *jīva* is the same and not the same. The difference between the soul and the Lord is incontrovertible. Plurality will lead to transmigration of soul in *Brahman*. Both are unacceptable to Nimbārka. Human souls are the part and parcel of the nature of God. They are dependent on Him for their essence, existence and activities (*tadāyatta-svarūpa-sthiti*).

There are two kinds of souls – *baddha* (bound) and *mukta* (liberated). The souls in bondage are surrounded by beginningless *māyā* and are associated with physical bodies, while the liberated souls are free from the clutches of *karma* and matter. They possess the celestial body.

THE NATURE OF THE WORLD

Brahman, *jīva* and the world are three real entities according to Nimbārka. The world is a modification (*pariṇāma*) of *Brahman*. *Pariṇāma* here means potency of *Brahman*. Thus the objection, that there cannot be any modification in *Brahman* as *Brahman* is all-pervading, does not stand here. It is not *svarūpa-pariṇāma* of Sāṁkhya philosophy; it is, as Śrīnivāsācārya puts, *śakti-vikṣepa-lakṣaṇa-pariṇāma*, which means "a *pariṇāma* is nothing but the power of ejection".

The world is neither a modification of a part of *Brahman* nor of the whole of *Brahman*. *Brahman* is partless and untainted. It is

[51] V.P.S. II.1.22.

an expansion of his power (*śakti*). His essential nature remains unchangeable like spider which remains intact while its power is modified into a cobweb. The imperfection of the world does not touch Him. The universe never cuts off from *Brahman* as part but inheres in Him during creation as well as dissolution.

The world is not an illusory appearance. It is inadmissible to believe that *māyā* as the world principle produces the world in cooperation with *Brahman*. *Brahman* cannot be the substratum of *avidyā*.

The inanimate is of three kinds – (a) *aprākṛta*, (b) *prakṛta*, and (c) *kāla*. *Aprākṛta* is immutable matter of which divine body is made. It is like the *nityavibhūti* of Rāmānuja. *Prākṛta* is derived from *prakṛti*. It is the stuff of the whole universe. It is as eternal as soul yet it has *Brahman* as its cause. It consists of three *guṇas* – *sattva*, *rajas* and *tamas*. Nimbārka accepts the Sāṁkhya view of creation in general. *Kāla* is another species of *acit*. Nimbārka has not gone in detail about the meaning of *aprākṛta* or *kāla*.

THE CONCEPT OF SALVATION AND WAYS TO ATTAIN IT

Mukti, according to Nimbārka, consists in the experience of the nature of God (*tadbhāvāpatti*) which is the supreme end of life. This experience is feasible due to the complete destruction of the nescience and potencies of actions in consequence of divine grace. A liberated soul attains similarity (*sāmya*) with the Lord in nature and quality. *Sāmya* means similarity and never identity. For him, the bondage of *jīva* is real as well as the dissolution of bondage too is real. In bondage, souls forget their affinity with God and feel themselves independent. The ultimate end of life is to live in eternal bliss in his devotional contemplation of God. He feels these to be one with God (*tad-tādātmyānubhava*) and bliss in Him as a part of His energy. This realization destroys all the *karmas* – *sañcita*, *kriyamāṇa* and *prārabdha*. In *mukti* there is establishment of an incessant devotional fellowship with God. This is like return to his original abode. A liberated soul remains in God as His distinct energy and is never sent back to this world.

Like other Vaiṣṇavites, Nimbārka also accepts four kinds of

liberation: proximity of God in His abode (*sāmīpya*), residence in His abode (*sālokya*); similarity of form with Him (*sārūpya*) and merging in Him (*sāyujya*). They merge in God without losing the separate identity. They are full with the ecstasy of delight. They move about in God as the delightful fishes swim in water. He achieves the nature of *Brahman* as well as possesses an infinite knowledge and bliss. The attainment of the nature of *Brahman* (*brahma-svarūpa-lābha*) is only one aspect of *mokṣa* and not the whole of it. The other important aspect is the realization of one's own nature (*ātma-savarūpa-lābha*). *Mokṣa* is thus "a full development of one's own individuality". Salvation never implies identity of soul with *Brahman*. This means the full manifestation of its real nature as consciousness through and through untainted by matter. The real nature of self remains hidden by *avidyā* like the rays of a lamp within a pot. When this veil of *avidyā* is cast off the soul shines in pristine purity and brilliance. The non-distinction of *jīva* is not incompatible with its distinction from *Brahman*.[52]

The *abheda* (similarity) between *Brahman* and *mukta jīva* consists in the following facts.

The liberated souls are also free from transmigration and suffering; they too are omniscient; they too enjoy supreme majesty. *Chāndogya Upaniṣad* too quotes: "When he becomes bodiless, pleasure and pain do not touch him."[53] He becomes as self ruler.[54] He enjoys all pleasures together with *Brahman*. He enjoys the world by the means of body created by God Himself. He always follows the Lord's will.

The *bheda* (difference) between the *mukta* (freed) soul and God consists in the following facts:

(a) The freed soul, in spite of possessing Supreme Majesty, can never create or maintain or destroy the world. Only the Lord

---

[52] *muktaḥ parasmād ātmānaṁ bhāgāvirodhinā avibhāgenānubhavati* I
– V.P.S. IV.4.4

[53] *aśarīraṁ vāva santaṁ na priyāpriye spṛśatah* I – Chā.U. VIII.12.1

[54] *muktaḥ āvirhūta-satya-saṅkalpatvādevānanyādhipatiḥbhavati* I
– V.P.S. IV.4.9

is capable of such activities.[55]

(b) It is atomic in size but *Brahman* is all-pervading. Though atomic, it enjoys the pleasure of several bodies simultaneously through its all-pervading quality of knowledge like the rays of a lamp.[56] Roma Bose (1943: 45) says: "The state of salvation is a definite acquisition – a positive state of Supreme self-development, knowledge and enjoyment and not a negative state of unconsciousness and blankness."

There are five means to attain liberation:

(a) *Karma* (work).

(b) *Jñāna* (knowledge).

(c) *Upāsanā* (meditation).

(d) *Prapatti* (self-surrender).

(e) *Bhakti* (devotion).

Karma is the indirect means of liberation because it gives rise to knowledge. Before the attainment of *vidyā* (knowledge) performance of action is essential.[57]

Jñāna is the second means. Only "the fire of wisdom reduces action to ashes".[58] The work is destroyed by knowledge.[59] The works are propaedeutic to *jñāna*. The fruit of *karma* is limited and surpassable but the fruit of *jñāna* is not limited. The soul desirous of emancipation should perform only the obligatory and occasional duties. Moreover, the continuous practice of *śravaṇa, manana* and *nididhyāsana* results in the realization of *Brahman*. He must listen to the instruction of the teachers, who have direct vision of truth. *Śravaṇa* generates the intuition of *Brahman*. *Manana* destroys doubts and illusions. It organizes our thought in such a way that it

---

[55] (a) V.P.S. IV.4.20.

(b) "He is the cause, the Lord of the Lord of causes." – Śve.U. VI.9

(c) "The controller of all, the ruler of all." – Bṛ.U. IV.4.22

[56] V.P.S. IV.4.15.

[57] Ibid. III.4.9.

[58] *Gītā* IV.37.

[59] V.P.S. III.4.16.

facilitates a favourable mental approach towards the knowledge of truth imparted by the teacher. The third stage is of *nididhyāsana* – it marshalls the inner psychical processes by repeated meditation. Thus one is totally convinced about the truths communicated by the teacher. The inefficacy of *karma* leads to an urge for the blissful knowledge of *Brahman*. *Śravaṇa*, *manana* and *nididhyāsana* are the means towards this end. When *jīva* realizes itself to be a part and parcel of *Brahman*, it abnegates the performance of actions and remains unaffected by them. It "lives in eternal bliss in devotional contemplation of God". It feels to be one with God. It abides in God as part of its energy. Its *sañcita*, *kriyamāṇa* and *ārabdha karma*s are destroyed, only *prārabdha* remains as the *prārabdha karma*s cannot be exhausted until their fruits are reaped.

Knowledge is produced by *karma* but that very knowledge destroys *karma*. *Karma* does not necessarily lead to salvation; it sometimes gives rise to merit that is heaven only. In fact, the spirit behind the performance of *karma* determines the end. Desireless performance of *karma* leads to salvation, but if attainment of heaven is the aim of *karma*, he goes to heaven and is born again.[60]

For the rise of knowledge the inner control of the sense is also incumbent.[61] He must be calm and self-controlled. He must bear "childlike simplicity",[62] unostentatiousness, profound thoughtfulness and the gift of silence. There are three sets of auxiliaries (*sahakārī*s) to knowledge – (a) performance of duties disinterestedly, (b) possession of self-control, and (c) possession of simple-heartedness, deep learning and ardent thoughtfulness. *Vidyā* is not necessarily dependent on *karma*. One can attain knowledge even without the help of *karma*. According to Nimbārka, renunciation of household duties is not an essential prerequisite from salvation. The only thing required is he should not lapse from his vow. There cannot be emancipation without the saving knowledge.

Pure food is necessary for *jñāna* for it leads to inner sense

---

60 V.P.S. III.4.32-34.

61 *vidyāṅgatayā śamādi-vidheḥ teṣāmavaśyaṇuṣṭheyatvāt* | – V.P.S. III.4.27

62 V.P.S. III.4.46.

(*sattva*) which again leads to the *dhruvā smṛti* (love for God).[63] Muttering of *mantra* purifies the inner self, which leads to true knowledge. *Maunavrata* (wow of silence) is also helpful for the attainment of true knowledge.

Upāsanā is the third means to attain liberation. A man desirous of salvation must meditate upon the essential nature of his own self, upon God as his own self[64] (*abhedopāsanā*). He is related to Him as *aṁśa* and *aṁśī*. *Gītā* (X.20) too says that the Lord is seated in the heart of all beings. Meditation should be done in the sitting posture. Mind can be firm only in this posture. He should meditate in a solitary place. This practice should be continued till the highest aim is achieved. Like knowledge, meditation too brings about the annihilation of all *karmas* leading to salvation.[65] Evil deeds do not cling to him as water does not cling to the lotus leaf.[66] All the three types of meditation are based on the real knowledge of the Lord. The first kind of meditation on the Lord as the self is based on the knowledge of God and soul and their relation. The second kind of meditation on God as the inner controller of the material world is based on the real knowledge of God and the matter. The third kind of meditation on the Lord Himself is based on the knowledge of essential nature of *Brahman*. *Brahma-jñāna* consists in influencing meditation on the nature of God and the participation in Him as His constituent.

Prapatti means a complete resignation or self-surrender to God. It is also an effective means of liberation. It consists in the total surrender in the hand of God leaving all the feelings of narrow individuality, relinquishing all other *sādhanas*. He feels utter helplessness and insignificance. He takes refuge in Him with all his mind and body. The Lord bestows all His blessings on those who take refuge in Him. He protects them against all pains and aflictions. The gate of self-surrender is open to all whether he is

---

63 *āhāra-śuddhau sattva-śuddhiḥ sattva-śuddau dhruvā smṛtiḥ* ।
– Chā.U. VII.26.2

64 *mumukṣunā paramapuruṣaḥ svasyātmatvena dhyeyaḥ* । – V.P.S. IV.1.3

65 V.P.S. III.2.25.

66 Chā.U. IV.14.3.

high or low, learned or ignorant, brāhmaṇa or śūdra. This is not the state of utter inactivity or apathy. He does all that to please God. Meditation directly generates intuition of *Brahman*.

Prapatti or *śaraṇāgati* is of two kinds – (a) surrender to God, and (b) surrender to *guru*. *Guru* is the intermediary link between the divotee and the Lord. He leads the devotee to the Lord.

Bhakti is the chief source of realizing godliness. It is not meditation (*upāsanā*) but love and devotion.[67] Meditation and devotion mutually involve each other. It involves knowledge of the Supreme Reality, the nature of soul and divine grace. Nimbārka was the first Vaiṣṇava philosopher, who has insisted on *mādhurya-pradhāna bhakti* (devotion based on the love of God's sweetness) in the place of *aiśvarya-pradhāna bhakti* (devotion caused by reverence for His greatness). Rāmānuja and Madhva support the second type of *bhakti*. In the domain of philosophy, Nimbārka has made his own place for the happy reconciliation of *bheda* and *abheda*. In the field of religion also he leaves his mark for his striking balance between a rigid intellectualism of Advaitavāda which decries personal tie with *Brahman* and the bare emotionalism of *bhakti* religion. In the ethical domain also he maintains the same balance by taking into consideration various types of human personalities.

Bhakti is the supreme *sādhana*. It can be obtained only through the grace of God. *Bhagvatkṛpā* (the Divine grace) generates in one the feeling of utter humility which leads to devotion. It is not the blind and irrational feeling, rather it is rational in its nature and is based on the knowledge of the individual, the world and God. It is unceasing love of God.

There are two kinds of *bhakti*: *parā* and *aparā* or *sādhana-rūpikā*. *Parā bhakti* is generated in the devotee by the grace of God. A man, who conscientiously performs his duty, pleases the Lord and gains in return. His favour which makes him realize his utter worthlessness and majesty of God generating in him a special love for Him. *Aparā bhakti* is gained through meritorious *sādhanā* like penance, charity and meditation. Devotion as an end is of the

[67] *prema-viśeṣa-lakṣaṇā* | – *Daśaślokī* 9

nature of intense love for God. It is "interrupted mental mode", undeviating love for God. Nimbārka prefers devotion nurtured by knowledge more than pure devotion. Wise devotee is more dear to Him.

When the fetters of *karma* are cast off, all the doubts are dispelled and *jīva* realizes its true nature as different as well as non-different from God and the true nature of *paramātman*. He knows Him to be all in all, to be the universe only by His grace. Unaided efforts on the part of the devotee is of no avail unless God chooses to help him. He may choose whichever path he likes – knowledge, meditation and self-surrender – he must evoke *bhagavadānugraha*. He has to depend on Him at every stage. It is the grace of God which evokes him to seek liberation and it is the grace of God that makes him free in the end. His dependence on *sādhana*s for the bestowal of His grace in no way snatches away His independence.

There are five auxiliaries (*sahakārī*s) to *sādhana*s for liberation:

(a) Reverence (*śraddhā*), means reverently accepting the truths of scriptures and *guru-vacana* (preceptor's saying).

(b) Straightforwardness (*ārjava*), means perfect harmony between mind, speech and body (*manasā*, *vācā* and *karmaṇā*). He should speak what he thinks and should do what he speaks.

(c) Faith (*viśvāsa*), means the unshaken belief in Lord and His protection.

(d) Company of good (*sat-saṅga*), means to be in the company of good persons, who are endowed with knowledge, detachment and devotion.

(e) Detachment (*virāga*), means absence of *rāga* and *dveṣa*, indifference to both pleasing and painful aspects of life.

Devotion accompanies all the five *sādhana*s, which are not mutually exclusive rather they involve each other. Nimbārka has never mentioned definitely, which of these *sādhana*s is the best. Each of them may lead to salvation in its own way. He sometimes mentions that *Brahman* is to be realized through *vidyā*,[68] sometimes

[68] *brahmaprāptiḥ vidhyātaḥ* I – V.P.S. III.4.1

Brahman realization is said to be possible through meditation.[69] He says at some other place that there is no way to salvation except surrender to the lotus feet of God.[70] And this surrender is possible only in the case of devout love for Him. He is to be realized through exclusive devotion.[71]

Thus, according to Nimbārka, any of these *sādhana*s may lead to *mukti* either by itself or in conjunction with each other. A *mumukṣu* can resort to any of these according to his capability. If one is to follow all the *sādhana*s the order will be the following – *karma* makes him fit for knowledge, *jñāna* generates *bhakti* which leads to meditation, meditation leads to *prapatti*, *prapatti* generates *bhakti* which induces the grace of God which brings about final emancipation.

Nimbārka believes only in instantaneous liberation (*sadyo-mokṣa*) and not into in gradual liberation (*kramika mokṣa*) like Śaṅkara, etc. the word *jīvanmukti* has no meaning to convey. To claim liberation even when the *prārabdha karma* is not exhausted by its *bhoga* is deceptive. In realization we constantly think of the Lord as in nescience we constantly think of the world. It is the realization of the true nature of the Lord (*bhagavad-bhāvāpatti*), the manifestation of consciousness and this is to be attained only at the fall of the body.

Thus, liberation means the realization of the nature of God possessed of infinite knowledge and bliss after the complete destruction of nescience. It is real and not merely phenomenal. The liberated soul exists in Him as His distinct energy and may be employed by Him for His purpose. He is the same as *Brahman* as well as not the same.

Śuddhādvaita of Vallabhācārya

Vallabhācārya is the protagonist of the Śuddhādvaita (pure non-dualistic) Vedānta. The compound Śuddhādvaita can be parted in two ways: *śuddhayoḥ advaitam* and *śuddham ca tad advaitam*. The

[69] Ibid. III.2.24-25.

[70] *Daśaślokī* 8.

[71] (a) V.P.S. III.2.24; (b) *Gītā* XI.54.

first interpretation suggests that soul and the world are one with *Brahman*. And the second interpretation also means in similar vein the non-duality of *Brahman* undefiled by *māyā*. Gosvami Giridhara explains the term *śuddha* as:

> *māyā-sambandha-rahitaṁ śuddham ityucatebudhaiḥ* ।
> *kāry-kāraṇa-rūpaṁ hi śuddham brahma na māyikam* ॥
> – *Śuddhādvaita-mārtaṇḍa* 28

And this is the manifestation of *Brahman* – *brahmaiva tadi daṁ tathā*. In the spirit of *Muṇḍaka Upaniṣad* (II.2.11), Vallabha also says that *Brahman* alone is in front of us, behind us, to the right and left of us and underneath us. The whole universe is the permeation of *Brahman*. All that is nothing but the self, nothing other than *Brahman*.[72] To accept *māyā* as the explanatory principle for world creation means to accept a second to *Brahman*. And according to Vallabha, *Brahman* needs no auxiliary for creation. He is of the nature of both the cause and the effect, both the creator of the universe and the universe itself.[73] There is nothing like real difference, everything is an explicit or analytical form of the Lord which was implicit in *Brahman* before creation. *Brahman* permeates everything through the manifestation of His qualities of existence, etc.[74] He is real and there is no other reality besides Him, no non-Being besides the Being.

He is *Saccidānanda*, the Absolute Being, Knowledge and Bliss which are ever present in Him in their fullness. In the world only the *sat* aspect of *Saccidānanda* is rendered perceptible through the will of the Lord; whereas in *jīva* both the *sat* and *cit* aspects are rendered manifest, the bliss aspect remains hidden; but in Him, all the three aspects – *sat*, *cit* and *ānanda* – are manifest.

God, according to Vallabhācārya, is *Puruṣottama*, the perfect person. He is no other than Lord Kr̥ṣṇa.[75] He is God in His fullness.

---

[72] *ātmaiva tad idaṁ sarvaṁ brahmaiva tad idaṁ taṭhā* । – Sarvanirṇaya chapter of *Tattvārtha-dīpa-nibandha*

[73] *Aṇubhāṣya* I.1.4.

[74] *asti-bhāti-priyatvenasaccidānanda-rūpeṇānvayāt* । – *Aṇubhāṣya* 1.1.3

[75] *paraṁ brahma tu kr̥ṣṇo hi* । – *Tattvārtha-dīpa-nibandha* 1.4.13 and also in *Siddāntamuktāvalī* 3

Ānanda is His chief quality, *sat* and *cit* serve only as foundation for His Bliss.

The distinction between *Para* and *Apara-Brahman* is not acceptable to Vallabha. *Brahman* is both *saguṇa* and *nirguṇa*. Vallabha shows full faith in scripture and that is the final authority for the existence of God. Such scriptures never speak in favour of *Saguṇa-Brahman* as distinct from *Nirguṇa-Brahman*. Even Bādarāyaṇa, in the opinion of Vallabha, has never advocated his concept in any of his *sūtras*. This fact is evident from the absence of any *sūtra* quoted by Śaṅkara in support of his view. Vallabha is emphatic on the point that Bādarāyaṇa refers to one and same *Brahman*. He possesses all wonderful powers.[76] He is never *nirviśeṣa*. M.T. Telivala says:

> The negation of negative Śrutis refers not to the divine attributes described of *Brahman* in the Upaniṣads, but to the *laukika* or *prākṛta* or *iyattāvācaka* ones. This seems to be the *yukti* to explain to those who cannot see their way to accept *Brahman* as possessed of even contrary attributes on the authority of the Vedic texts.
>
> – Mishra 1980: 68

The scriptural statement that He is incomprehensible implies the richness of His qualities and it does not refer to His being absolutely devoid of attributes.

According to Vallabha, *sūtrakāra* refers to *Brahman* as *sarvaśaktyupeta* thus he is *kartṛ*[77] and *bhoktṛ*, the agent and enjoyer both. According to him, the *kriyā śakti* (power of action) of *Brahman* is described in the Upaniṣads. But *Brahman* is associated with both *kriyā* and *jñāna* as in *Gītā* and *Bhāgavata*. Almost all the theists believe in *Brahman* on the grounds – (a) it will incur duality, (b) it will make *Brahman* imperfect (*apūrṇa*), (c) it will prove *Brahman* to be changeable (*vikṛti-doṣa*), and (d) finally it will deprive *Brahman* of its essential characteristic (*samatā*). The existence of evil with the perfect knowledge of *Brahman* will be inexplicable. To meet such objections Śaṅkara denies any activity in *Brahman* (as *nirguṇa*). According to him, all the activities are falsely superimposed on

---

[76] *sarvopetā ca taddarśanāt* | – B.S. II.1.30

[77] *kartā kārayitā 'haririti* | – *Aṇubhāṣya* I.1.3

Brahman through *māyā*. But according to Vallabha, the nature of *Brahman* is such that in the infinite diversity perfect non-duality is ever present. It expresses itself in diversity through its own ever-multiplying inherent power without undergoing change within itself. It is self-creation (*ātma-sṛṣṭi*).[78] There is no-duality between *śakti* and *śaktimān*, *dharma* and *dharmī*, *aṁśa* and *aṁśī*. *Āpta-kāma Brahman* works for its own *līlā*. The nature of *Brahman* is such that it acts naturally and yet it is free from the faults arising out of its *kartṛtva*. He is an independent *kartā* and not a *māyā*-environed *Īśvara*. Neither *jaḍa* of Sāṁkhya nor *māyā* of Śaṅkara nor *cidācidviśiṣṭa-śarīra* of Rāmānuja can be independent *kartā* as *kartṛtva* is possible in intelligent beings only. *Brahman* alone is the independent *kartṛ*. According to Vallabha, *kartṛtva* is as real an attribute of *Brahman* as truth (*satya*) is.

The Supreme *Brahman* is not only *kartṛ*, he is *bhoktṛ* (the enjoyer) also. But it is not *bhoktṛ* in the ordinary sense. Its *bhoktṛtva* is as divine as its *kartṛtva*, thus "*brahmatva* of *Brahman* remains as it is".

As *Brahman* is everything, even contradiction is *Brahman*. Contradiction (*virodha*) as such can rightly be said to be reconciled if both sorts of scriptural passage are given their due equally. The *niṣedha* should have reference to what we see and not to the qualities of *Brahman*. Contradictions in *Brahman* (from the worldly standpoint) do not speak of any *dūṣaṇam* (defect) rather they are *bhūṣaṇam* (ornament) because they underline the unfathomable majesty of God which is not to be grasped by reasoning unaided by devotion and Divine grace. The attributes seem to be contradictory because our limited reason is not able to understand their harmony in the Lord. There is harmonious blending of these attributes in the Lord who is perfectly simple. He is *viruddhadharmāśraya*. He is smaller than the smallest, greater than the greatest. He is one as well as many. He is the independent doer. He is *antaryāmī*, He is *aṅguṣṭha mātra* as well as *vaiśvānara*, He is *ānandarūpa*.[79] He is beyond *prakṛti* and its *guṇas*. The *nirguṇa* Śrutis do not deny the divine attributes of *Brahman*. Their genuine significance consists

---

[78] B.S. I.4.26.

[79] *ānandamayo 'bhyasat* – B.S. I.11

in denying the ordinary attributes only. *Brahman* develops itself into *jaḍa-jīvātmaka* universe without undergoing the least change and without ceasing to be *niravayava*.

Among His attributes, the most important ones are six, glory (*aiśvaryai*), power (*vīrya*), good repute (*yaśa*), power to attract other towards himself (*śrī*), knowledge (*jñāna*) and *virāgya* (detachment from the world). Kṛṣṇa has innumerable other divine powers like *puṣṭi, kānti, kīrti, ilā, ūrjā* and *tuṣṭi*.

Brahman is both the inherent (*samavāyin*) and efficient (*nimitta*) causes of the world. The substance and its attributes, the cause and its effect are identical. Vallabha rejects the relation of *samavāya* and explains it as *tādātmya*. The substance really appears as its attributes, the cause as its effect. Material (*upādāna*) cause really means inherent cause. God is not only the cause of world, He is the world itself. He, assuming the form of *akṣara*, creates the world. In the form of *akṣara* only that much of the divine bliss is manifested which is needed for the full manifestation of creation. It is an abode of the Lord. It represents the spiritual (*ādhyātmika*) aspect of the Lord while Puruṣottama Kṛṣṇa represents the celestial or fully divine (*ādhidaivika*) form of *Brahman*. He is dynamic. He wants to share His *rasa* with others, for this He incarnates Himself as a human being.

He is the inner controller (*antaryāmī*) of all alike. He controls from within not only the movement of the earth and planets but the activities of all living beings. He lives in the heart of all. He is transcendent as well because the whole of *Brahman* is not exhausted in the world. He is the warp and woof of all that exist. Vallabha is in no way a pantheist which confounds God with the world. His emphasis on the personality of the Lord and His transcendence holds sufficient evidence against the charge of pantheism. He never believes in the reality of the nature to the extent of its being God. Nature is always transient. M.C. Parekh (1969: 134) says:

> His Brahmavāda is only a vestibule to his religious teaching which is wholly centred in God, the supreme person and whatever pantheistic elements there may be in his philosophy, they have never been introduced so far in the practical life of his followers.

There is no difference (*bheda*) either homogeneous (*sajātīya*) or heterogeneous (*vijātīya*) or *svagata* in God. All the three forms – *jagat, jīva* and *antaryāmī* – are essentially identical with the Lord. He runs through all these. The world is His *līlā*, a divine sport. Manifestation (*āvirbhāva*) and concealment (*tirobhāva*) are said to be the inherent causal potencies of God which give rise to variety (*vaicitrya*). Viṭṭhalanātha explains *āvirbhāva* as "fitness for or capability of becoming an object of experience" and *tirobhāva* as "capability of not becoming an object of experience".[80] *Jīva* and *antaryāmī* represent the essential aspects of God in greater or lesser quantity – "their intimate reality never coming into being nor ceasing to be". Being means manifestation of certain aspects through the Divine will. Here the implicit becomes explicit, the homogeneous becomes heterogeneous. Non-being means the lapse of explicit into the implicit, *āvirbhāva* stands for *prākaṭya* (manifestation) and not *utpatti* (creation) whereas *tirobhāva* stands for absorption (*samāveśa*) and not dissolution (*pralaya*).

Brahman has four forms: Kṛṣṇa; *akṣara,* which is twofold; and the inner controller (*antaryāmī*). Kṛṣṇa is the highest *Brahman*. He is all-pervading. He is endowed with all auspicious qualities. He is the *Puruṣottama* of *Gītā*. He is God in His first and primordial self (*kṛṣṇastu bhagavān svayaṁ*) and not an incarnation.

In *akṣara,* the bliss is partially manifested. He is called *bṛhat*. The world originates from this only.

Following the spirit of Bhāgavata, Vallabha too believes in the manifestation of the Lord in different incarnations in order to punish the evil and prize the good. The incarnations differ in accordance with the use of his power of action or knowledge. The incarnation with his power of knowledge as Vyāsa or Dattātreya, etc. destroys inner suffering while incarnation with his power of action as Fish or Tortosie destroys the outward suffering. The deities are His *vibhūti*s or *aṁśa*s. Worship of the deities is fruitful but the Supreme Bliss is to be attained by the worship of Kṛṣṇa only. The *akṣara* transforms itself into many gods like Brahmā,

---

[80] *aṇubhavaviṣayatva-yogyatā āvirbhāvaḥ, tadviṣayatvā-yogyatā tirobhāvaḥ* ।
– *Vidvan-maṇḍanam*, p. 44

Viṣṇu and Rudra, who creates, sustains and destroys respectively. *Antaryāmī* is the incarnation of Viṣṇu. The *āveśāvatāra* is witnessed in living persons like Nārada.

Para-Brahman, *akṣara* and *antaryāmī* stand for the *ādhidaivika* (divine), *ādhyātmika* (spiritual) and *ādhibhautika* (elemental) conditions of *Brahman* who assumes different forms and still is unchanged. Mrudula Marfatia (1967: 42) says:

> Vallahba is looking for an Absolute that fulfils and explains not only the truth-seeking intellectual thirst of man, but also the inmost craving of man's heart that finds a fitting consummation in a loving self-surrender to God.

Brahmavāda of Vallabha was formulated mainly in antagonism to the Māyāvāda of Śaṅkara. His philosophy in general is based on *Brahmasūtra* but his conception of God is close to the teachings of Bhāgavata. His Brahmavāda is not an independent system of philosophy like that of Plato, Aristotle, Kant, Hegel or Spinoza. It creates an atmosphere of Divine love, serves as a background for the way of life and *mukti*.

THE NATURE OF SOUL AND ITS BONDAGE

The individual souls are eternal though atomic in size. For Madhva, soul is essentially different from God though it is His dependent part. For Nimbārka, soul is dependent on God, supported by God and in this sense it is different from God but at the same time it is part and parcel of *Brahman*. Its difference from *Brahman* is as important as its unity. But for Vallabha soul is identical with God but appears as different because of manifestation only of certain divine aspects while others remain obscured. They are related to *Brahman* as parts to a whole. Consciousness and bliss constitute His intrinsic nature hence they are same as *Brahman* but ordinarily bliss remains shrouded in them that is why they are in bondage. The individual soul is not *Brahman* clouded by *avidyā* but is itself *Brahman* with bliss aspect rendered imperceptible. The soul is a conscious reality, a part of *Brahman*, and not merely phenomenal. It comes out of very *svarūpa* of God, it is self-creation (*ātma-sr̥ṣṭi*) of the Lord. The Lord wished to be many and thus emerged innumerable *jīva*s out of His *akṣara* form like the sparks flying from the blazing fire.[81] They are neither caused nor created by any supernatural agency; they are the *aṁśa*s of the Lord Himself.

Absence of *utpatti* leads to the eternality of souls (*nityatva*). Birth and death are applied only to body.[82] The presence of *jīva* is felt because of its association with the body.

Jīva is intelligent, active and atomic in size. It is not *vibhu* (all-pervading) as Śaṅkara thinks. The atomic *jīva* itself resumes all-pervasiveness when its bliss aspect is manifested fully in it. The objection that *caitanya* of atomic *jīvātman* cannot be *sarva-śarīra-vyāpī* does not hold true. Vallabha cites the example of sandalwood which, though applied to one part of body, produces coolness in the whole body. Again, on the analogy of the diamond or the lamp the spread of *caitanya* all over body is explained. As the light of diamond or lamp spreads over a wider space than is occupied by it, *jīvātman* resides in heart still it permeats the whole body. Another objection is that if *jīvātman* resides in the heart and is atomic in size his consciousness will not be *sarva-śarīra-vyāpī*. This objection is met on the analogy of *gandha*. *Jīvātman* is called *vibhu* only to declare his Brahmanhood. *Jīva* is identified with *Brahman* only because the qualities of *Brahman* form its essence and make it different from the non-sentient world.

Śaṅkara advocates the *vibhutva* of *ātman* on the ground of its non-*utpatti* (eternity of the human soul). But Vallabha asserts that the denial of *utpatti* does not conclusively prove the *vibhutva* of *Jīvātman*. It can't be asserted that *jīva* is *Brahman* and hence *vibhu* just because it is eternal (*anādi*). This argument is detrimental for his concept of *avidyā* which is also *anādi* according to Śaṅkarācārya. If eternity is the criterion of *brahmatva, avidyā* is also *Brahman*. If *anādi jīva* is *vibhu, avidyā* too is *vibhu*. And this conclusion will never be acceptable to Śaṅkara. The *aṁśa, jīvātman,* is *ananya* with *Brahman, viśeṣaṇa* is *ananya* with *viśeṣya Brahman,* thus the knowledge of *Brahman* includes knowledge of *jīva*. Just as the crown prince becomes king, *jīva* becomes *Brahman* and it

[81] Aṇu.B. II.3.18.

[82] Ibid. II.3.16.

experiences *vibhutva* and all the *dharmas* of *Brahman* in spite of its *aṇutva*. Once this Brahmanhood of *jīvātman* becomes manifest it continues to experience *brahmatva* as well as *vibhutva* for ever. "Soul knowing *brahman* becomes *tādṛk* not *tat*…" *vibhutva* is latent in *jīva*.

According to Śaṅkara, *kartṛtva* is a product of ignorance, in fact, the human soul is *akartā* (inactive). But according to Vallabha, *jīvātman* is both *kartā* and *bhoktā*. As the carpenter having made the chariot, rides in it, *jīvātman* does something and enjoys it. *Kartṛtva* is in no way *duḥkha-rūpa* (unpleasant). There is *svābhāvika kartṛtva* (natural doership) in *jīva*. Śaṅkara puts the following arguments in his favour:

(i) If *kartṛtva* is *svābhāvika*, *jīva* will never be free from doership like fire which is never free from heat,

(ii) *kartṛtva* is *duḥkha-rūpa*,

(iii) liberation bestows on *nitya-śuddha-buddha-mukta* soul, and

(iv) some Śrutis teach *jīva*'s *kartṛtva* as product of ignorance.

None of the arguments is acceptable to Vallabha. If individual soul's doership is declared to be *Brahman*'s, there seems to be no valid objection. Even *Gītā* says that *jīva* has to be *kartā* with *Brahman* by his side. Misery is caused by egoity and not by doership of *jīva*. Bādarāyaṇa advocates the same in *parāttu tacchruteḥ* (B.S. II.3.41), human activity has its source in *Brahman*. *Brahman* manifests Himself in *jaḍa* and *jīva* for the sake of *līlā* and still remaining transcendent, determines the activities of His *aṁśa*, *jīvas*. As *aṁśa*, *jīvas* are *ananya* with *Brahman*. They have to play their allotted role. When they forget that their *kartṛtva* is *Brahman*'s they invite misery. *Brahman* is the source of all activities. *Jīvātman*'s *kartṛtva* is not a product of *upādhi* (nescience).

Jīva is *aṁśa* of *Brahman* as spark is of fire, it is *bhinnābhinna*. But Śaṅkara says that *aṁśa* should be taken in the sense of *aṁśatva*. Bhāskara interprets *aṁśa* as *upādhyāvacchinna ananya-bhūta*. Rāmānuja takes the word in the sense of *viśiṣṭa-vastvekadeśa*. *Brahman* is *viśeṣya* and *jīva* is *viśeṣaṇa*. Nimbārka interprets *aṁśa* as *śakti*. *Jīva* is *aśakti* of *Brahman*. According to Madhva, *aṁśas* are different like sons and others. All theses Vedāntists accept difference between *Brahman* and *jīva* to be natural but Vallabha takes this difference to be *aicchika*. *Jīva* is *aṁśa* of *Brahman*, still *Brahman* is *adhika*, greater than *jīva*.

Jīva, according to Vallabha, is a part of the Lord and not a reflection (*pratibimba*) because "a thing which permeates another thing cannot cast its reflection on that thing".

Jīva emerges out of *Brahman* like the ring from gold, or like the pot from clay. Antagonists of Vallabha raise the objection that if *jīva* is a part of *Brahman*, how can it miss one of the inherent qualities of *Brahman* – bliss. To this Vallabha's answer is: *ānanda* is only suppressed in *jīva* like the potential masculine feature in a male child. Owing to this suppression (*tirobhāva*) of the bliss in *jīva*, *jīva* does not possess any of the six divine qualities, i.e. sovereignty (*aiśvarya*), valour (*vīrya*), fame (*yaśa*), splendour (*śrī*), knowledge (*jñāna*) and detachment (*vairāgya*). Because of suppression, *jīva* turns away from its true nature of reality and involves itself into the cycle of birth and death. It acquires these qualities along with bliss by the grace of God only. The atomic *jīva* resumes all-pervasiveness when bliss is fully manifested in it, still the individual distinction is not completely lost in case of *jīva*s. R.G. Bhandarkar (1965: 78) says:

> The individual soul is not a form of the supreme soul altered by a third thing being involved in it, such as the *māyā* (illusive power), but is itself the same substance as the supreme soul with one attribute rendered imperceptible. The relation between the two is thus that of identity (Advaita), both being in the pristine unchanged form, i.e. identity of untransformed souls (Śuddhādvaita).

Radhakrishnan (1953, vol. II: 758) says:

> Vallabha, on the one hand, gives us something like Schelling's neutrum, where the differences are abolished, while Rāmānuja's view is more like Hegel's.

Vallabha explains the *mahāvākya*s *sarvaṁ khalvidam brahma* (all this is *Brahman*) and *tat tvam asi* (that thou art) in literal sense and not only in figurative sense. There is no complete identity between *jīva* and *Brahman*. It is one with *Brahman* but appears as different on account of its limited manifestation and obscuration of divine aspects. *Jīva* is not phenomenally real. The world and *jīva* as manifestation of *Brahman* are as real *Brahman*. The non-duality is established on the basis of the theory of part-whole-oneness. It is non-difference which admits difference (*bheda-sahiṣṇu abheda*). The difference is *jīva*'s own making. The individual self is not the Supreme, clouded by *avidyā*, but is itself *Brahman* with one attribute rendered imperceptible.

Vallabha puts three sets of classification for *jīva*s – (i) *puṣṭi, maryādā* and *pravāha jīvas*; (ii) *śuddha, saṁsārī* and *mukta jīvas*; and (iii) *ajña, durajña* and *sambaddha jīva*s.

*Jīva*s are free (*mukta*) and *baddha* (conditioned). The free *jīva*s are of two types – *jīvanmukta* and *videhamukta*. Among conditioned *jīvas*, some are divine (*daivī*) and some are demonic (*asura*). The divine *jīva*s get liberation, the demonic are bound to this world. The divine *jīva*s are again divided into *maryādā* and *puṣṭi jīva*s. *Maryāda jīva* believes in human endeavour apart from the Divine grace while *puṣṭi jīva*s are wholly dependent on God's grace. *Puṣṭi jīva* may again be classified under two heads: (a) *śuddha* (pure), and (b) *miśra* (mixed). Pure *jīva*s partake of the bliss of Kṛṣṇa in Goloka. They work according to the will of God. They are the best type of devotees. Mixed types of *puṣṭi jīva*s are *puṣṭi-puṣṭi, maryādā-puṣṭi* and *pravāha-puṣṭi*. Such *jīva*s are sent to the world by the Lord for some sort of punishment. *Puṣṭi-puṣṭi jīva*s possess the knowledge of Lord as well as they are aware of their own mistakes, *maryādā-puṣṭi jīva* knowns only the attributes of the Lord while *pravāha-puṣṭi jīva* takes to worship in order to fulfil its own desires. Yet these mixed *jīva*s may prove their eligibility for the pure *jīva*s. *Maryādā jīva*s are ordinary *jīva*s since in them there is a blending of Divine and human aspects. The *cit* aspect predominates in them. *Parvāha jīva*s are devoid of the Divine grace. They contain chiefly the *sat* aspect in them. They attain the state devoid of joy and knowledge (*andhaṁ tamaḥ*). *Pravāha* soul seems to overlap another set of division, i.e. of *asura jīvas*. These are classified under two heads: (a) uninformed (*ajña*s), and (b) malinformed (*durajña*s). *Ajña*s are misled temporarily but they come back to right path soon because the possibility of liberation has not finally been precluded for them. But *durajña*s are doomed for ever to eternal darkness. There is one more type of *jīva* referred by Vallahba, viz. *sambandhī* (intermediary) souls who sometimes do good, sometimes bad.

Vallabha sacrifices the freedom and dignity of human endeavour on the altar of "Divine wish". To prove the supremacy of the Divine Will, Vallabha makes everything dependent on God. The doctrine of *karma* carries out only the Divine dictates.

THE NATURE OF THE WORLD

The world, according of Vallabha, is the translation of *Brahman*'s innate desire for self-expression. "*Brahman* desired to be many[83] and manifested Himself in *jīva* and *jagat*." The world is *brahmātmaka* (of the nature of *Brahman*). Both for its creation and sustenance, the world is dependent on the will of *Brahman*. Thus it is as real as *Brahman* Himself. In fact, the effect is not different from its cause, like the gold ornaments and gold. Thus the world is essentially identical with *Brahman* though only *sat* aspect of *Brahman* is manifested in it. It is deprived of conscious and bliss aspects of *Brahman*. All the three forms – *jagat*, *jīva* and *antaryāmī* – are identical with *Brahman* while *jīva*s are more similar to Him (*sajātīya*), the world is *vijātīya* to Him. *Antaryāmī* is inside Him (*svagata*).

This world is the *kṛti* or *pariṇāma* of *Brahman*. *Brahman* is both the efficient and material causes of the world. Rāmānuja accepts *cidācidviśiṣṭa Brahman* as *upādāna*. Nimbārka accepts *Brahman*'s *śakti* as *upādāna* and Madhva accepts *prakṛti* as *upādāna*. Śaṅkara delegates *Brahman*'s *upādāna* to *avidyā*, whereas Vallabha accepts *Brahman* as both the *upādāna* (material) and *nimitta* (efficient) causes of the world. *Brahman*, according to Vallabha, is not exhausted in the world like the Absolute of Spinoza, He exists separately also. In one way *Brahman* is the material cause of the world, in another way He is pure and object of devotion. The rudiments of the material and the spiritual world associated with God as His characteristics (Rāmānuja) or as His body (Nimbārka) or as His power (Bhāskara), only undergo development, He Himself remaining pure.

---

[83] Bṛ.U. I.4.3.

Vallabha's view is neither Vivartavāda nor Pariṇāmavāda. It is *avikṛta* Pariṇāmavāda. The universe is not merely an appearance, but a reality. At the same time it is not a *pariṇāma* for this manifestation does not bring any transformation in the Lord. Thus it is called *avikṛta* Pariṇāmavāda. The universe is a natural emanation from Him. It is an effect of *Brahman* (*brahmakārya*) thus it is neither an illusory appearance nor is it different from *Brahman* in essence. It is in truth *Brahman*. *Avikṛta* Pariṇāmavāda of Vallabha turns out of court the Vivartavāda of Śaṅkara as well as Pariṇāmavāda of Sāṁkhya. The emanation of *Brahman* into the world is neither real like change of milk into curd nor unreal like change of rope into snake. After His transformation into the world also He is immutable and unmodified. Vallabha's is the theory of Immutable Transformation. God does not lose His essence even if He is moulded into different ornaments. His qualities of *sat*, *cit* and *ānanda* are manifested in *jīva*, *jagat* and *antaryāmī* without effecting any change in Him. The defects of change cling only to the earthly material cause and not to *Brahman*. Vallabha is well aware of the possible objection that "the real changing pots cannot be made of unchanging clay". As answer to this objection he says that "difference and changes are only partial–successive manifestation of the Immutable Absolute: yet that Absolute has no separable layers internally and externally, none else to manifest them to".

Vallabha distinguishes between *jagat* or *prapañca* and *saṁsāra*. *Jagat* is the real manifestation of *Brahman*, it never ceases to exist. The world cannot be unreal as it is being perceived by everybody. The world has been called *māyika* (a product of nescience) in the Purāṇas, etc. only to produce an attitude of renunciation. *Saṁsāra* may cease to exist but not *jagat* as it is a manifestation of the Lord. *Saṁsāra* is imagined by soul on account of ignorance. It is subjective and fictitious. The bliss aspect is obscured in *jīva;* consequently the six divine qualities (sovereignty, valour, fame, splendour, knowledge and detachment) are veiled in *jīva*s and misery, poverty and sorrow take their place. The obscuration of first four divine qualities results in *jīva*'s entanglement in *saṁsāra* while the concealment of the last two qualities brings perverted notion of reality. The ignorance is fivefold: (a) *ajñāna* of the real nature of soul, (b) false identification with the body, (c) with the senses, (d) with the vital breath, and (e) with the internal organ. *Jīva* is caught in the clutches of *saṁsāra* due to this fivefold ignorance. He is confused under the spell of *avidyā* and is unable to perceive the things in their right perspectives. He is inflected by the perversity of misconception. Thus the perception of ignorant *jīva* is unreal and not the world itself. As a person in a moving vehicle feels as if the objects he is passing through are moving but reality is something else, similarly we perceive this world ignorantly to be unreal; in fact it is nothing but *Brahman*. *Jagat* is the *ādhidaivika* (empirical) form of *Brahman*. The wrong perception of the world is unreal and not the world itself. *Saṁsāra* comes to end when *jīva* by means of devotion casts off the veil of ignorance but not the *jagat*. *Jagat* can be brought to end only if the Lord wishes it to be so. *Brahman* assumes the form of *akṣara* to manifest Himself in the world.

The world is a stage for Divine *līlā* (sport). God is engaged in such sports simply on His own accord. *Āvirbhāva* (manifestation) and *tirobhāva* (concealment) are the inherent causal potencies in *Brahman* which give rise to manifoldness (*vaicitrya*). Just as cotton spreads itself as threads, so does God spread Himself as this universe. Creation means manifestation of *Brahman* in diverse forms (*āvirbhāva*), dissolution means withdrawal of this manifestation by *Brahman* within Himself (*tirobhāva*). This manifestation of *Brahman* possesses a part of His essence and is similar to Him while it is not the same *Brahman* as some of His essential aspects remain hidden. Viṭṭhalanātha explains *āvirbhāva* as "fitness for or capability of becoming an object of experience" and *tirobhāva* as "capability of not becoming an object of experience".[84] In *āvirbhāva* the homogeneous becomes heterogeneous, the implicit becomes explicit, in *tirobhāva* the heterogeneous becomes homogeneous, and the explicit lapses back into the implicit. A pure and real *jagat* emerges from a pure and real *Brahman*. Manifestation and concealment are led by the Divine wish. When He wishes to be many, there is manifestation, when He desires not to be perceptible, concealment takes place. World as *māyā* refers to the world of

[84] *anubhava-viṣayatva-yogyatā āvirbhāvaḥ tadaviṣayatva-yogyatā tirobhāvaḥ* |

erroneous perception (*viṣayatā*) and not the real world (*viṣaya*) which is as real as *Brahman*. If the world is unreal we cannot say that it is one with *Brahman* as an unreal phenomenon cannot be identified with the real entity. The world comes out from the very essence of *Brahman* (*svarūpa-pariṇāma*). It is not a *vivarta* of *Brahman* but "a real wilful *pariṇāma*" of the Supreme Lord. It is "*ātma-kṛti* or *ātma-pariṇāma*" of *Brahman*. It gives an idea of the majesty of God. One who realizes His greatness cannot but worship Him.

LIBERATION

Vallabha's scheme of liberation, which emphasizes more on the deeper religious values than metaphysical subtlety, gives greatest possible premium to *bhakti* and grace. *Bhakti*, to him, "is a perfectly steady and unsurpassed love for God accompanied by the knowledge of His grandeur and excellence".[85] It is a firm and an excessive affection for the Lord. It is a service to God through affection. Gopeśvara, the author of *Bhaktimārtaṇḍa*, interprets *bhakti* as "state of mind which gradually suppresses the mental repercussions and acquires oneness with God". True love for God makes the devotee see Him in all and all in Him (*sarvātma bhāva*). The identity is not the result of *jñāna* (as in Absolute Monism) but that of "self-forgetting, self-attaining oneness in single-minded devotion". He becomes God-intoxicated. He feels God's presence even if He is not there, and even in His presence he wails for the pang of His separation.

Vallabha treats knowledge only as an auxiliary or a stepping stone to *bhakti*. Undoubtedly he has recognized the importance of *jñāna* as a means to dispel ignorance or erroneous perception of the world. *Karma* has been subordinated to *jñāna* and *jñāna* to *bhakti*. *Bhakti* technically means "mental service in the form of love". It gradually suppresses the mental repercussions. No desire is left in the mind of devotee. There is only one desire, viz. to rest at the lotus feet of God. He is free even from the desire of his own salvation. And this goal is to be achieved only when the soul is purified by the actions of the right kind and illumined by

---

[85] *māhātmya-jñānapūrvastu sudṛḍhaḥ sarvato 'dhikaḥ* |
sneho bhaktiriti proktastayā muktirna cānyathā || – T.D.N. I.42

the knowledge of reality. It is neither worship nor knowledge but love that plays dominant role in liberation. It is gained through the grace of God which is to be won by the purity of heart only. The highest goal is no liberation but eternal service to Kṛṣṇa and participation in His *līlā*.

Connotation of *bhakti* includes both service (*sevā*) and love. Without service love is empty and without love service is merely a formality or a "dry drudgery".

Bhakti consists in profound admiration for Divine majesty coupled with spontaneous love and respect for the Supreme.[86] It is means as well as end (*prāpti-sādhana* and *prāpti-rūpa*). There is full desirelessness (*ahaitukī bhakti*). It is of the nature of *amṛta* (immortality). *Chāndogya Upaniṣad* too says that he who has devotion to God becomes immortal.

Bhakti, being a transcendental experience of bliss, is not ordinary love. It is not merely emotional excitement or eroticism. The love in *bhakti* is on the Divine plane. It is not to be confused with fanaticism which leads to sectarian quarrel. It is "a firm and supreme love for God preceded by a full comprehension of His greatness". It includes training of will as well as intellect. It vividly perceives the Supreme Reality. In *Tattvārtha-dīpa-nibandha*, Vallabha says that *Gītā* is the only scripture sung by the son of Devakī, the only God is Kṛṣṇa and the only activity is the service of that Deity.[87] Purity of heart is the principal means to the attainment of *bhakti*. This highest sentiment of love may flourish only in the person who possesses Divine seed. This is unearthly and spiritual love. The clamour of his passion and craving is drowned completely.

The life of devotion is not necessarily a life of inaction rather we should lead an active life completely dedicated to God. *Niṣkāma karma* goes hand in hand with *bhakti*

(a) *Śravaṇa* (hearing),

(b) *kīrtana* (praising),

(c) *smaraṇa* (remembering),

---

[86] *sā parānuraktirīśvare* | – *Śāṇḍilyasūtra* 2

[87] . . . *karmāpyekaṁ tasya devasya sevā* | – T.D.N. I.4

(d) *pādasevana* (worshipping the feet of God),

(e) *arcana* (ceremonial worship of God),

(f) *vandana* (bowing, etc. to God),

(g) *dāsya* (personal serving of God),

(h) *sakhya* (friendship with God), and

(i) *ātmanivedana* (complete surrender to God).

Bhakti is real *sevā* (service) to God. The initiation of "Śrī Kṛṣṇa is my refuge (*śrī kṛṣṇaḥ śaraṇaṁ mama*)" leads to total surrender in the name of God. This initiation carries with itself forgiveness on the part of God. As the dirty rivulets when submerged in Gaṅgā wash their dirt in it, *jīva*s forgiven by Kṛṣṇa wash away all their sins.

The truest type of *bhakti*, in Vallabha's opinion, is *prema-lakṣaṇa bhakti*, where love is the chief criterion. This love grows into intense attachment (*āsakti*). There is passionate desire for God. It is a spontaneous flow of heart which corresponds to spontaneous grace of God. It leads to *rāga-vināśa*. Glamour of passion is drowned for ever.

The ideal *bhakta*s, according to Vallabha, are Nanda–Yaśodā and Gopīs. In them *bhakti* is realized in *vātsalya-bhāva*, and *dāsya-bhāva* or *sakhya-bhāva*. God is love in the terms of human relationship at their deepest and best. *Śṛṅgāra* or *mādhurya bhakti* also is valued mostly by some of the followers of Vallabha. It is the relation between a lover and his beloved. But it is spiritual love and self dedication. The only difference is that the object of love here is God Himself who is the fountain of beauty and joy. This is supranatural (*alaukika*) lust (*kāma*). One should bear in mind that *mādhurya bhakti* is not meant for all. It nowhere includes the earthly "instinct-bound passion". It rises only in the heart who has Divine seed in him.

Vallabha interprets *rāsalīlā* both in literal and metaphorical senses. In literal sense Vallabha wants to show that there is no tinge of sensualism as the Lord is free from all passion. *Rāsalīlā*, on the other hand, purifies the spirit of man and engenders in him devotion to the Lord. In metaphorical sense Vedas, etc. are the *gopī*s always connected with God, Kṛṣṇa. Human colourful description raises misunderstanding about it. But we should always bear in mind that it is "the spiritual ideal of unselfish devotion, amounting to a complete self-surrender and a total dedication at the Divine feet".

The devotee realizes *sarvātma bhāva*. He experiences all things as God Himself does. He becomes one with God not in the sense of Śaṅkara's Advaita but in that in which the lover is absolutely united with his beloved. It is not a complete absorption in the Lord, eternal rhythm of separation and union is present there. "It is a perfect union in and of love."

The rise of *bhakti* may be gradual or spontaneous. *Bhāva, prema, praṇaya, sneha, rāga, anurāga* and *vyasana* (passionate attachment) are the seven steps in the gradual rise of *bhakti*. Among these seven, the last *vyasana* is most important. In this surging motion he forgets everything (*yajjñātvā matto bhāvati, stabdho bhāva ti, ātmārāmo bhāvati, yat prāpya na kiñcid vāñchati*).

Bhakta's experiences take the form of two states of consciousness: *viyoga* (separation) and *saṁyoga* (union). Vallabha takes *viyoga* as most important. The pang of separation fans out the love for God more than union.

Although *bhakti* is itself the end, Vallabha has spoken incidentally of its *phala* (fruits) also. The first reward the devotee gets is *alaukika sāmarthya* (supernatural power). It is not a miraculous power, it is a power of pure love. God is at the disposal of His devotees. Leaving His infinite glory God develops human relationship like any common person. The second *phala* is *sāyujya* (association with God). The other three are *sālokya* (residing with God), *sārūpya* (having the likeness of God) and *sāmīpya* (closeness to God). *Sāyujya* is the final state. The next *phala* is *sevopayogī deha* (a body fit for service to God). Soul puts on a celestial body. It is a body made of *ānanda* so that it may serve God in the fullness of spirit.

Vallabha's faith remained a living religion only because it offered an equal opportunity to all, viz. śūdras, women and vaiśyas who were desirous for spiritual elevation. Service to child Kṛṣṇa is an important phase in the life of a devotee. The service is threefold, offered with the aid of body, wealth and mind. The last is the highest since here all our mental activities are centred around God. The love of *gopīs* is the highest ideal for the religion of love. God is full of *rasa* and out of eight *rasas* Śṛṅgāra is most prominent.

Public worshipping or going to temple is an important aspect of Vallabha's school. God is not a being seated high up in the heaven and passing out judgements but appears as an innocent child whose sweet behaviour becomes an object of affection culminating in *vātsalya bhakti*. This Child-God governs all affection and respect of devotees. Devotees do *sevā* and not *pūjā* as *pūjā* is offered with sectarian *mantras*, it is a conventional affair with much paraphernalia but in *sevā,* love is important. The image of God is not a symbol of God but God Himself. *Sevā* is an eightfold *darśana*. *Maṅgalā,* the first *darśana*, takes place in the morning. It means awakening Him. The next *darśana* is *śṛṅgāra*, when Kṛṣṇa is dressed up. The third *darśana* is in the form of *gvāla*, going out with cows. The fourth is *rājabhoga* when He takes lunch in the forest with His companions. The fifth is awakening Him after day-nap, *utthāpana*. The sixth is *bhoga*. The seventh is *sandhyā* when He brings the cows back from the meadows. The eighth is *śayana* when he retires to bed.

Vallabha does not believe in asceticism rather he believes that since God has created the world, it is good and beautiful, and there is no sense in relinguishing it. Everything can be made holier and better by using it in the service of God. All beautiful things are used as "sacramental sense foods". The body itself is a temple of God and there is no sense in mortifying it.

DIVINE GRACE OF PUṢṬI MĀRGA

Effort on the part of devotee is not enough. Unless the Lord bestows His blessings, his sin cannot be destroyed. *Bhakti* is generated by God Himself. The path of devotion characterized by the grace of God (*puṣṭi*) is the highest *puruṣārtha* according to Vallabha. This grace aspect of devotion forms the keynote in Vallabha *sampradāya*. The three *sādhanas* of God-realization have lost their efficacy in the present-day perspective. Divine grace is the sheet anchor of souls who find themselves helpless. Grace has an enviable status in Śuddhādvaita Vedānta which is known as *puṣṭi mārga*. Bliss is purely a gift of the Lord and is not to be obtained by any human effort.

The word *puṣṭi,* meaning nourishment, is found in Vedas. This nourishment can be physical or spiritual. Vallabha uses the word *puṣṭi* in spiritual sense. *Bhāgavata* explains it as *poṣaṇaṁ tadaṇugrahaḥ*. It is a favour of God. Upaniṣads declare: "him alone does He cause to undertake good deeds whom He wishes to uplift."

The devotion with *puṣṭi* signifies that ever performance of duty is dependent on God's wish. No other means is efficient to produce the desired effort unless God wishes it to be so. God plants in His devotee the love for God in order to attain Him. The chosen souls are called *puṣṭi* souls. He is the only saviour of all destitutes. The follower of *puṣṭi-mārga* needs no knowledge, no deed and no effort.[88] The only thing required is total surrender to God and detachment from worldly pleasures. The concepts of love and self-surrender are the keytone of *Gītā* and *Bhāgavata*.

The human souls, according to Vallabha, are of three kinds, viz. *puṣṭi*, *maryādā* and *pravāha*. All these are different from each other in their origin, nature and final end. Leading to nature of these souls there are three paths, viz. *puṣṭi mārga*, *maryādā mārga* and *pravāha mārga*.

The Lord creates the *pravāha mārga* out of His mind. Here there is no grace, no law but continuous motion which is the meaning of *pravāha*. *Pravāha* soul lives and moves in self-will. It is again and again absorbed in *avidyā* at the end of the cycle.

The path of *maryādā* is generated from God's speech. This path is governed not by grace but by law. *Maryādā* souls are called *vaidika* souls who live, move and have their being in accordance with Vedic injunctions. They perform their ritualistic duties in

---

[88] *puṣṭimārgaḥ anugrahaika-sādhyaḥ, pramāṇamārgādvilakṣaṇaḥ* |
– *Aṇubhāṣyam* IV.4.7

order to gain some material prosperity. They evolve from this state and soon get absorbed in *akṣara*. It is *dharma-karma-mārga*. God bestows His blessing according to their actions. Everything is dependent of their personal efforts.

The highest path or the highest soul is the *puṣṭi mārga* or *puṣṭi* soul where there is total surrender in God. It is issued from the bliss aspect of God. These souls are *aṁśa* of His body, He being *aṁśī*. They have Divine seed in them. *Puṣṭi bhakta*s do not envisage the necessity of personal effort. They are dedicated to God wholeheartedly. They rest assured that grace of God is the only saviour of their lives. *Puṣṭi bhakti* is devotion born of grace.[89] Grace is the only decisive factor here. It speaks utter futility of all means except God who is both the means and the end. It is a single-minded devotion. He alone whom He chooses can attain Him. Wish of God is the prime factor. Later He submits Himself to the *puṣṭi bhakta*s. It is the path of single-minded devotion where absence of means acts as means. He loves God so intensely that he gives up all earthly love and ignores all his duties of class (*varṇa*) and order (*āśrama*).

According to Vallabha, Divine grace has not the least reason behind it as to why God has accepted that particular person as His own.[90] The fitness or antecedent merit is no criterion for being chosen for this boon. The blessed *jīva* dedicates everything at the feet of the Lord.

If *puṣṭi* means utter futility of human efforts that means dignity of endeavour has no meaning. If God is the prime regulator of man's destiny, men may not be held responsible for their deeds. Thus the human responsibility will be thrown overboard. In order to safeguard the position Vallabha allows a bit of liberty (*kiñcit svātantryam*). *Jīva* shows an inclination towards the path to be followed.[91] But if this "inclination" is also to be seeded by God in soul, this little liberty is a misnomer, it is pseudo-liberty. Divine

---

89 *sā 'pi kṛṣṇecchayā jātaḥ puṣṭimārgaḥ sa kathyate* | – Quoted in P.R., p. 102

90 *svīyatvenāṅgīkāraḥ* | – P.R., p. 20

91 *kṛtaprayatnāpekṣastu vihitapratiṣiddhāvaiyarthyādibhyaḥ* |
– *Aṇubhāṣya* II.3.42

grace makes human effort futile. Later Vallabha accepts in *Aṇubhāṣya* that the Lord takes into account the *karma* performed by *jīva*.[92] God is not an arbitrary ruler.

The path of *puṣṭi* is open to all. Even the females and śūdras may be liberated. There is no distinction of caste, creed and nationality. The *puṣṭi mārga* is the means for those who are utterly helpless and destitute but desirous of getting liberation. *Gopī*s were born in low family, they were unassuming, illiterate but by the grace of God they cherished love for Him. The episode speaks volume about *puṣṭi mārga* for the realization of Divine. When God is pleased, He keeps the devotees near to Him so that He may enjoy their service.

To the question why God caused the separation of souls from Himself resulting in *jīva*'s suffering, Vallabha gives a peculiar answer that "it is God's wish, His sovereign pleasure", "it is an integral part of the Divine *līlā*". All other philosophers hold *karma* to be responsible for this. Making God responsible for this will take away to some extent His infinite glory. But to Vallabha, "any other cause of this kind would itself be a detraction from God's absolute independence". Such souls experience the Divine communion again. And this communion after separation is more valuable. As a matter of fact the state of solitude is more important in the eyes of Vallabha than union. In solitude he finds God everywhere while in union at one place only.

Puṣṭi bhakti is of four kinds:

(a) *pravāha-puṣṭi bhakti,*

(b) *maryādā-puṣṭi bhakti,*

(c) *puṣṭi-puṣṭi bhakti,* and

(d) *śuddha-puṣṭi bhakti.*

Pravāha-puṣṭi class belongs to the world; they are engaged in "me and mine" attitude though they have come under the operation of God's active grace. *Maryādā-puṣṭi bhakta*s relinquish all worldly activities and are devoted to contemplation of God. Grace of God is working in them. The *puṣṭi-puṣṭi bhakta*s do not

[92] *Aṇubhāṣya* II.3.42.

surrender themselves fully in the hands of God. Their life is full of grace but still there is some lacking in them which debar them from the highest end. In *śuddha-puṣṭi bhakti* is generated by God Himself. They have no other desire except the desire of God. Even the grandeur of heaven does not allure them, they are happy in hell if God so desires for them. They are unaffected by sobs and throbs of life. In God's good world nothing is amiss for them. Their love is perfect. By haunting passion about *hari* everything becomes an object of love for them. Their inner as well as outer world is full of Puruṣottama. The highest aim of man's life is to live in Vaikuṇṭha where Kṛṣṇa lives with Rādhā and to participate in the Divine sport. He is in intense love for God. He is God-intoxicated.

5

The Integral Advaitism of Sri Aurobindo

THE Absolute (*Brahman*) is, according to Sri Aurobindo, the fundamental reality. It is one "From that all variations begin, in that all variations consist, to that all variations return" (Aurobindo 1970, vol. I: 33). "It is the truth of all life and existence" (ibid.). "It is one, the universal and supreme, the Eternal and the infinite" (Aurobindo 1950b: 279). There is nothing outside. Whatever is, is in *Brahman*. According to Sri Aurobindo, "All this is a manifestation of *Brahman*, by *Brahman* and in *Brahman*, therefore, all is real as *Brahman* itself" (Pandit 1959: 3). It is the fact behind all dualities, which we come across in our life.

The Absolute in itself is indeterminate and unknowable; it is an ineffable transcendental reality. Its character is neither to be determined by affirmation nor by negation. "The first aspect of cosmic existence is an Infinite which is to our perception an indeterminate, if not indeterminable" (Aurobindo 1970, vol. II, pt I: 296). Absolute is, according to Sri Aurobindo (1970, vol. II, pt I: 636):

> not a rigid determinable oneness, not an infinity vacant of all that is not a pure self-existence attainable only by the exclusion of the many and the finite, but something which is beyond these definitions, beyond indeed any description either positive or negative. All affirmations and negations are expressive of its aspects, and it is through both a supreme affirmation and a supreme negation that we can arrive at the Absolute.

It is above all still holds all in its essence. It is not known by our finite mind but can be known by the supramental consciousness. This Absolute manifests itself in our consciousness as a triune principle of Existence, Consciousness and Bliss, i.e. Saccidānanda. The Absolute is both immanent as well as transcendental reality.

It is immanent in the world and man and at the same time transcends them. In its immanent aspect, this Absolute (*Brahman*) is Supermind and in its transcendental aspect, it is Saccidānanda. When turned towards manifestation, this indeterminate absolute reality determines itself as Supreme Existence; it is *sat*, something which exists by itself. It does not only exist but it is "actively aware of itself, dynamic with self-knowledge, it is conscious-force". And "the very nature of this existence innate with consciousness is an utter delight. This is the triune status, existence, consciousness and bliss, in which the reality perceives it in its poise for manifestation" (Pandit 1959: 4). Thus it is called Saccidānanda, *sat, cit* and *ānanda*.Maitra (1968: 59) says:

> The highest conception of reality which the genius of India could evolve was the conception of it as Saccidānanda. . . . It is the greatest single achievement of Indian philosophy. It brings out clearly the relation between Existence and Value by showing that Existence itself is a Value.

Existence (Sat)

The Absolute is pure existence; it dwells equally in all existences. It is a supremely transcendental principle which is immanent as well. Saccidānanda is both transcendental as well as immanent, Being as well as Becoming. It is pure existence at the same time movement, energy and process. To quote Sri Aurobindo (1970, vol. I: 78):

> The pure Existence is then a fact and no mere concept, it is the fundamental reality. But let us hasten to add, the movement, the energy, the becoming are also a fact, also a reality.

The Buddhists, Heraclitus and Henri Bergson assert becoming as the Ultimate Reality. They totally refuse to accept reality as pure immutable existence. But Sri Aurobindo (ibid.: 75) says:

> . . . it brings us to a last abruptly ceasing stair of ascent which leaves the whole staircase without support, suspended in the void.

For the Vedāntists, Being is the essence, the Ultimate Reality, but they refuse to give any transcendental importance to Becoming.

Becoming is only phenomenally real but transcendentally unreal. Sri Aurobindo does not deny the reality of Becoming. Being is the very substance of Becoming, it constitutes its essence. Sri Aurobindo (1970, vol. I: 75) says:

> The very conception of movement carries with it the potentiality of repose and betrays itself as an activity of some existence; the very idea of energy in action carries with it the idea of energy abstaining from action; and an absolute energy not in action is simply and purely absolute existence.

The Vedāntists conceive existence to be "universal and ineffable reality". Sri Aurobindo too agrees with it but his way of demonstration is somewhat different. Sri Aurobindo says that when we view the world with inquisitive and dispassionate eye free from personal or egoistic considerations, we perceive "boundless energy of infinite existence, infinite movement, infinite activity" expressing itself in limitless space and eternal time. And this energy is nothing but pure existence in action.

Sense experience knows nothing about pure existence whatsoever. Sense experience is conditioned by space and time, forms and movement and observes things in this context. But reason cannot logically deny the reality of pure existence. According to both Śaṅkara and Sri Aurobindo:

> Thought is constrained to posit the reality of pure existence or the Absolute in order to understand the rationale of world process.
>
> –Misra 1957: 30

All beginning and end presuppose something which is beyond beginning and end, an absolute beginning or absolute end is contradiction in terms if it is a fiction. Thus reason cannot deny pure existence; denial of pure existence will mean denial of one's own self or *Brahman* as existence is the underlying reality both for the world and the individuals. Thus pure existence is not an imaginary idea. It is the Absolute underlying all phenomena.

It may be objected that scriptures advocate the theory of Non-Being (*asat*), which is contrary to the theory of pure existence as the ultimate nature of reality. *Taittirīya Upaniṣad* says: "There was only *asat* formerly, being come out of Non-Being". But Sri Aurobindo says that *asat* does not mean negation of *sat* but *sat* transcending all mental categories. Non-Being is only a word.

> This nothing then is merely a something positive conception. We erect a fiction of nothingness in order to overpass, by the method of total exclusion, all that we can know and consciously are. Actually when we examine closely the Nihil of certain philosophies, we begging to perceive that it is a zero which is All or an indefinable Infinite which appears to the mind a blank, because mind grasps only finite constructions, but is in fact the only true Existence. – Aurobindo 1970, vol. I: 28

According to Sri Aurobindo, when we speak of Being appearing from Non-Being we are perceiving in terms of time that which is beyond the unit of time.

> We give the name of Non-Being to a contrary affirmation of Its freedom from all cosmic existence-freedom, that is to say, from all positive terms of actual existence which consciousness in the universe can fromulate to itself, even from the most abstract, even from the most transcendent. – Ibid.: 28-29

Chāndogya Upaniṣad VI.2.2 too says: "How can being be born out of Non-Being. Being can only come out of being, and not out of Non-being".[1] Absolute does not have that kind of existence which worldly things have. Absolute is *asat* from a particular standpoint.

Basant Kumar Lal says that in talking about the pure existence, Sri Aurobindo makes a distinction between (a) what is revealed of pure existence to our insight; to our attempts to see the world, and (b) what pure reason is able to conceive about it (Lal 1973: 167). The former draws the picture of existence in terms of space and time; it pictures existence actually existing, the latter transforms the spatial and temporal distinctions; it forms the concept of existence. But he reconciles the two pictures by suggesting that these two pictures are the result of looking at pure existence from the different viewpoints. The Being and the Becoming, the stability and the world movement, are only the two aspects of the reality which transcends them equally. *Brahman* is the all-pervading Truth

---

[1] *kutastu khalu somyaivaṁ syāditi hovāca kathamasataḥ sajjāyeteti* ।

behind all appearance and is equally present in all "from the solar system right down to the anthill".

Saccidānanda, in its aspect of self-existence, manifests Itself to us in three forms: *Ātman*, *puruṣa* and *Īśvara*. Pure existence is unknowable according to Sri Aurobindo. It can neither be described by negation *neti, neti* nor by affirmation, *iti iti*. But it is not unknowable altogether. As Non-Being does not mean in Sri Aurobindo's philosophy the negation of being, similarly unknowable does not mean, as agnostics believe, that the Absolute is altogether unknown and unknowable by human reason. Reality is not unknown and unknowable as Kant thinks. It is unknown to finite consciousness only. Man is capable of piercing the veil of finite consciousness attaining a sacramental consciousness which has an all-embracing vision of the Absolute. "The Absolute is the ultimate of philosophy and the limit of man's intellectual aspirations" (Reddy 1966: 170).

According to Maitra:

> This value of existence is the passport to the admission of anything to the city of philosophy. Whatever other values a thing may possess, unless it possesses the essential value of existence, it cannot enter the portals of philosophy. But the peculiarity of this value of existence is this, that although without it a thing cannot enter the domain of philosophy, with it, it cannot remain long in it.[2]

Thus Absolute is not only existence but conscious-force too.

Conscious-Force

Sri Aurobindo agrees with the ancient Indian thinking that force is inherent in existence. Absolute *Brahman* is not only existent but conscious too. *Brahman* is not only conscious, as Śaṅkara and others have asserted, it is conscious-force (*cit-śakti*). It is dynamic and creative and not passive. Both Śiva and Kāli are equally true. World is a product of force. Force is not contradictory to existence. It is inherent in existence. Force may be static and dynamic both.

---

[2] Presidential Address at the Indian Philosophical Congress, 1948, pp. 28-29.

Now two questions may be asked: first, what is the relation between the pure existence and force? Second, what is the nature of this force?

Absolute, in the state of equipoise, is pure existence, is concentrated energy. It is the aspect of being, but in its dynamic state, it creates the world, it is becoming. Force is inherent in existence. *Brahman* and *śakti*, Śiva and Kālī are one and inseparable. This force may be at rest or in motion. This dual character of conscious-force, this alternative possibility of rest and movement averts the opposition between existence and force. Giving an independent and ultimate place to it will mean movement even in pure existence. This view will go against the very spirit of Absoluteness of the pure existence. Thus conscious-force is inherent in the pure existence; it is not independent of it. Sri Aurobindo says that as we cannot separate fire and power of fire, we cannot separate the Divine Reality and its *cit-śakti*.

Saccidānanda is never overpowered by this force; rather it is the controller of its *śakti*. It is never compelled by its *śakti*. There is no fundamental opposition between them. It manifests itself as *śakti* in both dynamic and static aspects at the same time. According to Sri Aurobindo, the questions regarding the "how" and the "why" of the movement are illegitimate. Why should this force manifest itself? Why should this force of existence not remain static? These questions do not arise if we take "Existence to be non-conscious and consciousness only a development of material energy which we wrongly suppose to be immaterial". There is no cause to ask why for that which is self-existent by nature.

> Both existence and force being inert-inert status and inert impulsion – both of them unconscious and unintelligent, there cannot be any purpose or intention. – Aurobindo 1970, vol. I: 84

There is freedom of choice of *Brahman*. It is not compelled or determined by this force. To quote Sri Aurobindo:

> A *Brahman* compelled by *prakṛti* is not *Brahman*, but an inert infinite with an active content in it more powerful than the continent, a conscious hold of Force of whom his Force is master. If we say that it is compelled by itself as force, by its own nature,

> we do not get rid of the contradiction, the evasion of our first postulate. We have got back to an Existence which is really nothing but Force, Force at rest or in movement, absolute Force perhaps, but not absolute Being. – Aurobindo 1970, vol. I: 84

The second question is what is the nature of Force? Is it unconscious energy or an intelligent power or a chemical force or a conscious energy? Sri Aurobindo boldly asserts that it is consciousness. By consciousness we generally mean our waking mental awareness. We are not said to be conscious when we are fast asleep or when we fall into a swoon. But, according to Sri Aurobindo, this narrow concept of consciousness is to be outgrown with a view to appreciate its nature and extent properly. This superficial consciousness is merely "a narrow strip of our entire conscious being". Consciousness is no more synonymous with mentality, it is a "self-aware force of existence of which mentality is a middle term; below mentality it sinks into vital and material movement which are for us sub-conceit; above, it rises into the supramental which is for us the super conceit. But in all it is one and the same thing organizing itself differently. This is, once more, the Indian conception of *cit* which, as energy, creates the worlds." (ibid.: 88).

There are various forms of consciousness: unconsciousness, sub-consciousness, subliminal consciousness and super-consciousness. To suppose all types of consciousness as mental consciousness is erroneous.

> Below this surface-consciousness there is a much vaster region of consciousness the subliminal mind, which is capable of attaining to heights which are far beyond the capacity of the waking mind. – Banerjee 1957-59: 59

Human consciousness ordinarily is too narrow and forms only a small part of our total consciousness.

Sri Aurobindo disagrees with the materialistic contention that consciousness is a by-product of matter and is so organized that it gives rise to consciousness. Matter, according to Sri Aurobindo, is veiled spirit and in its essence it is nothing but a product of consciousness itself. In the course of cosmic evolution, matter will become progressively conscious and it has the ultimate destiny of being transformed into super-nature. It is, therefore, evident that consciousness is continuous and immanent in all types of existence. It does not come to halt at the level of the plants or matter, though it is in latent manner there.

No doubt, it is very hard for us to believe that there can be inert or suppressed consciousness in the earth. It is difficult to realize that consciousness is the inherent reality behind the trace-like sleep of matter. *Ex nihilo nihil fit* from nothing, nothing comes and unless consciousness was there involved in matter from the very inception of this material world, it could not have gradually emerged during the process of evolution (ibid.: 62-63). Further there is no ground to suppose that there is sudden break of unity at a particular stage. And if we take the unity to be unbroken, we will find existence of consciousness in all forms of the force working in the world.

The presence of consciousness in creative force may be also proved by the fact that there is design seen behind the nature. What to tell of rational human beings, even in the minutest movement of the animals, birds, beasts and tiniest insects, there is clear indication of purposefulness. They carry on their daily routine as if being guided by some conscious force from behind. Furthermore in the working of what we call inanimate nature, there is a sign of working of a supreme hidden intelligence.

It has been charged against this conception of conscious-force that nature is wasteful. If some conscious-force is working behind nature why is it not following the direct path saving itself from waste? Sri Aurobindo says that such misconceptions are born out of the limitation of human intelligence. We apply our reason on world-force. We judge only the surface; we are completely ignorant of the real purpose, the truth behind the world movement. What we call waste may be good from the standpoint of nature's ulterior purposes.

This supreme consciousness is universal and cosmic. It is equally present in the deep sea as well as in the sky. The supreme conscious-force is transcendental, universal and individual.

It is transcendent to the world and is unmanifest. It is universal

> and cosmic also because it creates the world, supports and inheres in it. It is at the same time individual in the sense that it is found in all individuals. –R.S. Srivastava (1968: 30)

Sri Aurobindo (1978: 33) states the triple status of conscious-force thus:

> transcendent, the original supreme Śakti, she stands above the world and links the creation to the ever unmanifest mystery of the Supreme. Universal, the Cosmic Mahāśakti, she creates all these beings and contains and enters, supports and conducts all these million processes and forces. Individual, she embodies the power of these vaster ways of her existence, makes them living and near to us and mediates between the human personality and the divine Nature.[3]

In relation of this universe, the fundamental principle of existence manifests itself as self (*ātman*), spirit (*puruṣa*) and God (*Īśvara*). And the conscious-force manifests itself as *māyā*, *prakṛti* and *Śakti* corresponding to the three aspects of existence: *ātman*, *puruṣa* and *Īśvara*, respectively. Thus *ātman–māyā*, *puruṣa–prakṛti* and *Īśvara–Śakti* go together. These are the three aspects in which the Absolute (*Brahman*) manifests itself in the universe. These three aspects taken together give full view of the relation between the existence and conscious-force. They also throw light on the fact that there is no contradiction between the individual, cosmic and transcendental Existence. In the first two there is apparent duality. Existence and force seem to separate from each other. There is apparent duality between conceit *puruṣa* and the active *prakṛti*, between static *ātman* and dynamic *māyā*. In the aspect of *Īśvara–Śakti* we realize that being and conscious-force cannot be fundamentally dual. They are rather complementary to each other. *Īśvara* is the Lord of *Śakti* and of all things. Their unity is the final, truth and not their duality. Misra (1957: 118) says:

> The consciousness-force as *māyā* is "conceptively creative of all things", as *prakṛti* it is "made dynamically executive", working out all things under the witnessing eye of the conscious Being, the self or spirit, as *śakti*, it is both conceptively creative and

[3] *The Mother.*

dynamically executive of all the divine workings.

Thus, existence and consciousness-force, in their ultimate analysis, are one and the same. Śiva and Śakti are one transcendentally. Saccidānanda appears to be dual in the forms of *Īśvara–Śakti*, *ātman–māyā* and *puruṣa–prakṛti*. But the supreme unity of Saccidānanda remains unaffected in spite of its multiple expressions as the creative force. It is conscious in nature and is one with absolute existence. Misra (1957) says:

> He (Sri Aurobindo) has been able to arrive at his integral Advaitism by his conception of the ultimate creative force as conscious in nature.

With his concept of creative principle as conscious energy, Sri Aurobindo is able to avoid the difficulties related to the concept of unconscious teleology. There remains no problem for explaining the harmony and purpose present in the nature.

One very illuminating idea presented by Sri Aurobindo is this that conscious-force (*cit*) is called mother. He conceives it as Divine Śakti which is the principle behind the world-process. It is the operative principle which is behind the creation and maintenance of the universe. She is veiled by her *yogamāyā* so long as she is working in the lower hemisphere. In all that is done in the universe, the Divine through his *śakti*, is behind all actions but he is veiled by his *yogamāyā* and works through the ego of *jīva* in the lower nature.[4] The mother is the Divine *śakti* behind the world-process. The universe is created and sustained by this *śakti*. Śiva and Śakti are ultimately one. There is no duality in transcendental status, in manifestation merely it appears in dual character, Śiva and Śakti. Śakti is not opposed to Śiva in the absolute unity of transcendental reality. Śiva and Śakti remain intact in an inseparable manner. She is the dynamic aspect of Saccidānanda. Sri Aurobindo says elsewhere:

> All is she, for all are parcel and portion of the divine conscious-force. Nothing can be here or elsewhere but what she decides and the Supreme sanctions, nothing can take shape except what

[4] *The Mother*, p. 9.

> she, moved by the Supreme, perceives and forms after casting it into seed in her creating Ānanda.[5]

To quote Srivastava(1968: 31): "All things are in the Mother, the Mother is in all things and all things are nothing else than the Mother."

BLISS

The existence and consciousness are related to the "how" of creation, while Bliss is concerned with the "why" of creation. Bliss constitutes the very nature of Saccidānanda. This is the most important of all the constituents of Saccidānanda. If the Absolute is self-content and needs nothing for its realization, it should be of the nature of bliss necessarily. *Taittirīya Upaniṣad* says:

> From *ānanda* all existents are born, by *ānanda* they remain in being and increase, to *ānanda* they depart.

Kena Upaniṣad too says:

> The name of that is Delight as the Delight we must worship and seek after it.

In the words of Sri Aurobindo (1970, vol. I: 101):

> Delight is existence, Delight is the secret of creation, Delight is the root of birth, Delight is the cause of remaining in existence, Delight is the end of birth and that into which creation ceases.[6]

The Absolute creates the world for the sake of self-delight. All illimitableness, all infinity, all absolute is pure delight.[7] Ultimate existence, according to Sri Aurobindo, is not bare existence; it is not merely conscious existence whose consciousness is crude, rather "it is a conscious existence, the very term of whose being, the very term of whose consciousness is bliss" (1970, vol. I: 91).

Bliss is not pleasure in ordinary sense. It is more comprehensive and universal and is quite different from pleasure. Universal delight of existence is something different from ordinary pleasure.

---

5 *The Mother*, p. 35.

6 Ibid.

7 Ibid., pp. 91-92.

It is more essential and wider. Bliss "comprehends both pleasure and pain which are its positive and negative currents. They are the first positive and negative phenomenal manifestations of Bliss. But these rise to a Supreme Bliss of existence where they are transcended into a unity" (R.S. Srivastava 1968: 33). *Chāndogya Upaniṣad* says: "That which is infinite is bliss, there is no bliss in the finite". Finite pleasure is not everlasting. It is full of desire and desire is the root cause of suffering but infinite is of the nature of bliss as it is free from desire which leads to suffering. The joy found in the world is a part and parcel of the absolute bliss. Śaṅkara in his *Bhāṣya* on *Bṛhadāraṇyaka Upaniṣad* says that the empirical bliss is the part of the bliss of *Brahman*.

The bliss represents the value aspect of Saccidānanda. Misra (1957: 131) says:

> It is the content of value aspect of the absolute that gives concreteness to it. Without content or value, the Absolute will be a mere abstract unity. To call the Ultimate Reality merely existence or existence-consciousness and ignore its aspect of bliss or value is to give a one-sided view of it. To take away its value aspect means depriving it of all its concreteness.

Most of the Western philosophers have drawn distinction between value and existence and they have come to the conclusion that the value is unreal. S.K. Maitra (1968) says:

> Can there be anything more absurd than this – this assertion by any value philosophers that value is unreal?

Every reality must possess three kinds of value: (a) the value of existence or objectivity, (b) of consciousness or logic, and (c) of bliss or spiritual value. Thus in Saccidānanda the existential aspect is expressed by *sat*, logical aspect by *cit* and value aspect by *ānanda*. In *Bṛhadāraṇyaka Upaniṣad* (III.9.28) we have similar statement where *Brahman* is, *vijñanam ānandaṁ brahma*. All worldly things as the expressions of this Saccidānanda are permeated by existence, consciousness and bliss. Sri Aurobindo says:

> All things that exist are what they are as terms of that existence, terms of that conscious-force, terms of that delight of being.

He again says:

> In everything that is, dwells the conscious-force and it exists and is what it is by virtue of that conscious-force; so also in everything that is there is the delight of existence and it exists and is what it is by virtue of all delight. – 1970, vol. I: 92

The bliss of *Brahman* is not limited to its being aspect only, it manifests itself in Becoming as well. Sri Aurobindo says:

> The self-delight of *Brahman* is not limited, however, by the still and motionless possession of its absolute self-being. Just as its force of consciousness is capable of throwing itself into forms infinitely and with an endless variation, so also its self-delight is capable of movement, of variation, of reveling in that infinite flux and mutability of itself represented by numberless teeming universes. To lose forth and enjoy this infinite movement and variation of its self-delight is the object of its extensive or creative play of force. – ibid.

The bliss cannot be intellectually understood, but can be intuitively apprehended. Our sense and intellect can give us only shadow of the absolute bliss.

In answer to the question why does the absolute, infinite and perfect *Brahman* create the world, Sri Aurobido says that it is all for delight. There is no lacking in *Brahman* which is to be fulfilled by creation. It is perfect in every sense. A purpose in creation will mean it lacks something. *Brahman* is sportive and creates the world for the sake of sport (*līlā*) Misra (1957: 136) says:

> It creates out of Bliss, by Bliss and for Bliss. *Līlā* indicates a spontaneous sportive activity of *Brahman* as distinguished from a self-conscious volitional effect. The concept of *līlā* signifies freedom as distinguished from necessity.

The whole of the universe is a play of joy, a spontaneous activity of God for the sake of *līlā*. Sri Aurobindo says:

> Again if we look at the world-existence rather in its relation to the self-delight of eternally existent being we may regard, describe and realize it as *līlā*, the play, the child's joy, the poet's joy, the actor's joy, the mechanician's joy of the soul of things eternally

> young, perpetually inexhaustible, creating and recreating Himself in Himself for the sheer bliss of that self-creation, of that self-representation-Himself the play. Himself the playground.
>
> – Ibid., 1970, vol. 1: 102-03

Now the question arises, if the world is an expression of the delight, how can we account for the suffering of the world? All being Saccidānanda how can suffering at all exist? If the world would have been an expression of only the existent aspect that is conscious force merely, there would have been no problem but it is an expression of existence that is also infinitely delightful. Then how can suffering be accounted for? Unless we are in a position to claim that this suffering is not a negation of bliss but only a mode of its expression, our assumption that bliss is inherent in nature everywhere will fall flat. Bliss is inherent characteristic of all existence, of every finite being and of all cosmos. But it is there in latent manner.

This problem of evil is a hard nut to crack for monastic philosophy. Evil seems to be contradictory of bliss; thus to accommodate evil in the monistic scheme of reality is a task for them. To give evil an independent position is to accept fundamental dualism which is not at all acceptable to Sri Aurobindo. Thus evil cannot be given an independent status as opposed to the bliss of the Absolute if monism is to be maintained. A monist can neither reconcile evil with the Absolute nor can he provide evil an independent position. In both the cases, their monism will be seriously jeopardized.

> In most of the monistic systems evil seems to maintain jealously its identity and existence like lonely island in the ocean of the infinite. Thus it has proved a stumbling block to all monistic system.
>
> – Misra 1957: 140

William James, the pragmatist, regards the inescapable fact of evil as the rock on which all forms of monism are wrecked.

Sri Aurobindo is never a pessimist; rather he is a supreme optimist. According to Haridas Chaudhary (1972), his optimism does not rest "upon a denial of the existence of evil or the working of the devil but upon his emphatic refusal to accept them as essentially unconquerable forces and as ultimately independent principles. Like Bergson, he believes that the duality of pain and pleasure is capable of being transmuted into pure unalloyed joy, as in his view that duality is essentially a distested reflection of the pure delight of existence upon the realm of ignorance."[8] According to Sri Aurobindo, if we will make a dispassionate evaluation we shall find that the sum of pleasure far exceeds the sum of suffering of existence. Pleasure is the normal state but pain is "a contrary occurrence temporarily suspending or overlaying that normal state". Lesser pain affects us more than greater pleasure only because pleasure is our normal state. It is unobservable unless it "intensifies into some acuter form" or into "way of happiness" or into "a crest of joy or ecstasy".

The solution of the problem of evil depends on the relation between the world and evil. If we imagine God to be extra-cosmic, the problem of evil will never be solved. A God, living aloof from the world and inflicting pain on his creation, no more satisfies the religious consciousness. Sri Aurobindo (1970, vol. I: 94-95) says: "On no theory of an extra cosmic moral God, can evil and suffering be explained."

In Vedāntic scheme, the Absolute is one without second, "all that is, is He". It bears the evil in the creature as it is embodied there. But still the problem is not solved wholly. How does Saccidānanda admit into itself that which is not of the nature of bliss? Thus suffering and evil seriously challenge the validity of monistic philosophy.

Sri Aurobindo quietly meets the difficulty and says that all the problems arise when we look at things from an individualistic point of view and try to impose our ethical concept on the whole of nature. He says:

> ". . . we do not live in an ethical world. The attempt of human thought to force an ethical meaning into the whole of Nature is one of those acts of wilful and obstinate self-confusion, one of those pathetic attempts of the human being to read himself his limited habitual human self into all things and judge them from

[8] Sri Aurobindo Mandir, 1950, *Annual*, 9.

> the standpoint he has personally evolved, which most effectively prevent him from arriving at real knowledge and complete sight."
>
> – 1970, vol. I: 96

J.S. Mill (1874) too says:

> In sober truth, nearly all the things for which men are hanged or imprisoned for doing to one another, are nature's everyday performance. Killing the most criminal act recognized by human laws, nature does once to every being that lives. . . . A single hurricane destroys the hopes of season.

The modern idealistic thinkers like F.H. Bradley, Bernard Bosanquet and J.S. Mackenzie assert that morality is a peculiar phase of human life only and cannot be treated as the ultimate characteristic of the reality. For Bradley (1893: 430):

> Evil and good in short are not ultimate; they are relative factors which cannot retain their special character in the whole.

He elsewhere says (1893: 202):

> The discord as such disappears if the harmony is made wide enough.

Bosanquet (1913: 209, 217) too says:

> Evil, one might say, is good in the wrong place. There is nothing in evil which cannot be absorbed in good and contributory to it, and it springs from the same source as good and value.

Thus ethics is only a stage in evolution. Ethical life is possible in human stage merely. There was no ethics before the emergence of human life. At supra-human level too, there is no need of ethics. The common feature of all stages is an urge of Saccidānanda towards self-expression.

> This urge is at first non-ethical then infra-ethical in the animal, then in the intelligent animal, even anti-ethical for it permits us to approve hurt done to others which we disapprove when done to ourselves. In this respect man even now is only half ethical. And just as all below us is infra-ethical, so there may be that above us whither we shall eventually arrive, which is supra-ethical, has no need of ethics. – 1970, vol. I: 97

Thus the world has three layers, infra-ethical, ethical and supra-ethical. Ethical impulse, which is so dear to humanity, is a means to shed off individual discords so that a higher harmony may be acquired. But it shall bear no meaning after that goal is achieved as the opposition on which it depends will naturally disappear in the final reconciliation. Ethics or morality has great relevance for man but it does not constitute the nature of reality as a whole. Ethical standpoint has a temporary phase of existence and cannot be applied to the whole. Similar is the concept of Bradley. Maitra (1993: 13) refers Bradley in support:

> Bradley says that morality is an appearance for it rests upon a fundamental opposition between the ideal that is to be achieved and the actuality that falls far short of it. The highest condition, the ultimate nature of reality is thus, beyond Good and Evil.

Thus it is clear that evil is not an essential character of the world. It emerges at certain stage of evolution and that is in the plane of mind. It is an expression of Saccidānanda in the world of ignorance which is destined to disappear in the higher stages of evolution. Pleasure and pain are nothing but positive and negative currents of the delight of the Absolute. They are the results of ignorance; they will be dissolved in Absolute when ignorance gives place to knowledge.

> The Supreme Absolute in its Blissful activity takes a plunge into darkness of inconscience and ignorance. This plunge into darkness is for the sake of its conquest and for fuller self-assertion. The opposition of good and evil is a necessary antithesis in the dialectical movement of divine self-realization. The dual and hostile forces are created out of its power of darkness, the forces that check all movements towards the Divine Light and Supreme Bliss. The dark forces are also the forces of the Divine. It is not a negation of Bliss nor is it an illusion. It is a creation of the spirit. The evil is the lowest form of Bliss where it completely but apparently negates itself.
>
> – R.S. Srivastava 1968: 35

Śaṅkara is forced to call evil unreal in order to make the path smooth for his Advaitism but Sri Aurobindo boldly and squarely faces it, and accepts its reality and shows the way how it may finally be transformed into Good. It is not contradictory to Good rather it is lesser Good. Leibnitz too says that in spite of all the difficulties, the world is the best possible world.

Sri Aurobindo says in *Savitri*:

> *Bliss is the secret stuff of all that lives*
> *Even pain and grief are garbs of world-delight*
> *That hides behind thy sorrow and thy cry.*[9]

Sri Aurobindo writes (vol. 10: 1396):

> I am a tāntric, I regard the world as born of *ānanda* (bliss) and living by *ānanda*, wheeling from *ānanda* to *ānanda*. *Ānanda* and *śakti* these are the two real terms of existence.

He further says:

> A transcendent being, unimaginable and inexpressible by the mind and speech, is the nature of the ineffable. That broods immanent and secret in the whole universe and in everything in the universe. Its presence is described as a secret ether of the bliss of being, of which the scripture says that, if this were not, none could for a moment breathe or live. And this spiritual bliss is here also in our hearts. – 1950b: 532

INTEGRAL ADVAITISM

Sri Aurobindo's philosophy is Advaitic in character but it is not absolute Advaitism but integral Advaitism. It is Advaita because he regards *Brahman* as one and the fundamental reality. But this Advaita is called integral as it does not maintain infinite at the cost of the finite, the Absolute at the cost of the reality of any aspect of existence.

> The philosophy of Sri Aurobindo may aptly be described as integral non-dualism (Pūrṇa Advaita) or Integral idealism (Pūrṇa-vijñāna) or just integralism (Pūrṇavāda).
>
> – Banerjee 2012: 19

In integral Advaitism of Sri Aurobindo, there is complete synthesis of physical, vital, logical and mental realities, "Absolute is the unity of rich diversity". It reconciles all the opposites in a comprehensive

[9] *Savitri*, part II, book VI, canto 11, p. 98.

whole. According to Sri Aurobindo, the real monism or true Advaitism accepts all things as one *Brahman*. It does not bisect its existence into two incompatible entities as an eternal truth and an eternal falsehood, *Brahman* and non-*Brahman*, self and not-self. "If it be true that the Self alone exists, it must be also true that all is the self" (Aurobindo 1970, vol. I: 31). It looks upon difference as eternal development within the framework of all inclusive reality. Integral Advaitism integrates the difference between ethics, religion, logic and metaphysics without depreciating their value and importance. It reconciles thought and existence in the "unity of integral experiences, integral living and the integral sweep of cosmic evolution". In integral scheme of Sri Aurobindo, the value of differences between real and unreal, good or bad is not fixed as dualistic thinkers say. They are real but do not indicate any ultimate division in existence. According to integralism, the opposition between higher and lower develops within the cosmic self-expression of the same Ultimate Reality. Reality is non-dual, non-conceptual and at the same time it manifests itself in the form of the world and the individual. This constitutes the meaning of the integral Advaitism of Sri Aurobindo. This view steers clear both extremes of the complete affirmation and absolute denial. According to the materialists, spirit is a by-product of matter whereas spiritualism denies the reality of matter. According to Sri Aurobindo, matter and spirit, are the expressions of the Absolute and as such the lowest and the highest terms of existence. Thus an integral view of reality cannot overlook any of these realities. To quote *Taittirīya Upaniṣad*: "Matter is also *Brahman*."[10] All this is: *Brahman*. Monism which utters a profound truth in proclaiming the fundamental unity of existence, commits the rationalistic fallacy of identifying reality with a conceptually formulated principle or intellectual scheme. According to non-dualism (Advaita) reality is beyond one and many, beyond substance and quality.

Matter and spirit will no more be two opposite ends if we will consider the intervening grades between them, i.e. life, mind and supermind. Asceticism has rendered great services to life

[10] *Annaṁ brahmeti vyajānāt.*

and humanity. According to Sri Aurobindo "the reality which the *saṁnyāsin* seeks has been grasped in its full height, but not in its full extent and comprehensiveness". We owe great debt to materialism for it has freed human mind from dogmas and superstitions to a great extent and to asceticism for rising to a great extent spiritual and moral life. Both spirit and matter are the expressions of Absolute and contribute equally to our understanding of life and reality as a whole.

Unity is the keynote of Sri Aurobindo's philosophy, that one is pre-eminently real but it never denies the many as the figment of the mind. Sri Aurobindo (1951b: 37) says:

> *Brahman* is one, not numerically but in essence. Numerical oneness would either exclude multiplicity or would be a pluralistic and divisible oneness with the many as its parts. That is not the unity of *Brahman*, which can neither be diminished nor increased, nor divided.

Sri Aurobindo arrives at integral Advaitism without denying the reality of the phenomenal world and the individual souls. He has been able to arrive at his integral Advaitism by his concept of creative-force as conscious in nature.

THE CONCEPT OF SUPERMIND

The concept of supermind is the pivot over which the whole integral philosophy of Sri Aurobindo rotates. According to Sri Aurobindo, the world is the manifestation of Saccidānanda. But the diametrically opposite nature of the world and Saccidānanda "does not warrant a smooth transition". This creation of a finite world out of an Infinite Absolute demands an intermediary principle, a principle which can associate the finite world with the infinite reality. And this link cannot be the mind as "mind distorts reality by arbitrary division. It believes in dichotomy. It is not sufficient to fathom the mystery of existence in the universe and Being mainly because it is governed by the formal laws." "Mind may divide, multiply, add, subtract but it cannot get beyond the limits of this mathematics" (Aurobindo 1970, vol. I: 162). It views everything from its own viewpoint excluding all others. It "clamps everything in rigidly fixed forms". If matter is matter and soul is soul how can the gulf be bridged. If the world is world and God is God, how can the twain meet. Second, because it is itself a product of the free creativity of being, it cannot cross its own limitation. Third, it cannot transcend the dichotomy of subject and object as this is ingrained in the intellect.[11] Mind deals with appearance and not with reality. Reality cannot be known by mind. Thus this intermediary link should be something higher than mind and Sri Aurobindo calls this principle Supermind. It is the Supreme Truth Consciousness. It finds no opposition between Being and becoming, one and many. Contradiction remains in our limited mind and not in reality. The whole credit of Sri Aurobindo consists in his maintenance of the oneness of the Absolute without denying the reality of the many. The Advaitin maintains the one at the cost of many; the pluralist maintains many at the cost of one, but the beauty of integral philosophy of Sri Aurobindo consists in its maintenance of unity without denying multiplicity. This is made possible by his concept of the Supermind. It is "the culmination and consummation of Mind. It is all that Mind strives to be but cannot attain" (Maitra 1993: 19). This Supermind is non-dichotomous as it grasps the reality intuitively.

The idea of Supermind is completely Sri Aurobindo's own discovery; he has not borrowed it from any secondary source. He has intuited it himself. He has himself said:

> I did not learn the idea from Veda or Upaniṣad and do not know if there is anything of the kind there, what I received about the Supermind was a director, not a derived knowledge given to me, it was only afterwards that I found certain confirmatory revelation in the Upaniṣad and Veda. – Aurobindo 1953b: 173

Sri Aurobindo (1970, vol. I: 124) accepts that Vedas and Upaniṣads conceive Supermind

> as a vastness beyond the ordinary firmaments of our consciousness in which truth of being is luminously one with all that expresses it and assures inevitably truth of vision,

[11] Chaudhary, 1942: 20.

> formulation, arrangement, word, act and movement and therefore truth also of result of movement, result of action and expression, infallible ordinance or law.

Sri Aurobindo has himself accepted that he arrived at this concept of Supermind by his own direct experience of truth-consciousness and its comparison and contrast with mental consciousness yet its germs are found in the Vedas and the Upaniṣads. In *Ṛgveda* it is said that *ṛta* was produced first of all. The harmony, law and peace are prevailing in the world due to *ṛta*. H. Chaudhary (1972: 16) says:

> The Supermind is what the Vedic seers described as *satyam ṛtam bṛhat* – the vast truth-consciousness which is at once self-shining and self-effectuating in character. It is what the Upaniṣadic *ṛṣis* glimpsed as the *vijñāna, turīya śakti* – the creative medium of self-manifestation of the super-natural trinity, Saccidānanda.

Supermind is in between one and many.

THE SUPERMIND AS CREATOR

The Supermind is the creative aspect of Saccidānanda. As Sri Aurobindo calls it, it is the creatrix. Saccidānanda has infinite truth, infinite existence, infinite bliss, infinite power and infinite potentiality. It is not possible to manifest simultaneously its all creativity or potentiality. It is the Supermind which selects some of them and actualizes them in explicit manifestation. If all the creative powers are manifested at a time, there will be creation of a chaotic world and not of a cosmos. In the absence of Supermind, the potentiality of Saccidānanda would not have manifested. The infinite conscious-force has to abide by certain laws in order to manifest the universe. As Sri Aurobindo (1970, vol. II: 115) says:

> Infinite consciousness in its infinite action can produce only infinite results; to settle upon a fixed Truth or order of truths and build a world in conformity with that which is fixed demands a selective faculty of knowledge commissioned to shape finite appearance out of infinite Reality.

It manifests some of its potentiality and preserves the rest. It is the guiding truth. But it does not work in an arbitrary way rather it works according to some fixed truth, some definite principle or law. Sri Aurobindo says that the Supermind "does not work directly or with a sovereign irresponsibility like a magician building up worlds and universe by the mere fiat of its word. We perceive a process, we are aware of a law." The law and order in the universe are maintained by Supermind which is the other name of the conscious-force working according to some fixed truth, some definite order. The Supermind is nothing but Saccidānanda in space and time. While Saccidānanda is spaceless and timeless Absolute, the Supermind is Saccidānanda manifested in spatial and temporal world. It is the God aspect of the Absolute. Saccidānanda is Absolute in its totality; Supermind is the Absolute as creator or sustainer of the world. Sri Aurobindo says:

> No doubt, it is Saccidānanda not resting in its pure infinite invariable consciousness, but proceeding out of this primal poise or rather upon it as a base and in it as a continent, into a movement which is its form of energy and instrument of cosmic creation.[12]

The Supermind is the intermediary principle between Saccidānanda and the universe. Sri Aurobindo defines Supermind as:

> A principle of active will and knowledge superior to Mind and creatix of the world is then the intermediary power and state of being between that self-possession of the One and this flux of the Many.

Above the Supermind is "the unitarian or indivisible consciousness of pure Saccidānada which knows no separation and below the Supermind is the "analytic or dividing consciousness of mind" which proceeds only by differentiation and division. The Supermind falls in between this one and many, in between his unitary and differenciating consciousness. It is one-in-many as well as many-in-one. It is originally one that is potentially many. The unity is Saccdānanda's primary unity, the original unity but in supermind it is a modified one. This intermediary principle is the beginning and the end of all creation, "the Alpha and the Omega, the starting-point of all differentiation, the instrument of all unification, originative, executive and consummative of all

[12] An article in *Annual* of Sri Aurobindo Mandir, 15 August 1944.

realized or realizable harmonies" (Aurobindo 1970, vol. I: 126). It can draw the one in multiplicity; it manifests the many but is never lost in it. It bridges the vast gulf between the finite and the infinite. Sri Aurobindo calls the Supermind the child of Saccidānanda and the parents of the mind. Revelation of Saccidānanda through the Supermind is the ultimate fact of this universe. It is only through the creative Supermind that the two extremes, Saccidānanda and the world are united.

SUPERMIND AS TRUTH-CONSCIOUSNESS

The Supermind is called by Sri Aurobindo, "Real Idea", "Truth Consciousness", "Seer Will", "the creative idea", "the creator" and so on. By giving it the name "Real Idea", Sri Aurobindo (1970, vol. I: 117) emphasizes the fact that the Supermind is

> a power of conscious-force expressive of real being, born out of real being and partaking of its nature and neither a child of the void nor a weaver of fictions. It is conscious reality throwing itself into mutable forms of its own imperishable and immutable substance.

Again Sri Aurobindo calls it truth-consciousness, a name which he has borrowed from *Ṛgveda* and "uses it to delimit the connotation of the more elastic phrase, Supermind". By truth-consciousness Sri Aurobindo means the principle of Conscious-Force, the Divine law. It is also called real idea. It is not mental awareness rather, it is a self-aware truth of being. The supermind is the consciousness of essential truth of being (*satyam*), of ordered truth of active being (*ṛtam*) and the vast self-awareness (*bṛhat*) in which alone this consciousness is possible. There is infinite potentiality in Saccidānanda which is being guided by truth-consciousness. We perceive law and order in the manifestation of this world due to the presence of this truth-consciousness. The truth-consciousness is present in the world everywhere as ordering self-knowledge by which the One manifests the harmonies of its infinite potential multiplicity. Without this the world would have been a "shifting chaos", "a teeming, amorphous, confused uncertainty" because infinite potentiality may lead to "a play of uncontrolled unbounded chance". The truth-consciousness is well aware of all potentialities and harmonious relationship. It knows well both "the what" and "the how" of things. It maintains law and order in the universe. It keeps law in the world, the creation does not mean coming out of anything new. It is all contained there in its potential form.

In this truth-consciousness, the trinity of knowledge (knower, knowledge and known are not different entities but are basically one. The distinction is made on mental level only. We posit three entities in *sat* (existence), consciousness and bliss and unite them to arrive at a trinity. But it is merely a mental procedure, for unitary consciousness such a division is inadmissible. Existence is consciousness, consciousness is Bliss, and there is no distinction between them. In Supermind, knowledge, force and being are not self-divided as in the mind. "The Supermind is the vast-*satyamamṛtam bṛhat*, one vast will."

The Supermind acts fundamentally on the truth of unity. It sees the universe and its contents "in a single indivisible act of knowledge, an act which is its life, which is the very movement of its self-existence". The indivisibility of the comprehensive Supermind is truth upon which Sri Aurobindo has always advised us to insist. Supermind is the power of conscious-force which creates the cosmos and manifests in it. Universal force and universal consciousness are one – cosmic force in the operation of cosmic consciousness.

It should not be thought that this principle is entirely alien to us. It does not belong to a Being which is entirely other than ourselves, from where we have been dethroned for ever. Though it is far off from us still we have access to it. We cannot infer that truth but we can realize it and the realization of this truth is the supreme ideal of our life.

The relation of Supermind to the Absolute is that of identity.

> It is of the very essence of Sri Aurobindo's metaphysics to deny the reality of separate entities as such. Supermind is then identically the Absolute under its aspect of becoming, which coexists with the aspect of motionless being. – Feys 1973: 44

Again, Supermind is not mind raised to its highest degree, but it is totally different from the consciousness. It is above the triple principle of life, mind and matter and is below the triune principles of *sat*, *cit* and *ānanda*. It may be called the creative power or *sat*.

Supermind is not only a superlative necessity – it is also vitally or practically important, for the theoretical is subordinate to the practical in Sri Aurobindo. Its exact function is to realize multiplicity without doing harm to unity. Here it is distinct from mind which is divisive. Mind proceeds by division and distinction. It distorts the reality. It expresses only relative truth. It does not reveal the omniscient knowledge. It always creates distinction and has no vision of true unity; it has no vision of creation of many out of the one. It is an instrument of analysis and synthesis and not of essential knowledge. Sri Aurobindo says:

> Mind is the nodus of the great Ignorace because it is that which originally divides and distributes, and it has even been mistaken for the cause of the universe and for the whole of the divine *māyā*.

It proceeds by exclusive concentration of consciousness. It tries "to clamp everything into rigidly fixed forms and apparently unchanging or unmoving external factors". Mind is a passage not a culmination. It is Supermind which has the vision of Saccidānanda and holds in its creative will, the secret of the development of multiplicity from unity. Mind cuts up the Absolute being into smaller wholes, into atoms.

> Behind this dividing action is the saving knowledge of the Supramental which knows every whole, every atom to be only a concentration of all-force, of all-consciousness, of all being into phenomenal forms of itself. – Aurobindo 1970, vol. I: 166

> Whereas mind makes the paralysing fissure between thought and reality in Supermind all being is consciousness, and all consciousness is equally a vibration of being pregnant of itself.
> – Chaudhary, Haridas 1972: 29

Besides, mind sees only a given time and space. It sees only the bare present surface things but Supermind sees the whole extension of time and space.

It is only after the veil is lifted and the dividing mind is overpowered that the mind gets back to the truth of things. Mind is really a subordinate instrumentation of the truth-consciousness. The fundamental error of the mind is "this fall from self-knowledge". If it returns back to truth from which it has fallen, it becomes the final action of truth-consciousness. Mind cannot see the things as a whole. The difference between mind and supermind lies in their manner of apprehending reality. While Supermind perceives the unitary picture of reality, mind bisects the whole into parts. Bergson too says that mental knowledge suffers from a fundamental defect. "Mind saves itself by becoming more than mind, by transforming itself into the Supermind" (Maitra 1993: 21).

THE ABSOLUTE AND THE SUPERMIND

There are systems of philosophy which believe in God but not in Absolute; there are also other systems which affirm the existence of Absolute but not of God. But a few philosophers have tried to reconcile the Absolute and the personal God. Advaita Vedānta is one of them. But for Advaitist, the Absolute is the only reality, God is only phenomenally real and for this they take shelter under Māyāvāda. The world is given only phenomenal reality. But in the philosophy of Sri Aurobindo, the Supermind or God is the real Creative power of Saccidānanda. Sri Aurobindo is the first modern philosopher who equally accepts Absolute as well as God and sees, some sort of synthetic oneness in them. The difficulty in the reconciliation of the Absolute and God is due to the fact that they are taken to be distinct realities. For Sri Aurobindo the immanent aspect of Saccidānanda is as real as the transcendental aspect. Supermind is not an illusory power of Saccindānanda taken in the context of the world. It cannot be differentiated from Saccidānanda. It is in between the world and Saccidānanda, ever busy in manifestation of infinite potentiality of Saccidānanda with certain laws and principle. Supermind is "such a continuous and synthetic reality which has the absolute synthesis of the spaceless and timeless Saccidānanda, and also the projected world of manyness in space and time" (R.S. Srivastava 1968: 47). According to Sri Aurobindo (1970, vol. I: 132):

> this all-containing, all-originating, all-consummating Supermind

> as the nature of the Divine Being, not indeed in its absolute self-existence, but in its action as the Lord and creator of its own worlds. This is the truth of that which we call God.

Saccidānanda is the precosmic and primal absolute, the Supermind is the cosmic Absolute. Again "The primal transcendent reality in its Absolute self-possession is Saccidānanda and its secondary poise is the Supermind". The three aspects of Saccidānanda, namely, existence, consciousness-force and bliss are its transcendental aspect, whereas it has also a fourth and immanent aspect which is Supermind. Supermind, the God of Saccidānanda, is different from *Īśvara* of Vedānta or the Demiurge of Plato. *Īśvara* of Vedānta is Absolute seen in and through its reflection in *māyā*. In the words of Maitra (1993: 17):

> *Īśvara* of the Vedānta is not the Absolute in its pure untarnished form. It is the Absolute seen through its reflection in *māyā*, which reflection partially disguises and even distorts its true nature. Sri Aurobindo in this matter wants to go back to the unsystematized Vedānta of the Upaniṣads, which is innocent of this conception of a *māyā*-ridden *Īśvara* and to the standpoint of the Vedas. The sages who said, *yato vā imāni bhūtāni jāyante yena jātāni jīvanti, yat prayantyabhisaṁviśanti* did not contemplate a creator who was himself shrouded in *māyā*.

The creative principle that is *Īśvara* in the Advaita Vedānta is not conceived as ultimately real and the world is also ultimately reduced to reality. Just to provide Absolute the perfect integrity and transcendence, Śaṅkara reduces the world to unreality from the ontological viewpoint. Sri Aurobindo lays great stress on the fact that creatorship is not incompatible with Absoluteness. His assertion that the Absolute is above all relations never advocates the falsity of the relational world. It is imperfect no doubt, but never false. Sri Aurobindo's integral Advaitism never neglects the world and this is possible only with the supposition of supermind as the creative principle. But this Supermind is not the whole of the Absolute reality, it is only its creative and dynamic aspect. His conception of the Supermind is most illuminating portion of his philosophy. The explanatory principle *māyā* treats the world as a "meaningless show", but Supermind provides fullest reality to it. The difference between Saccidānanda and Supermind is that while Supermind is differentiated unity, Saccidānanda is undifferentiated unity. The apparent opposition between the world and the Absolute is reconciled by Supermind.

> The Supermind is at once the creative medium of God's descent into cosmic being and the illuminating medium of man's ascent into this unfathomable mystery. It is not a super eminent capacity lifted above ordinary mentality but a radically changed function of consciousness . . . it is at once the instrument of all unification and the starting point of all differentiation.
>
> – Chaudhary, Haridas 1972: 28-29

It creates the many but never loses itself in this many.

THE TRIPLE STATUS OF SUPERMIND

The Supermind has three ways of action in its three poises or status, which are called comprehending consciousness, apprehending consciousness and projecting consciousness.

In its first poise of comprehending consciousness, it is one with Saccidānanda. It is "unitarian consciousness". In its second poise, it has potentiality of cosmic evolution. Here it is like Hiraṇyagarbha; the great cosmic potentiality or cosmic egg from which the universe is born. It has the potentiality to manifest the power of Saccidānanda. In the third poise (projecting consciousness), actually there is creation of the cosmos with matter, life and mind. All these poises are supra-terrestrial.

The first poise is the causal state (*kāraṇāvasthā*) in which everything is potentially ready for the Supermind to initiate the play of creation. The second stage is the effect of the first stage in which the play has begun. The third is fully manifest state, *pūrṇa vyakta avasthā* in which creative process is fully at work and consciousness is expressed in all forms and centres. Sri Aurobindo (1970, vol. I: 145-46) says:

> the first finds the inalienable unity of things, the second modifies that unity so as to support the manifestation of the Many in One and One in Many; the third further modifies it so as to support the evolution of a diversified individuality which, by the action

> of ignorance, becomes in us at a lower level the illusion of the separate ego.

According to Sri Aurobindo (1970, vol. 1: 144), Supermind and Saccidānanda are equally real but Supermind is

> Saccidānanda not resting in its pure infinite invariable consciousness but proceeding out of this primal poise or rather upon it as a base and in it as continent, into movement which is its form of energy and instrument of cosmic creation.

This Supermind is the dynamic aspect of *sat*. It is wholly responsible for the creation. In its primary status it has unity with Saccidānanda. It comprehends the cosmos in complete oneness and unity. It finds here the inalienable unity of things. Saccidānanda is always transcendental. It is pure unity where consciousness is existence, existence is bliss and bliss is existence. These three are not divided in Saccidānanda. But the primary status of Supermind is not the pure unitary consciousness which is a spaceless and timeless concentration of Saccidānanda that contains the universe in eternal potentiality. It is self-extension of Saccidānanda which is still one all-constituting, all-possessing and all-comprehensive consciousness. Unity is the dominant character of the Supermind in its first poise. It holds infinite potentiality in unity. In this poise there is no difference between matter and spirit as everything is here in the form of Spirit.

Again, here there is no difference between conscious-soul and force-soul for "all force would be action of consciousness". There is no difference between subject and object. There is no sense of otherness here. The manifold creation to this stage is not anything than itself.

The Supermind here is not divided. It is one and single *Brahman* everywhere. It pervades the whole creation as one. This all comprehensive status of the Supermind may be well expressed by the formula, "All this is, indeed, *Brahman* (*sarvaṁ khalvidam brahma* – Chā.U. III.14.1)".

> It is the unity that holds the whole world of diversity in its close embrace. The diversity is real because it is ultimately nothing but *Brahman*. Not only the reality underlying all these existence

> is *Brahman* but all these existences themselves are nothing but the forms of *Brahman*. – Misra 1957: 190

The second poise of the Supermind is named as the apprehending consciousness (*prajñāna*). In this poise, the Supermind supports the manifestation of manyness from the one. Here the first division appears between Divine Consciousness and its force, between *puruṣa* and *prakṛti*, between self and not-self, though there is no essential difference between self and not-self; only practical differentiation is created. In all forms it realizes itself, no doubt, as "one stable conscious-self and also as the one supporting each individual play of movement and its differentiation". They all are one in soul-essence but not in soul-form. The Divine Consciousness, which creates the multiplicity, is also well aware of its existence as the one in essence and reality. Here Supermind supports manyness, the individual distinction in its oneness. Here we meet with the fundamental distinction between subject and object (*puruṣa* and *prakṛti*) or self and not-self though it is not an essential difference but practical only. Here there is beginning of creation but still they are in united form. The apprehending consciousness is the support of the movement, but it is indifferent to any sort of movement. *Gītā* XIII.16 too says:

> Though itself indivisible it seems to distribute itself in the forms of nature.[13]

Sri Aurobindo (1970 vol. 1: 146) says:

> In each name and form it would realize itself as the stable Conscious-Self, the same in all; but also it would realize itself as a concentration of Conscious-Self following and supporting the individual play of movement and upholding its differentiaton from other play of movement, the same everywhere in soul-essence, but varying in soul-form.

Sri Aurobindo sets an example of a poet to illustrate this point. A poet thinks his own creation put before him as if they were things other than the creator himself; yet they are nothing but "the play of self-formation of his own being in itself and indivisible there

---

[13] *avibhaktaṁ ca bhūteṣu vibhaktamiva ca sthitam* | – 6

from their creator".

In the first poise there is only consciousness of unity, in the second, unity in multiplicity. Here there is identity-in-difference. Here Many is conscious of Oneness, and the One manifests itself in Many. Only a practical difference is drawn between knowledge, knower and known. By the comprehending consciousness it realizes its unity with the one but by apprehending consciousness it realizes its difference from One and other Soul-forms. We never forget unity though we are amidst the multiplicity. Here too unity is predominating. The "Many does not appear as Many but as one". It proceeds from unity to resultant multiplicity, "it comprehends all things in itself as itself", "it proceeds in its action from the unity to the multiplicity and from multiplicity to unity" (Aurobindo 1970, vol. I: 146).

The third poise of Supermind is called the projecting consciousness. It projects itself into the multiplicity and identifies itself with each form. Multiplicity is distinctively emphasized here. In comprehending poise; there is pure unity, in apprehending poise, there is consciousness of unity-in-diversity. In projecting poise, there is full emphasis on multiplicity. Here *jīvātman* thinks himself to be different from other soul-forms. This projecting consciousness is wholly responsible for the feeling of individuality and manyness which is so contrary to the universal Divine consciousness. Here conscious-self projects itself into the multiplicity and gets involved in it. But *avidyā* is not a necessary consequence of this poise.

> This tertiary poise would be therefore that of a sort of fundamental blissful dualism in unity – no longer unity qualified by a subordinate dualism – between the individual Divine and its universal source, with all the consequences that would accrue from the maintenance and operation of such a dualism.
>
> – Aurobindo 1970, vol.I: 147-48

In the higher poise unity is dominant; variation is only a play of this unity. Here too individual Divine would be conscious of itself as the result of that one. This true spiritual individual will never show arrogance by providing itself independent and separate existence. Sri Aurobindo further observes:

> It would only affirm the truth of differentiating movement along with the truth of the stable unity regarding them as the upper and lower and poles of the same truth, the foundation and culmination of the same divine play: and it would insist on the joy of the differentiation as necessary to the fullness of the joy of the unity. – Ibid.: 148

Sri Aurobindo affirms that no philosophy (even Vedānta) would ever deny the priority or eternal dependence of Many on the One. The Supermind has three types of activity in three poises but they are not different from each other. In the words of Chaudhary (1942: 136):

> The comprehending consciousness of the Supermind ensures the truth of the self-containing all things, the apprehending consciousness ensures the truth of the self-inhabiting all things, and the projecting consciousness ensures the truth of the self-becoming all things.

Many is only a static self-diffusion and self-differentiation. Not only one is divine but many too is divine. Many is nothing but "self-differentiated existence of the one in the play of delightful creativity of the Supermind". If one manifests itself as many, many too has to come back to once again. One is logically prior to many and many is eternally dependent on one. Both are equally true. None is to be accepted at the cost of other. In fact, unity is the basis of multiplicity and multiplicity is the basis for its return to unity. In the Supramental plane, the soul is aware of unity but on empirical plane, it forgets its real abode due to ignorance.

SUPERMIND AND OVERMIND

The Overmind is "in its nature and law a delegate of the Supermind to the ignorance. The Supermind acts on the world of ignorance through the Overmind." How does the self-luminous Supreme spirit descend into the inconscience of matter? How does mind in ignorance fall from supramental truth consciousness? Sri Aurobindo replies that it is all done by Supermind. Supermind is the medium between the unmanifested spirit and manifested world. This Overmind forms the transitional link between the upper and the lower hemisphere; it is the meeting ground of mind and Supermind.

The general tendency of the Overmind is towards separation. It does not enjoy the integral unity of the Supermind. It is not able to transform wholly the ignorance and inconscience. Its descent does not change the nature of terrestrial existence. It still proceeds on the basis of ignorance. The Overmind is distinguished from the Supermind by a transparent veil.

Supermind communicates all its realities to the Overmind yet the Overmind is "a first parent of the ignorance, because the integrality of the Supermind is lacking there". It weaves each aspect of reality into an independent reality, in this way the integrality of Supermind, which tries to bind the diversities in one whole, is spoiled by Overmind. The Supermind maintains the integrality but in the Overmind this integrality is no longer there. Yet the Overmind is aware of essential truth of things, it knows their oneness; it is not directly determined by it. Thus the integrality and unity of Supermind is destroyed by Overmind. Sri Aurobindo (1970, vol. I: 279) further says:

> In Overmind we have the origin of the cleavage, the trenchant distinction made by the philosophy of the Saṁkhyas in which they appear as two independent entities, *prakṛti* able to dominate *puruṣa* and cloud its freedom and power, reducing it to a witness and recipient of her forms and actions, *puruṣa* able to return to its separate existence and abide in a free self-sovereignty by rejection of her original overclouding material principle.

Overmind allows each of different aspects of the all-comprehending One to create the nest of its own. It erects each power of the Supreme Reality into a separate reality.

The Overmind is "a principle of cosmic Truth and a vast and endless catholicity is its full spirit" (Aurobindo 1970, vol. I: 183). It is a sort of inferior Supermind.

To the Overmind, all religions would be true as development of one eternal religion, all philosophies would be valid in their own respective fields. It is creator of the truth and not of illusions or falsehood. Maitra (1993: 28) says:

> Where the mind sees irreconcilable differences, the Overmind intelligence perceives coexistent correlatives; what to the mind are contraries are to the Overmind complementaries.

Sri Aurobindo's Conception of Man and His Bondage

In spite of being most close to us, the concept of self always puts us in riddle as to its real nature. It is really difficult to grasp what is self after all. The dispute about the nature and concept of the self which is so close and dear to us is most perplexing. Some identify it with ego, others know it as an imaginary focus behind the five sheathes. But according to Sri Aurobindo (2003: 3):

> *Brahman* is, subjectively, *ātman*, the self or immutable existence of all that is in the universe. Everything that changes in us, mind, life, body, character, temperament, action is not our real and unchanging self, but becoming of the self in the movement, *jagati*. – vv 6-7

He again says:

> *Ātman*, our true self is *Brahman*, it is pure indivisible Being, self-luminous, self-concentrated in consciousness, self-concentrated in force, self-delighted. Its existence is light and bliss. It is timeless, spaceless and free. – Aurobindo 1951b: 44

THE CONCEPT OF THE INDIVIDUAL SELF

The problem of individuality is closely connected with the conception of self. Our individualization is only a superficial formation, a practical selection and limited conscious synthesis for the temporary utility of life in a particular body. Individuality is a necessary presumption for ethics and religion. Denial of individuality is equivalent to the denial of moral responsibility and religion. The personalists and the theists assert individuality but an Absolutists like Śaṅkara denies individuality of the soul. According to him, *ātman* is *Brahman*. Due to false identification of *ātman* with psycho-physical organism, the sense of egoity develops. Liberation means the relation of the identity of soul with *Brahman*. Sri Aurobindo agrees with Śaṅkara when he says that souls is one in essence with *Brahman* but disagrees when he denies individuality. He takes side of Rāmānuja when Rāmānuja says that the individual self is real eternally. The true individuality persists even after liberation. It is only false ego that disappears. T.D. Chatterjee (1970: 40) opines that according to Sri Aurobindo:

> The individual is God himself but in a particular poise or mode of manifestation. Every self is a centre of action, a channel of expression of God. Ego is abolished but the central personal being has to remain as an instrument for the Divine's work in the world.

This problem of individuality is the greatest hindrance in the way of spiritual monistic theism. If the whole existence is embraced in one Absolute, there is no room left for the individuality of the self. The self as individual will mean one independent existence and a free will to choose. For Sri Aurobindo (1970, vol. I: 38): "Individual salvation can have no real sense if existence in the cosmos is itself an illusion". It is not the Supreme self benefited by liberation, not the world; rather it is the individual soul who is benefited but for an illusionalist the individual is an illusion. Sri Aurobindo (ibid.) says:

> Therefore we arrive at the escape of an illusory non-existent soul from an illusory non-existent bondage in an illusory non-existent world as the Supreme Good which non-existent soul has to persue.

Chaudhary (1943: 181) says:

> If ultimate reality be the Absolute in the true sense of the term, we should reduce the individual either like Spinoza to a mode of consciousness of the one infinite substance which the Absolute is or like Bradley to a mere appearance which is bound to be lost or dissipated in the life of the Absolute. The modal or adjectival theory of the individual seems to be a necessary consequence of the absoluteness of reality.

If individuality is not denied the result will be atomism, separatism and pluralism. John McTaggart exalts the individual selves to the rank of eternally perfect and self-subsistent spirits and reduces ultimate reality to an impersonal unity of these spirits having no centralized consciousness of its own. But such theory is not satisfactory at all. Here speculative thinking clashes with spiritual experience. Atomic theory too is one sided. According to Josiah Royce, the individuals are the self-representatives of Absolute. Their uniqueness is denied as it is "the fulfilment of a certain purpose which belongs to the will of God". Pringle Pattison maintains that the individual is a "standing differentiation of the Absolute" and focalized expression of the universe. Sri Aurobindo may be credited for solving this problem of individuality in a unique way. Individual is not mere appearance or "an illusory product of ignorance" or "a vanishing quality" rather it belongs to the final structure of the Ultimate Reality. The individual "lives in God, by God for God". Individuality is never lost, never fused even after the soul has attained freedom. Only false idea of individuality is dissolved. Individual is none but God himself in a particular poise of being, He is the nucleus of action of Divine. According to Sri Aurobindo the contradiction between acceptance of individuality and Absolute unity of *Brahman* originates because of one-sided view. They approach this problem with the help of finite reason and not through the logic of infinite. Sri Aurobindo asserts without any difficulty the reality of the individual souls and at the same time their oneness with the absolute *Brahman*. The self is one in its being, still it is capable of differentiating itself from cosmic individuality. Misra (1998: 409), says:

> The soul, according to Sri Aurobindo, can enjoy unity both in its essence and in its power. To become one with the Divine, to enjoy unity with it only in essence and not in its aspect of power is a partial and one-sided unity and not a perfect and integral unity.

The unity will be perfect only when it participates in its aspect of being as well as in its aspect of power, in its transcendental as well as individual aspect. Sri Aurobindo very emphatically asserts the importance of individual in the world-process. To the question why individual is necessary Sri Aurobindo's (1970, vol. I: 37) reply is:

> The individual is still necessary to the action of the Transcendent in the universe and that action in him does not cease to be possible by his illumination on the contrary, since the conscious

> manifestation of the Transcendent in the individual is the means by which the collective, the universal is also to become conscious of itself, the continuation of the illumined individual in the action of the world is an imperative need of the world-play.

The universe and the individual are one and not exclusive to each other. And the liberation of this individual soul is, according to Sri Aurobindo (ibid.: 40),

> the keynote of the definite divine action; it is the primary divine necessity and the pivot on which all else turns. It is the point of Light at which the intended complete self-manifestation in the many beings to emerge.

But the unity of liberated soul is incomplete without its unity with the many. It should extend its perception of unity "horizontally as well as vertically". Sri Aurobindo is empathic in his view that "we can attain to the highest without blotting ourselves out from the cosmic extension. *Brahman* preserves its two terms of liberty within and formation without." So can individual soul do.

The individual has come to this world to play an inalienable role and the world is his necessary counterpart. It is by means of universe that the individual is impelled to realize himself. Both the universe and the individual are necessary to each other in their ascents. Sri Aurobindo (1970, vol. I: 45) says:

> Always indeed they exist for each other and profit by each other. Universe is a diffusion of the divine all in infinite Space and Time, the individual its concentration within limits of Space and Time.

According to Sri Aurobindo, the individual must necessarily universalize and impersonalize himself in order to realize divinity in all which is his reality too. But impersonalization never means depersonalization; the essence of personal existence must persist.

> Yet is he called upon to preserve, even when he most extends himself in universality of consciousness, a mysterious transcendent something of which his sense of personality gives him an obscure and egoistic representation. Otherwise he has missed his goal, the problem set to him has not been solved, and the divine work for which he accepted birth has not been done.
>
> – Ibid.: 45-46

The importance of individual is realized by Sri Aurobindo even by the intermediate role assigned to the individual consciousness. He recognized three terms: an inferior term of animal life, the middle term, which is characterized by the consciousness of mind, and a supreme term, which is superior to man's present self. The human stage is a transitional stage but it is an indispensable stage as it is through the human being that the divine realizes himself in the universe. Sri Aurobindo calls man as supremely capable of incarnating God. Thus for Sri Aurobindo:

> The divine is the fulfilment of man and no longer entails the obliteration of the person. – Feys 1973: 44

With the elimination of the personality we do not eliminate our individuality. Sri Aurobindo (1970, vol. I: 58-59) says:

> The limited ego is only an intermediate phenomenon of consciousness necessary for a certain line of development. Following this line the individual can arrive at that which is beyond himself, that which he represents, and can yet continue to represent it, no longer as an obscured and limited ego, but as a centre of the Divine and of the universal consciousness embracing, utilizing and transforming into harmony with the Divine all individual determination.

The individual soul can realize itself as individual, universal and transcendental. It can maintain its relationship with other souls of the world, still it can maintain its unity with the Divine. It appears to be self-contradictory only to our abstract logic. But according to Sri Aurobindo, the transcendental has to be judged by its own logic, i.e. logic of the infinite. Viewing the reality from the point of view of mundane logic, will mean to tear asunder its very spirit and will always land in contradiction. He himself observes at one place in the *Life Divine* (1970, vol. 1: 372):

> The whole difficulty and conclusion into which the normal reason falls is that we are speaking of a higher and illimitable self-experience founded on divine and infinite and yet are applying to it a language formed by this lower and limited experience which bases itself on finite appearances and the separative definitions by which we try to distinguish and classify the phenomena of

the material universe.

Thus all these words man, apparent, real, individual have to be taken in relative sense with a full awareness of their inability to express the things that we mean. The individual lives in God, by God and for God. Only a higher reason can well understand the true relationship between the individual and the Divine. Liberation is not cessation of individual but divine perfection of it.

THE DOUBLE SOUL

Sri Aurobindo is well aware of the fact that the man as it appears to us through our senses is not the real man, at least he is not a complete man. But he holds that man can know himself in his true perspective. He conceives the double soul in man – the psychic being (*ātman*) and the central being (*jīvātman*). "The surface desire-soul which works in our vital cravings, our emotions, aesthetic faculty and mental seeking for power; knowledge and happiness, and a subliminal psychic entity, a pure power of light, love, joy and refined essence of being which is our true soul behind the outer form of psychic existence we so often dignify by the name" (Aurobindo 1970, vol. I: 220).

The psychic being, according to Sri Aurobindo, is inside the evolutionary process, whereas *jīvātman* is beyond evolution. Psychic being is a deputy of *jīvātman* expressing itself in individual life and existence, and supporting it. We have the outer soul as well as the inner soul. The psychic soul is the outer soul and *jīvātman* is the inner soul. *Jīvātman* is the part and parcel of Saccidānanda. It is the "centre of the spirit in the cosmos", *jīvātman* is a spark of Divine, a portion of *paramātman* and is transcendent to individuality. It is the transcendental entity, an eternal and ever pure being. It does not participate in the affairs of the world. It is eternal, immutable, everlasting, omniscient, omnipotent, bliss and perfect Reality. It is Saccidānanda itself. It is the same in all individuals. It is the universal *ātman*. It rules over the psychic being.

The psychic being is the representative of *jīvātman*. It is the soul in us. It secretly participates in our daily life. It does not perish with our body, rather it transmigrates from one life to another.

The psychic being actively participates in the activities of an individual and helps him in transformation of his lower nature into higher nature. Sri Aurobindo (ibid.: 226) says:

> It is the psychic personality in us that flowers as the saint, the sage, the seer, when it reaches its full strength, it turns the being towards the knowledge of self and the Divine, towards the supreme Truth, the supreme Good, the supreme Beauty, Love and Bliss, the divine heights and largenesses, and opens us to the touch of spiritual sympathy, universality, oneness. On the contrary, where the psychic personality is weak, crude or ill-developed, the finer parts and movements in us are lacking or poor in character and power, even though the mind may be forceful and brilliant. . . .

Jīvātman is a sport of divinity and a portion of *paramātman*, but the psychic being is the flame of divinity and deputy of *jīvātman*. Psychic being is this spark flaming into fire. *Jīvātman* is the transcendental portion of the psychic being. The psychic being is still not indentified with *jīvātman* which is none but Saccidānanda seated in us. According to Sri Aurobindo (ibid.: 225), subliminal self is

> a flame born out of the Divine and, luminous inhabitant of the Ignorance, grows in it till it is able to turn it towards the Knowledge . . . it is the inner light or inner voice of the mystic.

The psychic being is the principle of individuality. It is dynamic part of *jīvātman*. Sri Aurobindo says that we know by psychological experiments that subliminal mind receives the inner touches of things which the surface mind ignores "so also we shall find that the subliminal soul responds to the *rasa* or essence in experience, of these things which the surface desire-soul rejects by distaste and refusal or ignores by netural unacceptance". Sri Aurobindo observes that if we live only by the surface desire soul, we are no better than the plant or stone.

This theory of double soul should not lead us to the illusion that Sri Aurobindo preaches two independent souls. It simply means that our inner being is related with Saccidānanda while our outer being is participating in the wordly affairs. Everything speaks of manifestation of *Brahman*; thus both psychic being and *jīvātman* are expressions of the Divine.

Sri Aurobindo opines that the psychic being has not yet completely manifested in human level. We are governed not by soul but by mind. The working principle in us is not soul. Only a psychic person will remove our ignorance and incite us towards Divine Consciousness. The psychic being can at first exercise only a concealed, partial and indirect action through the mind, life and body. Transformation of our personality is possible only by the development of this psychic soul. The psychic being is the lower portion of the divine, *jīvātman* is the upper portion of the divine. In its fulfilment the psychic being relates itself to its divine sources. Sri Aurobindo says (1970 vol. 1: 230):

> The psychic being uplifted by that Light and Force can unite itself with the original Delight of existence from which it came; overcoming the dualities of pain and pleasure delivering from all fear. . . .

Although it is a truth that psychic being brings vital changes in us, still it is not all. It alone cannot take us far in the path of spiritual realization. Sri Aurobindo observes that though the psychic transformation is an important phase of the total transformation, it is not all that is required for spiritual change. It is only when the Supermind descends in us that complete transformation is possible. The psychic soul opens only the gate of divine transformation. And it may be well said that there is no need of any intervention of a superior truth-consciousness or of the principle of the Supermind to assist us in getting divine perfection. Sri Aurobindo (ibid.: 226-27) observes:

> If the secret psychic Person can come forward into the front and, replacing the desire-soul, govern overtly and entirely and not only partially and from behind the veil this outer nature of mind, life and body, then these can be cast into soul images of what is true, right and beautiful and in the end the whole nature can be turned towards the real aim of life, the supreme victory, the ascent into spiritual existence.

EVOLUTION

Evolution is made of two words "E + volvere" meaning "unrolling". Evolution, as used in modern science, does not mean arbitrary derivation of anything from anything else, rather it means the growth of an indefinite incoherent homogeneity, into a definite coherent heterogeneity. The concept of evolution is the root of Sri Aurobindo's integralism. The contradiction between matter and spirit, between different grades of reality is resolved with the assertion that matter is not something inert or full but expression of Saccidānanda. In fact, they are not contrary to spirit but one is essence. Matter, according to Sri Aurobindo, is not destined to be inert for ever but in due course of evolution it has the capacity to rise up to the status of spirit. The peculiarity of Sri Aurobindo's conception lies in the fact that there is not only the descent of Absolute into the material world but there is ascent too of grades of existence into spirit again. There is not only evolution but a prior involution too. Evolution is "the process of rising or ascent of matter to its essential and supreme level, viz. the principle of spirit is known as the process of evolution". And involution is the descent of spirit into the principle of ignorance. Says Sri Aurobindo (1970, vol. II, pt 1):

> Evolution is an inverse action of the involution, what is an ultimate and last derivation in the involution is the first to appear in the evolution, what was original and primal in the involution is in the evolution the last and supreme emergence.

Involution means manifestation of spirit in matter or lower forms of reality and evolution means the return of spirit to its original form. In involution it "projects itself out of itself" whereas in evolution it returns back to its original status. It is "the home-coming of the spirit". It goes out of itself again to come back to itself. Ascent would have been impossible without descent. As there is descent of spirit in matter, matter can evolve. It could not have evolved if spirit would not have descended in it. In the words of Sri Aurobindo (1970, vol. I: 3):

> ... there seems to be no reason why life should evolve out of material elements or Mind out of living form, unless we accept

> the Vedāntic solution that life is already involved in Matter and Mind in life because in essence Matter is a form of veiled Life, Life a form of veiled Consciousness.

SPIRITUAL EVOLUTION

Spirit, according to Sri Aurobindo, is the source of creation, evolution and the end of all realization. Evolution is essentially spiritualistic. He presents an integral, cosmic, spiritual and dynamic philosophy of evolution.

> All spiritual evolution, an evolution of consciousness in Matter in a constant developing self formation till the form can reveal the indwelling spirit, is then the keynote of the central significant motive of the terrestrial existence.[14]

Actually evolution, which means the return of Spirit to itself and its self-projection in the world process, carries no meaning if it is not spiritual in character. But for Sri Aurobindo, mechanical evolution is contradiction in terms. It cannot be called evolution in true sense of the term.

According to Hegel, evolution must be a spiritual evolution or no evolution at all. Hegel is right so far; but he wrongly identifies spirit with reason. According to Sri Aurobindo, a true view of evolution must transcend reason. Spirit is on much higher level. The whole scheme of evolution cannot be chalked out with reason as Hegel asserts. Evolution has always something novel, something new in its store for us. Sri Aurobindo (1970, vol. 2, pt 2: 703) observes:

> An evolution in the Inconscience is the beginning, an evolution in the Ignorance is the middle, but the end is the liberation of the spirit into its true consciousness and an evolution in the knowledge.

Spiritual evolution is not the scientific evolution. The scientific theory is concerned only with the outward mechanical process, with physical development of things in matter only. According to Sri Aurobindo, the vitalistic theories too fail to explain evolution

---

[14] Reddy 1966: 270.

as in the ordinary sense of vitalism, there is no goal but only ceaseless process. No doubt, they take life, the dynamic principle, as the creative principle, but for them evolution is only a wayward movement. The mentalistic or rationalistic view of evolution too cannot explain emergence of the higher spiritual and Divine Principles. The divine evolution of Sri Aurobindo views the evolutionary process as unfoldment of spirit in higher and higher degree. Sri Aurobindo (ibid.: 824) observes:

> A Spiritual evolution, an evolution of consciousness in Matter in a constant developing self-formation till the form can reveal the indwelling Spirit, is then the keynote, the central significant motive of the terrestrial existence.

Evolution is cosmic but also individualistic. According to Sri Aurobindo, the evolutionary process will go on till there is complete rising up of the revealed spirit. Evolution is not at random. It has some purpose, some end. The aim is "the concretization, the materialization which includes, of course, vitalization and mentalization of the spirit and the spiritual values". It leads to establishment of divine kingdom on terrestrial existence. There is manifestation of spirit not only in individual but in cosmos too. Not only the individual realizes the Divine, the world is also transformed into the Divine. The individual and the cosmos act reciprocally to realize the Divine in each other. It is wrong to think that only man is spiritualized. It is "the spirit that plunged into a stupor of inconsciene at the inception of creation and it is the spirit again that is gradually waking up from its stupor step by step, through a slow difficult process till the spirit" is fully awake, that is to say, "till there is a complete manifestation of the spirit".

Sri Aurobindo's view of evolution is integral in character:

> Integral evolution means that when the higher principle emerges the lower principles are also transformed. . . . The new principles which emerge out of the lower ones are even effecting their transformation and thus endeavour to lift them up.
>
> – R.S. Srivastava 1968: 88

New principles do not obliterate all connections with past in order to emerge new qualities rather they carry the whole past with them. Lower principles are not abandoned by the emergence of higher principles, but transformed and integrated into higher principles. Samuel Alexander too thought of emergence of new qualities is the course of evolution but the higher there has no capacity to transform the lower. Evolution means, according to him, emergence of novel beings and not ascent of the lower principles into higher ones. Lower principles are lower and higher principles are eternally higher forever, no integral relation between these two principles is possible. According to Alexander, the lower principles are negated and left alone with the emergence of new qualities. As against Alexander, Sri Aurobindo conceives an integral ascent of all these lower principles. The lower principles are also the forms of Absolute Spirit. For Sri Aurobindo (1970, vol. 2: 728):

> Our mental, physical, vital existence need not be destroyed by our self-exceeding, nor are they lessened and impaired by being spiritualized, they can and do become much richer, greater, more powerful and more perfect, in their divine change they break into possibilities which in their unspiritualized condition could not be practicable or imaginable.

While some thinkers believe that lower principles should be outcast to realize spirituality, they do not cooperate in any way in the spiritual ascent of man, Sri Aurobindo believes that in supramentalized condition, body, life and mind are transformed and not rejected in onward journey towards spirit. Integration includes all aspects of man: his work, his body and his world, "it is this evolution which will enable him progressively to manifest God in the holy". In Sri Aurobindo's philosophy, spirit and matter are not closed in watertight compartments like other thinkers. Matter is concealed spirit and is destined to rise up again to the status of Divine in its slow but steady transformation. Transformation takes place gradually, step by step. As three constituents of Saccidānanda (i.e. existence, consciousness and bliss) are one in being but serve different purposes, similarly matter, life and mind are spirit at different stages integrated finally by the action of Supermind.

Man occupies the central position in Sri Aurobindo's scheme of evolution because "the role he fulfils in its development and from the place he finds at its term: the divine is realized both through and in man. This is then what we mean by anthropocentrism" (Feys 1973: 72). The Divine must integrate the man. In fact, Divine is the culmination of man.

P.T. Raju (1953) says that "what is the evolution of Western thinkers is involution of Sri Aurobindo". Sāṁkhya theory of evolution is also different from Sri Aurobindo's theory. No doubt, the theory of involution finds its national justification in Satkāryavāda. Sri Aurobindo adheres to this theory. The effect is pre-existent in the cause. "Matter is the form of veiled life. Life is a form of veiled consciousness." Though Sri Aurobindo borrowed the theory of causality from Sāṁkhya, his evolutionary theory is distinct from that of Sāṁkhya. True, in Sri Aurobindo as well as in Sāṁkhya, evolution is a process of manifestation, but the concept of *pralaya* in Sāṁkhya is different from the concept of involution. While in *pralaya*, manifested materials are back to unmanifest matter, involution is the Spirit concealing in matter. Involution proceeds evolution as condition of the latter.

The monism of Sri Aurobindo accepts intermediaries or gradation in order to integrate different realities.

> Without these one may assert the synthesis, but fail to see how it is brought about. A conceptual transition between extreme terms becomes possible only across a series of intermediate principles. Thus, after laying down the fundamental identity of spirit and matter Sri Aurobindo establishes the rational law which will rule all further synthesis: extreme opposites postulate the existence of link-terms. – Feys 1973: 60

Sri Aurobindo (1970, vol. I: 6) says:

> Nor, so far divided apparently are these two extreme terms, . . . is that identification convincing to the rational intellect if we refuse to recognize a series of ascending terms (Life, Mind, Supermind and the grades that link Mind to Supermind) between spirit and matter. Otherwise the two must appear as irreconcilable opponents bound together in an unhappy wedlock and their

> divorce the one reasonable solution.

A human being cannot remain satisfied with barren contradiction. He always seeks a luminous reconciliation. The principle of intermediaries underlies the whole scheme of Sri Aurobindo's integral metaphysics. Spirit is the highest, matter is the lowest and in between them are the connecting links. The intermediaries are not independent realities, unconcerned with each other.

> Rather, the gradations and intermediaries represent logical stepping-stones in the intellectual transition between two logical extremes. They are a conceptual link which permits reason to understand how contradictories can be identified. The principle of intermediaries justifies the synthesis of opposites, negatively, it frees "integral monism" from the charge of latent dualism.
>
> – Feys 1973: 62

This intermediary principle is a static principle, it is comprehended by another dynamic principle that of involution–evolution.

> What affects the synthesis of opposites is not so much the series of intermediate terms as rather the movement which runs through them. It is this dynamic process which is to be thought of as real, while the various terms which mark out its course are real only as phases of that process and not as isolated entities.
>
> – Feys 1973: 62

This process has two directions: ascent and descent, which is technically called by Sri Aurobindo as evolution and involution respectively. Evolution means "the upward movement of ascent and of spiritualization of the world. It is movement towards Saccidānanda." But involution means the movement of Divine for the creation of the world. The Absolute descends into matter to rise up again to the heights of spirit. The process of evolution is cyclic in the sense that the "final term coincides with initial term".

We may draw the inverted order of the ascent and descent of Divine existence as follows:

Existence	-	Matter
Conscious	-	Life
Bliss	-	Psychic
Supermind	-	Mind

Sri Aurobindo (1970, vol. II, pt 2) says that evolution is a process of ascent from "matter through developing life, soul and mind as the illuminating medium of Supermind towards the divine being". The evolution so far has reached up to the mind as the highest emergent principle. But this is not the end. Mind is not the highest peak. Mind is unable to understand the Absolute. It has still to rise up higher and higher. This is what he means by cosmic evolution. But evolution is also individual. Maitra (1993: 46) says:

> It may be said to have, like God Śiva, a triple eye, an eye turned upwards, an eye turned downwards, and the eye turned inward. We have so far spoken of its upwards eye, its downwards eye, its ascent and its integration. But it has also an eye turned inward, that is, towards that small thing, no bigger than a man's thumb, as *Kaṭhopaniṣad* calls it, which is our soul. Evolution is as much individual as it is cosmic.

Anthropocentrism may be well said to be a characteristic feature of Sri Aurobindo's theory of evolution. This is clear both from the role he fulfils in its development and from the place he finds at its term, the divine is realized in man and through man. Truly, anthropocentrism has no place in system where the concept of Absolute prevails. Feys (1973: 71) says:

> In the case of Sri Aurobindo, then, anthropocentrism is evidently not opposed to theocentrism. Rather, the divine and the human are concentric: all evolution tends to manifest the divine, and the locus of that manifestation is not other than man.

If man culminates in the divine, it is not because human effects are made as such but because the divine is also at work in the individual and the society.

> The individual is not a mere accompaniment or an auxiliary product of the play of consciousness in the body but is a persistent reality, an eternal portion of the Eternal Spirit.
>
> – Maitra 1993: 47

He is the medium through which the spirit discloses its being. H. Chaudhary defines individuality as

> It is neither an unreal appearance nor a self-subsistent entity. It

> is real and significant centre of self-expression of being.[15]

The individual *puruṣa* has to assume a body in working out his cosmic relation with the Supreme Spirit. This is the first step towards his expression in the universe. This is called birth. Birth is thus an essential condition for *puruṣa* in order to manifest himself in the universe. This birth is the prerequisite condition for the appearance of man. The importance of the body is very obvious. Sri Aurobindo (1970, vol. 1: 231) says:

> Equally, it can only be by developing a body or at least a functioning of the physical instrument capable of receiving and serving a still higher illumination that he will rise above himself and realize, not merely in thought and in his internal being but in life, a perfectly divine manhood.

But birth is not an isolated phenomenon. It has its past, it has its future. The body is enjoying or suffering the deeds performed in the last birth and is storing for the future birth. There is a process in the individual evolution as there is certain process in cosmic evolution. If rebirth is denied, the evolution of soul, too, is bound to be denied.

TRIPLE CHARACTER OF THE PROCESS OF EVOLUTION

The evolutionary process, according to Sri Aurobindo, follows the triple character: widening, heightening and integration. Widening means proceeding from simple to more and more complex; heightening means ascent from lower grade to higher grade and integration means a vital transformation of the lower in order to adjust with the higher. In this process of transformation, the lower principle is not simply lifted up and transformed but assumes some newness.

Widening is the first condition of the principle of evolution. In the process of evolution the lower principle should make itself fit receptable for the emergence of the lighter principles. It should be adaptive when it has to ascend. Life appears in matter only when it is sufficiently organized and becomes subtle and complex. For the emergence of the higher principle of consciousness the

---

15 Chaudhary, 1967, *Philosophy of Integralism*, p. 128.

widening of lower principles of matters is an essential condition. It is because the bodies of men are more complex, the organism more subtle than that of the animals, that mind has its indwelling in men and not in animals. The aim of the evolutionary process is to raise matter and for this, widening of the lower principles to receive the higher is the first prerequisite of evolution.

Second, there is a heightening or ascent from lower grade to higher grades. Sri Aurobindo (1970, vol. II, pt II: 726) observes:

> All evolution is in essence a heightening of the force of consciousness in the manifest being so that it may be raised into the greater intensity of what is still unmanifest, from matter into the life, from life into mind, from the mind into the spirit. It is this that must be the method of our growth from a mental into a spiritual and superamental manifestation, out of still half-animal humanity into a divine being and divine living.

Matter evolves into Life, Life into Mind, Mind into Higher Mind, Illumined Mind, Intuitive Mind, Overmind, etc. till the Divine manifests fully. The emergence of the higher principle from the lower is not only caused by intensification of lower conscious-force but is also caused by the higher planes which help in the emergence of the new principle. Whenever there is ascent from one principle to another, we observe that conscious-force is heightened. A change to higher form of consciousness is the very nature of evolution. Sri Aurobindo (ibid.: 727) observes:

> To heighten the force of consciousness until it passes from a mental, vital and physical instrumentation into the essence and power of the spirit is the indispensable thing. . . .

Higher planes too help the emergence of new principles. At the end of this process, the action of the ignorance will be changed into action of knowledge, inconscience into complete consciousness which exists at present in superconscience. The aim of evolution is divinization of the whole process. This is the law or method to be followed by evolutionary process.

> It is an evolution slowly becoming conscious of itself the future must be a more and more conscious evolution of the spiritual being until it is fully delivered into a self-aware action by the

> emergent gnostic principle. – Ibid.: 707

Thus evolution is in essence nothing but heightening of the conscious-force so that greater intensity of consciousness may be achieved gradually. There is a growth of the mental from material, spiritual from mental and supramental from spiritual. A new spiritual height, an elevation, expansion, plasticity, integral capacity of our being is to be achieved in due course.

Integration is the third principle of the evolutionary process. Integration means the process of transforming the lower grades by a higher principle. It transforms the essential character of the lower principles. In this process of transformation the lower principles are not rejected and left aloof; rather they are integrated, harmonized into the higher one. Sri Aurobindo (1970, vol. II, pt II: 711) says:

> But it must be observed that this ascent, this successive fixing in higher and higher principles, does not carry with it the abandonment of the lower grades, any more than a status of existence in the lower grades means the entire absence of the higher principles.

It is not only lifted, rather it assumes some new form. At each step of the ascent, there is not merely an ascent of the higher principles, the lower principles are also integrated. Integration means descent of the higher principle into the lower actually.

> It is ascent through descent. Thus when the principle of mind evolves, there is not merely the emergence of this new principle but a descent of it into all the lower ones, leading to an uplifting and transformation of matter and life, so that life and matter become different after the emergence of mind from what they were before its emergence. – Maitra 1993: 43

The principle of integration is a unique contribution of Sri Aurobindo which is not to be found in any evolutionary concept whether Eastern or Western. Maitra presents a proper simile. According to him the usual view of evolution may be compared to "the march of an army which advances without keeping its lines of communication with the base intact". But Sri Aurobindo's conception of evolution may be compared with

> the march of an army which advances with the whole force, keeping all its lines of communication perfectly intact. An evolution, which is merely the isolated lifting of a part of the nature of a being by dissociating it from the other parts, is of as little significance from the evolutionary point of view as the isolated landing of some advanced troops into enemy territory.
>
> – Maitra 1993: 43

Sri Aurobindo feels that this is the reason why the world has not been transformed so far in spite of so many individual salvations. In order that there may be total transformation of nature, a supramental principle must emerge. Sri Aurobindo (1970, vol. II, pt. II: 705) observes:

> If there is to be an entire transformation, it can only be by the full emergence of the low of the spirit; its power of Supermind or gnosis must have entered into Matter and it must evolve in Matter. It must change the mental into the Supramental being, make the inconscient in us conscious, spiritualize our material substance, erect its law of gnostic consciousness in our whole evolutionary being and nature.

It is an evolution slowly becoming conscious of itself. There should be more and more conscious evolution of being till it is finally delivered into "a self-aware action by the emergent gnostic principle".

Due to this triple process of evolution, there is a rapid change of the basis of inconscience into a basis of complete consciousness, a change of action of ignorance into the action of knowledge. Evolution, thus according to Sri Aurobindo, is not the isolated raising of any principle to the higher level, rather all the principles transformed. The principle of integration as a vital part of evolution is in the words of V. Madhusudhan Reddy (1966: 253), "a wonderful stroke of genius of Sri Aurobindo". It provides a new dimension to the theory of evolution which was so far only an ascent from the lower to the higher. Herbert Spencer speaks of differentiation and integration as the two necessary constituents of the evolutionary process. But this integration is usually the structural integration of the part and not the transformation of the lower part with the emergence of the higher. Also, Spencer fails even to maintain perfect continuity of evolution in the transition from matter to life or from life to mind.

THE TRIPLE TRANSFORMATION

The secret of evolution consists, according to Sri Aurobindo, not in liberation from the material or psychic realms but by their transformation by a higher principle. Liberation of spirit is partial. It does not transform the whole of man. But evolution, according to Sri Aurobindo, means a transformation of the whole of our terrestrial existence, material, mental and vital. Even at the height of intellectual development man is not able to achieve a perfect integration of his personality. He is perturbed by discords there too. Only the supramental transformation can redeem him from the fetters of bondage, mental or physical. But a mental man has no access to Supermind. First of all the gulf between mind and Supermind is to be bridged and this can only be done by triple transformation, namely, the psychic, the spiritual and the supramental. Before the advent of man upon this earth, there were only animals, then came man, the next and the ultimate stage of the evolutionary movement will produce supramental beings in whom Supermind will be the normal nature as mind is the normal nature in man and vital is the normal nature of the animals. And this goal can be achieved by this triple transformation.

The concept of transformation is the original contribution of Sri Aurobindo like the concept of Supermind.

> Transformation is a word that I have brought in myself (like Supermind) to express certain spiritual concept and spiritual facts of the integral *yoga*. Purification of the nature by the influence of the spirit is not what I mean by transformation, purification is only part of a psychic change or a psycho-spiritual change. . . . What I mean by the spiritual transformation is something dynamic (not merely liberation of the self or realization of the one putting of the spiritual consciousness dynamic as well as static in every part of the being down to the subconscient. . . . It means a bringing down of the divine consciousness static and dynamic into all these parts and the entire replacement of the present consciousness by that. – Aurobindo 1953b: 168-69

By transformation he never means yogic *siddhis* or ethical perfection or a "transcendental *cinmāyā* body". Transformation means to him a complete and radical change of consciousness which brings "an assured step forward in the spiritual evolution of the being of greater kind".

The word transformation is used by Sri Aurobindo in accordance with its grammatical sense *anyad rūpam rūpāntaram*. Transformation is the divine change of the whole consciousness of man. Transformation, according to Sri Aurobindo, is always dynamic as it is not one day's achievement. This process of transformation is going on from the very beginning of the creation. Matter was transformed into life, life into mental consciousness. The history of growth from matter to plant, from plant to animal and from animal to man depicts the story of transformation. And Sri Aurobindo believes that the next and the final stage will be supramental stage which transforms mind, life and body by the descent of Supermind. Our yogic processes seek liberation beyond life. Transformation is not their aim but Sri Aurobindo believes in "... a full descent of a new consciousness into the whole nature from top to bottom to transform life here" (Aurobindo 1953b: 169). He wants to fill the life, nay, the whole nature with Supramental consciousness, to bring heaven on earth. The problem before him is not the triumph of spirit over matter but the spiritualization of matter.

There are three stages in transformation:

i. Psychic
ii. Spiritual
iii. Supramental

Sri Aurobindo (1970, vol. II, pt II: 891) says:

> . . . there must first be the psychic change, the conversion of our whole present nature into a soul-instrumentation; on that or along with that there must be the spiritual change, the descent of a higher Light, Knowledge, Power, Force, Bliss, Purity into the whole being, even into the darkness of the life and body, even into the darkness of our subconscience; last, there must

> supervene the supramental transmutation – there must take place as the crowning movement the ascent into the Supermind and the transforming descent of the supramental Consciousness into our entire being and nature.

This triple transformation brings down the supramental consciousness into the terrestrial existence. It makes the direct communion of the spirit with the cosmos and the mental individual. This aim is not to be achieved by evolutionary process merely. The evolution does not incur the complete or radical change which brings a permanent new order to terrestrial nature. Only a few persons here are aware of their souls; they are put into communion with divinity but this is not all. At this stage only a spiritual man has evolved but not the supramental being. The spiritual experience no doubt brings some change in the nature of the seekers but that is not integral transformation which will bring forth a new delight, namely, the supramental delight on this earth. This aim can be achieved by this triple transformation. It finalizes the evolutionary process.

PSYCHIC TRANSFORMATION

The first step of this triple transformation is the psychic change. Although soul is that by which we survive as individuals in Nature; it is nearer to us than our nearest still it is an entirely veiled part of us. It is fundamentally the same in us always. Sri Aurobindo (ibid.: 891) opines:

> . . . it is not limited by what it manifests, not contained by the incomplete forms of the manifestation, not tarnished by the imperfections and impurities, the defects and deprivations of the surface being. It is an ever-pure flame of the divinity in things and nothing that comes to it; nothing that enters into our experience can pollute its purity or extinguish the flame.

It uses mind, life and body as its instruments but by itself it is unaffected by their operations. The soul is the Divine light in us but it is so thickly covered that we do not know the secret light within us, it is hidden in the "heart's innermost sanctuary". We are totally unaware of it. Thus, the revelation of the soul and consequent transformation of our lower nature, mind, life and body is the first condition of this psychic transformation. Psychicization removes the veil of the psychic beings, when its light falls down on the imperfect nature it is transformed immediately. It brings right vision into the mind, right impulse into the vital, and right movement into the physical – all turning to Divine. It effectuates a true harmonization in our being. This psychicization, the removal of the veil, is the first principle we do get in our normal life. We do recognize it as the part of divine living in us as we say that a man who has no sensitive feeling for *satyam, śivam* and *sundaram* has no soul at all. But that should not be all what is required in full transformation of mind, life and matter into this psychic being, "the conversion of our whole present nature into the soul instrumentation". No doubt the psychic being is constantly sending impulsions to the surface for guiding us but we are not ready to grasp it, we are unable to detect their source. We do not appreciate them as they are mixed up too much with mental stuff before they come on the surface. A twist is given, a wrong direction is imparted. The ultimate goal of the soul personality is to liquidate the sense of ego and to be the guide of human spiritual endeavours, although at the very beginning of our journey we have only the faintest idea of the soul as something which survives our death.

If the soul would not have been the veiled part of ourselves then the human evolution would have been very smooth and swift. It would not have been disfigured as it is. The psychic being does not emerge fully grown. Our psychic being is not born in us as fully armed. It gradually evolves. It is never impure but imperfect. It passes through very slow development. It develops through the process of evolution. How much strength it has gained, depends upon the power of the soul that has succeeded in asserting itself on our surface consciousness against the violent opposition of inconscience. One has to go a long way before the secret psychic principle develops in him as a person. As there is greater emergence of soul in nature, there is further possibility of communion with the soul and improvement in its communication with the physical and mental existence. It can transmit its intimation to the mind, heart and life with a greater purity and force, it can strongly react against false mixture and more and more it is felt as a power in the nature. Sri Aurobindo says in *Savitri*:

> *Our soul from its mysterious chamber acts,*
> *Its influence pressing on our heart and mind,*
> *Pushes them to exceed their mortal selves,*
> *It seeks for Good and Beauty and for God,*
> *We see beyond self's wall's our limitless self,*
> *We gaze through our world's glass at half seeing vasts.*
> *We hurt for the Truth behind apparent things.*

Sri Aurobindo describes the relation of the psychic entity to mind, life and body as that of a king to his minister. They are his subordinates whom he could overrule if he so wished. But its character is to integrate them and not to subdue them. The psychic entity may allow its ministers to rule and keep itself as "a secluded king in a screened chamber". But these three fail to combine in a harmony, "this aggregate is, because of its composition, a heterogeneous compound not a simple harmonious and homogeneous whole" (Aurobindo 1970, vol. II, pt 2). In that case human personality will be one-sided. A true harmony is possible only if the psychic self controls the three secondary selves – physical, vital and mental – without suppressing them:

> It is by the coming forward of this true monarch and his taking up of the reins of government that there can take place a real harmonization of our being and our life. – Ibid.: 900

The emergence of the psychic self which is the sole aim of psychic transformation can be attempted in various ways, through mind, through heart and through the separation of *puruṣa* and *prakṛti*. The thinking mind is drawn always towards the impersonal. It strives towards Supreme Bliss. Sri Aurobindo (ibid.: 901) says:

> There is a pressure from this Impersonality that seeks to mould the whole mind into a form of itself; at the same time the impersonal secret and law of things become more and more visible.

Such is the case with the higher mental thinker. The second approach made by the soul is through the heart. It is an approach of a devotee, a *bhakta*.

> It is through love and adoration of the All-Beautiful and All-Blissful, the All-Good, the True, the spiritual Reality of love, that the approach is made; the aesthetic and emotional parts join together to offer the soul, the life, the whole nature to that which they worship. – Ibid.: 902

Here mind goes beyond "impersonality to the awareness of a Supreme Personal Being":

> . . . he becomes directly aware of his soul and its dictates, unites his emotional with his psychic personality and changes his life and vital parts by purity, God-ecstasy, the love of God and men and all creatures into a thing of the spiritual beauty, full of divine light and good, he develops into the saint. . . . – Ibid.: 903

The dualistic solution of *Puruṣa,* divorced from *Prakṛti* evidently cannot be satisfactory for that will not bring transformation. There are three essential conditions of psychological transformation. First, the development of psychic transformation according to Sri Aurobindo, will be very slow, if it is left entirely to its own accord. It is comparatively rapid when man feels the need of the growth of our psychical being. We must culture ourselves to feel the need of such psychic growth to transform our surface life into psychic personality. Thus there should be "sufficient preparation quieting of all turbidities and turbulence, a tranquillizing purification of the external nature". Second, the psychic personality should be so developed that the soul can effectively change the whole pattern of life. Third, "in order that the psychic transformation may be complete there must be a cracking of the crust of outer nature, a breaking down of the walls of inner separation, a joining of the depths of our being to the surface". Consciousness has to shift its centre from surface being to the inner being.

SPIRITUAL TRANSFORMATION

But this psychic transformation is not sufficient for the realization of Supramental Divine. The second step required for the ascent of the mind to the Supermind is spiritual transformation. The spiritual transformation is distinguished from the psychic as the upward from the inward.

> The psychic movement inward to the inner being, the self or Divinity within us, must be completed by an opening upward to a Supreme Spiritual status. – Ibid.

Psychicization only facilitates the ascent of the spiritual life. Here Sri Aurobindo differs from Vedānta and other *yogas*. In Advaita Vedānta the fulfilment of the destiny of man consists in the realization of identity of soul with *Brahman*; whereas in integral Advaitism of Sri Aurobindo, the realization of the essential nature of soul is undoubtedly important; at the same time, the realization of *prakṛti* and its oneness with the Absolute are not less important. Not only the soul is the part and parcel of the divine, matter too is one with *Brahman* ultimately. His *yoga* is integral *yoga* as against the partial *yoga* of other schools. Only spiritual liberation is not sufficient, it is not final, the whole nature is to be transformed.

The fundamental requirement of the spiritual transformation is an upward movement of the mind to the higher ranges of superconscience. Higher consciousness should be descended so that every inch of the lower being may be taken up for inner transformation. This transformation of the lower nature by the power and bliss descending from above is known as spiritualization. Such transformation brings in us the abiding spiritual awareness of the infinite with a greater extention of the nature.

The higher principles of consciousness between the mental and supramental, which bring about the spiritual transformation, are the Higher Mind, Illumined Mind, Intuitive Mind and the Overmind. These are not modes of cognition or ways of knowing reality; rather they are "domains of being, grades of the substances and energy of the spiritual being, fields of existence which are each a level of the universal Consciousness-Force constituting and organizing itself into a higher status". Mind cannot itself enter into the nature of Supermind. It can look through these higher approaches. These grades are nothing but hierarchical manifestations of the Supermind.

HIGHER MIND

The first step of ascent of mind in its upward march towards

Supermind is into a Higher Mind. Here an individual has a direct and spontaneous knowledge. It has greater light and clarity than our normal mind. It is mind of truth-thought, whereas in ordinary mind we may have thoughts which are not true. It can think mass of knowledge in a single view but its activity of consciousness is dominated by thought. Normal mind gathers knowledge from sense perception, inference, induction and deduction, etc. Higher Mind has not to depend upon these limited sources, it can see truth at a single glance and it has not to take resource to logic for showing a rational consistency between these ideas. In fact, "this thought is a self-evolution of eternal wisdom, not an acquired knowledge". It is "a luminous thought-mind, a mind of spirit-born conceptual knowledge". This is the cognitive aspect of Higher Mind. In the aspect of will there is a dynamic effectualism of the truth. Here it is a dynamic force. The feelings and actions originating from Higher Mind become the vibration of the higher wisdom. It is, in fact, the first towards the change of mind with a new consciousness; it is prepared for a superior truth. It is not a vision but an idea, it is not intuition. The Higher Mind is a spiritual consciousness which is characterized by all-awareness, swift, conceptual and firm valid knowledge. Its thoughts are self-revelation of higher wisdom, not an acquired knowledge. The descent of this higher mind changes entire being. We become more responsive to the light ideas and vibrations, but it is not able to effect a complete transformation as it does not diminish inconscience altogether. It helps man to considerable extent but Sri Aurobindo (ibid.: 944) says:

> The power of the spiritual Higher Mind and its idea-force, modified and diminished as it must be by its entrance into our mentality, is not sufficient to sweep out all these obstacles and create the gnostic being, but it can make a first change, modification that will capacitate a higher ascent and a more powerful descent and further prepare an integration of the being in a greater force of consciousness and knowledge.

ILLUMINED MIND

The next higher ascent of the mind after Higher Mind is Illumined Mind. It is "mind no longer of higher thought but of spiritual light". It is the mind of spiritual illumination, of spiritual vision. It does not work primarily by thought but by vision, the thought is only subordinate here. For an ordinary mind thought is the higher process of knowledge, but in the spiritual process thought is made secondary. "Thought creates only a representative image of truth. . . ." The truth itself can be grasped only by spiritual sight. The consciousness of the seer, according to Sri Aurobindo, is a greater power for knowledge than the consciousness of the thinker. The perceptual power of the inner sight is far greater than the perceptual power to the thought. Human mind has no access to the actual stuff of the objects but spiritual sight gets directly into the very body of the truth of things. Higher Mind brings greater consciousness through the spiritual idea and its truth power but the Illumined Mind brings still greater consciousness through a truth-sight and truth-light and its power of seeing and seizing. It illumines the thinking mind with inner insight and inspiration, and develops spiritual sight into the heart; it brings a more powerful and dynamic integration, imparts to the life-force a spiritual urge. It breaks the limitation of the physical mind. Distinguishing the Higher Mind from the Illumined Mind, Sri Aurobindo (1970, vol. II, pt 2: 946) says:

> In the transformation by the higher mind the spiritual sage and thinker would find his total and dynamic fulfilment; in the transformation by the illumined mind, there would be a similar fulfilment for the seer, the illumined mystic, those in whom the soul lives in vision and in a direct sense and experience: for it is from these higher sources that they receive their light and to rise into that light and live there would be their ascension to their native empire.

But the knowledge of Illumined Mind also undergoes a modification and distortion due to resistance of the surface nature. It has still to go higher and this higher consciousness which is the source of Illumined Mind is intuition.

INTUITIVE MIND

Intuition is direct awareness of object. It is the outcome of the meeting subject-consciousness with object-consciousness. The subject goes out of itself to meet the object. Sri Aurobindo (ibid.: 946-47) says:

> Intuition is a power of consciousness nearer and more intimate to the original knowledge by identity; for it is always something knowledge by identity; for it is always something that leaps out direct from a concealed identity. It is when the consciousness of the subject meets with the consciousness in the object, penetrates it and sees, feels or vibrates with the truth of what it contacts, that the intuition leaps out like a spark or lightning-flash from the shock of the meeting; or when the consciousness, even without any such meeting, looks into itself and feels directly and intimately the truth or the truths that are there or so contacts the hidden forces behind appearances, then also there is the outbreak of an intuitive light.

Intuition has direct perception of the Supreme Reality. It is the power of knowledge by the identity of consciousness not by conceptual analysis. The first blaze of intuition casts off the mass of ignorance. It does not study only the appearance of things as other sources of knowledge do, it studies reality as such.

No doubt, human mind often receives the flashes from intuition but it fails to receive intuition; mind interprets it in its own light; "... it is subject there to an invading mixture or a mental coating or an interception and substitution" (ibid.: 947). And as such intuition ceases to bear any sense for us. Intuition being overburdened with mental mode is not in position to provide us with the integral homogeneous experience. It is only when mind rises to the planes of the Higher Mind and Illumined Mind, it recognizes intuition directly descending from the supramental plane.

R.S. Srivastava (1968: 132) says:

> Intuition in its native consciousness is a projected consciousness of the Supermind into the human consciousness.

Aurobindo (1970, vol. II, pt. II: 948) says:

> Intuition is always an edge or ray or outleap of a superior light; it is in us a projecting blade, edge or point of a far-off supermind . . .

Higher Mind operates by means of thoughts. Thus it exceeds mere mind which works by reasoning. Illumined Mind proceeds by vision. Intuition comes nearer to knowledge by identity.

Intuition, according to Sri Aurobindo, has a fourfold power, a power of revelatory truth-seeing, inspiration or truth-hearing, truth touch and a true automatic discrimination of the relation between Truth and Truth; these are the fourfold potencies of intuition. Intuition can perform all the actions of reason without any failure anywhere. It can transform into its own substance not only the mind but life and heart too. Sri Aurobindo (1970, vol. II, pt II: 949) says:

> It can thus change the whole consciousness into the stuff of intuition; for it brings its own greater radiant movement into will, into the feelings and emotions, the life-impulses, the action of sense and sensation, the very workings of the body-consciousness; it recasts them in the light and power of truth and illumines their knowledge and their ignorance.[16]

The ascent of the place of intuition is followed by the descent of the consciousness into the human organism. But this intuition is not the highest form of mind as it does not bring in the whole mass or body the identity of knowledge. The next ascent of mind towards the Supermind is Overmind.

OVERMIND

The Overmind is the link between mind and Supermind. It is delegate of the Supermind to the ignorance. It is "parent of ignorance", an intermediary principle between knowledge and ignorance. Supermind acts on the world through this Overmind. Its inclination is for separation and not for unity. It enables one to manifest itself as many, keeping unity in the background. Sri Aurobindo (ibid.: 279) says:

> The overmind is well-aware of essential Truth of things; it embraces the totality; it uses the individual self-determination without being limited by them: but although it knows their

16 The concept of Overmind has already been discussed in detail in the section on Supermind, pp. 233-34.

> oneness, can realize it in a spiritual cognition, yet its dynamic movement, even while replaying on that for its security, is not directly determined by it.

It represents the highest stage of spiritual consciousness yet it is a stage which falls under ignorance. It cannot bring integral transformation of nature. The basis of nescience is still there, thus there is always a possibility of regression or total disintegration.

SUPRAMENTAL TRANSFORMATION

The psychic and spiritual transformations are different stages towards the superamental transformation, which are still within the boundaries of ignorance. After supramental transformation evolution through ignorance is stopped. There is transition from ignorance to knowledge. Sri Aurobindo says that the supramental Divine may take over the lead of the evolution from the Overmind and build the first foundation.

The supramental gnosis takes charge of the evolution from Overmind. A supramentally transformed individual becomes one with conscious-force of the divine. The psychic or spiritual transformation only produces in us an urge for Supermind. It makes us "receptive and capable of surrender to the Supermind". Supramental consciousness cannot be forced to descend. We can cultivate such personality as to make us competent to receive it. An individual must be the first field of transformation but only the transformation of individual is not sufficient. Sri Aurobindo (1970, vol. II: 962) says:

> These must be an emergent supramental consciousness-force liberated and active within the terrestrial whole and an organized supramental instrumentation of the spirit in the life and the body.

The descent of the Supermind will bring a radical transformation in all existence, material, vital and spiritual. Man will become a gnostic being. The whole human race will not be a race of superman in a day. First there will be some persons to receive this delight; later on the whole race will be divinized.

The supramental descent will affect the lower evolutionary stage as well, "its light and force will permeate downwards and awaken in the lower regions a greater realization of the hidden truth within them" (R.S. Srivastava 1968: 138).

> On this basis the principle of a divine life in terrestrial Nature would be manifested; even the world of ignorance and inconscience might discover its own submerged secret and begin to realize in each lower degree its divine significance.
>
> – Aurobindo 1970, vol. II, pt II: 963

The Destiny of Man

The destiny of man is the stark question facing mankind in the present crisis. The present age is the age of humanism. The philosophical interest has shifted from God, matter, etc. to man. In the words of Radhakrishnan (1940: Preface), "Man has become spectator of man". The whole philosophy centres round the welfare of man. And Sri Aurobindo advocates more strongly than any other philosopher the spirituality of man and his higher goal ahead.

Man is not a meek person in the hand of nature; rather he is embodiment of the Divine. And the destiny of man consists not only in the liberation of spirit but in getting rid of all sorts of limitations: physical, vital and mental. Divinity does not consist in getting out of mind, life and body; it is possible for him to become a divine being here on this earth continuing all contacts with the physical universe. His destiny is not to be confined eternally to his present life, it has to exceed his present life and search of divine life which is lying in the core of his heart. Maitra (1968: 107) observes:

> No philosopher in ancient or modern times has a higher conception of the destiny of man than he. No one has announced with greater conviction than he that man must exceed himself, that his destiny is not to be mere man but to be something infinitely higher.

Man is divine by nature, he has to realize that divinity in actual life. He has not only to realize the divinity in the unchanging aspect of his being rather in changing aspect too. Not only the soul but the whole universe is being permeated by divinity. And this task can be performed only by the descent of the Supermind. This descent will lead the whole to divinity, it will divinize it.

H.G. Wells says that the kingdom of God on earth is not a metaphor, not a mere spiritual state, not an uncertain project . . . it is the close and inevitable destiny of mankind.[17] To this Sri Aurobindo adds that "the kingdom of God within is the sole possible foundation of the kingdom of God without, for it is the spirit by which man lives that conditions out the outer forms of his life" (Aurobindo 1914: 16). And identity of the Divine within is not enough. One has to achieve identity with the Divine without.

> For the Divine which manifests in the individual is manifested in the universe also. Only there is an extended manifestation. The truth of my being is not complete without the truth of my neighbour. – Pandit 1959: 13

The Divine in the individual is none but the Divine in the universe as they are both manifestations of one Divine which transcends both the individual and the universe. *Śvetāśvatara Upaniṣad* VI.11 too quotes "One godhead occults in all beings, the inner self of all beings, the all persuading, Absolute without qualities".

M.P. Pandit (1959: 14) says, according to Sri Aurobindo:

> It is the Supreme Divine that individualizes itself as the divine self of the individual upholding his existence; it is the same transcendent Divine which likewise formulates itself as the divine self of the universe basing All-existence. Hence both the self of the individual and the self of the universe are identical in their origin.
>
> Man is the vehicle in which God seeks to manifest Himself fully. The importance of man is that he gives to the world for the first time a development of consciousness by which a full self discovery becomes possible, a fulfilment and realization of God in life. Man must enclose himself without losing himself, he must become God without ceasing to be man.

Against the theory of Nicolai Hartmann's "God or man", Sri Aurobindo maintains the thesis "God in man".

> Man's freedom does not mean freedom to be damned, but freedom to be saved. And saved he is and saved he can be only

[17] Quoted by Sri Aurobindo 1914, *Views and Reviews*, p. 16.

> by being linked with God. If freedom in the Hartmannian sense is to be looked upon as the prerogative of man, evil will become permanent for him as there will be no possibility of his ever getting rid of it.
> – Maitra 1968: 230-31

What he calls freedom is egoism, which is the self-assertiveness of the finite. This self-assertiveness is, in Sri Aurobindo's view, the root of all evil. This means, according to Sri Aurobindo, negation of man, destruction of all his future hope, whereas Sri Aurobindo's man is to be a divine man or a gnostic being. Hartmann's conception will leave no room for the destiny of man which is present in Sri Aurobindo's imagination.

Sri Aurobindo is an optimist, his vision of the future is optimistic.

> But the source of his optimism is not morality but spirituality . . . this optimism consists in his view of man as having higher destiny, to become more than man, to become Superman. A spirit of harmony will then descend even to the lower order of creation.
> – Olsson 1958: 34-35

A standard of man is as he is destined to be, not as he is now. His destiny is to be a God–man who far exceeds a common man in spiritual qualities. As to the possibility of such consummation, Sri Aurobindo says that it is not "a possibility but an inevitability". The force working for the result is not the individual human power but the Divine himself labouring for the destined end. The advent of the superhuman or divine race can become a thing of practical actuality.

According to Henri Bergson the ultimate destiny of man is to be one with the life-current. And as he equates God with life-current we may say that the destiny of man for Bergson is to be one with God. But Maitra (1968: 102) asks:

> What does this identity with God mean? Does it mean a mere pantheistic absorption? If it does, then this destiny cannot kindle any enthusiasm in us, for what alone can satisfy us is the assurance that, retaining our individuality as men, we can still become Divine. Does Bergson give us this assurance?

In his book, *The Two Sources of Morality and Religion*, Bergson says about the mystic's love of humanity that it can do wonderful things what we may regard otherwise an impossible thing such as converting the human species into the creative effort itself. Bergson's "love of humanity" never conveys his faith in the higher destiny of man. He never foresees that evolution must produce a higher type of man, radically different from the man of today. The ideal of humanity in Bergson is an ideal for the present mankind. It needs no transformation of the nature of man.

What makes Sri Aurobindo think of man's higher destiny? We may say in a very nutshell: it is discovery of the spirituality of man. He is divine in potentiality; he should be divine in actuality. In everybody dwells a spark of divinity; we are required to develop our personality in such a way that, that spark may illumine our inner being as well as our outerbeing. And man is ultimately destined to illumine that spark. Man is the first being in whom consciousness appears but the malady of the world is that an individual seldom finds his real self. The idea is not certainly new altogether. In Vedic age we find reference of the Divine birth in man, Vedic seers prayed for the descent of God in man. From Purāṇa, we get the idea of Satya Yuga; in *Gītā*, of the reign of righteousness (*dharma rājya*); in Jew religion, the city of God; in Christianity, the kingdom of heaven on earth. Adolph Harnack (p. 9) says: "Christian religion means one thing only: Eternal life in the midst of time by the strength and under the eyes of God". And this idea of kingdom of heaven on earth gets a logical justification in the scheme of Sri Aurobindo. It seems like an impossibility at first sight. Sri Aurobindo (1970, vol. I: 56) is well aware of this difficulty when he says:

> His (man's) dream of God and Heaven is really a dream of his own perfection, but he finds the same difficulty in accepting its practical realization here of his ultimate aim as would the ancestral Ape if called upon to believe in himself as future man. His imagination, his religious aspirations may hold that end before him, but when his reason asserts itself, rejecting imagination and transcendent intuition, he puts it by as a brilliant superstition contrary to the hard fact of the material universe. It

> becomes then only his inspiring vision of the impossible. All that is possible is a conditional, limited and precarious knowledge "happiness, power and good".

Today even science has started believing in better possibilities for man. There can be no limit put before the man's onwards march. Pessimism is vein and misleading.

We must clearly bear in mind that Sri Aurobindo does not mean any humanism for one reason. Maitra (1968: 108) says:

> In fact, humanism is not consistent with faith in the higher destiny of man. If the end of man is not to end as man, if his destiny is to rise to higher state of being, then no point of view which cannot look beyond human needs and condition can be said to be adequate.

Again there are regions where humanism cannot be applied for. Sri Aurobindo himself does not appreciate the attempt of human thought to force an ethical meaning into the whole of nature. "The motive force of evolution is not ethical principle but the urge of the spirit towards self-expression. This urge is at first non-ethical, then infra-ethical, partly also anti-ethical, and it will be supra-ethical when evolution will reach a stage higher than the mental." Only at the present stage, ethics is required. People breathe sigh of relief when they say "our *yoga* is not for ourselves but for humanity". N.K. Gupta observes that when Sri Aurobindo saw that the very core of his teaching was being missed by this common interpretation of his saying, he changed the word, "our *yoga* is not for humanity but for Divine", though this change was not welcome by many quarters. As Gupta (1955, part 1: 9) suggests, we may combine the two mottoes he has given, and says that

> His mission is to find and express the Divine in humanity. This is the service he means to render to humanity, viz. to manifest and embody in it the Divine, his goal is not merely an amelioration, but a total change and transformation, the divinization of human life.

We must guard against an error here. Transformation of life does not mean that the entire humanity will be changed into the race of God; it means the evolution or appearance on earth of superior type of humanity, even as man evolved out of animality as a superior type of animal, not that the entire animal kingdom was changed into humanity. Such transformation of man into Divine is not a possibility but an inevitability according to Sri Aurobindo as the force working for this goal is not the human power but the Divine himself labouring to bring this into effect. The appearance of the Superman is a practical actuality, it is bound to appear sooner or later. God must be revealed in man. This revelation is a dual revelation for it also reveals man's true nature to himself. Liberated self extends its perception of unity horizontally to other selves as well as vertically to God.[18]

> Its unity with transcendent One is incomplete without its unity with the cosmic Many. – Aurobindo 1970, vol. I: 40

Man does not become *Brahman*, he is *Brahman*. This conception well suits with the concept of *bodhisattva*. A *bodhisattva* takes a vow not to make the irrevocable crossing unless the whole mankind is not liberated. He enjoys *nirvāṇa* only when there is nobody left on earth undelivered from the knot of suffering.

Sri Aurobindo calls the liberated state the Divine life. It is "the necessary concomitance of the supramental consciousness". The being in that state is called the Gnostic Being and the avenue to that state is the integral *yoga*. "To be perfect as He is perfect is the condition of His integral attainment" (ibid.). He does not live for his ego or for any collective ego, rather "he lives in and for the Divine in himself, in and for the Divine in the collectively, in and for the Divine in all beings" (Chand 1969: 210). To grow within or to live within is the cardinal principle for divine life, "to be and to be fully" is Nature's aim in us. But what does this "to be fully" mean? It is to be aware wholly and integrally of one's own being. The harmony of internal and external life is the condition of the life that aims at being really Divine. To be perfect as He is perfect is the condition of His integral attainment.

Sri Aurobindo (1970, vol. II, pt II: 1024) says:

> . . . to be fully is to have the intrinsic and integral force of one's

18 Organ, 1962, "The Status of Self in Aurobindo's Metaphysics and Some Questions".

> being; it is to come into possession of all one's force of self and of all its use.

Again he says:

> To be fully is to have the full delight of being. Being without delight of being, without an entire delight of itself and all things is something neutral or diminished; it is existence, but it is not fullness of being. This delight too must be intrinsic, self-existent, automatic. – Ibid.: 1024-25
>
> To become complete in being, in delight of being and to live in this integrated completeness is the divine living. – Ibid.: 1025

Again to be fully is to be universally. To live within the limitation of ego means imperfect existence. All beings are ultimately one and to be fully means to be all that is. It includes all in one's own being, to feel delight of being as one's own being, to feel integrated in force with the universal force are the necessary conditions of the integral divine living. Not to be held in the body or by the body, but to use the body only as an instrument is, according to Sri Aurobindo, the first condition of divine living. Again to transcend mind as an instrument and not to hold it as subject to ignorance is the second condition of divine living. The third condition is "to be by the self and Spirit, not to depend upon life, not to be identified with it, to transcend it and control and use it as an expression and instrumentation of the self" (ibid.: 1026). His life, mind and physicality – all must be converted into the terms of supramental. He should evolve out of ignorance into knowledge.

His sole aim should be living within and not living without. The transcendental being lives in our secret self. To look within is the first necessity for the transformation of the nature and for the divine life. This inward turning is not imprisonment in personal self, it is rather the first step towards a true universality. Living for others is possible only by an inner spiritual force of love and sympathy. Sri Aurobindo (ibid.: 1030) observes:

> As he does not live for a separate ego, so too he does not live for the purpose of any collective ego; he lives in and for the Divine in himself, in and for the Divine in the collectivity, in and for the Divine in all beings.

He always emphasizes the primacy of the inward over the outward. Here Sri Aurobindo should not be misunderstood. Feys (1973: 160) remarks:

> The "conscious unanimous", of which Aurobindo speaks later as the basis and structure of gnostic society, cannot therefore be taken too literally: it is not so much the coalescence of a multiplicity of spirits as rather the constitution of one single soul: unanimism in the strict sense of the word. Nor is this all. Not only would each centre consciousness communicate directly with the other spiritual centres, but also the material barriers would vanish.

Gnostic Being

Sri Aurobindo has used the term gnostic being as almost equivalent of the term "superman". As the consequence of supramental descent, the spiritual being is transformed into the gnostic being, *aparā prakṛti* is transformed into *parā prakṛti* or *cit-śakti*. The gnostic beings are men of knowledge. Their perfection and completeness are the result of the highest possible integration both within and without. He is completely a divinized spirit. In gnostic being, it is the psychic aspect which determines its nature and not the physical aspect. He acts "in a universal awareness and a harmony of his individual self with the total self, of his individual will with the total will, of his individual action with the total action". As a result of supramental transformation, there is distinct change in the working of mind, life and body where their own ways are not annihilated but "perfected and fulfilled by the self-exceeding".

In the gnostic being, the process of knowledge undergoes a fundamental change. Mental thought is based on the consciousness of the finite, but supramental thought is based on the consciousness of Infinite. It sees things through the spectacles of oneness, while mind sees through division and distinctions. The supramental or the divine life is "a life of essential, spontaneous and inherent unity". Senses and mind are the chief sources of knowledge in an ordinary sense but in gnostic personality mind is replaced by fundamental consciousness of unity. Sri Aurobindo (1970, vol. III, pt II: 965) says:

> The mind acts by intellectual rule or device or by reasoned choice of will or by mental impulse or in obedience of life-impulse; but supramental nature does not act by mental idea or rule or in subjection to any inferior impulse: each of its steps is dictated by an innate spiritual vision, a comprehensive and exact penetration into the truth of all and the truth of each thing; it acts always according to inherent reality, not by the mental ideas, not according to an imposed law of conduct or a constructive thought or perceptive contrivance.

A mind can describe the supramental only in the terms of abstract or mental figures which are never true to its nature. Mind cannot anticipate the process of supramental working as they are far-off from the laws and self-vision of supramental nature. Only Supermind can make a more living picture of the gnostic being, mind can draw only an abstract line of it. He seeks *Brahman* in all material things, a beauty in the life of matter.

A gnostic being will not differentiate not-self from self as contradictory of each other, rather they will be complementary for him. He will realize the matter as the projection of self in the order of space and time. The Divine consciousness will descend on earth, consequently the conscious-force will manifest its nature. Sri Aurobindo expresses this transformation in *Savitri* as follows:

> *When superman is born as Nature's King*
> *His presence shall transfigure Matter's world:*
> *He shall light up Truth's fire in Nature's night,*
> *He shall lay upon the earth Truth's greater law;*
> *Man too shall turn towards the Spirit's call.*
>
> – Book XI, canto I, p. 331

In an ordinary person, body is governed by subconscious or unconscious force but in gnostic being will or spirit controls the movements and the workings of the body. The whole of evolutionary process cannot remain but be affected by the presence of the Supramental life. Previously the evolutionary process was working through ignorance but after supramental descent it will continue through knowledge. A principle of harmony would impose itself on the life of the ignorance. A free play of intuition and sympathy will penetrate into human life. Sri Aurobindo (1970, vol. II, pt II: 969) says:

> Instead of a constant intermixed and confused struggle between the growth of consciousness and the power of the inconscience, between the forces of light and the force of darkness, the evolution would become a graded progression from lesser light to greater light; in each stage of it the conscious beings belonging to that stage would respond to the inner consciousness-force and expand their own law of cosmic nature towards the possibility of a higher degree of that nature.

This intervention of the gnostic being would not paralyse the evolutionary process but it would harmonize, facilitate and tranquillize the difficulties coming in the way to evolutionary emergence. It would not lose its unitarian trend, its push towards integration or its harmonic influence. It allows contradiction and discord but makes them a part of the cosmic whole; they share the whole. They accept contradiction but feel that it is coming from one and will ultimately lead back to the path of Oneness. He will perceive the principle of harmony hidden in ignorance. He will link the contradictions in a true order.

A gnostic race of being will not be a race of colourless identity of beings where all diversities are totally annulled, it will be a race of unity-in-diversity. Basically the gnostic consciousness will be the same but it will express itself in different degrees in hierarchical grades. As there is difference of individuality and personality between ordinary beings, there will be differences in the case of gnostic beings also, but there will be no ignorance in the case of gnostic beings. The supramental consciousness does not abolish the diversity; rather it fulfils it. A gnostic being is at once well aware of his "individuality, universality and transcendence". Sri Aurobindo (ibid.: 971) has himself said:

> A supramental or gnostic race of beings would not be a race made according to a single type, moulded in a single fixed pattern; for the law of supermind is unity fulfilled in diversity, and therefore there would be an infinite diversity in the manifestation of the gnostic consciousness would still be one in its basis, in its constitution, in its all-revealing and all-uniting order.

Each individual will possess a distinct personality, it is one in its basis but different in its nature. Misra (1957: 325) says:

> Sri Aurobindo does not contend that unity can be established only by effacing or abolishing diversity altogether. The diversity cannot be reconciled with unity so long as it is subject to ignorance and limitation. When the ignorance is cancelled, the diversity is seen as nothing else but the manifestation of unity. So man, according to Sri Aurobindo, realizes his highest destiny not by sacrificing his individuality and personality on the alter of bare and abstract unity but by raising them to their highest status of development by the realization of his universal and transcendent nature. The gnostic being realises the highest status or destiny when he becomes one with the Absolute in both status and dynamic. So the diversity exists side by side of the principle of unity and there is no opposition felt between them in supramental or gnostic consciousness.

Thus supramental unity, according to Sri Aurobindo, will be unity-in-diversity. He has said elsewhere:

> But in the supramental race itself, in the variation of its degress, the individuals would not be cast according to a single type of individuality; each would be different from the other, a unique formation of the Being, although one with all the rest in foundation of self and sense of oneness and in the principle of his being. – 1970, vol. II, pt II: 971

The gnostic personality is the consummation of the spiritual man, ". . . . his whole way of being, thinking, living, acting would be governed by the power of a vast universal spiritualiy. All the trinities of the Spirit would be real to his self-awareness and realized in his inner life. All his existence would be fused into oneness with the transcendent and universal. Self and Spirit, all his action would originate from and obey the supreme Self and Spirit's divine governance of Nature. All life would have to him the sense of the Conscious Being . . ." (Ibid.: 971-72).

He will feel the presence of divine everywhere, in every vibration, in every cell of life. He will feel workings of the supreme world Mother everywhere. He will feel all beings as his own self. In *Savitri,* Sri Aurobindo says:

Thus shall the earth open to divinity?
And common natures feel the wide uplift,
Illumine common acts with the Spirit's ray
And meet the deity in common things
Nature shall live to manifest secret God,
The Spirit shall take up the human play,
This earthly life becomes the life Divine.
– Book XI, canto I, p. 331

A gnostic individual may be in the world or above the world, but he will necessarily live in his self of transcendence. He would be individual but would not be ruled by separative individualiy. He individualizes in the universe for the complete individual is the cosmic individual. According to Sri Aurobindo, our individuality can be completed only when we take the universe into ourselves and transcend it. Gnostic being constantly lives in the consciousness very different from ours. Whereas a normal being is cooped within the four walls of his egoistic ignorance unaware of the truth of his own being or of the cosmos, "the gnostic being is constantly self-aware of all the trinities of the spirit and lives in a consciousness not of narrow individuality but in one of a vast universal spirituality" (Banerjee 1957-59, pt II: 256).

A supramental being is well aware of the self-manifestation of the spirit in himself as well as in others, thus he will seek that delight in himself as well as in others as other's joy will also be a part of his own joy of existence. To share the joy or grief of others as if it is his own is, according to Sri Aurobindo, is sign of the liberated spiritual man. For supramental being there will be no contradiction between his good and the good of others. There will be a cosmic sympathy in him, "his cosmic sympathy will be part of his inborn truth of being and not dependent on a personal participation in the lesser joy and suffering; it will transcend what it embraces and in the transcendence will be its power" (Aurobindo 1970, vol. II, pt II: 976). This feeling of universality will be a spontaneous state a natural movement. There will be no place for limited self or desire in him. Unhappiness and grief, pain and suffering belong to ego and not to the truth of the Spirit. The normal human being acts from some necessity, whatever it may be. Moreover a normal mind does not know what it should will, it proceeds from ignorance but the gnostic being has no want, no desire to be fulfilled. It has full knowledge of what is to be willed. His knowledge is not ideative, it is the Real-idea of the Supermind. The gnostic living is the life of inner-living. The world will be connected with his inner life. His self will not be the mental ego but the spirit that is pervading everywhere.

PLACE OF PERSONALITY IN THE GNOSTIC BEING

Now the question naturally creeps in: Is the gnostic being a person? What is the place of the ethical element in gnostic being? For common people, ego is the self and the centre of personality and it makes them distinct from other. And if this sense of egohood disappears in a higher consciousness, it means loss of personality. And if the personality, the individuality is extinguished, there is no question of ethical element in the gnostic being. Thus common-sense logic will say gnostic individual should be impersonal and as such every gnostic being would be exactly the same in pattern and nature as the other one as there will be nothing to mark off one being as different from the other. But this conclusion can be drawn only when we take personality and impersonality as opposite principles. This is the mental solution rather than the supramental solution of the problem. According to Sri Aurobindo (ibid.: 992-93):

> In the Supermind consciousness, personality and impersonality are not opposite principles; they are inseparable aspects of one and the same reality. This reality is not the ego but the being, who is impersonal and universal in his stuff of nature, but forms out of it an expressive personality which is his form of self in the changes of Nature.

In Advaitic scheme of *videhamukti*, individuality and personality of a man completely cease to be. But according to Rāmānuja individuality is not incompatible with salvation. Sri Aurobindo here seems to agree with Rāmānuja. In liberation what is annihilated is the ego and not the individuality. But still they differ at a point when Rāmānuja says that full liberation can be attained only after death, after full exhaustion of all *prārabdha karmas*. But for Sri Aurobindo, liberation can be attained here on this earth without any cessation of individuality or personality. Sri Aurobindo (ibid.: 994) says:

> A supramental gnostic individual will be a spiritual person, but not a personality in the sense of pattern of being marked out by a settled combination of fixed qualities, a determined character; he cannot be that since he is a conscious expression of the universal and the transcendent.

But let it not be supposed that in the absence of personality a gnostic being would be "some sort of impersonal flux throwing up various waves of personality out of the sea of gnostic consciousness". In common sense of the term personality is used in very limited sense but this is not the case with the gnostic personality. A gnostic being is not a surface personality.

> The gnostic individual would be such an inner person unveiled, occupying both the depths – no longer self-hidden – and the surface in a unified self-awareness; he would not be a surface personality partly expressive of a larger secret being, he would be the *puruṣa*, the inner conscious Existence self-revealed, and would have no need of a carved expressive mask or persona.
>
> – Ibid.: 995

> The gnostic being would be an universal being suggesting through the individual self-formation its eternal self and consciousness and the inherent truth of its existence.
>
> – Banerjee 1957-59: 76

With the acceptance of personality the ethical question, with regard to the place of ethics in the life of gnostic being, naturally creeps in. But according to Sri Aurobindo, there is no ethical problem for a gnostic being. The purpose of ethics is to regulate the conflicting ideas which prevail in human mind and society due to ignorance prevailing in man's character. But there is no such ignorance in a gnostic being leading to wrong will to inflict harm on others. All actions are automatic self-expression contributing towards good of all. Sri Aurobindo (1970, vol. II, pt II: 997) observes:

> All ethics is a construction of good in a Nature which has

> been smitten with evil by the powers of darkness born of the ignorance.

The conflict between good and evil, virtue and vice disturbs only an ordinay human being. The force of darkness (*tamas*) is constantly trying to pull his leg down to the depth of vices. There, an ethical norm is necessary to guard him against this pull; but a gnostic being attains real consciousness and he is ever guided by this truth consciousness, thus the conflict between virtue and vice, good and evil has no meaning for him. There is no fixed norm of behaviour no "categorical imperative" no cardinal virtue for him, nay, his behaviour rather fixes the norm of behaviour, the cardinal virtues. The problem stands only before those who are ever groping in ignorance, they have excelled this ignorance. Sri Aurobindo observes (1970, vol. 2: 997):

> All entire freedom of the spirit, an entire, self-existent order, self-creating, self-effectuating, self-secure in its own nature and inevitable movement, is the character of this dynamic of the gnostic supernature.

A gnostic being expresses only the truth of the will of *Īśvara*. This is present in each gnostic individual. He is in full accord and harmony. His activity is not a compelled one rather it would have the infinite freedom. This freedom is "the freedom of the light and not of darkness". His freedom is not a licence to do wrong to others rather it is a spontaneous overflow of his universal personality. His idea will be ever flourished by the universal love, sympathy and oneness, thus the ethical problem never stands in his way to make him perturbed.

DIVINE LIFE

The life of gnostic being, carrying the evolution of supramental status, may fitly be characterized as a divine life for it will be a life in the Divine. All spiritual life is, by principle, a development into divine life. We cannot draw a bifurcating line between the place where the mental ceases and divine life beings. A man of spiritual realization lives acts and behaves in Divine. His liberation is in nature and not from nature. *Gītā* too says: "He lives and moves in

Me." He lives inwardly a divine life. Sri Aurobindo (ibid.: 1023) says: "To be and to be fully is Nature's aim in us"; and to be fully means "to have the full delight of being". Sri Aurobindo (ibid.: 1025) says:

> To become complete in being, in consciousness of being, in force of being, in delight of being, and to live in this integrated completeness is the divine living.

Again to be fully means to be universal. Pain and suffering are caused by imperfection. All being is one and to be fully is to be all that is. To feel one's own being in the being of all, to be "conscious of consciousness of all", to realize all selves as dear as one's own self, to feel the pleasure of other as one's own pleasure, etc. are the necessary conditions of divine life. He lives for others out of spiritual force of love and sympathy. To live within is the first necessary condition of divine life. This inward turning does not mean to be confined to selfish motives, this is the primary stage towards universality:

> A realization of spiritual unity, a dynamization of the intimate consciousness of one-being, of one self in all beings, can alone found and govern by its truth the action of the divine life.
>
> – Ibid.: 1030

6

A Summing up of the Journey of Advaita from Śaṅkara to Sri Aurobindo

THE philosophy of Advaita constitutes that lofty eminence of thought which gives either origin or inspiration to different Vedāntic schools. Because of remarkable speculative genius the Kevalādvaita of Śaṅkara had, it had its sway on the mind of pursuer of truth for centuries to come. Evaluation of his contribution will be incomplete if we assess only his positive contribution; his negative contribution gave birth to Bhakti-Vedānta. His denial of the reality of the world, his all-embracing absolutism could not keep under spell those who were eager to have loving communion with God. Consequently a new school of Vedānta, viz. Bhakti-Vedānta came into existence. The Ultimate Reality is not impersonal, unqualified *Brahman*; rather he is *Īśvara* full of all auspicious qualities. They never cancel the world as unreal as it is a product of God Himself. The self too is not to be blown off in liberation. It is the egoity that is destroyed not the individuality. The individual enjoys loving communion with God. Unity at the cost of multiplicity is no unity. The Bhakti-Vedānta school works as a transitional link between the Absolute monism of Śaṅkara and the integral Advaitism of Sri Aurobindo. He is an Advaitist but he never propounds his Advaitism at the cost of the reality of the world. The world as the expression of *Brahman* is too great to be cancelled as unreal. A divinized man can only emerge in a divinized cosmos.

Theistic Vedānta accepts the reality of the world as against Māyāvāda of Śaṅkara but they do not accept the indeterminate Absolute. Sri Aurobindo's higher logic could easily reconcile the concept of the indeterminate Absolute with the creation of a real world and the existence of individual souls.

For both Śaṅkara and Sri Aurobindo, Saccidānanda is the Absolute. Both of them felt the need of a link between *Brahman* and the world. Śaṅkara calls this link *Īśvara* but Sri Aurobindo calls it the Supermind. *Īśvara* is not an "irrelevant intrusion" rather it has practical utility. It is the creator of the world. According to Sri Aurobindo, Saccidānanda has infinite power, infinite energy, infinite potency. If Supermind would not have intervened, the world would not have been a cosmos but a chaos. It is both the beginning and end of all creation and arrangement. Supermind is the immanent aspect. Both Śaṅkara and Sri Aurobindo believe that the whole universe is a play of joy, a spontaneous activity of God. It is creation out of bliss, by bliss and for bliss. *Brahman* transcends the cause–effect relationship. It is all inclusive. It cannot be distinguished from what it is not. It is immanent as well as transcendent.

In spite of all these similarities there is ample difference too. The *Brahman* of Śaṅkara is indeterminate, unknowable and static whole; Saccidānanda of Sri Aurobindo is both static and dynamic, being and becoming, consciousness and force. Absolute is not a rigid indeterminate oneness, not an infinity vacant of all that is not a pure self-existence and at the same time movement, process and energy. Being is the very substratum of becoming. *Brahman* of Śaṅkara is pure existence. He conceives this existence to be a "universal and ineffable reality". A transcendental and static *Brahman* cannot be thought to evolve in world process. Becoming is, therefore, an appearance and not reality.

For Śaṅkara, *Brahman* is consciousness as such, it is *cit*, but for Sri Aurobindo it is conscious-force, *cit-śakti*. It is dynamic and creative. Force is existence. Śiva and Śakti are one, not two. *Cit-śakti* is the root principle of creation; he calls it by the name mother. Here the influence of Tantra philosophy on Sri Aurobindo is evident. Mother is the divine Śakti behind this world process.

Both of them conceive *Brahman* as bliss. Now the question is how can the evil of the world be justified with the concept of bliss? Śaṅkara is forced to call evil unreal in order to make room for his Advaitic philosophy, but Sri Aurobindo never feels shy of evil. He boldly accepts its reality and shows the way how it can be finally transformed into good in the course of cosmic evolution. Evil is the garb of world's delight, it is not contradictory to good.

Śaṅkara's Advaitism maintains the infinite at the cost of finite. It maintains the one at the cost of many, unity at the cost of diversity. But Sri Aurobindo's Advaitism is integral Advaitism which includes all things as one *Brahman*. Here there is complete synthesis between matter and spirit, between the impersonal and the personal, etc. The one is maintained not at the cost of many, but in and through many. For the maintenance of infinite there is no need to deny finite. Reality includes all aspects of existence in it but it transcends them as well.

Śaṅkara maintains identity at the cost of difference, *Brahman* at the cost of the reality. But Bhakti-Vedāntists as well as Sri Aurobindo grant full reality to the world as the creation or expression of *Brahman*. For Rāmānuja as an attribute of *Brahman* the world is not different from Him. The effect is as real as cause. For Madhva too, creation is a real fact and has its cause in God's will. Nimbārka and Vallabhācārya too have a realistic attitude towards the universe. The universe, according to Vallabha, is a natural emanation from Him. It is *brahmakārya*, an effect of *Brahman*. The ornament is not something different from gold. All Bhakti-Vedāntists accept world to be real. It is a product of *māyā* which is to be cancelled at the time of liberation. But Sri Aurobindo goes even far. The whole universe is to be supramentalized as it is a descent of the Divine. This involution is the result of the self-concealment of the Divine in the universe. But this is not all. The spirit has to return to itself. There should be ascent from a less manifest condition of the consciousness-force to a more manifest condition. The dormant spirit in matter feels an inner urge to rise above. Thus the universe is not to be cancelled at the time of liberation. In Śaṅkara's philosophy objects are given only empirical status and not ontological status, but in Sri Aurobindo's philosophy objects too are conceived ultimately as *Brahman*.

Śaṅkara, to save his Advaitism, did not concede reality to the immanent aspect; theistic Vedānta did it but they could not place it on any sound foundation of logic. Sri Aurobindo thinks he could do it successfully with his logic of the infinite. There is no provision for such reconciliation of contradiction in Śaṅkara's philosophy.

In Advaita Vedānta God has only practical utility. The moment the reality of the world is sublated, God is sublated. It is product of *avidyā*. But Supermind, possessing integral consciousness, is a reality. It presents the integral view of the Absolute. It reconciles the opposition between Saccidānanda and the world and makes integral aspect possible. It is absolute itself in its creative aspect. Saccidānanda is undifferentiated unity but the supermind is the differentiated unity. Since supermind is the creative aspect of Saccidānanda both the aspects of Saccidānanda, its determinability and indeterminability are made possible. There is no opposition between Saccidānanda as active, i.e. as supermind and Saccidānanda as passive.

The world-creating power, the *cit-śakti* is as real as *Brahman* for Sri Aurobindo, but Śaṅkara, the staunch non-dualist, thinks the world creative power *māyā* as unreal as the world itself. They appear to be real till we are in ignorance. An independent importance of *māyā* will put his monism at stake. He is an uncompromising monist, thus besides that One Reality, all else is figment of *ajñāna*.

Brahman cannot be both changing and changeless, as it involves self-contradiction. But Sri Aurobindo says that the word "changeless" does not mean it is incapable of change, rather it means it is unaffected by change or becoming of the world. It is "boundless totality", "a multitude". *Brahman* is indeterminate does not mean it is incapable of determination rather it means it is beyond all determination. The change takes place not according to the mathematics of the infinite. Upaniṣadic philosophy says:

> *pūrṇamadaḥ pūrṇamidam pūrnātpurṇamudacyate* ।
> *pūrṇasya pūrṇamādāya pūrṇāmevāvaśiṣyate* ॥
> – Bṛh.U.-Śānti Pāṭha

> This is the complete, and that is the complete; substract the complete from the complete, the complete is the remainder.

The One does not cease to be one by manifesting the manifold objects of the world out of it or in it. His manifestation is as real as his transcendence as these are two poises of his being. His creatorship is not incompatible with his Absoluteness. Sri Aurobindo does not say that the exclusive realization of the transcendent aspect of the Absolute is not possible, what he means to say is, we can realize the nature of the Absolute fully only when we relate it with the individual and the universal. The polarity can be well understood by the logic of the infinite. Our reason is "the instrument of ignorance with a very limited vision". It cannot reconcile being with becoming, one with many. But the logic of the infinite "is a greater reason, a greater logic because it is more vast, subtle, complex in its operation: it comprehends all the data which our observation fails to seize, it deduces from them results which neither our deduction nor induction can anticipate because our conclusions and inferences have a meagre foundation and are fallible and brittle" (Aurobindo 1970, vol. I: 329).

To say *Brahman* is beyond cause is one thing, and to say *Brahman* as creator is unreal is another thing. A man can be the father, the son, the husband and the brother, etc. in relation to different persons, still his individuality is unaffected. He transcends all relationship; similar is the case with *Brahman*. His creatorship is not incompatible with his transcendence. In order to save the being, denial of becoming is not essential for Sri Aurobindo. Relational categories are not false but imperfect. An integral study of Absolute will include the study of being as well as of becoming.

Sri Aurobindo feels that if we make Absolute relationless and as such incapable of manifesting itself in relation, we are imposing limitations upon Absolute. The perfect freedom means freedom from all relations and at the same time its freedom to manifest relation.

Sri Aurobindo's integral outlook is not altogether a new concept. The term may be found in Upaniṣads, but his approach to the problem is new.

Śaṅkara's theory is supported by modern scientific theory of relativity. The distinction between appearance and reality is a necessary corollary of the theory of relativity. Jean James (1981: 193) says:

> We may picture the world of reality as a deep-flowing stream, the world of appearance is its surface below which we cannot see.

Albert Einstein looks at the world from the point of view of a scientist. He accepts that our physical reality can never be final. We must be ready to change it always. There is something ineffable about the real. Arthur Eddington too says that table presented to sense is but an unreal appearance of the real table which belongs to the shadow of world of physics. Śaṅkara with these scientists says that spatio-temporal world is unreal (the term unreal is not used in ordinary sense of illusion). Thus in view of Advaita Vedānta the question whether the world is real or unreal is one of "evaluation or axiology", and that its answer is relative to the spiritual achievement of the person concerned.

Śaṅkara presents an ultimate standpoint of philosophical way of thinking. The credit of Sri Aurobindo lies in its being integral in nature. He is a compromising Advaitist. He never turns a blind eye to its extent or comprehensiveness. An integral Advaitism has more appeal only for a common man who finds no reason to declare the world to be illusory as dream and its sublation after liberation.

Sri Aurobindo reconciles being and becoming with the help of the logic of infinite but his logic of infinite could not get a specific shape in his philosophy. This integral approach is a trial for synthesis, it does not get a strong logical footing. To reconcile reason, experience and revelation is undoubtedly a bold and appreciable step of Sri Aurobindo, but how far it is practicable one cannot say. It is difficult to make an assessment. How far it goes to dissolve the contradiction is a matter of speculation. *Brahman* is to be realized by intuition and not by reason.

All the Vedāntists feel that the present state of man is not the final state. Man, as he appears to our senses, is not the real man or at least he is not the "complete man". To fulfil God in life is man's manhood. The real self is behind this surface self. Its existence cannot be denied as denial will itself prove its existence. Pleasure and pain are the properties of mind but bliss is of the self.

In spite of these similarities there is ample difference in their way of thinking.

Soul, for Śaṅkara, is identical with *Brahman*.[1] And this identity is to be fully realized in the state of liberation. For Rāmānuja and other Bhakti-Vedāntists soul attains the nature of God, but not the identity. Individual soul is a mode of God, it is atomic in size. Egoity is opposed to liberation and not individuality. In liberation souls enjoy divine communion with God. But in Sri Aurobindo's philosophy both identity and individuality are maintained. The self is one in fact, but it is capable of cosmic differentiation and multiple individuality. It expresses itself in the individual, the universal and the transcendental. The individual and cosmos are the expressions of transcendent self. The transcendent self does not contradict the individual self or the cosmos. He too does not deny individuality in liberation. The individual must be there to enjoy the bliss. Our identification with temporal individualization is abolished, not the individuality itself. Here the individuality embraces both the "world-material and its individualized experience of spatial and temporal activities in a free and enlarged consciousness". In this new consciousness he realizes that his true self is one with the transcendence and individuality is not more than "a formation for world-experience". He transcends the sense of separative egoity. By individuality we wrongly presume a separative consciousness. A true individual, according to Sri Aurobindo (1970, vol. I: 373), is nothing "but a conscious power of being of the eternal, always existing by unity, always capable of mutuality. It is that being which by self-knowledge enjoys liberation and immortality". The soul can enjoy unity with Divine in essence as well as in power. We have perfect union with Divine as well as differentiated unity. Differentiation is means of greater unity.

In Advaita Vedānta *ātman* is a passive principle. For Rāmānuja, etc. it is atomic in size, it is of the nature of knowledge. It is the controlled (*niyama*) and God is its support (*niyantā*). But for Sri Aurobindo it is dynamic being, omniscient and omnipotent. It takes the control of our lower nature, i.e. body, life and mind. When the soul fully controls the physical body, etc. a soul personality gets developed in man. It is to be transmuted into the divine

---

[1] (a) *tvameva sarvasyātmabhūtasya* | – Śve.U.Ś.B. 4.4

(b) *bheda vyavahāra upādhikṛtaḥ* | – B.S.Ś.B. I.2.21

state of personality. Self is "equally real and truly individual". Sri Aurobindo say: "We can attain the highest without blotting ourselves out from the cosmic extension."

In Śaṅkara's philosophy soul enjoys only indentity and not fellowship with Him. To Rāmānuja, etc. it means annihilating the very existence of the man after liberation who aspires for it. They say that if individuality is saved, their interest in religion and morality is saved. But for Śaṅkara loss of individuality is not loss but gain. It regains its lost glory. *Ātman* is in fact *Brahman*.[2] After identity how can individuality be left apart. To say that *jīva* becomes *Brahman* is a verbal statement only (*upacāramātra*) as *jīva* is already *Brahman*.

All the Vedāntists believe that man's involvement into finitude is caused by *avidyā*. According to Śaṅkara, it is *avidyā-kalpita* or *avidyā-pratyupasthāpita*. He uses another expression, *adhyāsa* is the root cause of the world-process. But this involvement in finitude is the temporary phase. *Ātman* is finally to be withdrawn from this structure. Ultimately it is possible only through knowledge. Sri Aurobindo too realizes fully that *ātman* is to be conceived as different from the body. But he does not believe in withdrawal from the nature wholly. He does not aim at individual liberation, but his goal is complete transformation of nature. Not only individual persons but the whole nature is to be supramentalized. And this supramentalization is possible only through cosmic evolution. The indivinity is to be realized not merely in the unchanging aspect of his being but in the psycho-physical organism as well. Not only the spirit is to be divinized but also physical, vital and mental aspects of man's personality. His aim is total divinization of life. As the creation of Saccidānanda, it has its own claim to be supramentalized.

Śaṅkara believes in total unity of soul and *Brahman*; individuality is completely lost in divine. Bhakti-Vedānta maintains the individuality of soul to enjoy the fruits of his liberation. It is only egoity which is lost in *mukti*. But Sri Aurobindo goes even

---

[2] *eṣa ātmā bhavatām svarūpam* – Chā.U.Ś.B. VIII.1.5.

further. His liberation means spiritualization not only of spirit but of the whole cosmos as well.

Man is not a meek personality left at the caprice of chance; rather he is Divine in essence. And his destiny consists in realizing the Divine in the core of his heart. He is Divine in essence, he must be Divine in actuality. The cosmic expansion of self (*sarvātma bhāva*) is the *summum bonum* of human existence, it is the greatest value of human life.

But Śaṅkara lays emphasis on the liberation of soul only and not of nature, whereas for Sri Aurobindo it is not an isolated raising of any single principle, rather a genuine upliftment of the whole nature of man. Freedom does not mean cessation of worldly existence merely. Salvation means transmutation of man into gnostic being. It is to live a divine life on earth. It is the life of gnostic being. It does not mean freedom from the transmigration of soul as other Vedāntists think. A gnostic being takes birth again and again and helps people in their moral upliftment. After the supramental descent, evolution proceeds through knowledge.

In Śaṅkara's scheme of liberation the world is to be negated as it is a product of *avidyā*. But Sri Aurobindo believes that a divinized man can emerge only in a divinized universe. Body is not a cage for soul from where it is to be set free for higher realization rather the divination and integration of the lower nature are an essential part of liberation. Bhakti-Vedāntists too do not believe in the negation of the world.

Śaṅkara does not believe in any supramental transcendence of the world but Sri Aurobindo foresees teleology behind the evolutionary process; it is the descent of the Supermind into the world of life. After supramental descent, the evolutionary process rises to the total victory of spirit over matter and total divinization of life. The conscious-force of the Divine is to descend permanently on earth.

While Śaṅkara calls the liberated soul *jīvanmukta*, Sri Aurobindo calls it gnostic being. His life is divine life. In *jīvanmukti* only spirit enjoys complete freedom but Sri Aurobindo stresses not only the liberation of spirit but also of psycho-physical organism. Even the physical organism transcends all sorts of limitation. Body does not cease to work, rather it obeys the higher principle of spirit. All his actions and thoughts are guided by Divine will. The body of the *jīvanmukta* is governed by *prārabdha karma*, but that of superman is ever free from the fetters of all kinds of *karma*.

Jīvanmukti is an individual liberation. He never tries to bring down the higher light in the flux of evolution. He is a silent spectator of the nature. But the emergence of gnostic being affects the whole of nature. He has grasped reality "not only in its full heights but also in its extent and comprehensiveness". He has not only glimpsed the spirit in its native splendour but has also perceived the meaning of the spirit in matter. Superman is necessarily *jīvanmukta puruṣa* but all *jīvanmukta*s are not supermen. Choudhary says: There have indeed been so many *Jīvanmukta*s "but superman is yet to emerge." He acts in full awareness of harmony of the universal self and his individual self. The individual is only a unit of the race. This transformation of man into a Divine man is precisely the chief message of Sri Aurobindo's philosophy.

Śaṅkara advocates the path of knowledge as true means to liberation. He does not even entertain the idea of *karma-jñāna-samuccaya*. Bhakti-Vedānta deems devotion to be the chief means of liberation. But Sri Aurbindo like his integral Advaitism preaches integral *yoga*. Fullness of being, fullness of consciousness and fullness of life must be the end of the history towards which we are moving, and which will manifest sooner or later.

The Advaita Vedānta of Śaṅkara does not believe in historical interpretation of history. Following the ancient Hindu tradition it believes in the cyclic view of history. It does not believe that history is heading towards perfection. But Sri Aurobindo advocates historical interpretation of history. It is not only the self which is to be redeemed from the clutches of ignorance but the whole universe. He believes in the salvation of the whole personality as well as of human race in general. History is heading towards fulfilment. But Śaṅkara along with the Hindu tradition as a whole does not agree with this view. He believes in the absolute freedom of spirit and not of history. Only psychological self is to be expanded in cosmic self and not the whole universe which is subject to the law of emergence or evolution and dissolution. He just sees the possibility of the world coming into existence and passing away. It is to be taken as a non-historical interpretation of history. It may also be called the cyclic interpretation of history.

Thus, Śaṅkara, as a staunch Advaitist, believes in one and only one reality, the rest is illusion. Bhakti-Vedānta is realistic in approach and gives due importance to the world as a creation of God. Sri Aurobindo goes still further. The world is not only real; "a self-finding and self-unfolding of the spirit, a self-revelation of Divinity in the universe" is its ultimate destiny. Sri Aurobindo believes that the idea of spiritual individual was dominant in ancient Indian thought but in recent times, the whole stress is on the life of the race, the individual is only a unity of the race. As we move towards spiritual freedom, we also move towards spiritual oneness. True perfection means "the sovereignty and self-effectuation of the spiritual reality in all the elements of our nature". His philosophy is of Advaita but it is integral Advaita as against Kevalādvaita of Śaṅkara.

7

Advaita and Modern Science

RIGHT from the Vedic period, the keynote of Indian philosophy is Advaita which sees its highest bloom in Śaṅkara's philosophy of Kevalādvaita. Even today Śaṅkara's theory has full support of modern physics. N.C. Panda (1991: 440) comments that "Advaita Vedānta is more scientific than science itself." He again says (in Prologue on page xiii):

> Advaita Vedānta is found to be the only philosophy that has capacity to be scientific. It can absorb all the modern concepts of science without any contradiction.

According to Einstein, philosophy is the "mother of all sciences". It owes the development of all later thoughts whether cosmological or psychological or scientific. During the period of Greek philosophy, philosophy, science and religion were not separated. Aristotle laid more emphasis on human soul and contemplation of God than on the material world. In the medieval period, philosophy was handmade to religion but in the modern period science has settled at the hard rock of reality which is purely materialistic in nature. With the appearance of Descartes, the diehard dualist, an antagonism between mind and matter, between "I" and "the world" emerged. The belief of the people was that the objective picture of the world without any mention of the human observer was possible and this objective description became the ideal of all scientific discoveries. Cartesian dualists with their view, that matter functions as a machine "bereft of any spiritual value, wrenched us from the familiar religion and culture".

Philosophy of Descartes left immense effect on classical physics of Isaac Newton. From the second half of seventeenth century to the end of nineteenth century, there was tremendous impact of Newtonian mechanics. With the "relentless withdrawal of the transcendental deity from the scheme of things", human consciousness knew nothing but itself. Pierre-Simon Laplace, the great mathematician of that time, wrote a book titled *Mécanique céleste* on the system of the universe and presented it to Napolean who when commented on it that he had not mentioned the creator of the universe anywhere, his reply was "I had no need for that hypothesis".[1]

For them, the mechanical view of the world was deterministic and self-sufficient to solve all the riddles of the world. It was that age of physics in which the future was determined by the past.

The modern physicists never say that Newton is wrong, they only show that Newtonian physics is limited. Religion was a matter of fundamental interest to Newton. He believed that the world is created by God and He rules the world from above. Everything which happens is predetermined and cannot be proved or disapproved by the scientific standard.

The classical physics of Newton with mechanical and deterministic view gave a static model of the world. It transmuted the purposeful cosmos driven by love of God of Greek and medieval period into a "dead clockwise machine". His mechanical model was the "blueprint of an entirely lifeless design". The immutable law of history pictured by Marx, the Darwin's blind evolution and Freud's "theory of dark psyche" were all inspired by Newton's theory. Russell rightly remarks that we were steeped in unyielding despair. We were forced to live willy-nilly in the age of existential here forgetting all about its spiritual heritage by turning blind eyes to wholistic knowledge. To quote Vedic seers, "Knowledge comes to those who are wide awake, for those who know it not, what the knowledge will do".[2]

With the belief that the course of the universe can be completely

---

[1] Quoted from Capra 1975: 58.

[2] *yojāgāraḥ taṁ ṛcā kāmayante*
tasmin devaḥ adhiviśve niṣedhuḥ ।
yaścanna veda kim ṛcā kariṣyati
–Quoted from R.K. Pandey, 1976-77 "Yoga: The Mechanics of Consciousness," *Prajñā*, vol. 21.

determined by the coherent mathematical laws which assert that each event is followed by a necessary consequent event "man was put into a terrible low profile". John Keats blamed Newton for destroying the rainbow by saying that "only white light is real all else is illusion".

After the appearance of Einstein with the theory of relativity the whole castle of Newtonian classical physics was exterminated. He believed that invention is not the work of logical thinking, it is the result of intuitive realization. "The domain of intuition is sweeter than the nightmare of logic". Upaniṣad too says, the reality is not to be known by mind: *yanmansā na manute* (Ke.U. 1.5), reality is to be revealed and not to be grasped by logical categories; *naiṣa tarkena matirā paneyā* (K.U. 1.2.9). It is erroneous to say that science proceeds mainly from empirical foundation. There is no logical path here. Only intuition, based on sympathetic understanding of experiences, can realize it. "Intellect has little to do on the path of discovery."

Einstein accepts that cosmic religious feeling is the strongest motive of scientific research. He strongly believed in nature's inherent harmony and his major concern was "to find out a unified foundation of physics". He believed that without the inner harmony of the world there can be no science. He says:

> I cannot conceive a genuine scientist without the profound faith. The situation may be expressed by an image: science without religion is lame, religion without science is blind.[3]

His formula of $E = mc^2$ brought revolution in the world of physics. The concept that mass is a form of energy obliterated the idea of material substance. Quantum theory reached out to the basic oneness of the universe. Once you know the parts we can derive at least the dynamics of the whole. The scientific knowledge is no more a catalogue of the properties of matter, rather it is an understanding of nature.

The classical physics, with its deterministic and mechanical

---

3 Selection from and on Einstein, Indian National Science Academy and CSIR, 1984.

view, gave a static model of the world but by reducing physical world into "a dynamic unitary substratum", modern physics paved the way for the mystic view of the world, "where something that can't be proved true may not necessarily be said to be false".

The theory of relativity discovers the ontological contents of reality, Einstein realizes that we can't take Galileo's suggestion that God's book of nature is written in the alphabets of mathematics or Baconian that we must put nature on a rack and with a screw draw out its secrets. Max Planck believes that science is moving towards the aim "where poetic intuition may apprehend but intellect can never fully grasp". They are fastly realizing that "we cannot know anything unless we know everything" (Zukav 1979: 313).

The scientific researches were gradually leading to a point where the demarcation between the subjective and the objective disappears. The modern physics realizes that when the separation between the subject and the object ceases, the mind takes a quantum jump from reason to intuition, from wisdom to intelligence. The physicists accept that while doing physics, they are getting the glimpse of "central order of things". They are realizing that they are "confronting the ineffable".

Today the entire field of physics is "quivering with anticipation"; they are realizing the futility of mechanical process. In the process of scientific analysis we sacrifice the whole for the parts banishing our soul into eternal exile. As against the concept of singularity and indeterminacy of earlier physics, quantum physics reveals a basic oneness of the universe and the knowledge of this oneness cannot be obtained by observation but by full participation with the whole.

To quote Capra (1975: 131):

> The basic oneness of the universe is not only the central characteristics of mystical experiences but is also one of the important revelations of modern physics.

It is the whole which determines the behaviour of the parts. Renée Weber (1986: 29) says: "the major role, the real music of the universe is the unity of unity and diversity or the wholeness of the whole and parts".

Ken Wilber (1996: Prologue, 3) puts the question: " Has the nature laboured these billions of years just to bring forth the egoic mouse?" Simply by drawing the line in the middle of blank page we divide it into right and left and generate a sense of opposition; we forget that the dividing line is only apposition. Reality is unity, a "no boundary truth".

Zukav (1979: 282) says:

> One of the implications of Bell's theorem is that at a deep and fundamental level the separate parts of the universe are connected in an intimate and immediate way. In short, Bell's theorem and enlightened experience of unity are very compatible.

David Bohm too says: "We must turn physics around." Instead of starting with parts and showing how they work together we start with the whole. "It leads to the notion of 'unbroken wholeness' which is in his words 'that-which-is'" (quoted in Zukav 1979: 305-06).

Sri Aurobindo (1970, vol. 1: 14) feels that "significant especially is the drive of science towards monism towards the Vedic idea of the essence with its many becoming". Earlier science monopolized the "kingdom of mind to the exclusion of metaphysics", but now scientists are of strong feeling that what they need is a "dose of metaphysics". To quote Zukav (1979: 114) "if the new physics had led us anywhere it is back to ourselves which of course is the only place that we could go". It challenges the concept of value-free science and imbibed the concept of science with values. Now it is not only a search for "what is", but also "what ought to be".

The modern scientists are realizing that science has paid a high price for excluding the subject of cognizance from the objective world. This is as if the "original sin" committed by earlier scientists. The deepest mystery that quantum physics reveals is that the man of science, in the larger interest of the whole humanity, must atone for their initial fault of banishing their souls into eternal exile. Their predecessor sacrificed the whole for the parts, consciousness for the matter but Eugene Wigner (1970: 172) says: "It was not possible to formulate the laws of quantum theory in the fully consistent way without reference to the consciousness."

Max Planck in Advaitic spirit of Śaṅkara says: "Consciousness, I regard as fundamental, I regard matter as derivative from consciousness." Schrödinger, in the spirit of Vedānta, adds to it that "consciousness is never experienced in the plural, only in the singular". He feels that the present way of thinking does need to be amended perhaps, "by a bit of blood transfusion from Eastern thought". These physicists frankly accept that their physics sound very much like old Eastern mysticism.

Capra comments that both mystics and the physicists confirm the ancient wisdom that the ultimate reality without is identical with the reality within. The acceptance of the scientists that all conclusions are only hypothetical as no conclusion can be claimed as final has the support of *Bṛhadāraṇyaka Upaniṣad*'s concept of *neti, neti*. Robert Oppenheimer says:

> . . . if we speak for instance whether the notions of electron remains the same, you must say no, if we ask whether the electron's position changes with time we say no. If we ask whether the electron is at rest we must say no, if we ask whether it is in motion we must say no. . . .[4]

James Jean realizes that the days of small hard atoms are gone and what is left is somewhat mental. Quantum physics never takes the objective world independent of the subject who is the observer. Heisenberg, Schrödinger and Eddington assert that in the texture of reality the subject and the object are one. The man is no more an observer but a participator. The new science is wholistic science which includes in itself both within as well as without. Krishnamurti too says: "The observer is the observed, the thinker and his thought are one."[5] In the *Dṛgdṛśyaviveka*, it is said in the similar vein that all the scenes before us are projections of our intellect, the only seer is Self (the pure consciousness) inside us. Vivekananda in his lectures on *bhakti* accepts that the external world is only the world of suggestion. All that we see, we project from our own mind. Vedāntins say that it is our consciousness that creates the world outside.

---

[4] Oppenheimer 1954: 42-43.

[5] Ojai, California, 6th public talk, 1946.

This realization that the observer is the observed gives us the awareness of the wholeness as the feature of reality which takes in its fold both the subjective and the objective as well as it transcends them both. For Heisenberg, Capra says that he has pursued his discipline to the point of complete self-realization. He feels that we cannot speak about nature without speaking about ourselves. Heisenberg himself accepts that "at least at subconscious level his work has been influenced by Indian philosophy".

Zohar (1991: 6) quotes:

> Quantum physics reveals a basic oneness of nature. Consciousness like matter emerges from the world of quantum events that the two, though wholly different from each other, have a common mother in quantum quality.

It has foundation which can support both physics and philosophy.

Capra (1988: 39) comments:

> The mystics and the physicists arrive at the same conclusion, one starting for the inner realm and the other from the outer world: *Brahman* the ultimate reality without is identical with *Ātman* the reality within.

All the modern theories of science can be assimilated by Advaita Vedānta in its fold. The modern physicists accept that the solution of their problem lies in the ancient wisdom of the Upaniṣad about which Schopenhauer says: that

> From the very sentence deep, original and sublime thoughts arise and the whole is pervaded by high and holy and earnest spirit. . . . In the whole world there is no study, except that of originals, so beneficial and so elevating as that of Oupnekhat. It has been solace to my life, it will be solace to my death.
>
> — quoted from Müller 1879: Introduction, xi

John Wheeler too realizes that the thinkers of the East knew it all and if we could only translate into our language we would have answer to all our questions.

Modern science is moving towards an aim which the intellect can never fully grasp. They are realizing that beyond a certain point there is no logical path, only intuition can reach there. They invoke a conscious force, spirit in the backdrop of all physical events. Barnett Lincoln (1949: 101) says:

> In the evolution of scientific thought one fact has been impressively clear that there is no mystery of the physical world which doesn't point to a mystery beyond itself.

Generally the colleagues of Max Planck attributed that his achievements were the result of his extraordinary will-power, but Einstein, in his address on Max Planck's 60th birthday, delivered at the Physical Society in Berlin, said that mind which enables a man to do work of this kind is akin to that of "the religious worshipper or the lover … the effect comes directly from heart."

Today the "cosmic religious feeling" is the basic motive for scientific researchers. Bohm (2005: 116) says:

> We are led to propose that more comprehensive, deeper and more inward actuality is neither mind nor body but rather a yet higher dimensional actuality which is their common ground and which is of the nature beyond both.

The concept of Advaita, especially Advaita Vedānta, has never been rejected by scientists of today or spiritualists of past. The fundamental interrelatedness and interdependence of all phenomenon and intrinsically dynamic nature of reality are common. Swami Vivekananda also feels that science has really made the foundation of religion strong. Now, the fact that the whole universe is one can be scientifically demonstrated.[6]

Panda (1991: xiii) says:

> The Advaita Vedānta and the modern science when fused together may "give rise to a synthetic integral philosophy which when translated to action of being, becomes cosmic religion".

Śaṅkara's philosophy has great affinity with the modern science but the advantage of Śaṅkara's philosophy is that he virtually visualizes the reality but science doesn't because it is speculative in nature and hedged around with unexplored limitations. But without conviction in the inner harmony of the world, science

---

[6] Vivekananda, 1947, vol. 7: 50.

cannot succeed. Śaṅkara's intuitive method shows the way to enter into the domain of reality and realize it practically. The aura of Advaita has not diminished even today; rather it is more strengthened, more embellished by modern science.

A day is bound to come when the antagonism between science and spirituality will be a matter of past. "Cosmic religious feeling" will be the noblest cause of all scientific researches. That will be an age of "scientific spirituality".

Bibliography

Agrawala, V.S., 1962, *Sparks from the Vedic Fire*, Varanasi: Banaras Hindu University.

Apte, R.N., 1986, *Doctrine of Māyā*, Bombay: University of Bombay, Government Central Press.

Aurobindo, Sri, 1914, *Views and Reviews*, Madras: Sri Aurobindo Ashram Library.

———, 1935, *Lights on Yoga*, Pondicherry: Sri Aurobindo Ashram.

———, 1941, *Thought and Glimpses*, Calcutta: Arya Publishing House.

———, 1946, *Ideal and Progress*, Calcutta: Arya Publishing House.

———, 1949, *Letters of Sri Aurobindo*, 1st to 4th Series, Bombay: Sri Aurobindo Circle.

———, 1950a, *The Superman*, 4th edn, Pondicherry: Sri Aurobindo Ashram.

———, 1950b, *Synthesis of Yoga*, New York: Sri Aurobindo Library.

———,1950c, *The Human Cycle*, New York: Sri Aurobindo Library.

———, 1951a, *Savitri*, Pondicherry: Sri Aurobindo International University Centre Publication.

——— (tr. and com.), 1951b, *Isha Upanishad*, Pondicherry: Sri Aurobindo Ashram.

———, 1951c, *The Riddle of the World*, 4th edn, Pondicherry: Sri Aurobindo Ashram.

———, 1952a, *The Supramental Manifestation Upon Earth*, Pondicherry: Sri Aurobindo Ashram.

———, 1952b, *Kena Upaniṣad*, Pondicherry: Sri Aurobindo Ashram.

———, 1953a, *Eight Upaniṣads*, 1st edn, Pondicherry: Sri Aurobindo Ashram.

———, 1953b, *Sri Aurobindo on Himself and the Mother*, Pondicherry: Sri Aurobindo Ashram.

———, 1959, *Essays on the Gita*, Pondicherry: Sri Aurobindo Ashram.

———, 1963, *Reason and Beyond Reason*, Bombay: Bharatiya Vidya Bhavan.

———, 1964a, *The Ideal of Karma Yogi*, Calcutta: Arya Publishing House.

———, 1964b, *On the Vedà*, Pondicherry: Sri Aurobindo Ashram.

———, 1969, *The Destiny of Man* (compiled by Rishabha Chand and S. Jhunjhunwala), Pondicherry: Aurobindo Society.

———, 1970, *The Life Divine*, vols I-II, Pondicherry: Sri Aurobindo Ashram.

———, 1971, *Letters on Yoga*, Pondicherry: Sri Aurobindo Ashram.

———, 1978, *The Mother*, Pondicherry: Aurobindo Ashram Press.

———, 1998, *The Secret of the Veda*, The Complete Works of Sri Aurobindo, vol. 15, Pondicherry: Sri Aurobindo Ashram.

———, 2001, *Yogic Sadhana* (Complete Works of Sri Aurobindo, vol. 10, ed. Uttara Yogi, Sri Vani Vilas Press.

———, 2003, *Isha Upanishad* (Complete Works of Sri Aurobindo, vol. 17), Pondicherry, Sri Aurobindo Ashram.

Banerjee, Aparna, 2012, *Integral Philosophy of Sri Aurobindo*, Delhi: Decent Books.

Banerjee, Siddheswar, 1957-59, *A Short Treatise on the Life Divine*, 2 vols, Pondicherry: Sri Aurobindo Ashram.

Barth, A., 1963, *The Religions of India*, Varanasi: Chaukhamba Sanskrit Series Office.

Belvalkar, S.K., 1939, *Vedānta Philosophy*, Poona: Bilvakury Publishing House.

Belvalkar, S.K. and R.D. Ranade, 1933, *History of Indian Philosophy*, Poona: Aryabhushan Press.

Bhandarkar, R.C., 1965, *Vaiṣṇavism, Śaivism and Minor Religious Systems*, Varanasi: Indological Book House.

Bharadwaj, Krishna Datta, 1958, *The Philosophy of Rāmānuja*, New Delhi: Sir Shankar Lal Charitable Trust Society.

Bhatt, S.R., 1975, *Studies in Rāmānuja Vedānta*, New Delhi: Heritage Publishers.

Bhattacharya, A.C., 1972a, "Sri Aurobindo: His View of Reality", *Darshana International* (April).

Bhattacharya, A.C., 1972b, *Sri Aurobindo and Bergson: A Synthetic Study*, Varanasi: Jagabandhu Prakashan.

Bhattacharya Shastri, D.C., 1986, "Advaita Vedānta according to Swami Vivekananda", *BRMIC*, 37: 3-8.

Bhattacharyya, Haridas, 1937, "The Advaita and Its Spiritual Significance", *Cultural Heritage of India*, vol. III, Calcutta: The Ramakrishna Mission Institute of Culture.

Bhattacharyya, K.C., 1909, *Studies in Vedāntism*, Calcutta: University of Calcutta.

Bohm, David, 2005, *The Essential*, ed. Lee Nichol, London and New York: Routledge Taylor & Francis Group.

Bosanquet, B., 1913, *The Value and Destiny of the Individual*, London: Macmillan.

Bose, Roma, 1943, *Vedānta Pārijāta Saurabha of Nimbārka and Vedānta Kaustubha of Śrīnivāsa*, Bengal: Royal Asiatic Society of Bengal.

Bradley, F.H., 1893, *Appearance and Reality: A Metaphysical Essay*, London: George Allen & Unwin.

Browning, Robert, 1855, "Bishop Blougram's Apology", in *Men and Women*, London: Chapman and Hall.

Buch, Maganlal A., 1921, *The Philosophy of Śaṅkara (Essays)*, Baroda: Vidya Vilas Press.

Bultemen, J.A.B. van, 1974, *Rāmānuja on Bhagavadgītā*, Delhi: Motilal Banarsidass.

Burtt, Edwin Arthur, 1923, *The Metaphysical Foundation of Modern Physical Science: A Historical and Critical Essay*, London: Kegan Paul, Trench and Trübner.

Capra, F., 1975, *Tao of Physics*, Boulder, CO: Shambhala Publications.

———, 1982, *The Turning Point: Science, Society and the Rising Culture*, New York: Bantam Books.

———, 1988, *Uncommon Wisdom: Conversations with Remarkable People*, New York: Simon & Schuster.

Chakraborty, Nirod Baran, 1967, *The Advaita Conception of Falsity: A Critical Study*, Calcutta: Calcutta Sanskrit College.

Chakraborty, Suresh Chand, 1921, *Philosophy of Upanishad*, Calcutta: Bhut Nath Palit.

Chakraborty, V.R. Srisaila, 1974, *The Philosophy of Sri Rāmānuja*, Madras.

Chand, Rishabh, 1955, *Integral Yoga of Sri Aurobindo*, parts I and II, Pondicherry: Sri Aurobindo Ashram.

———, 1969, *The Destiny of Man*, Pondicherry: Sri Aurobindo Ashram.

Chatterjee, T.D., 1961, *A Handbook of Sri Aurobindo's Yoga*, Calcutta: Anita Printers.

———, 1970, *Sri Aurobindo's Integral Yoga*, Pondicherry: Sri Aurobindo Ashram.

Chattopadhyay, Devi Prasad, 1986, *History of Science and Technology in Ancient India*, Calcutta: Firma K.L.M.

Chaudhary, Haridas, 1942, "The Supermind in Sri Aurobindo's Philosophy" in *Sri Aurobindo Mandir Annual*, Calcutta: Sri Aurobindo Pathamandir.

———, 1943, "Sri Aurobindo and Absolutism", *Sri Aurobindo Mandir Second Annual*, Calcutta: Sri Aurobindo Pathamandir.

———, 1972, *Sri Aurobindo: The Prophet of Life Divine*, Pondicherry: Sri Aurobindo Ashram.

Chaudhary, Haridas et al. (eds), 1960, *Integral Advaitism of Sri Aurobindo*, London: George Allen & Unwin.

Chaudhary Haridas, 1967, *Philosophy of Integralism — The Metaphysical Synthesis in Sri Aurobindo's Teaching*, Pondicherry: Aurobindo Ashram.

Clayton, A.C., 1913, *The Rig-Veda and Vedic Religion*, London and Madras: Christian Literature Society of India.

Coode Adams, W.B.C., 1927, *A Primer of Occult Physics*, 2010 edn, Whitefish, MO: Kessinger Publishing.

Das, A.C., 1958, *Sri Aurobindo and Some Modern Problems*, Calcutta: General Printer and Publisher.

Das, R., 1935, "Vedanta and the Common Sense", *Prabuddha Bhārata*, XL.

———, 1968, *Introduction to Śaṅkara*, Calcutta: Firm K.L.M.

Das, Rasvihary, G.R. Malkani and T.R.V. Murti, 1933, *Ajñāna*, Amalner: Indian Institute of Philosophy.

Das, Saroj Kumar, 1937, *A Study of the Vedānta*, Calcutta: University of Calcutta.

Dasgupta, Surendra Nath, 1922, *History of Indian Philosophy*, Cambridge:

Cambridge University Press (repr. 1997, Motilal Banarsidass, Delhi).

———, 1933, *Indian Idealism*, London: Cambridge University Press.

———, 1941, *Philosophical Essays*, Calcutta: University of Calcutta.

Date, V.H., 1954, *Vedanta Explained*, vol. II, Bombay: Bookseller's Publishing Co.

Datta, Bhagavad, 1968, *The Story of Creation as Seen by the Seers*, Delhi: Itihasa Prakashana Mandala.

———, 1972, "Extraordinary Scientific Knowledge in Vedic Works", in *Proceedings of the All-India Oriental Conference.*

Datta, D.M., 1950, *Chief Currents of Contemporary Philosophy*, Calcutta: Calcutta University Press.

Deussen, Paul, 1906, *Outline of the Vedanta System of Philosophy according to Shankara*, New York: Grafton Press.

———, 1912, *The System of Vedānta*, tr. Chairles Johnson, Chicago: The Open Court Publishing Company.

———, 1966, *The Philosophy of Upanishads*, New York: Dover.

Deutsch, Eliot, 1969, *Advaita Vedānta: A Philosophical Reconstruction*, Honolulu: East–West Center Press.

Devanandan, Paul David, 1950, *The Concept of Māyā*, London: University Press.

Devaraja, N.K., 1962, *An Introduction of Śaṅkara's Theory of Knowledge*, Delhi: Motilal Banarsidass.

Devaraja, N.K. and Hirematha, 1971, *A Source Book of Śaṅkara*, Varanasi: Centre for Advanced Study in Varanasi, Banaras Hindu University.

Dharmaraja, Dhvarindra, 1967, *Vedānta Paribhāṣā*, tr. Vidyanand Jijñāsu.

Dongre, N.G., 1994, *Physics in Ancient India*, New Delhi: Wiley Eastern.

Donnelly, Morwenna, 1958, *Founding the Life Divine: Integral Yoga of Sri Aurobindo*, Bombay: Jaico Publishing House.

Dravid, Raja Ram, 1972, *The Problem of Universe in Indian Philosophy*, Delhi: Motilal Banarsidass.

Dukas, Helen and Banesh Hoffmann (eds), 1976, *Albert Einstein: The Human Side*, New Jersey: Princeton University Press.

Einstein, Albert, 1949, *The World as I See*, New York: The Wisdom Library.

———, 1954, *Ideas and Opinion*, New York: Dover.

Farquhar, J.N., 1920, *The Crown of Hinduism*, London: Oxford University Press.

Feys, J., 1973, *The Philosophy of Evolution in Sri Aurobindo and Teilhard de Chardin*, Calcutta: Firma K.L.M.

Gakak, V.K., 1973, *Sri Aurobindo: Seer and Poet*, New Delhi: Abhinav Publication.

Gandhi, Kishore, 1973, *Contemporary Relevance of Sri Aurobindo*, Delhi: Viveka Publishing House.

Garg, R.K., 1978, *Upaniṣadic Challenge to Science*, Delhi: Sandeep Prakashan.

Geden, A.S. (tr.), 1908, *The Philosophy of the Upanishads*, Edinburgh: T. & T. Clark.

Giridharajee, Mahārāja, 1906, *Śuddhadvaitamārtaṇḍa*, Varanasi: Chaukhambha Sanskrit Series.

Gopinatha, Kaviraj, 1966, *Aspects of Indian Thought*, Burdwan: The University of Burdwan.

Gosvami, Acharya Lalita Krishna, 1963, *Sri Nimbārka Vedānta*, 1st edn, Allahabad: Sri Nimbārka Pīṭha.

Gough, A.E., 1903, *The Philosophy of Upaniṣads and Ancient Indian Metaphysics*, London: Kegan Paul, Trench Trübner & Co.

Grant, Allen, 1903, *The Evolution of the Idea of God*, London: Watt and Co.

Green, T.H., 1906, *Prolegomena to Ethics*, ed. A.C Bradley, Oxford: Clarendon Press.

Greenlees, D., 1953, *The Gospel of Advaita*, Adyar: The Theosophical Society Publishing House.

Grinnell, Frederick, 1992, *The Scientific Attitude*, New York and London: The Guilford Press.

Gupta, Nolini Kanta, 1946, *The Approach to Mysticism*, Pondicherry: Sri Aurobindo Ashram.

———, 1955, *The Yoga of Sri Aurobindo*, Madras: Sri Aurobindo Library.

Gupta, Sanjukta, 1966, *Studies in the Philosophy of Madhusudana Saraswati*, Calcutta: Sanskrit Pustak Bhandar.

Harnack, Adolph, 1902, *What Is christianity?*, New York : G.P. Putnam's Sons.

Hastings, James (ed.), 1910, *Encyclopaedia of Religion and Ethics*, vol. II, New York: Charles Scribner's Sons.

Hasurkar, S.S., 1958, *Vācaspati Miśra on Advaita Vedānta*, Darbhanga: Mithila Institute.

Heisenberg, Werner, 2000, *Physics and Philosophy: The Revolution in Modern Science*, London and New York: Penguin.

Hiriyanna, M., 1932, *Outlines of Indian Philosophy*, London: George Allen & Unwin.

———, 1952, *The Quest After Perfection*, Mysore: Kavyalaya Publishers.

———, 1955, *Essentials of Indian Philosophy*, London: George Allen & Unwin.

———, 1957, *Indian Philosophical Studies*, Mysore: Kavyalaya Publishers.

Horrwitz, Ernst P., 1937, *Veda and Vedanta*, Mayavati:Advaita Ashram.

Hume, R.E. (tr.), 1921, *The Thirteen Principal Upanishads*, (repr edn 1934), London: Oxford UniversityPress.

Huxley, Aldous, 1969, *The Perennial Philosophy*, London: Chatto & Windus.

Isherwood, C., 1952, *Vedānta for Modern Man*, London: George Allen & Unwin.

Iyer, M.K. Venkataraman, 1964, *Advaita Vedanta according to Sankara*, Bombay: Asia Publishing House.

Jacob, G.A., 1934, *Vedāntasāra*, 4th edn, Bombay: Pandurang Jawaji.

James, Jeans, 1948, *The Growth of Physical Science*, Cambridge: Cambridge University Press; New York: Macmillan.

———, 1981, *Physics & Philosophy*, New York: Dover Publications.

Joad, C.E.M., 1924, *An Introduction to Modern Philosophy*, London: Oxford University Press.

———, 1932, *Philosophical Aspects of Modern Science*, London: George Allen & Unwin.

Karmarkar, R.D., 1962, *Śrī Bhāṣya of Rāmānuja*, University of Puna Sanskrit Patrika.

Kirtikar, V.J., 1924, *Studies in Vedanta*, Bombay: D.B. Taraporevala Sons & Co.

Lal, Basant Kumar, 1973, *Contemporary Indian Philosophy*, Delhi: Motilal Banarsidass.

Langley, G.H., 1949, *Sri Aurobindo: Indian Poet, Philosopher and Mystic*, London: David Marlowe.

Lincoln, Barnett, 1949, *The Universe and Dr. Einstein*, London: Victor Gollancz Ltd.

Londhe, D.G., 1930, "The Advaita Philosophy of Śaṅkara and Its Later Development", *Review of Philosophy and Religion*, 1(1): 30-52.

Mādhvācārya, *Sarvadarshana Samgraha*, 1964, tr. Umashankar Rishi, Varanasi: Chaukhamba Vidya Bhavan.

Madhusūdana Saraswatī, 2014, *Śrīnyāyāmṛtādvaita Siddhi*, parts I and II, Varanasi: Chaukhamba Vidya Bhavan.

Mahadevan, T.M.P., 1937, "The Religio Philosophico Culture of India", in *Cultural Heritage of India*, vol. 1, ed. Suniti Kumar Chatterji et al., Calcutta: The Ramakrishna Mission Institute of Culture.

———, 1954, *Gaṇḍapāda: A Study in Early Advaita*, Madras: University of Madras.

———, 1957, *The Philosophy of Advaita*, Madras: Ganesh & Co.

Maitra, S.K., 1968, *The Meeting of East and West in Sri Aurobindo's Philosophy*, Pondicherry: Sri Aurobindo Ashram.

———, 1993, *An Introduction to the Philosophy of Sri Aurobindo*, Pondicherry: Sri Aurobindo Ashram.

Malkani, G.R., 1916, *Metaphysics of Advaita Vedānta*, Madras: G.S. Press.

———, 1966, *Philosophy of the Self: Or, a System of Idealism Based upon Advaita Vedānta*, New York: Johnson Reprint Corp.

Malkani, G.R., R. Das and T.R.V. Murti, 1933, *Ajñāna*, London: Luzac & Co.

Marfatia, Mrudula, 1967, *The Philosophy of Vallabhacharya*, Delhi: Munshiram Manoharlal.

———, As quoted in Max Muller, 1879, "Preface", *Sacred Book of East*, vol I, Oxford: The Clarendon Press.

Max Müller, F., 1879, "Preface", *The Upanishads*, Sacred Book of East, vol. I, Oxford: The Clarendon Press.

———, 1893, *Theosophy of Psychological Religion*, London: Longmans, Green and Co.

———, 1952, *Vedānta and Pūrva Mīmāṁsā*, Calcutta: Susil Gupta.

———, 1964a, *Six Systems of Indian Philosophy*, Varanasi: Chaukhamba

Sanskrit Series.

———, 1964b, *Six Lectures on Origin and Growth of Religion*, Varanasi: Indological Book House.

———, 1967, *Three Lectures on Vedānta Philosophy*, Varanasi: Chaukhamba Sanskrit Series.

Mill, J.S., 1874, *Three Essays on Religion*, New York: Henry Holt & Co.

Mishra, Adya Prasad, 1967, *The Development and Place of Bhakti in Śāṅkara Vedānta*, Allahabad: The University of Allahabad.

Mishra, K.N. (ed.), 1980, *Śuddhādvaita Brahmavāda: The Complete Works of M.T. Telivala*, Delhi: Anand Prakashan.

Misra, R.S., 1957, *The Integral Advaitism of Sri Aurobindo*, Benares: Banaras Hindu University (1998 edn, Delhi: Motilal Banarsidass).

———, 1971, *Studies in Philosophy and Religion*, Varanasi: Bharatiya Vidya Prakashan.

Miśra, Umesh, 1940, *Nimbārka School of Vedānta*, Allahabad: Tirabhukti Publication.

Miśra,Vācaspati, 1933, *Bhāmatī*, tr. S.N. Shastri and C.K. Raja, Adyar Theosophical Publishing House.

Mitra, Sisir Kumar, 1965, *An Inroduction in the Philosophy of Sri Aurobindo*, Pondicherry: Sri Aurobindo Ashram.

———, 1968, *The Meeting of the East and West in Aurobindo Philosophy*, Pondicherry: Sri Aurobindo Ashram.

———, 1972, *Sri Aurobindo: The Quest of Divine Consciousness*, New Delhi: Indian Book Company.

Modi, P.M, 1985, *Siddhantabindu of Madhusudana Sarasvati*, translated to English, Allahabad: Vohra Publishers and Distributors.

Moore, Charles A. (ed.), 1967, *The Indian Mind: Essentials of Indian Philosophy and Culture*, Honolulu: University of Hawaii Press.

Mudgala, S.G., 1975, *Advaita of Śaṅkara: A Reappraisal*, Delhi: Motilal Banarsidass.

Muirhead, John Henry, 1892, *The Elements of Ethics — An Introduction to Moral Philosophy*, New York, Charles Scribner's & Sons.

Mukerji, A.C., 1943, *The Nature of Self*, Allahabad: Indian Press.

Mukherjee, Satkari, 1975, "Buddhism in Indian Life and Thought", in *Cultural Heritage of India*, vol. 1, ed. Sarvepalli Radhakrishnan,

Calcutta: The Ramakrishna Mission Institute of Culture.

Mukherji–Sastri, Nalini Mohan, 1942, *A Study of Śaṅkara*, Calcutta: University of Calcutta.

Murty, Satchidananda, 1974, *Revelation and Reason in Advaita Vedānta*, Delhi: Motilal Banarsidass.

———, 2007, *Hinduism and Its Development*, New Delhi: D.K. Printworld.

Narain, K., 1962, *An Outline of Madhva Philosophy*, Allahabad: Udayana.

———, 1964, *A Critique of Madhva Refutation of the Śaṅkara School of Vedānta*, Allahabad: Udayana.

Naravane, V.S., 1964, *Modern Indian Thought: A Philosophical Survey*, Bombay: Asia Publishing House.

Naulakha, R.S., 1964, *Śaṅkara's Brahmavāda*, Kanpur: Kitab Ghar.

Niels, Bohr, 1958, *Atomic Physics and Human Knowledge*, New York: Wiley.

Nimbārka, *Vedānta Pārijāta Saurabha*.

———, *Dasaślokī*.

Nirodbaran, 1966, *Talks with Sri Aurobindo*, Calcutta: Pathamandir.

———, 1972, *Twelve Years with Sri Aurobindo*, Pondicherry: Sri Aurobindo Ashram.

Olsson, Eva, 1958, *The Philosophy of Sri Aurobindo*, Mysore: Christian Library.

Oppenheimer, J.R., 1954, *Science and the Common Understanding*, New York: Simon and Schuster.

Organ, Troy Wilson, 1962, "The Status of Self in Aurobindo's Metaphysics and Some Questions", *Philosophy East and West*, 12(2): 135-51.

Otto, Rundolf, 1932, *Mysticism: East and West – A Comparative Analysis of the Nature of Mysticism*, London: Macmillan.

Panda, N.C., 1991, *Māyā in Physics*, Delhi: Motilal Banarsidass.

Pandey, R.C., 1966, *The Panorama of Indian Philosophy*, Delhi: Motilal Banarsidass.

Pandey, R.K., 1976-77 "Yoga: The Mechanics of Consciousness," *Prajñā*, vol. 21.

Pandey, Sangamlal, 1974, *Pre-Śaṅkara Advaita Philosophy*, Allahabad: Darshan Peeth.

Pandit, M.P., 1959, *The Teaching of Sri Aurobindo*, Madras: Sri Aurobindo

Study Circle.

———, 1969, *Sri Aurobindo: Studies in the Light of His Thought*, Pondicherry: Sri Aurobindo Ashram.

Parekh, M.C., 1943, *Śrī Vallabhācārya: Life, Teachings, and Movements*, Rajkot: Sri Bhagavata Dharma Mission.

Peacock, Arthur, 1993, *Theology for Scientific Age: Beings and Becoming – Natural, Divine, and Human*, Minneapolis, MN: Fortress Press.

Pearson, N., 1952, *Sri Aurobindo and the Soul Quest of Man*, London: George Allen & Unwin.

Plott, John C., 1974, *The Philosophy of Devotion*, Delhi: Motilal Banarsidass.

Prabhavananda, Swami, 1963, *Spiritual Heritage of India*, New York: Doubleday & Company.

Pringle-Pattison, A.S., 1920, *The Idea of God*, New York: Oxford University Press.

Purani, A.B., 1955, *Sri Aurobindo Address on His Life and Teachings*, Pondicherry: Sri Aurobindo Ashram.

———, 1961, *Evening Talks with Sri Aurobindo* (Recorded), Pondicherry: Sri Aurobindo Ashram.

———, 1966, *Sri Aurobindo's Life Divine: Lectures Delivered in the USA*, Pondicherry: Sri Aurobindo Ashram.

Radhakrishnan, S., 1966, *Indian Philosophy*, vols I-II, London: George Allen & Unwin.

———, 1940, *Eastern Religions and Western Thought*, London: Oxford University.

———, 1948, *The Bhagavadgītā*, London: George Allen & Unwin.

———, 1952, *History of Philosophy: Eastern and Western*, vol. I, London: George Allen & Unwin.

———, 1960, *The Brahmasūtra: The Philosophy of Spiritual Life*, London: George Allen & Unwin.

———, 1964, *Idealistic View of Life*, London: Unwin Book.

———, 1965, *Hindu View of Life*, London: Unwin Book.

Radhakrishnan, S. and J.H. Muirhead, 1958, *Contemporary Indian Philosophy*, London: George Allen & Unwin.

Radhakrishnan, S. and Charles A. Moore (eds), 1957, *Source Book of Indian Philosophy*, Princeton, NJ: Princeton University Press.

Radhakrishnan, S. et al. (eds), 1960, *The Concept of Man*, London: George Allen & Unwin.

Raja, C. Kunhan, 1960, *Some Fundamental Problems in Indian Philosophy*, Delhi: Motilal Banarsidass.

Raju, P.T., 1953, *Idealistic Thought of India*, London: George Allen & Unwin.

Ramachandran, T.P., 1969, *The Concept of Vyāvahārika in Advaita Vedānta*, Madras: Centre for Advanced Study in Philosophy.

Ranade, R.D. and S.K. Belvalkar, 1983, *History of Indian Philosophy*, vol. 2, Pune: Aryabhusan Press.

Ranade, R.D., 1968, *Constructive Survey of Upaniṣadic Philosophy*, Bombay: Bharatiya Vidya Bhavan.

Rao, P. Nagaraja, 1943, *The Schools of Vedānta*, Bombay: Bharatiya Vidya Bhavan.

Ray, Binoy Gopal, 1947, *Contemporary Indian Philosophers*, Allahabad: Kitabistan.

Ray Chaudhuri, Anilkumar, 1950, *The Doctrine of Māyā*, Calcutta: Dasgupta & Co.

———, 1955, *Self and Falsity of Advaita Vedānta*, Calcutta: Progressive Publishers.

Reddy, V. Madhusudan, 1966, *Sri Aurobindo's Philosophy of Evolution*, Hyderabad: Institute of Human Study.

Reichenberg, H., 1944, *Philosophical Foundation of Quantum Physics*, Berkeley and Los Angeles: University of California Press.

———, 1951, *Rise of Scientific Philosophy*, Berkeley, Los Angeles and London: University of California Press.

Rhys Davids, 1967, "Mokṣa" in *Encyclopedia of Religion and Ethics*, vol. III, ed. James Hastings, London: Collier Macmillan.

Roy, Alur Venkat, 1954, *A Handbook of Sri Madhavacharya: Poorna Brahman Philosophy*, Dharwar: Navajeevan Grantha Bhandar.

Roy, Anil Baran, 1940, *Sri Aurobindo and the New Age*, Madras: Jupiter Press.

Roy, M.N., 1947, *Science and Philosophy*, Calcutta: Renaissance Publishers.

Roy, S.S., 1965, *The Heritage of Śaṅkara*, Allahabad: Udayana Publications.

Ruth, Reyna, 1962, *The Concept of Māyā: From the Vedas to the 20th Century*, Bombay: Asia Publishing House.

Sadanand, 1967, *Vedāntasāra*, tr. Pt. Shree Ram Govind Shukla, Varanasi: Bharatiya Vidya Prakashan.

Saksena, S.K., 1971, *Nature of Consciousness in Hindu Philosophy*, Delhi: Motilal Banarsidass.

Śaṅkara, 1967, *Śāṅkarabhāṣya on Brahmasūtra*, tr. Hanumāndasji Ṣaṭśāstri, Varanasi: Chaukhamba Vidya Bhavan.

———, *Śāṅkarabhāṣya on Bhagavadgītā*, Gorakhpur: Gita Press.

———, *Śāṅkarabhāṣya on Aitareya, Chāndogya*, Gorakhpur: Gita Press.

———, *Śāṅkarabhāṣya on Bṛhadāraṇyaka*, Gorakhpur: Gita Press.

———, *Śāṅkarabhāṣya on Kaṭha, Kena, Māṇḍūkya*, Gorakhpur: Gita Press.

———, *Śāṅkarabhāṣya on Muṇḍaka, Praśna, Śvetāśvatara*, Gorakhpur: Gita Press.

———, *Śāṅkarabhāṣya on Taittirīya, Gauḍapāda Kārikā*, Gorakhpur: Gita Press.

Śaṅkara, 1910, *Collected Works of Śaṅkara*, vol. XIV, Srirangam: Vanivilas Press.

———, 1929, *Dasaślokī*, tr. P.M. Modi, Baroda: Arya Sudharaka Press.

———, 2009, *Upadeśa Sāhasrī*, tr. Swami Jagadānanda, Madras: Sri Ramakrishna Math.

———, *Vivekacūḍāmaṇi*, Gorakhpur: Gita Press.

Sarasvatī, Madhusūdana, 1933, *Siddhānta Bindu*, Baroda: Oriental Institute.

Sarvajñātmamuni, 1967, *Saṅkṣepaśārīraka*, Varanasi: Chaukhamba Vidya Bhavan.

Sastri, Kokileshwar, 1926, *An Introduction to Advaita Philosophy*, Calcutta: Calcutta University Press.

———, 1931, *A Realistic Interpretation of Śāṅkara Vedānta*, Calcutta: University of Calcutta.

———, 1937, *Māyā in Śaṅkara's Vedānta*, Poona: Oriental Book Agency.

Sastri, N., 1942, *Introduction of Vedānta Philosophy*, Calcutta: University of Calcutta.

Sastri, Suryanarayan, 1961, *Collected Papers of S.S. Sūryanārāyaṇa Śāstrī*, Madras: University of Madras.

Sastri, Suryanarayan, 1941, *Life and Teaching of Śaṅkarācārya*, Madras: G.A. Natesan and Co.

Sastry, T.V. Kapali, 1966, *Sri Aurobindo: Lights on the Teaching*, Amudasuradi Press.

Satprem, 1968, *Sri Aurobindo, or the Advent of Consciousness*, tr. Tehmi, Pondicherry: Sri Aurobindo Ashram.

Schrader, Otto, 1916, *Introduction to the Pāñcarātra and the Ahirbudhnya Saṁhitā*, Madras: Adyar Library.

Schrödinger, 1964, *My View of the World*, Cambridge University Press.

Seal, B.N., 1915, *Positive Sciences of the Ancient Hindus*, London: Longmans, Green and Co.

Sengupta, Anima, 1967, *A Critical Study of the Phiolosophy of Rāmānuja*, Varanasi: Chowkhamba Sanskrit Series.

Sengupta, B.K., 1953-54, "Devotionalism in Advaita Vedānta", *Vedānta Kesarī*, vol. xl.

Sethna, K.D., 1968, *The Vision and Work of Sri Aurobindo*, Pondicherry: Sri Aurobindo Ashram.

———, 1973, *Teilhard de Chardin and Sri Aurobindo*, Varanasi: Bharatiya Vidya Prakashan.

Sharma, B.N.K., 1960/61, *A History of Dvaita School of Vedānta and Its Literature*, vols I-II, Bombay: Book Seller's Publishing Co.

———, 1962, *Philosophy of Śrī Madhvācārya*, Mumbai: Bhartiya Vidya Bhavan.

———, 1971, *The Brahmasūtra and Their Principal Commentaries: A Critical Exposition*, Bombay: Bharatiya Vidya Bhavan.

Sharma, C.D., 1952, *Indian Philosophy*, Varanasi: Nandkishore and Brothers.

———, 1960, *A Critical Survey of Indian Philosophy*, Delhi: Motilal Banarsidass.

Sharma, Ram Nath, 1960, *The Philosophy of Aurobindo*, Lucknow: Bharatiya Prakashan Mandir.

Shastri, A.B., 1936, *Studies in Post-Śaṅkara Dialectics*, Calcutta: University of Calcutta.

Shastri, Prabhu Dutt, 1911, *The Doctrine of Māyā in the Philosophy of Vedānta*, London: Luzac & Co.

Singh, R.P., 1949, *The Vedānta of Śaṅkara: A Metaphysics of Value*, Jaipur: Bharat Publishing House.

Sinha, J.N., 1952, *A History of Indian Philosophy*, Calcutta: Sinha Publishing House.

———, 1963, *Outlines of Indian Philosophy*, Calcutta: Sinha Publishing House.

———, 1971, *Problems of Post-Śaṅkara Advaita Vedānta*, Calcutta: Sinha Publishing House.

———, 1972, *The Philosophy of Rāmānuja*, Calcutta: Sinha Publishing House.

———, 1973, *The Philosophy of Nimbārka*, Calcutta: Sinha Publishing House.

Sircar, Mahendranath, 1934, *Hindu Mysticism According to Upaniṣad*, London: Kegan Paul.

———, 1975, *The System of Vedāntic Thought and Culture*, New Delhi: Oriental Book Reprint Corporation.

Sivaraman, Krishna (ed.), 1989, *Hindu Spirituality: Veda through Vedānta*, Delhi: Motilal Banarsidass.

Srinivasachari, P.N., 1946, *The Philosophy of Viśiṣṭādvaita*, Adyar: The Adyar Library.

Srivastava, R.S., 1966, *Contemporary Indian Philosophy*, Delhi: Munshiram Manoharlal.

———, 1968, *Sri Aurobindo and the Theories of Evolution*, Varanasi: Chaukhambha Sanskrit Series Office.

Srivastava, S.N.L., 1937, "What Vedantism Is?", *Prabuddha Bharata*, vol. XLII.

———, 1968, *Śaṅkara and Bradley*, Delhi: Motilal Banarsidass.

Sureśvarācārya, 1970, *Naiṣkarmya Siddhiḥ*, Eng. tr. K.V.S. Aiyar, Shreerangam: Sree Vani Vailas Mudranalaya.

Tagore, Rabindranath, 1949, *Salutation to Sri Aurobindo*, Pondicherry: Sri Aurobindo Ashram.

Taylor, A.E., 1961, *Elements of Metaphysics*, London: Methuen.

Thachil , Jose, 1993, *The Upaniṣads: A Socio-Religious Appraisal*, New Delhi: English Intercultural Publications.

Thibaut, George, 1957, *Vedānta Sūtra*, The Sacred Book of the East Series, Delhi: Motilal Banarsidass.

Upadhyaya, Veermani Prasad, 1959, Lights of Vedānta, Varanasi: Chowkhamba Sanskrit Series Office.

Vallabhācārya, 1897, *Aṇubhāṣya*, ed. Pandit Hemachandra Vidyāratna, Calcutta.

Vidyaranya, Swami, 2008, *Panchadaśi*, tr. Swami Swahananda, Madras: Sri Ramakrishna Math.

Vidyarthi, P.B., 1978a, *Knowledge of Self and God in Rāmānuja*, Calcutta: Oriental Publishers & Distributors.

———, 1978b, *Divine Personality and Human Life in Rāmānuja*, Calcutta: Oriental Publishers & Distributors.

Vireswarananda, Swami, 1948, *Brahmasūtra*, Calcutta: Advaita Ashram.

Vivekananda, Swami, 1947, *Complete Works of Swami Vivekananda*, vol. 7, Calcutta: Advaita Ashram.

Warder, A.K., 1971, *Outlines of Indian Philosophy*, Delhi: Motilal Banarsidass.

Warrier, A.G. Krishna, 1961, *The Concept of Mukti in Advaita Vedānta*, Madras: University of Madras.

Weber, Renée, 1986, *Dialogues with Scientists and Sages: The Search for Unity*, London: Routledge & Kegan Paul.

Whitehead, A.N., 1925, *Science and the Modern World*, New York: Macmillan.

Wigner, G.P., 1970, *Symmetries and Reflections: Scientific Essays*, Cambridge, MA: MIT Press.

Wilber, Ken, 1996, *A Transpersonal View of Human Development*, 2nd edn, Madras, Quest Books and Theosophical Publishing House.

——— (ed.), 2001, *Quantum Questions: Mystical Writings of the World's Great Physicists*, Boulder, CO: Shambhala.

Zimmer, Heinrich, 1953, *Philosophies of India* (ed. Joseph Campbell), London: Routledge and Kegan Paul.

Zohar, Danah, 1991, *The Quantum Self: Human Nature and Consciousness Defined by the New Physics*, New York: William Morrow Paperback.

Zukav, Gary, 1979, *The Dancing Wu Li Masters: An Overview of the New Physics*, New York: Bantam Books.

Index

ābhāsa 74
Ābhāsavāda 52
abheda 162, 170, 172, 176
abhedopāsanā 175
abhyāsa 141
abhyudaya 104
abhyudayārthāni 111
Absolute (*Brahman*) 201-02
  Being 25, 179
  Ego 53
  of Spinoza 189
  Space 59
  Spirit 246
Absolutism 4
Acintya-bhedābhedavāda 5
acintya-rūpam 148
acit 122, 126, 165, 168, 171
acosmism 57, 68
adhama bhakta 160
ādhāra-ādheya 132
ādhārādheya bhāva 125
adharma 114
ādheyatva 131
ādhibhautika 170, 184
ādhidaivika 170, 182, 184, 191
adhikārī-bheda 159
adhyāropa 75
adhyāsa 75-76, 85, 87-88, 115
ādhyātmika 170, 184
adṛṣṭa 152
Advaita 2-3, 16, 25, 27-28, 71, 91, 195, 218-19, 292, 301
  focus of 1
  philosophy 28
Advaita Vedānta vii, 2, 7-8, 26, 30, 35-37, 70, 76-77, 96, 111, 118, 136, 148, 151, 160, 162, 227-28, 260, 285, 287, 291, 293, 300
  ātman 288
Advaitasiddhi 90
Advaitic
  sādhaka 102
  Vedānta 6
Advaitism 103, 217
āgāmī karmas 113
Agni 11-12, 20
agrahaṇātmikā 82
ahaitukī bhakti 193
ahaṁ-pratyaya-viṣaya 58
ahiṁsā 107, 141
āhlādinī 6
aiśvarya 163, 187
aiśvarya-pradhāna bhakti 176
Ajātivāda 74
ajña 188
ajñāna 75, 81, 83, 87, 89, 114, 190
  is *bhāvarūpa* 78

locus of 80
ajñānamaya avidyā 106
akartā 186
akrodha 107
akṣara 182-85, 191, 198
Akṣara Puruṣa 20
Alātaśānti Prakaraṇa 74
alaukika 194
sāmarthya 195
Alexander, Samuel 246
all-comprehensive consciousness 230
alphabets of mathematics 296
amṛta 193
aṁśa 155, 175, 181, 198
as *śakti* 186
aṁśatva 155
aṁśāvatāra 166
aṁśī 175, 181, 198
ānanda 140, 179-80, 187, 190, 195, 202, 211, 218, 226
is essential to *Brahman* 43
ānandamaya 69
ātman 43
Brahman 44
is the Supreme Bliss 69
maya of 44
ānandarūpa 181
ānandasvarūpa Brahman 97
anantaṁ brahma 32
anāropitam 145
anavasāda 141
anavasthā doṣa 50
ancillary to revelation 51
andhaṁ tamaḥ 188
Anekajīvavāda 70
an exalted ideal of superman 116
aṅguṣṭha mātra 181
Aniruddha 129-30, 150, 166
anirvacanīya 75
annamaya 69
antagonism between *karma* and *jñāna* 105
antaḥkaraṇa 59, 63, 70
vṛtti 60
antaryāmī 122, 129, 155, 166, 181-84, 189-90
is the incarnation of Viṣṇu 184
Aṇu-bhāṣya 199
anubhava 142
aṇuddharṣa 141
anurāga 195
aṇutva 131
aparā
bhakti 176
prakṛti 273
Apara-Brahman 32, 46, 49, 123
aparokṣa
jñāna 161
jñānī 161
apavarga 104
of Nyāya 98
aprākṛta 171
attributes 126
aprāptamiva prāpnoti 98
apṛthak siddhi 3, 127
Āpta-kāma Brahman 181
apūrṇa 180
apūrva, Mīmāṁsā's theory of 50
ārabdha karma 174
Āraṇyaka
period 18
theology 17

Āraṇyakas 1, 17
arcā 129
arcanā 142, 194
Aristotle 184, 293
ārjava 141, 177
Arjuna 101
arthādhyāsa 86
Āruṇi 21, 73
Aryaman 12
asakṛdāvṛttiḥ 142
asat 204
āśrama 198
asteya 107
Atharvaveda 71
ātmajñāna 108, 110
ātman 3, 54, 59, 61, 73, 84, 86, 88, 109, 114, 151, 156, 161, 205, 209, 240, 289
  and
    Brahman identity of 64
    jīva relation between 58
  is
    Brahman 21, 235
    homogeneous consciousness 55
    Universal Self 58
    verily Saccidānanda 7
  oneness of 96
  too is *Brahman* vii
ātmanivedana 194
ātman–māyā 209-10
ātmānanda 114
ātmanikṣepa 143
ātma-pariṇāma 192
ātma-samarpaṇa 143
ātma-savarūpa-lābha 172
ātma-sṛṣṭi 181, 184
ātmatva 131
Atomic theory 237
ātyantika-duḥkha-nivṛtti 160-61
Aupaniṣadic Mīmāṁsā 25
Aurobindo, Sri viii-ix, 2, 6-7, 18-19, 127, 201-15, 217-18, 220-24, 226, 229, 231, 233-47, 249-56, 258-68, 270-92, 297
Avacchedavāda 52
āvaraṇa śakti 78
āvaraṇātmakatvād avidyā 82
avatāra 128-29
avataraṇam 127
avatāras 150, 166
āveśāvatāra 184
avibhaktāvasthā 81
avidyā 3, 46, 61, 63, 70, 75-76, 78-80, 84, 88, 127, 135-36, 138, 151-52, 157, 168, 171-72, 184-85, 188, 191, 232, 285, 290
avidyā-kalpita 83, 289
avidyā-nimitta 83
avidyā-pratyupasthāpita 83, 289
avidyāropita 83
avidyātmaka 83
avikṛta pariṇāmavāda 4-5, 190
āvirbhāva 183, 191
avyakta 75
ayam ātmā brahma 154

Baconian 296
Bādarāyaṇa 2, 26, 31, 180, 186
baddha 152, 170, 188
  jīva 135, 168
bādhārahita 90
bādhva 34
bala 129, 163
Ballantyne, J.R. 68

Banerjee, Aparna 218
Banerjee, Siddheswar 277, 279
Barnett, Samuel 300
Barth, Auguste 127
Bāṣkali 34
Becoming, reality of 203
Bell's theorem 297
Belvalker, S.K. 16
Bergson, Henri 34, 202, 215, 227, 268-69
bhāga-tyāga-lakṣaṇā 65
bhagavadānugraha 177
bhagavad-bhāvāpatti 169, 178
Bhagavadgītā 48
bhagavad-rāga 144
Bhāgavata 180, 197
bhagvatkṛpā 176
bhakta 258
  and *bhagavān* duality of 130
bhakti 110, 138, 140, 142, 144-45, 154, 157-59, 161, 173, 176, 192-93, 195
  is the supreme *sādhanā* 176
  religion, emotionalism of 176
Bhaktimārtaṇḍa 192
bhaktirūpāpanna jñāna 139
Bhakti-Vedānta viii-ix, 2, 282, 289, 291-92
Bhakti-Vedāntists 284, 288-90
bhakti-yoga 144
Bhandarkar, R.G. 187
bhāra samarpaṇa 143
Bhāskara 167
Bhatt, S.R. 123
Bhattacharya, D.C. 27
Bhattacharyya, Haridas 86
Bhattacharyya K.C. 55, 110
Bhāṭṭa Mīmāṁsā 40
bhāva 195
bhāviśreyaska 169
bheda 87, 162, 172, 176, 183
bhedābheda 130, 146, 154, 167
Bhedābhedavāda 4, 162
bheda-sahiṣṇu abheda 188
bhoga 196
bhoktā 153, 186
bhoktṛ 181
bhoktṛtva 55
bhrama 75
bhrānti 75
bhūmā 166
bhūṣaṇam 181
bhūti 129
bījaśakti 75
bimbatva dharma 62
blind voluntarism 139
Bliss of *Brahman* 43, 45
bodhisattva 271
Bohm, David 297, 300
Bosanquet, Bernard 126, 216
Bose, Roma 173
Bradley, F.H. 34, 126, 216-17, 236
Brahmā 24, 100, 183
brahma-caitanya 79
brahmaivāham 63
brahma-jñāna 106, 109, 113, 175
brahmakārya 284
Brahman viii, 1-5, 7, 10-12, 19-24, 28-33, 35-36, 39-42, 44-45, 48, 50-52, 61, 63-65, 67-68, 71, 75, 77, 80-81, 84-85, 87, 89-97, 99-100, 103-05, 108-09, 111, 113-15, 117-

25, 127, 133-37, 146-49, 154-56, 162-64, 167-72, 174-75, 177-79, 182, 184, 187-92, 203, 206, 212-13, 219-20, 230, 235, 237-38, 242, 260, 271, 274, 282-85, 287-89
- and *ātman* spiritual identity of 19
- and the universe duality between 19
- Bliss of 43, 45
- characteristic of 43
- concept of 52
- definition of 34, 36
- *dharmas* of 186
- essence of 192
- Existence is 36
- impersonal aspect of 126
- in *vyācikīrṣitāvastha* 76
- manifestation of 11, 179
- of logic 6
- realization 178
- reflected in
  - *avidyā* is 84
  - *māyā* is *Īśvara* 84

Brahman as
- an abyss of negative infinitude 52
- Bliss 42, 45, 283
- *cit* 39
- Consciousness 39
- *jāyamānaprakṛtitvena nirdiśya* 76
- *nirguṇa* 70
- *saccidānanda* 33
- Śaṅkara 153
- *satkāryābhimukha* 76
- *satya* 37

Brahman is
- all-pervading Truth 204
- both *saguṇa* and *nirguṇa* 180
- Kṛṣṇa 164
- *kūṭastha nitya* 36
- light 40
- necessarily *saguṇa* 147
- *nirguṇa* 35
- pure existence (*sat*) 39
- unexcellable bliss 42
- *viśeṣya* 186

Brāhmaṇas 1, 17-18
Brahmanhood 185
Brāhmanism 117
brahmānubhāva 34, 109
Brahma-Pariṇāmavāda 156
Brahmasiddhi 107
Brahmasūtra 26, 31, 43-44, 49, 111, 160
Brahmasūtra-Bhāṣya 40, 47
brahma-svarūpa-lābha 172
brahmātmaka 189
brahmatva 185-86
- of *Brahman* remains as it is 181

Brahmavāda 118, 182, 184
brahmavidyā 106
Bṛhadāraṇyaka Upaniṣad 43, 49, 59, 72-73, 106, 122, 157, 212, 298
Bṛhaspati 12
bṛhat 224
Browning, Robert 77
bubhukṣu 169
Buddha 113
buddhipratyaya sākṣin 61
Buddhists 202

Caird, E. 68
caitanya 185
caitanyānandaghana 55
cakra 165
Capra, F. 296, 298-99
Carlyle, Thomas 108
Cartesian dualists 293

Cārvāka 108
  philosophy 153
caturvyūha 150
cause–effect relationship 283
cetanatva 131
Chand, Rishabh 271
Chāndogya Upaniṣad 37-38, 73, 116, 126, 141, 172, 193, 204, 212
Chatterjee, T.D. 236
Chaudhary, H. 214, 222, 226, 229, 233, 236, 249
Christian ethical ideal 67
cidācidviśiṣṭa Brahman 3
  as *upādāna* 189
cidācidviśiṣṭa-śarīra 181
cinmātra-jyotiḥ 33
cit 122, 126, 165, 168, 179, 190, 202, 207, 226
  is the locus of *ajñāna* 80
cit-śakti 206, 273, 283, 285
citśaktisvarūpamātra 60
Citsukhācārya viii, 120
Citsukhī 115
citta 161
cittaśuddhi 107
cold intellectualism 139
completest consciousness 53
concept of
  Absolute 249
  avatāra 127-28
  bhakti rūpa jñāna 6
  Brahman 52
  creative-force 220
  evolution 243
  indeterminate Absolute 282
  neti 298
  salvation 171
  soul of Upaniṣad 54
  supermind 220
  Ultimate Reality 145
  personal gods and goddesses 16
conception of
  evolution 252
  God 4
  jīvanmukti 95
  māyā as the causal willpower 75
  mukti 115
  quantitative *Brahman* 121
Conscious Being 276
conscious-force 205, 210, 212-13, 222-25, 251, 265, 274, 290
conscious-self 231-32
conscious-soul 230
consciousness
  and Bliss 201
  dawn of 71
consciousness-force 228, 260, 275
cosmic
  avidyā is *māyā* or *prakṛti* 80
  consciousness 225
  differentiation 288
  evolution 249, 284, 289
  individual 277
  moral God 215
  religious feeling 301
  sympathy 277
Cosmic Self 59
Cosmic Soul 13
creative idea 224
crest of joy or ecstasy 215
crown of moral perfection 47
cyclic interpretation of history 292

dama 100-101

dāna 141
darśana 196
darśana-samānākāratā 142
Darwin, Charles 294
Daśaślokī 34
Das, R. 79, 90, 95-96
Das, Saroj Kumar 14, 16, 104
Dasgupta, S.N. 50, 71, 77, 103, 132
dāsya-bhāva 194
Date, V.H. 99
Dattātreya 183
dayā 141, 163
dead clockwise machine 294
deceitful demons 145
dehātma-buddhi 99
Dehātmavāda 153
Demiurge of Plato 228
Descartes, René 54-55, 102, 293
Deussen, Paul 30, 35, 45, 49, 51, 57, 85, 102, 117
Deutsch, Eliot 32, 35, 38, 47, 58, 64, 99
Devadatta 64, 134
Devakī 193
Devanandan, Paul David 75
Devaraja, N.K. 56, 77, 93
dhairya 107
dharma 99, 114, 128, 181
  of *jīva* 167
  rājya 269
dharmabhedavāda 151
dharma-bhūta-jñāna 132
dharma–dharmī bhāva 167
dharma-karma-mārga 198
dharmas of *Brahman* 186
dharmī 181
dharmin 146
dharmisvarūpa 151
dhruvā smṛti 140, 175
dhyāna 140, 142, 161
die-hard realism 151
difference between
  ātman and *sākṣin* 61
  jīva and *ātman* 58
  jñāna and *karma* 106
  tat and *tvam* 66
  vijñānātmā and *paramātma* 66
distinction between *ātman* and *sākṣin* 61
Divine
  Consciousness 231, 242
  dictates 189
  evolution 245
  Light 217
  līla 199
  Majesty 158
  Mother of the universe 129
  Principles 245
  Reality 206
  Śakti 210
  Will 143, 150, 189
  wish 189
divinize the human 26
doctrine of
  Dvaitādvaitavāda 162
  karma 152, 189
  māyā 25, 70-71
  prapatti 143
  universal immanence of an intelligent monism 15
Dṛgdṛśyaviveka 92, 298
duḥkha-rūpa 186
durajña 188
Dvaita viii, 26

Dvaitādvaita viii, 26, 121
Dvaita Vedānta 4, 121, 145, 148, 162
dveṣa 177
Dyaus 10
dynamic
- philosophy 6
- truth vision 26

Eastern
- mysticism 298
- thought 298

Eckhart, Meister 67, 97
Eddington, Arthur Stanley 57, 287, 289
eight *rasas* 196
Einstein, Albert ix, 287, 293, 295-96
Ekajīvavāda 70
Ekātmavāda 70
Eleatic Being 53
enlarged consciousness 288
essence of
- *Brahman* 192
- self 55

essential nature of *māyā* 82
eternal
- coexistence of God and the world 22
- exile 296

Eternal Absolute 67
Existence triune principle of 201
expansiveness of the dynamic consciousness 135
external exile 297

Farquhar, J.N. 117
fetters of *karma* 165, 168-69, 177
Feys, J. 225, 239, 247-49, 273
Fichte, J.H. 53
Fitzgerald, James 68
force-soul 230
four
- forms of *vyūhas* 166
- stages of *jīva* 168
- types of *mukti* 159

Freud, Sigmund 294
fruit of
- *jñāna* 173
- *karma* 173

full *svarūpa* 166
fundamental consciousness of unity 273

gadā 165
Galileo 296
Gandharva 12
gandharvanagara 90
Gaṅgā 194
Garg, R.K. 21
Gauḍapāda 10, 25, 27, 73-75
Geden, A.S. 22
ghaṭākāśa 59
Gītā 28, 73-74, 101, 107-08, 111, 115, 130, 138, 141, 175, 180, 186, 193, 197, 231, 269, 280
Gītā-bhāṣya 143
gnostic
- being 271, 273-77, 279-80, 290
- consciousness 275, 279
- personality 279
- principle 253
- race 275
- supernature 280

God
  aspect of the Absolute 223
  as *saviśeṣa* 147
  great magician 74
  kingdom of 267
  realization 157
God in
  jīva, presence of 154
  Platonic sense 68
God is
  Absolute 125
  a personal 145
  God 165
  niyāmaka 132
  Lord of *māyā* 62
  Pure and Perfect 165
  upakāraka 62
Godless ritualism of Pūrva-Mīmāṁsa 145
God of
  devotion 13
  religion 6, 124
  Saccidānanda 228
God-conscious 141
God's creative energy personification of 4
Goddess Durgā 112
God-ecstasy 259
God-intoxicated 140, 200
golden web of Vedānta 27
Gopāla 165
Gopeśvara 192
gopīs 194, 196, 199
Gosvami, Giridhara 179
Gough, A.E. 9, 23, 73
Govindānanda 87, 101
Greek philosophy 293
Green, T.H. 37
guṇas 162, 181
guṇāvatāra 166
Gupta, N.K. 270

Hamlet 117
hari 200
Harnack, Adolph 269
Hartmann, Nicolai 267-68
Hastings, James 80, 97
Hegel 36, 53, 184, 187, 244
Hegelian
  mode of expression 53, 133
  position 37
Heisenberg, Werner 298-99
henotheistic polytheism 17
Heraclitus 202
higher
  consciousness 260
  principles of consciousness 260
Higher Mind 251, 260-64
Highest Glory 129
Hillebrandt, Alfred 30, 35
Hiraṇyagarbha 12, 69
Hiriyanna, M. 33, 60, 99, 110
Hume, Robert Ernest 15

idealistic pantheism 22
identity-in-difference 232
ilā 182
Illumined Mind 251, 260-64
illusory
  nature of the world 74
  product of ignorance 237
immortalize the mortal 26
Immutable Absolute 190
Indian

pantheism 22
philosophy, keynote of 293
indivisable mass of bliss 164
Indra 10, 71-72
indra-jāla 90
Indra–Pūṣan 12
Indra–Soma 12
Indra–Vāyu 12
Indra–Viṣnu 12
Infinite Absolute 220
infra-ethical 216
instinct-bound passion 194
integral
Advaitism ix, 2, 218-20, 260, 284, 287, 291
consciousness 285
monism 248
transformation 256
yoga 260, 291
Integral Advaita viii
internal and external life, harmony of 271
intuition fourfold, potencies of 264
intuitive
realization 295
Mind 251, 260, 262
Īśopaniṣad 19, 73, 107
Iṣṭasiddhikāra 80
Īśvara 46-50, 52, 61-63, 76, 80, 82, 84, 132, 148, 205, 209
and *jīva* are only appearances (*vivarta*) of *Brahman* 52
is *Brahman* 49
of Vedānta 228
Īśvara-prasāda 161
Īśvara–Śakti 209-10
Iyer, M.K. Venkataraman 47, 65, 115

Jacob, G.A. 83
jaḍa 181, 186
jaḍa-jīvātmaka 182
jagat 183, 189-91
jāgrata 68
Jaina 113
Jainism 145
James, William 214
Jean, James 102, 286, 298
jīva 59, 61-63, 65, 69-70, 80, 120, 132-34, 136-37, 151, 153-54, 167, 169-72, 177, 183, 186-87, 189-91, 198-99, 210, 289
four stages of 168
jīva and
Brahman identity between 187
Īśvara unbridgeable gulf between 61
jīva is
aṁśa of God 168
aśakti of *Brahman* 186
atomic 167
Brahman 185
called *aja* 168
empirical self 58
viśeṣaṇa 186
jīvanmukta 112-16, 161, 290-91
puruṣa 291
jīvanmukti 112-13, 116, 144, 161, 178, 290-91
jīvas 89, 152, 155, 163, 165, 188, 194
are *ananya* with *Brahman* 186
jīvātmā 153-54
jīvātman 43, 167, 185-86, 232, 240-42
jñāna 89, 105, 107-11, 129, 132,

138-40, 153, 157-58, 163, 173, 180, 182, 187, 192
generates *bhakti* 178
is *jñānaniṣṭhā* subject of 106
or *māyā* is the matrix of the manifold 78
yajña ix
jñānādhyāsa 86
jñāna-karma-samuccaya 107, 138
Jñāna-karmasamuccaya-vāda 105
jñāna-mārga 144
jñānamaya 106
jñānarūpa 22-23
jñānāśraya 167
jñāna-svarūpa 151, 167
jñāna-yoga 108
*jñānendriya*s 69
jñātṛ 151
Joad, C.E.M. 29, 119

kaivalya of *yogin* 98
kāla 171
kālatraya-sattāvat 2
Kālī 205-06
kalpanā-lāghava 89
kalpita 74
kalyāṇa 141
kāma 194
Kant, Immanuel 50-51, 53, 57, 149, 184, 205
kānti 182
kāraṇa śarīra 58
kāraṇāvasthā 229
karma 103, 105, 107-09, 112, 130, 133, 135, 138-40, 153, 158, 162, 168, 173-75, 192, 291
and matter clutches of 170
inefficacy of 174
law of 50, 143, 164
karma-jñāna-samuccaya 158, 291
karmakāṇḍa 88
karmaṇā 177
karma-yoga 108, 138-39
kārpaṇya 143
kartā 153
kartṛ 181
kartṛtva 55, 131, 136, 181, 186
Kaṭhopaniṣad 7, 23, 73, 107, 113, 138, 249
Keats, John 295
Kena Upaniṣad, 40, 211
Kevalādvaita viii, 26, 29, 282, 292-93
keyūra 165
kirīṭa 165
kīrtana 193
kīrti 182
Kirtikar, V.J. 49, 51, 53, 67, 112
kramika mokṣa 178
Krishnamurti, Jiddu 298
kriyā 129, 141, 180
kriyamāṇa 171, 174
*karma*s 132
Kṛṣṇa 5, 74, 101, 115, 162, 165, 182-83, 188, 193, 196, 200
kṣamā 107
kṣetrajña 166
Kuntī 101
kūṭastha nitya 95

Lakṣmī 4, 129, 150, 152
lakṣya–lakṣaṇa-bhāva 66
Lal, Basant Kumar 204

Laplace, Pierre-Simon 294
latent dualism 248
later Vedāntists 2
laukika pramāṇa 92
Leibnitz, Gottfrid Wilhelm 68, 130, 218
līlā 164, 183, 191, 193, 213
līlāvatāra 166
liṅga śarīra 58
Lohita 77
Londhe, D.G. 83
Lord Kṛṣṇa 6, 179
Lotze, Hermann 126

Mackenzie, J.S. 216
Mādhavācārya 86, 92
mādhurya 123, 163
  bhakti 194
mādhurya-pradhāna bhakti 176
Madhva viii, 3-6, 26, 121, 145-57, 159-61, 176, 184, 186, 284
  is a rank dualist 145
madhyama bhakta 160
Mādhyamika Buddhism 86
Māgha 82
Mahābhārata 73, 126
Mahadevan, T.M.P. 11, 36, 38, 74, 88
mahāvākya 65, 68, 134
Mahāyāna Buddhism 145
Maitra, S.K. 202, 205, 212, 217, 221, 227-28, 235, 249, 252-53, 266, 268, 270
Malkani, G.R. 37, 49, 65, 78, 83, 108, 118
manana 103, 161, 173-74
manas 166
manasā 177
man, destiny of 266
Māṇḍūkya Upaniṣad 25, 69
manomaya 69
mārdava 163
Marfatia, Mrudula 184
Marx, Karl 294
maryādā 188
  jīva 188
  mārga 197
maryādā-puṣṭi 188
  bhaktas 199
  bhakti 199
mataikya 154
Mātariśva 11
mathematics, alphabets of 296
maunavrata 175
māyā 5, 7, 48, 56, 62-63, 74-77, 80, 82-84, 89, 91, 145, 168, 171, 179, 181, 191, 209, 226, 228
  idea of 72-73
  doctrine 73
  is *Brahman* itself in a particular state 76
  is *jñāna-virodhinī* 78
  is the *prakṛti* 72
Māyāvāda 28, 184, 227, 282
māyika 190
McTaggart, John 126, 236
Mill, J.S. 216
Mīmāṁsakas 86, 121, 139
Mishra, K.N. 180
Miśra, Maṇḍana 107
Misra, R.S. 203, 209-10, 212-14, 231, 237, 276
Miśra, Vācaspati viii, 28, 87, 120
mithyā 74, 90

jñāna 86
Mitra, Sisir Kumar 12, 71
Modi, P.M. 34
mokṣa 96-99, 104-05, 108, 110, 117, 119, 136, 138-39, 144, 156-57, 160-61, 172
Monotheism 12
monotheistic mysticism 17
Muir, John 14
Muirhead, John Henry 108
Mukerji, A.C. 57, 60
Mukherji–Sastri, Nalini Mohan 34, 81, 85, 91
Mukherji, Satkari 27, 43, 47, 54
mukta 152, 155, 170, 172, 188
mukta jīva(s) 135, 159, 169, 172, 188
mukti 97, 121, 136, 139, 159, 168, 171, 178, 184, 289
four types of 159
of Sāṁkhya 98
mūla-prakṛti 62, 75, 89
Müller, Max 9, 27, 49, 53, 63, 67-68, 96, 102, 117-18, 299
mumukṣu 169, 178
disciple 103
puruṣa 103, 113
mumukṣutva 100, 102
Muṇḍaka Upaniṣad/ Muṇḍakopaniṣad 62, 117, 132, 148, 179
Murti, T.R.V. 89
Murty, Satchidananda 28

Naciketā 100, 104
Nāgārjuna 25, 94
Naiṣkarmyasiddhiḥ 54, 57, 104
nāma–rūpa 75, 80, 94
Nanda–Yaśodā 194
Nārada 184
Narain, K. 149
Naulakha, R.S. 30, 35, 59-60, 63, 118
Nayanaprasādinī 115
neti 298
is a characterization 147
Newton, Isaac 7, 293-95
Newtonian
classical physics 295
mechanics 293
physics 294
nididhyāsana 103, 161, 173-74
Nietzsche, Friedrich 116
nightmare of logic 295
niḥśreyasa 98, 104, 106
nijasvarūpāpatti 169
Nimbārka viii, 3-5, 26, 113, 121, 162, 164-67, 169-71, 174, 176-78, 184, 186, 189, 284
nimitta 182
nimitta-kāraṇa 126
nirāspada 92
nirātmaka 92
niravayava 182
nirguṇa 4, 147
Śrutis 181
Nirguṇa-Brahman 3, 30, 32-35, 46-47, 53, 99, 123, 180
nirupādhika 86
nirvāṇa of the Buddha 98
Nirvirodhavāda 27
nirviśeṣa 122
caitanya 55
niṣedha 181

niṣkāma karma 115, 138-39, 158, 193
niṣpāpa 129
niṣprapañca 55
nitya 152
  jīvas 135
  vṛndāvana dhāma 6
nityabodha-svarūpa 55
nityabuddha 164
nityamātmasvarūpam 100
nityamukta 164, 169
nityānitya-vastu-viveka 100
nitya-saṁsārī 152, 169
nitya-śuddha 113
nitya-śuddha-buddha-mukta 186
nityatṛpta 113, 164
nityatva 185
nityavibhūti of Rāmānuja 171
nivṛtti mārga 158
nivṛttimātra 89
niyama 288
niyāmya 168
niyantā 288
niyantṛtva 168
Non-Being of the Absolute Being 81
non-historical interpretation of history 292
Nyāya 105
Nyāyāmṛta 147, 161
Nyāya-Vaiśeṣika 78, 86, 125
Nyāya-vivaraṇa 147

object-consciousness 262
Oldenberg, Hermann 30
Olsson, Eva 268
One Eternal Being 23
oneness of
  ātman 96
  Absolute 221
ontological principle of unity 38
Oppenheimer, Robert 298
original sin 297
Otto, Rundolf 49, 97
Overmind 233-34, 251, 260, 264

pādasevana 194
Padmapāda 28
pañcabheda 151
Pañcadaśī 41, 63, 84, 115
Pāñcarātra theism 124
Panda, N.C. 300
Pandit, M.P. 202, 267
Pāṇini 59
pantheism 151
para 129
parā
  bhakti 176
  prakṛti 273
Para-Brahman 32, 46, 49, 123, 184
parādhīnakartṛtva 131
parama
  bhakti 142, 144
  puruṣārtha 97
paramānandāvāpti 161
paramārtha 26
paramārtha-tattva 33
pāramārthika 28
  dṛṣṭi 25
  sattā 91-92, 94
paramātman 44, 167, 170, 177, 240-41

Parama Puruṣa 13
paratantra 146
  sattābhāva 167
Parekh, M.C. 182
parikara 135
pariṇāma 170
Pariṇāmavāda 5, 190
pariṇāmī nitya 95
Pattison, Pringle 237
Paul, St. 68
phala samarpaṇa 143
philosophical tradition of India vii
philosophico-religious thought 145
philosophy of
  unity 8
  Upaniṣads 25
Physical Society 300
picturesque recklessness 53
Planck, Max 7, 296, 298
Plato 93, 184
Prabhavananda Swami 22
Pradyumna 129, 150, 166
Prajāpati 10-13, 53
prajñā 114
prājña 68
  Brahman 70
prajñāna 231
prajñānaghana 40
prakāra–prakārin 132
Prakāśānanda 70, 80, 84
Prakaṭārtha-Vivaraṇa 62, 84
prakṛta 171
prakṛti 136, 150, 155-56, 181, 206, 209, 231, 234, 258-60
  as *upādāna* 189
pralaya 168, 183, 247
pramāṇas 145
pramitiviṣaya 145
prāṇamaya 69
praṇaya 195
prapañca 190
prapatti 142, 144, 173, 175
  is the very spirit of *bhakti* 143
prāpti-rūpa 193
prāpti-sādhana 193
prārabdha 171
  karma 113, 115, 132, 161, 174, 178, 279, 291
prasāda 161
Praśna Upaniṣad/Praśnopaniṣad 49, 72
prātibhāsika 92
  sattā 91-92, 94
pratibimba 187
pratibimbatva 159
  dharma 62
Pratibimbavāda 52
pratyaktva 131
pravāha
  jīvas 188
  mārga 197
pravāha-puṣṭi 188, 199
  bhakti 199
prema 195
prema-lakṣaṇa bhakti 194
principle of
  cosmic Truth 234
  harmony 274-75
  illusion 81
  intermediaries 248
  unifying contradiction 81

projecting consciousness 229
psychological identity of self 96
psycho-physical organism 235
puṇḍarīkākṣa 126
Purāṇas 125
Pure
  and Perfect 165
  Being 46
  Bliss 46
  Consciousness 39, 45-46, 59, 64, 131
  Existence 45
  Spirit 62
  Unity 48
Pūrṇa Advaita 218
Pūrṇādvaita of Sri Aurobindo 26
pūrṇatva 148
Pūrṇavāda 218
pūrṇāvatāra 166
pūrṇa-vijñāna 218
pūrṇa vyakta avasthā 229
puruṣa 15, 205, 209, 231, 234, 250, 258-59, 279
puruṣa–prakṛti 209-10
puruṣārtha 104, 107, 196
puruṣatantra 109
puruṣāvatāra 166
Puruṣottama 179, 182, 200
puṣṭi 182, 188, 196
  bhaktas 198
  bhakti 198-99
  jīvas 188
  mārga 197-99
puṣṭi-puṣṭi 188
  bhaktas 199
  bhakti 199
quantum
  physics ix, 296, 298
  quality 299
  theory 295
    laws of 297

Rādhā 6, 200
Radhakrishnan, S. 10, 15, 18, 23-24, 30, 32, 34, 47, 52, 58, 60, 64, 82, 84, 95, 98-99, 112, 119-20, 152, 164, 187, 266
rāga 177, 195
rāga-vināśa 194
Raghuvaṁśa 128
rājabhoga 196
rajas 78, 84, 89, 124, 152, 171
rājasika 152
Raju, P.T. 247
rajoguṇa 78
Rāmānuja viii, 3, 5-6, 26, 105, 113, 121-30, 132-33, 135-42, 144-45, 150, 162, 164, 176, 181, 187, 189, 236, 278, 288-89
  regards *ātman* as *aṇu* 131
Ranade, R.D. 16-17, 21, 46, 73-75, 117
rāsalīlā 194
rational idealist 145
Ratnāvalī 31
Ray Chaudhuri, Anil Kumar 49, 56
Real Idea 224
realization of
  Brahman 63, 103-04
  God in man 97
Reddy, V. Madhusudan 205, 253
retribution scene of 91
Ṛgveda 1, 9-16, 18-19, 71-72, 75,

222, 224
Rhys, Davids 97
Royce, Josiah 237
ṛṣis 222
ṛta 222
ṛtam 224
Rudra 184
Rukmiṇī 165
Russell, Bertrand 294

Saccidānanda 5, 179, 202, 205, 210-12, 214-16, 220, 222-23, 226-30, 240-41, 243, 246, 248, 283, 285, 289
sacramental sense foods 196
Sadānanda 113
sadasadanirvacanīya 76
sādhaka 100, 159, 161
sādhanā 135, 161
sādhana-bhakti 144
sādhana-catuṣṭaya 99
sādhana-rūpika 176
sādhana-saptaka 142
sādhanas 141, 175, 177-78
sādhāraṇa 107
sādharmya 135
sādhya 99
sadyo-mokṣa 178
sadyo-mukti 116
Saguṇa-Brahman 3, 30, 32, 35, 46-49, 80, 123, 180
sahakārī-kāraṇa 126
sahakārīs 174, 177
sahasrākṣa 13
sahasraśīrṣā 13
sajātīya 183
  bheda 122
sajātīya–vijātīya 36
sakhya 194
sakhya-bhāva 194
sākṣin 59-60
sākṣīpratyakṣa 155
śakti 81, 129-30, 150, 163-64, 171, 181, 206, 209-10, 283
śaktimān 181
śakti-vikṣepa-lakṣaṇa-pariṇāma 170
śaktyupeta 180
sālokya 113, 137, 172, 195
  mukti 159
śama 100, 101
samādhi 100, 169
samādhāna 102
samānādhikaraṇya 125, 127, 137
  jñāna 65
sāmānyāvasthā 81
samatā 180
samavāyin 182
samāveśa 183
sambaddha jīvas 188
Saṁhitā mythology 17
Saṁhitās 1, 17
sāmīpya 113, 172, 195
  mukti 159
Sāṁkhya 87, 113, 136, 181, 190, 247
  inert *prakṛti* of 44
  philosophy 170
Sāṁkhya-Yoga 60
saṁnyāsin 220
sampradāya 196
saṁsāra 26, 157, 160, 190
saṁsargādhyāsa 86
saṁsārī 188

saṁskāras 114
saṁśyopasthāpikā 82
samuccaya 105, 110
saṁvṛtti 74
sāmya 171
saṁyoga 195
sañcita 171, 174
  karma 113
sandhyā 196
Śāṇḍilya 6
Śaṅkara viii, 2-7, 20, 24, 26, 28-33, 36-37, 39-40, 42-48, 50-53, 55-56, 58-61, 63-64, 66-68, 70-71, 73, 75-76, 78-81, 86, 88, 90, 92-99, 103-13, 116, 118-20, 122, 124, 127, 136-37, 139, 145, 158, 167, 178, 180-81, 185-86, 189, 195, 203, 205, 212, 235, 282-92, 298, 300-301
  agrees with the Sāṁkhya thinkers 41
Śaṅkara's conception of *Brahman* 29, 52
Saṅkarṣaṇa 129, 150, 166
śaṅkha 165
Saṅkṣepaśārīraka 63-64
śaraṇāgati 176
Sarasvatī, Brahmānanda 31
Sarasvati, Madhusūdana 61, 80
sargonamukha 76
śarīra-śarīrī bhāva 127
sārṣṭi 137
sārūpya 113, 137, 159, 172, 195
sarvabhūtāntarātmā 23
Sarvajñātmamuni 80, 84, 116, 120
sarvapratyayadarśī 60
sarvapratyaya sākṣin 61
sarva-śarīra-vyāpī 185
sarvātma bhāva 3, 192, 195, 290
  of *mukta* 116
Śāstradīpikā 98
Śāstras 102
Sastri, Kokileshwar 11, 25, 28, 32, 76, 82, 85, 94-95
Sastri, P.D. 72
Sastri, Suryanarayan 116
sat 179, 190, 202, 226, 230
  aspect of Saccidānanda 179
satkarma 108
sat-saṅga 177
sattāprada 95
sattva 78, 84, 89, 124, 152, 171
sattvaśuddhi 105
sāttvika jīva 152
satya 107, 181
  śaṅkalpa 129
Satyabhāmā 165
satyam 121, 141, 224, 257
Satya Yuga 269
śauca 107
sauhārda 163
saulabhya 123
sauśīlya 123
saviśeṣābheda 146
saviśeṣa-svarūpa 157
Savitri 258, 274
Sāyaṇa 72, 75
śayana 196
sāyujya 113, 137, 144, 172, 195
  mukti 159
Schelling's neutrum 187
Schopenhauer, Arthur 68, 299
Schraeder, Otto 131
Schrödinger, Erwin 8, 298

scientific spirituality 301
Seer Will 224
self-differentiation 233
self-diffusion 233
self is bliss as such 56
Sengupta, Anima 126, 144
Sengupta, Bratindra Kumar 110
sentimental idealist 145
śeṣa 142
śeṣa–śeṣī-bhāva 132
sevā 193
seven spiritual preparations 141
Sharma, B.N.K. 16, 149, 154, 156, 158
Sharma, C.D. 10-11, 18, 84
Sharma, Ram Nath 51, 76
Shastri, Prabhu Dutt 75
Siddhāntabindu 31
Siddhāntaleśasaṁgraha 61
Siddhāntamuktāvalī 84
Sinha, J.N. 49, 55, 59-60
Sircar, Mahendranath 19, 22-23
Śiśupālavadha 82
Śiva 56, 112-13, 205-06, 210, 249, 283
śivam 257
  and *sundaram* are attributes of *Brahman* 121
six
  divine qualities 190
  systems vii, 25
smaraṇa 142, 193
smṛti 142
Smṛtis 125
sneha 195
so'ham asmi 134
Soma 12
sopādhika 86
soul-essence 231
soul-form 231, 232
soul is *niyamya* 132
spatio-temporal world 287
speculative monism 10
Spencer, Herbert 253
Spinoza, Baruch 53, 130, 184, 236
spiritual
  evolution 244-45
  force of love and sympathy 281
  freedom 292
  identity of *Brahman* and *ātman* 19
  monistic theism 236
  reality 292
  transformation 265
spiritualization of matter 255
spiritualize the material 26
śraddhā 101-02, 177
śravaṇa 103, 113, 142, 157, 161, 173-74, 193
śrī 182, 187
Śrī Bhāṣya 138
Śrī Harṣa 28
Śrī Kṛṣṇa 194
Śrīnivāsācārya 170
Srivastava, R.S. 209, 212, 217, 227, 245, 263, 266
Srivastava, S.N.L. 57
śṛṅgāra 194, 196
Śrutaprakāśikā 132
śruti 113
Śruti 4, 9, 51, 89, 94, 95, 112
Śrutis 123, 125, 156, 162, 169, 180, 186
sthita-prajñatā 145

sthūla śarīra 58
stuti 142
subject-consciousness 262
śuddha 188
Śuddhādvaita viii, 26, 121, 178, 187
Śuddhādvaita Vedānta 197
śuddha-puṣṭi bhakti 199-200
śukti-rajata 92
sundaram 257
Śūnyavāda Buddhism 145
super-consciousness 207
Superman 268, 271, 291
Supermind 202, 221-30, 232-34, 242, 246-47, 249, 254-55, 259-61, 263-66, 274, 278, 283, 285, 290
supra-ethical 216
supramental
  being 277
  Consciousness 256
  Divine 259, 265
  gnostic individual 279
Supreme
  Absolute 217
  Being 128, 130, 149-51
  Bliss 169, 183, 212, 217, 258
  Brahman 161, 181
  conscious-force 208
  Divine 267
  Ethical 127
  Existence 202
  God 12, 15, 126
  Good 236
  Lord 74, 159
  Majesty 172
  Personal Being 145, 259
  Real 121
  Reality 3, 124, 126, 161, 176, 234, 263
  Self 43, 132
  Spirit 250
  Truth Consciousness 221
  Value 121
Sureśvarācārya/Sureśvara viii, 57, 28, 104, 106, 120
Suri, Sudarsana 132
suṣupta puruṣa 114
suṣuptāvasthā 68
suṣupti 114, 133
  sthāna 165
sūtrakāra 180
svābhāvika kartṛtva 186
svagata 183
  bheda 36, 122
svaprakāśa 151
svarūpa 125, 146, 164
  lakṣaṇa 30-32
  samarpaṇa 143
svarūpa-pariṇāma 170
svarūpatādātmya 152
*svarūpa-viśeṣa*s 153
svatantra 146
  sattābhāva 167
Śvetaketu 21, 73
Śvetāśvatara Upaniṣad/ *Śvetāśvataropaniṣad* 19, 72, 77, 111, 113, 132, 138, 267

tādātmya 135, 182
tādātmyādhyāsa 86
tadāyatta-svarūpa-sthiti 170
tadbhāvāpatti 171
tad-tādātmyānubhava 171
taijasa 68
Taittirīya Upaniṣad 32, 38, 43-44,

169, 203, 211, 219
tamas 78, 84, 89, 124, 152, 171, 280
tāmasika 141, 152
tamoguṇa 78
tamoyogya 152
tāratamya 159
taṭastha lakṣaṇa 30-32
tattvābhyāsa 135
tattva-jñāna 135
tat tvam asi 2, 5, 21, 63, 68, 103, 134, 154, 169, 187
Tattvapradīpikā 61
Tattvārtha-dīpa-nibandha 193
Tattvatrayabhāṣya 129
Tattvavāda 145
Tattva-Viveka 89
Taylor, A.E. 29
tejas 129, 163
Telivala, M.T. 180
Temple, William 126
Tengaḷais 142
that thou art 65
that-which-is 297
theism of old monastic Upaniṣad 49
theistic Vedānta 6, 282, 284
theory of
- *adhyāsa* 87
- atomicity and plurality 167
- dark psyche 294
- double soul 241
- evolution 249
- Immutable Transformation 190
- *māyā* 73
- Non-Being (*asat*) 203
- part-whole-oneness 188
- pure existence 203
- relativity 295-96

Thibaut, George 72, 83
thou art that 64, 66
three
- *guṇas* 171
  - of *prakṛti* 147
- *sādhanas* of God-realization 196
- states of
  - *Īśvara* 71
  - *jīva* 68
- types of *avatāra* 166

tirobhāva 183, 187, 191
tīrthaṁkaras 145
titikṣā 100, 102, 116
traditional Hindu concept of liberation 7
transcendental
- *cinmāyā* body 255
- reality 201

transcendentalism 57
triguṇātmaka 77
triguṇātmikā 76
- *prakṛti* 42

trikālābādhita 36
trikāladarśī 163
trikāla-satya 2, 36, 38, 76, 90
Triple Reality 91
triple transformation 254, 256
truth-consciousness 222, 224-25, 227, 242
turīya 69
- *śakti* 222

turīyāvasthā 20, 69
tuṣṭi 182

Ultimate
- Bliss 17
- *Brahman* 45

destiny 292
God 11
Reality 13, 18, 24, 28-30, 50, 60, 202, 219, 237, 282
of Oneness 27
unbroken wholeness 297
uncritical realist 145
unitarian consciousness 229
unity-in-diversity 275
Unity is the keynote of Sri Aurobindo's philosophy 220
universal
and ineffable reality 283
spirituality 277
Universal Consciousness 66
Universal Space 59
unqualified *Brahman* 49, 122
upacāramātra 289
upādāna 126, 164, 182
upādāna-kāraṇa 126
Upadeśasāhasrī 56
Upadhyaya, Veermani Prasad 116
upahitarūpa 58
upajīvya 147
Upaniṣadic
Absolutism 124
philosophy vii, 1-2, 17, 19, 22, 27, 59, 72-73, 285
seers 19
Upaniṣads ix, 1-2, 12-13, 16-21, 23-26, 32, 42, 50, 73, 75, 87, 123, 138, 180, 197, 221, 228, 286
uparati 100-02
upāsanā 140, 161, 165, 173, 175-76
upāya-bhakti 144
ūrjā 182
Puruṣottama of *Gīta* 183
utkramaṇa 131
utpatti 183
uttama bhakta 160
utthāpana 196

Vāc, Ṛṣikā 13
vācā 177
vacana 142
Vācaspati 61, 80, 89
Vaḍagaḷais 142
vaicitrya 183, 191
vaidika souls 197
vaijayantī 165
Vaikuṇṭha 137, 159, 200
vairāgya 110, 187
Vaiśeṣika 105
Vaiṣṇava 121, 136
Vaiṣṇavism 5, 124, 127
Vaiṣṇavites 153, 171
vaiśvānara 181
vākyārtha jñāna 144
Vallabha 3, 5, 26, 113, 121, 180-82, 184-89, 192-96, 198-99
Vallabhācārya viii, 178-79, 284
Vāmadeva, Ṛṣi 13
vandana 194
vandanā 142
varṇa 198
varṇāśrama-dharma 107-08
Varuṇa 10-11, 12, 53, 71
vastutantra 109
Vāsudeva 129, 150, 166
is the *nirguṇa* aspect of *Brahman* 166
vātsalya 163
bhakti 196

vātsalya-bhāva 194
Vāyu 20
Veda 114
Vedānta 8, 11, 15-16, 24, 26-28, 36, 67, 77, 83, 88, 95-96, 99, 103, 116-17, 145, 155, 178, 233, 260
  as spokesman of pantheism 68
  means "spiritual insight" 117
  of tomorrow viii
Vedānta Paribhāṣa 59, 70, 89, 97
Vedāntasāra 76, 89
Vedāntic 282
  Brahman 53
  emancipation 118
  Īśvara 48
  liberation 97, 119
  philosophy cornerstone of 53
  psychology 130
  scheme of liberation 117
Vedāntins 298
Vedāntism 57
Vedāntists 3, 98, 186, 202-03, 290
Vedas ix, 15-16, 18, 26, 28, 194, 221, 228
Vedic
  age 269
  concept of Viśvadeva 23
  hymns 2
  philosophy vii, 1, 17
  rituals 135
  seers 294
veiled consciousness 244, 247
vibhava 129
vibhu 185
vibhūti 125, 183
vibhutva 186
  is latent in *jīva* 186
  of *ātman* 185
  of *Jīvātman* 185
videhamukti 112-13, 116, 144, 278
vidheyatva 131
vidyā 173-74, 177
Vidyāraṇya 61-62, 78, 84
Vidyarthi, P.B. 125, 127-28, 131, 133, 136-37, 143
vijātīya 183, 189
  bheda 122
vijñāna 169, 222
vijñānamaya 69
vikṛti-doṣa 180
viparītagrāhika 82
viparyaya 74
virāga 100, 102, 177
virāgya 182
virodha 181
viruddhadharmāśraya 181
vīrya 163, 182, 187
viṣaya 192
viṣayatā 192
viṣayatvāt mithyā 93
viśeṣa 81, 151
viśeṣa-dharma 107
viśeṣaṇa is *ananya* 185
viśeṣaṇāṁśā 126
viśeṣanaviśeṣya-bhāva 65
viśeṣya Brahman 185
viśiṣṭa 122
Viśiṣṭādvaita viii, 3, 26, 120-21, 127, 130, 162
Viṣṇu 4, 112, 124, 129-30, 151, 184
Viṣṇu Purāṇa 123, 126, 129
Viśvadeva 11
Viśvakarmā 12-13, 53
viśvāsa 177

vitatha 74
Viṭṭhalanātha 183, 191
Vivaraṇa school 80
Vivaraṇaprameyasaṁgraha 84
vivarta 75-76
of *Brahman* 192
Vivartavāda 5, 87, 156, 190
viveka 141
Vivekacūḍāmaṇi 91, 103
Vivekananda 11, 26, 298
viyoga 195
von Roth, Rudolph 30
vyakti 150
Vyāsa 183
vyasana 195
vyāvahārika 28
sattā 79, 91-92, 94
vyūha 129, 166
vyūhas, four forms of 166

Warrier, A.G. 45, 49, 78, 102
way of happiness 215
Weber, Renée 296
Wells, H.G. 267
Western
pantheism 22
philosophy 36
Wigner, Eugene 297
Wilber, Ken 297
Whitehead, A.N. 48
Woodroffe, Sir John 55
world as the countenance of God 24
world-negating philosophy 119

Yaduvaṁśa 128
Yājñavalkya 21, 55, 100
yaśa 182, 187
yātanā 142
yoga 125, 254, 260, 270-71
yogamāyā 74, 210
yogī 108
yogic *siddhis* 255

Zimmer, Heinrich 56
Zohar, Danah 299
Zukav, Garg 297